Time and the World

Time and the World

Every Thing and Then Some

M. ORESTE FIOCCO

OXFORD
UNIVERSITY PRESS

Oxford University Press is a department of the University of Oxford. It furthers the University's objective of excellence in research, scholarship, and education by publishing worldwide. Oxford is a registered trade mark of Oxford University Press in the UK and certain other countries.

Published in the United States of America by Oxford University Press
198 Madison Avenue, New York, NY 10016, United States of America.

© Oxford University Press 2024

All rights reserved. No part of this publication may be reproduced, stored in a retrieval system, or transmitted, in any form or by any means, without the prior permission in writing of Oxford University Press, or as expressly permitted by law, by licence, or under terms agreed with the appropriate reproduction rights organization. Enquiries concerning reproduction outside the scope of the above should be sent to the Rights Department, Oxford University Press, at the address above.

You must not circulate this work in any other form
and you must impose this same condition on any acquirer.

CIP data is on file at the Library of Congress

ISBN 978–0–19–777710–7

DOI: 10.1093/oso/9780197777107.001.0001

Printed by Marquis Book Printing, Canada

*This work is dedicated, with the greatest esteem and affection, to
Nathan Salmon
Tony Anderson
and the memory of Tony Brueckner,
my primary teachers at Santa Barbara. Three very different men; three exceptional philosophers. I learned a tremendous amount from each.*

"You're crazy," I say. "If you think I created that wall that cracked my head, you're a fucking lunatic."

—John Gardner, *Grendel*

Contents

Preface — xiii
Acknowledgments — xvii

PART I INTRODUCTION: CONFRONTING THE WORLD

1. What Is *All This*? — 3
   1.1. How This Inquiry Is Different — 12
   1.2. Overview of the Present Work — 20

PART II METAPHYSICS, ONTOLOGY, AND TIME: THE SIGNIFICANCE OF TIME

2. Metaphysics and Its Distinctive Problem — 33
   2.1. Metaphysics vis-à-vis *All This* — 33
   2.2. The Distinctive Problem of Metaphysics — 37
   2.3. A Critique of Contemporary Metaphysical Inquiry — 40
      2.3.1. Deflationary views of metaphysics — 41
         2.3.1.1. Metaphysics as a hodgepodge — 41
         2.3.1.2. Deflationary views that are based on substantive assumptions — 43
         2.3.1.3. Naturalized metaphysics — 45
      2.3.2. Metaphysics as autonomous — 51
         2.3.2.1. Autonomy and aprioricity — 51
         2.3.2.2. Metaphysics as first philosophy — 55
   2.4. Metaphysics and the Need for a Novel Method — 58
3. The Method of Original Inquiry — 60
   3.1. What Hangs on the Question of What a Thing Is? — 61
   3.2. Can This Question Be Answered? — 65
      3.2.1. Aristotle's argument that *being* is not a genus — 66
      3.2.2. The circularity of any explicative account of *thing* — 68
   3.3. The Means of Resolving the Distinctive Problem — 69
      3.3.1. The world as impetus to inquiry — 70
   3.4. What a Thing Must Be: A Natured Entity — 76
   3.5. Original Inquiry as Wholly Critical — 84

viii CONTENTS

4. Radical Ontology and Its Principles — 92
   4.1. The Structure in the World — 93
   4.2. What the World Is — 100
      4.2.1. The structure in the world is not a thing — 100
      4.2.2. The world just is the plurality of all things — 102
   4.3. Further Principles of Radical Ontology — 106
      4.3.1. The categories of *thing* — 107
      4.3.2. Being a thing is uniform (and so there are no non-existent beings) — 110
      4.3.3. Being a thing is compulsory (to bearing any property or standing in any relation) — 111
      4.3.4. Being a thing is determinate (so there is no ontological indeterminacy) — 112
      4.3.5. Being a thing is not fragmentary (so the world is complete) — 115
   4.4. The Means and Limits of Inquiry — 116

5. The Metaphysics of Time — 120
   5.1. Confronting Time — 122
      5.1.1. Differentiation and change — 124
   5.2. Moments and Time — 127
      5.2.1. Moments do not suffice to account for temporal differentiation — 128
   5.3. Time Is a Thing — 132
   5.4. Time in the World — 135

PART III A GENERAL ACCOUNT OF TEMPORAL REALITY: THE HETEROGENEITY OF THE WORLD IN TIME

6. Two General Views of Temporal Reality — 141
   6.1. Time in the World, the World in Time — 143
      6.1.1. What temporal reality is — 143
      6.1.2. Ecumenical accounts of time and temporal reality — 146
   6.2. Controversy Regarding the Metaphysics of Time — 147
   6.3. The Real Bone of Contention Concerning the Metaphysics of Time — 154
      6.3.1. Experience of inconstancy and constancy — 156
      6.3.2. Two general views regarding the world in time — 157
         6.3.2.1. The ontological homogeneity of temporal reality — 158
         6.3.2.2. The ontological heterogeneity of temporal reality — 160
   6.4. The Primary Issue Regarding the Metaphysics of Time — 161

7. Against the Ontological Homogeneity of Temporal Reality — 163
   7.1. Arbitrating the Pivotal Dispute — 164
      7.1.1. One's position must have an appropriate basis — 164

7.2.	The Experience of Temporal Differentiation	167
7.3.	Temporal Differentiation and the Ontological Homogeneity of Temporal Reality	170
	7.3.1. The myth of passage	170
	7.3.2. The ostensible ontological basis of inconstancy	173
	7.3.3. Ontological homogeneity and the experience of temporal differentiation	175
7.4.	Why the World in Time Is Not Ontologically Homogeneous	178
	7.4.1. An argument against the ontological homogeneity of the world in time: A farrago of experiences	179
	7.4.2. A further argument against the ontological homogeneity of the world in time: The crucial transition	184
	7.4.3. Why these compelling considerations have been overlooked in previous discussions	187

8. Against Mere Qualitative Heterogeneity in Temporal Reality — 190

8.1.	Qualitative Heterogeneity in Temporal Reality	191
	8.1.1. The traditional passage view: Change in moments	191
	8.1.1.1. McTaggart's Paradox	193
	8.1.1.2. The real problem: The view requires moments per se to both change and be immutable	195
	8.1.2. Moving spotlight views: Change in the things at a given moment	198
	8.1.2.1. Sullivan's minimal A-theory	200
	8.1.2.2. Cameron's moving spotlight theory	202
	8.1.2.3. Problems with moving spotlight views	204
8.2.	Ontological Transience: Absolute Annihilation, Ceasing to Be Simpliciter	211
	8.2.1. An argument that at least some things cease to be simpliciter	212
	8.2.2. Another argument that at least some things cease to be simpliciter	212
	8.2.3. The scope of ontological transience	213
	8.2.4. Ontological transience and temporal differentiation	215
8.3.	What the Foregoing Reveals About the Structure of the World in Time	216
	8.3.1. Growing block views must be rejected	216

9. Absolute Becoming and the Contingency in the World — 219

9.1.	The Structure of the World in Time Subsequent to Now	220
	9.1.1. Arguments from change in a moment and synchronous change applied again	221
	9.1.2. Rejection of any structure subsequent to this moment, now	224
	9.1.3. Temporal entities and the extent of the world in time	226
9.2.	Ontological Transience: Absolute Becoming, Coming to Be Simpliciter	228
	9.2.1. What temporal differentiation is	229

9.3.	Necessity, Contingency, and the World in Time	232
	9.3.1. The basis of possibility and the necessity in this moment, now	234
	9.3.2. The necessity of the past	238
	9.3.3. Contingency and the openness of what is to be	241

PART IV THE SPECIFIC ACCOUNT OF TEMPORAL REALITY: TRANSIENT PRESENTISM AND ITS LIMITATIONS

10.	Temporal Reality and Inconstancy	247
	10.1. On Presentism	249
	10.1.1. The triviality objection	250
	10.1.2. The multiplicity of "presentist" views	252
	10.1.3. Presentism and structure	255
	10.2. Dynamism and Inconstancy	256
	10.2.1. Change, ontological transience, and dynamism	257
	10.2.2. Dynamism as actualizable potential	260
	10.2.3. Independent bases of inconstancy (and of constancy)	261
	10.3. Objections to Transient Presentism	263
	10.3.1. The different motivations for holding standard presentism and transient presentism	264
	10.3.2. The Special Theory of Relativity	265
	10.3.3. The insurmountable problem(s) of constancy	268
11.	Atemporal Reality and Constancy	273
	11.1. Constancy in Original Inquiry	274
	11.1.1. The bases of constancy are not among the sparse structure in temporal reality	276
	11.1.2. Being so versus being true	278
	11.2. Timelessness and the World Without Time	280
	11.2.1. Attempts to reject timelessness altogether	280
	11.2.2. Two incorrect views of timelessness	281
	11.2.3. The world without time	282
	11.3. Atemporal Reality: The Things Independent of Time	284
	11.3.1. Some examples of atemporal entities	285
	11.3.2. Atemporal becoming	288
	11.3.3. Epistemic access to the world without time	290
	11.4. The Constancy in the World	293
	11.4.1. Simple facts	294

PART V CONCLUSION: THE WORLD IN ITS ENTIRETY

12. *All This* and Why It Matters   303

References   315
Index   323

Preface

There is certainly a world—but what is it? What hangs on this question? Maybe little. Once posed, though, it is intriguing. At least I find it so. There is indeed a world. Clearly it is not nothing at all, yet is the world a *thing* (a *being*, an *entity*, an *existent*)? This is, admittedly, a strange question. Nevertheless, it is the one that motivated this book. Like many other questions, one cannot answer this one without some account of what a thing is.

What, then, is a thing? Much hangs on this question, more than merely the prospect of saying what the world is. With a true account of what a thing is, one has insight into literally everything and, with it, the means to resolve some of the most basic and pressing questions in the tradition of grand metaphysical inquiry (such as, *is there necessity in reality independently of any thinking being?* and *what is fundamental in reality?*). Moreover, with this insight, one can discern some of the ground rules of inquiry in general, for all legitimate inquiry is directed at some thing or other. Inquiry inconsistent with the account of what a thing is is irremediably misguided and, hence, futile.

So how does one acquire such an illuminating and significant account? If one begins with an assumption about what is (or is not) a thing, this assumption might be incorrect. If it is, one's account of what a thing is would, obviously, be mistaken. To verify any initial assumption, one would need some grounds. Grounds, however, are things. If one just accepts these grounds, these things, as the basis of one's account of what a thing is, one introduces into that account an arbitrariness that is objectionably uncritical. To determine whether the grounds are actually things, though, requires an account of what a thing is. That is what one was seeking in the first place. One is led, via a circular route, to where one started, with seemingly no way forward.

The problem here is beginning with an assumption about what a thing is. To breach the circle, one must forgo any such assumption. But how can one progress in an inquiry about everything with no assumption about any thing? One must start with what is incontrovertibly there, the world—*all this*—not presuming anything about what it comprises or even that "it" is a thing. I propose a method whereby one can discern what a thing is by confronting the world in this innocent, open-minded way. To permit myself here a metaphor: by engaging the forest, nothing but trees, one comes to see what a tree is.

These reflections on what a thing is are prompted by curiosity about the world, *all this*. If one indulges in such reflection and then turns one's attention back to the world, one sees that it is different. Something or other is not as it was. Considering this difference, one becomes aware that the world is continuously going from one way to another and that one, as one engages the world, is continuously changing. The world goes from *thus* at one moment... to *as so* at another... to *as such* at the next... and so forth. Such inconstancy in the whatnot that is the world is indisputable.

Still, if, at this moment, one is considering the inconstancy in the world, then it is true—forevermore—that one is considering the inconstancy in the world at that very moment. This cannot (and will never) be otherwise. Even when one changes and has gone on to other things, that it is true that one is considering the inconstancy in the world at that very moment is not otherwise. But how can this be? How can it be true that one is considering the inconstancy in the world (at a given moment) even as one has changed so as *not* to be considering the inconstancy in the world at all? What goes for one considering the world goes for every other thing doing whatever it does: insofar as that very thing changes, its being one way is true even as it is an incompatible way. Thus, the prevalent inconstancy and constancy in the world seems paradoxical.

Accommodating both inconstancy and constancy in the world is requisite for any satisfactory account of *all this* because both phenomena are incontrovertible. Doing so indicates that the world has a certain *structure*, that is, the world is unique things related to others in specific ways. This structure includes time, a moment, and myriad temporal and atemporal things. Time is not a sequence or a set of moments; it is something else entirely. Getting clear on how things relate to this pivotal one, time itself, reveals temporal reality—the world in time—and atemporal reality—the world outside time. This structure, which includes the bases of inconstancy and constancy, is what enables anything in the world to happen.

Inquiry happens. It is a process that takes place in time. So an account of the structure in the world provides further ground rules for inquiry. If certain conditions have to be met for anything to happen, for any process to occur, these conditions must be met for inquiry in particular to take place.

Inquiry that proceeds on assumptions incompatible with these conditions is irremediably misguided and, hence, futile. Therefore, an account of what a thing is jointly with an account of the structure in the world—that recognizes the centrality of time itself—presents formal conditions on all inquiry, for they demonstrate the constraints on absolutely everything and on anything that happens.

The accounts I provide herein of what a thing is and of how the world is structured will be controversial. I maintain that the world is not a thing; that each thing is fundamental; that reality has no ontological levels and, hence, that no thing is grounded in or made to be by another. I maintain that time per se is distinct from any moment and that there is but one moment, this one, now. Consequently, there are no earlier moments, nor later ones; there is no past, at least not as it is familiarly conceived, and nothing at all to the future. Indeed, this moment, now, stands in no relation to any other moment simply because there are no other moments (though wait momentarily). There are also, I maintain, in addition to the world in time, things outside of time, some of which even *come to be*. Inconstancy and constancy, then, are both genuine phenomena with bases amid *all this*. I also maintain that *all this* is literally a different world from one moment to the next.

Some of these claims might strike one as bizarre or clearly false. I maintain they all follow, given logical principles informed by the world, from indubitable grounds available to anyone who, critically, confronts *all this* ... and confronts it again. Any critical inquirer, therefore, should take the claims very seriously.

MOF
Irvine, CA
September 22, 2023

Acknowledgments

This book was written over several years. During that time, it benefited from the thoughts and comments of many insightful people, as I benefited from our conversations and their support. Here I would like to express my profound gratitude to all those who contributed to this long project and to name some of these people.

I have many fine colleagues at the University of California, Irvine (both within my field and without). I am grateful for the discussions we have had on topics bearing, in one way or another, on this book. Thus, I would like to thank my friends Chris Bauman, Daniel Brunstetter, Ian Coller, Rob Edwards, Christophe Litwin, David Malament, JB Manchak, and Santiago Morales-Rivera.

Within the Department of Philosophy, I would like to thank, for their interest in this project and support of it, Jeff Helmreich, Margaret Gilbert, Aaron James, Ari Koslow, Casey Perin, Kate Ritchie, Karl Schafer (now of the University of Texas at Austin), and Martin Schwab. Duncan Pritchard is a dear friend and valued interlocutor. I deeply appreciate our many conversations and outings and all we share. David Woodruff Smith has been a mentor and source of encouragement since I arrived at Irvine. He, more than anyone else, encouraged me to be as intensely serious about *things* as I have become. My greatest debt here, though, is to Sven Bernecker. In a very real sense, I owe my academic life to him. I admire Sven in many ways, both professional and personal, and I am glad to have him as an ally and beloved friend.

I had been working on a book concerning some of the issues discussed herein basically since finishing my dissertation. However, I began work in earnest on what would become this book during an academic year (2015–16) I spent as a visitor in the Department of Philosophy at the University of Salzburg. I was supported that year by a Lise Meitner Fellowship from the Austrian Science Fund (grant M 1881-G24). Johannes Brandl was my co-applicant on the grant and host at Salzburg. I had met Johannes several years before when he was teaching in Irvine (and he had already hosted me once at

Salzburg). He is an excellent philosopher and an earnest and caring man who has supported many of my endeavors, including this book. I am very grateful for all he has done for me (and have for him the greatest affection). During my year at Salzburg, Lena Zuchowski organized a reading group in which many of us discussed early versions of several chapters of this book. I thank Lena and the other participants in that group. As Head of the Department, Alexander Hieke made possible the three (so far) extended visits I have had at Salzburg. I have always appreciated his help. I would like to thank Chris Gauker for wide-ranging philosophical discussion, much pertaining to issues in this book. I would also like to express special thanks to Julien Murzi, an estimable philosopher, person, and friend.

I spent the 2022–23 academic year on sabbatical at King's College London. There I began revising this book for publication in light of the two extremely incisive and constructive reports I received from anonymous referees for OUP. I would like to extend my sincere thanks to the Head of Department, Maria Alvarez, for making my visit at King's possible. I was treated like a member of the department and I am grateful for all the kindness shown to me. I would like to thank Julien Dutant, Clayton Littlejohn, Eliot Michaelson, and Massimo Renzo for many pleasant meals and engaging philosophical discussions. Mark Textor, in the fall, and Eliot Michaelson, in the winter and spring, allowed me to use their offices as my own (and I did on a daily basis). I thank them for their hospitality. Mark and I had a fruitful exchange of work; I am appreciative of the helpful comments he provided on parts of this book. Matthew Soteriou and Bill Brewer participated in a reading group in which we read all twelve chapters of this book. That group and the rich discussion we had in it, conducted with excitement and seriousness and open-mindedness, reminded me of the value of intellectual community after the isolation of the pandemic. Matt is a formidable philosopher, keenly discerning and interesting. He is also a wonderful human being, kindly, thoughtful, magnanimous. I and this book were the beneficiaries of all these admirable traits. I am pleased to have Matt as a friend. Bill was my host during the year I spent at King's and in that time became a very close friend. He is an extraordinary philosopher and we had hours and hours of discussion in which I learned a great deal. Bill imparted invaluable advice on a number of matters of much importance to me. His expertise, among other beneficial results, improved the quality of this book and helped make the process of getting it published more bearable. I will always be tremendously grateful to him.

While in London, I had the opportunity to spend time with friends in Oxford—and to make a couple of new ones. Over the years, I have enjoyed hours of philosophical discussion with Tim Williamson. I have very much benefited from these. I am not sure, though, that Tim and I have ever agreed on anything (even when we agree). I also profited from discussion (and meals) with Matthew Parrot and Jeff McMahan. I thank them for their hospitality. Adrian Moore is a remarkable philosopher and person; I find his work fascinating and greatly appreciate him and the encouragement and advice he gave.

In the spring of 2019, I was given, by the School of Humanities here at UCI, one of the first Mid-Career Faculty Manuscript Workshop Awards. This award provided funds to host a workshop at which Part I of this book was, for many hours, examined and discussed. I would like to thank Dean Tyrus Miller for having the awareness and initiative to institute the awards and Professor Julia Lupton, Associate Dean for Research at the time, and Dr. Amanda Swain, the Executive Director of the Humanities Center, for the sagacious implementation of them.

The official participants at the manuscript workshop were Shamik Dasgupta, Dan Korman, Kathrin Koslicki, and Tim O'Connor. These four are among the philosophers working today that I admire and respect most, so their participation was an honor. I could not have enjoyed more the time we spent together and our genuinely critical exchanges. The book was improved immensely by their scrutiny and comments. At the workshop, Dan and Tim provided written notes that were quite helpful. Later, Dan provided me with even more assistance. His additional comments were so considered and insightful—so prodigiously valuable—that this book would not have taken the form it now has without them. My appreciation of Dan and my regard for him, as a person and philosopher, are enormous.

I organized the first meeting of the SoCal Metaphysics Network to coincide with the manuscript workshop. The inaugural conference of the Network was held the day after that workshop, so there were other outstanding philosophers in town who attended and contributed crucially to it and, hence, to the book. These are Kim Frost, Michaela McSweeney, and Elanor Taylor. I thank them for their insights and support. My colleagues Jeff Helmreich, Duncan Pritchard, and Karl Schafer also attended the workshop, so I would like to thank them again here for their many positive contributions to my work (and life). That weekend, in December 2019, was a highlight of an era of my academic career.

xx ACKNOWLEDGMENTS

I have presented parts of this book to many audiences over the years and I was able to improve it immeasurably in light of the discussion throughout and following those talks. I have also presented, in related papers, issues so intertwined with those herein, that I was able to improve the book via these talks as well. So I would like to express my gratitude to all those at the following places who listened to me and engaged in discussion of my work: Oxford University (St. Hilda's College); 2018 New England Workshop on Metaphysics (held at Rhode Island College); 2017 Hylomorphism Conference (in Banff, Alberta); 2017 Inland Northwest Philosophy Conference (in Sun Valley, Idaho); California State University, San Bernardino; Time-Methods Workshop on Presentism at the Centre for Philosophy of Time at the University of Milan (in September 2016); XIIth Annual Estonian Philosophy Conference (in Tallinn in June 2016); University of Manchester; University of Nottingham; University of Neuchâtel; International Academy of Philosophy (in Liechtenstein); University of Maribor; Charles University (in Prague); University of Bologna; University of Ljubljana; University of Modena and Reggio Emilia, University of Salzburg; Stanford University.

In the spring of 2022, I presented material on presuppositionless inquiry at a conference celebrating Mark Sainsbury at the Institute of Philosophy in London. To be able to honor Mark in this way was, for me, a significant pleasure. Mark was a colleague for two years at the University of Texas at Austin, my first job. His attention and compassion and respect meant a lot to me as a novice. I benefited greatly not merely from our friendly conversations and philosophical discussions and from his advice, but from Mark's example.

There are several other philosophers who have contributed to this book through inestimably valuable discussion, advice, or encouragement (and, in most cases, a mix of all three). These include: Gordon Bearn, Jeremy Bendik-Keymer, Patrick Connolly, Jonathan Dancy, Matt Duncan, John Heil, Mark Heller, Dave Ingram, David-Hillel Ruben, Kathleen Stock, Tuomas Tahko, Jonathan Tallant, and Giuliano Torrengo. Thank you, my friends.

Special acknowledgment is also due to the following people.

E.J. Lowe demonstrated to me a different way of confronting the world and of doing metaphysics than ones I had been exposed to at Princeton, where David Lewis was my first instructor in metaphysics, and at Tufts and Santa Barbara, where Quine and Kripke were, respectively, the paragons of metaphysical inquiry. Jonathan's interests, less semantic, more ontological and of the world, enabled me to recognize my real interests and his approach to metaphysics was instrumental to me developing my own. I had the pleasure of interacting with him on several occasions in different parts of the world. He was always kind to me and generous with his time. I hold dear our philosophical conversations and exchanges. Jonathan was encouraging at the earliest stages of this project, when the book was only incipient. I remain grateful for his help and saddened by the untimeliness of his passing.

When I first began to consider seriously time and temporal reality, I was introduced to many key ideas and distinctions via the work of L. Nathan Oaklander. So to meet him years later and to have the opportunity to interact with him was a great pleasure. His work was hugely valuable in my formative years as a philosopher and continues to inform much of my thinking. Although Nathan and I disagree on many issues, he has always appreciated my work—just as much as I have always appreciated his. Nathan's support was so important to me in the early stages of my career that I really do not know if I would have a career at all without him. He enabled this book, in more ways than one, and for this I am profoundly grateful.

I met Yuval Avnur when he was an undergrad at Santa Barbara and I was a grad student. We connected again several years later when—to Yuval's astonishment!—we both ended up with positions in SoCal. Since then he has been one of my favorite people with whom to talk philosophy (or just talk to). He is an extremely good philosopher: perceptive, honest, open-minded. He is a sympathetic and enthusiastic interlocutor. Many of the papers I have written over the last several years have been made much better by his careful consideration and a good number of the ideas and arguments of this book have been honed through hours of discussion with Yuval. He has urged me to think with originality and has made me a better philosopher.

I cold-called Michael Della Rocca via email many years ago when I was a grad student at Santa Barbara. He responded with a graciousness and respect that at the time, sadly, I did not think I deserved. Since then, we have corresponded, exchanged work, spent time together. Michael is a bold and original thinker and a paradigm of professional excellence. I always get much out of engaging with him and his work because we have, I believe, the same interests and very similar philosophical temperaments and values. (Nevertheless, a key disagreement, about the scope of explanation, sends us in opposite directions!) Michael, perhaps more than any other person, enabled me to enhance this book by challenging me with penetrating questions and demands for clarification regarding its central claims and positions. He also played an essential role in its publication, strategizing with me and offering guidance and uplifting words. For all this, I am indebted to him and will remain eternally grateful.

I was first introduced to John Martin Fischer decades ago by Tony Brueckner, when I was a grad student at Santa Barbara. I was close to Tony; Tony was close to John; so John immediately accepted me as a good friend. Ever since, John has provided guidance, assistance, and wisdom. I have benefited not only from these, but from numerous discussions, philosophical and otherwise, as well as John's laudable work, which takes life and living more seriously than that of any other philosopher I know. John has been a great friend and a crucial ally at pivotal junctures in my career. (He was the one who introduced me to Peter Ohlin.) My debt to John is huge, and I will always remember and wholeheartedly appreciate what he has done for me.

I would like to acknowledge here and convey my substantial thanks to Peter Ohlin at Oxford University Press. He rescued this project when I was languishing and it was somewhere—or nowhere—in limbo. I will always be grateful to him for the advice he gave, which moved this book toward actualization, and for his subsequent assistance in actualizing it.

This book owes a great deal—the most, really—to several people outside of academia. I have discussed this book and writing more generally, among much else, with Maya Rupert, my most eminent former student. I thank her for all of her love and our dear friendship. I have tremendous gratitude (and love) for F. David and Susan Mistretta, whom I met when I was in high school and they were established professionals. For most of my life now they have provided me with guidance and support. In the summer of 2019, when I was nearing completion of the initial draft of this book, they provided me with a basement in which to work (a haven from the upstate New York heat and humidity) and a fine, mint-condition, mid-century enamel top dinette table on which to write. When Dave would return home for lunch—around ten in the morning—he would come down the stairs to check in on me. He has a genuine interest in my work and so my efforts to explain to him what I was up to gave me the opportunity to clarify many subtle points and to come to a better understanding of the issues myself. I cherish those casual conversations and all the many more serious ones I have had with Dave and Sue as we have grown old together. I would like to thank as well my esteemed friend Kevin Baumert, whom I met in college, in an airport, on our way to East Africa for the summer. Kev is not a philosopher by training, but by acumen and quality of mind is an impressive one. We have had innumerable discussions over the decades, in places far afield, that have provided me with illumination and inspiration. In the summer of 1994, I pretentiously announced to Kev a book on time. I have no idea now what I presumed the contents of that book to be; but here is another, better one. I owe an incalculable amount—indeed, *everything*—to my mother, Roxanne Roma, who nurtured me in Endwell with the love and confidence and freedom to become anything, even something as ridiculous as an academic philosopher.

I would be little more than a ridiculous academic philosopher were it not for my wife, Ashley, and our two marvelous boys, Campbell and Basil. Ashley is, and not merely metaphorically, the source of my adult life, a wondrous life for which words are inadequate to express my gratitude. I know Ashley is my greatest love and, when we are not butting heads, I can see this, too. Her loving sustenance for me (and the boys) has myriad forms: logistical, practical, intellectual, emotional, etc. I could not have devoted the yearslong attention, in quiet and solitude, needed to write this book were it not for Ash's ingenuity and sacrifices. Our boys are the basis of my greatest happiness and meaning—and the impetus for my greatest humility. I hope I serve you all well. My love and appreciation for Ash and the boys is everything . . . and then some.

PART I
INTRODUCTION
Confronting the World

1
What Is *All This*?

Curiosity leads most everyone, at some point, to question something. When such a question arises, one might do one's best to answer it—or one might not. Practical demands might lead one to the next thing, as might one's temperament or other interests. Some questions one does pursue can be answered with minimal effort, by asking someone or by just lifting the lid. Not all questions are so easily answered, though. If one has the inclination (and privilege) to pursue earnestly some difficult question, others arise before any satisfactory answer to the original. These further questions raise issues that are specific and confined, general and expansive and lead, of course, to yet more questions.

Some (or many) of these questions might never have been asked and most would pique relatively few, but no question should be dismissed merely because of its strangeness or lack of widespread appeal. If one inquires conscientiously, among one's questions will be those regarding authority and justification, for example, who is in the position to answer any of these questions and on what grounds. If one were to persist with one's questions, critically and honestly, more and more would arise until eventually one would come to question literally everything. One might ask what *any of this* is. Here one would have to stop—there is no more to query. At this terminus, one need not be in a state of *doubt*, feeling angst or despair, questioning the legitimacy of one's inquiry or what prompts it. One might be, rather, in a state of *perplexity*, stirred, never doubting the legitimacy of one's inquiry or *whatever* it is that motivates it, feeling only determination to confront this whatnot. One might be seeing more clearly without recognizing what one sees. Mundane concerns would draw one away, but once one gets to that point, returning is not difficult.

Lingering here, at this point of acute perplexity, there are ever so many questions; there can no longer be, however, any question of authority. Authority arises, in some context, when prior skills or knowledge give one's claims extra epistemic weight. Yet in this context, one is calling into question everything, the basis of all skill and any knowledge, and so no one can be more adept or know more here. When one questions everything, what is left is just *all this*, whatever "it" is, if any thing at all. Anyone, regardless of how benighted, gets on to *all this* as well as any other. This point of acute perplexity, which precludes dogma or preconceived ideas, is egalitarian, putting all inquirers on the same footing. Thus, anyone purporting to be authoritative at this point must be making presumptions—about what exists, how what exists is, how "it" can be engaged, how "it" is to be engaged—that are antithetical to the wholly critical context. Any presumed authority here is misguided; anyone deferring to such authority is even more so.

Recognizing this lack of authority should be empowering, for one might have worried, after millennia of great minds investigating, contemplating, pontificating, whether one might dare question *everything*, including all that each of them has said. But if nothing is taken for granted, all are equals and anyone who would know anything must begin at the same point: *here*, where every tradition, every school, every text, every figure, every science, every theory, every claim is exposed to the utmost critical scrutiny. What one seeks at this terminus is an appropriate, that is, a correct and grounded, answer to some—to *any*—question. Certainly a salient question at this point, and perhaps the only relevant one, is *what is all this*?

'All this,' taking nothing for granted, demonstrates the *world*. When one endeavors to begin inquiry making no presuppositions, it is not as if one must begin with nothing whatsoever, even if one forgoes at the outset the presumption that there are any *things*. Rather one begins with the world—*all this*—the whatnot that can induce perplexity and so move one to inquire. The world, confronted without assumption, is merely the *impetus to inquiry*. The impetus to inquiry, given one's lack of assumptions, is unconditioned and, hence, unrestricted. "It" is whatever is like, or unlike, what moves one to inquiry, to wit, *all this*. Call whatever is like or unlike, without condition, what moves one to inquiry what *is*, that is, what *exists*. The world, then, is whatever is (not whatever might be and certainly not what is not). The impetus to inquiry, therefore, includes—unconceptualized—whatever might, at a later stage of inquiry, be conceptualized as near or far; microscopic, enormous, or in between; concrete or abstract; mental or physical; perceptible or imperceptible; effable or ineffable; comprehensible or incomprehensible; etc. If God, Bigfoot, or the Bunny Man exists or there are particles, tables, planets, colors, minds, sense data, attributes, numbers, sets, ghosts, souls, gnomes—what have you—*all this*, regarded merely as the impetus to inquiry, includes that thing, and whatever bases it has, unrecognized and undifferentiated by any inquirer (though, if such a thing does, in fact, exist, it is differentiated per se). If God, Bigfoot, or the Bunny Man does not exist or there are no particles, tables, planets, colors, minds, sense data, attributes, numbers, sets, ghosts, souls, or gnomes, then *all this* includes no such thing.

In confronting *all this* as merely the impetus to inquiry, one engages a complete and absolute diverse array. Any two inquirers taking nothing for granted confronting this array engage an impetus to inquiry that is not relevantly different. Even if *all this* presents to one as *thus* and to another, differently—*thusly*—"it" is nonetheless, from this perspective, nothing but a comprehensive diverse array. (Here 'thus' refers to *all this*, but in a way that is supposed to draw attention to the precise arrangement of "it," i.e., the world. The importance of observing the exact arrangement of *all this*, in its tremendous complexity, becomes clear below.) So a Neanderthal gazing about, withholding discrimination (from a totality that another might characterize as containing a fire and trees and a starry sky); and a medieval anchorite, with their eyes closed, musing on, yet not classifying, what they are experiencing (a totality that another might characterize as containing a welter of subdued visual impressions, bodily feels, emotional and intentional states); and a modern scientist reflecting on what is present to them, eschewing any means of discernment (from a totality that another might characterize as containing a table, lab equipment, a dirty window, a pang of hunger, a twinge of anxiety) may inquire on the same basis.

The conceptualizations of *all this*, how it is discriminated and how sense is made from these discriminations, obviously differ among various groups of inquirers and are, perhaps, significantly different at distinct stages of human development. Nevertheless, at some innocent point, human inquiry begins with nothing but a diverse array. *Any* theory ultimately comes from this basis, even if that theory is derived, in one way or another, from other theories, presumed or challenged, and so every theory must be consistent with such bare diversity. Wholly critical inquiry would begin from this ecumenical basis to see what insight can be gained into the world—and, consequently, all apt theorizing—by examining, without taking anything for granted, this basis. Of course, one might question whether any insight can be gained by such a general pursuit, but the present work is an attempt to show that much can.

Call inquiry that begins from bare diversity, a point where no presupposition is made, where *all this* is regarded merely as the impetus to inquiry, *original inquiry*. The fruits of such wholly critical inquiry, if it is possible, would be welcomed by someone who, acutely perplexed by the world, queries what any of this is and desires a pristine answer, one free from any unwarranted assumption. The value of original inquiry, however, would go beyond resolving such acute perplexity. Original inquiry begins where any completely open-minded inquiry must begin, with *all this*, a diverse array. Its starting point is neutral, universal and, therefore, beyond controversy. What can be learned about the world through inquiry from this point, given that nothing about *all this* is taken for granted, would provide constraints on any inquiry. All inquiry is directed at the world (or some part of it) so any inquiry would have to be consistent with the principles apprehended here, which would be based on unadulterated confrontation with the world. Original inquiry could reveal, then, the ground rules for inquiry itself; the generality of the pursuit, its stringent openness, could illuminate the *form* of inquiry, what must be in place for inquiry to be possible at all. If some principle is necessary for inquiry, it can be known with assurance by any inquirer.

Moreover, since *all this*, the starting point of original inquiry, is beyond controversy, any controversy regarding the world or some phenomenon herein must arise from some assumption posterior to engaging the world as merely the impetus to inquiry. Disagreement must arise from divergence in one's response to bare diversity. Beginning at a neutral, universal starting point, where *all this* is regarded as merely the impetus to inquiry, provides the opportunity to identify the roots of divergence and to evaluate their motivation, in conflicting principle or value, from common ground. Hence, insight into such controversies—and perhaps the means of resolving them—could be gained via investigation by the light of what is not controversial, *all this*, and whatever principles original inquiry might provide.

So original inquiry, a pursuit undertaken without presupposition about *all this* to answer the question what "it" is, seems to me to be invaluable. One might, however, even already dismiss such a pursuit. Wholly critical inquiry, inquiry that takes nothing for granted about *all this*, is ultimately directed at an account of what (if anything) the world per se is. In other words, such inquiry is directed at insight, if it is available, into what *all this* is and how it is independent of any inquiry. Yet, one might maintain, the unconceptualized or unqualified or unconditioned engagement with the world requisite for such insight is impossible. One might object that even if one ignores—or purports to—the familiar ways of cognizing one's inner and outer domains, one does not thereby gain access to the world as it is prior to inquiry, for any engagement with the world by creatures like us is mediated by formal features of the human mind that structure and so alter what is there or by subpersonal physiological cognitive systems that process and organize and so modify what is. Some qualification of and, hence, conditions on what is, the objection continues, is a prerequisite for any engagement with anything at all. The world as it is in itself, therefore, is inaccessible; original inquiry into *all this*, in the sense I propose, is a silly, ignorant fantasy.

This objection is misguided. Although original inquiry is indeed directed at illuminating what (if anything) the world per se is, I do not assume that by confronting *all this* merely as the impetus to inquiry that one thereby engages the world as it is in itself. In original inquiry, one makes *no* assumptions about what one is confronting when confronting *all this*. In so confronting the world, one engages a diverse array, whatever "it" is. Even if *any* mental engagement with *anything* requires contributions of a mind (or brain), what is engaged is a diverse array. Confronting *all this* without presupposition provides unadulterated confrontation with the world; it is not assumed to provide confrontation with the unadulterated world, the world per se. Unadulterated confrontation is confrontation that accepts this diverse array as nothing but a diverse array, and not with theoretical assumptions about the basis, cause or structure of this diversity. This objection, then, reveals a misunderstanding, on the part of the objector, as to what original inquiry is, and so does not undermine the pursuit. Any inquiry that, in the end, reveals that one can have unadulterated access to what is *or that one cannot* (say, because of the ineluctable transformations of the mind or brain) arises—if it begins untendentiously—from the same basis, namely, bare diversity, and with neither outcome presumed. So if one wants to resolve this issue regarding access to the world per se, on the basis of particularly secure grounds, one should examine it from the point of original inquiry.

This wholly critical pursuit, original inquiry, is to be without dogma. But one might object that what I say about the world and about the point from which presuppositionless inquiry must begin are themselves dogmatic. I am, one might claim, just insisting that *all this* is a diverse array. I am not, though, and I do not see how what I am doing could be dogmatic. Dogma is doctrine, claims that are to be taken on authority, to be accepted uncritically. Original inquiry is simply introduced as inquiry that begins with (nothing but) *all this*. Yet *all this* is not a claim. The use of "all this" simply demonstrates this whatnot, whatever "it" is here to be confronted. "Its" diversity might be incontestably patent to some, but still it need not, nor should not, go unquestioned in wholly critical inquiry. Question it. The very effort to do so—to hold some whatnot at critical distance to assess "it"—provides a clear demonstration of the lack of uniformity in question. So, to be clear, at the outset of this proposed wholly critical inquiry, I am not *assuming* the world is a diverse array. I am not even assuming that the world *appears* to be a diverse array (thereby presupposing a distinction between appearance and reality). I am not *assuming* anything about the focus of inquiry, I am just demonstrating *all this*, the world, a diverse array. Any inquiry that takes nothing for granted about *all this* that ultimately reveals what the world is, even that "it" is an utterly uniform static monolith, or that justifies taking seriously some distinction between the world per se and how it appears when creatures like us engage it, must begin upon the same basis, namely, *all this*, a diverse array of whatnot. Hence, this starting point is neutral and universal.

Original inquiry, as an activity, cannot be without constraint—any activity must have norms if one is to perform that very activity rather than some other—and these constraints must be present at the outset of inquiry and, therefore, presupposed. Still, such presuppositions do not contaminate the *focus* of the inquiry, *all this* without condition. The purity of its focus is what makes the starting point of original inquiry neutral and universal, that permits its insightfulness and gives the inquiry its force. (I say more about original inquiry and its methodology in Chapter 3.)

Returning to a point of acute perplexity, considering the feasibility of wholly critical inquiry and pondering how to proceed, one notices that what one is confronting—*all this*, the world—shifts. It is not entirely different, but it is indeed different. There is among it both inconstancy and constancy. Even questioning everything, these phenomena of inconstancy and constancy are patent, seeming to pervade the world. Retreating from this terminus for the nonce, I want to make cogent, in a more straightforward way, the familiarity, yet vividness, of these phenomena, for they are crucial to understanding this project.

One's experience seems to reveal an inconstant world in which things continuously come into existence, change, and cease to be. The leaves outside my window move in the breeze, stop, and start again. There are new buds on some branches. Students walk by and cars pass. I hear sounds that break the silence and cease. I am in a state of frustration as I strive to find the words to express this point, and then the state is relieved. Yet if the leaves are moving at this moment, this—the leaves moving at this very moment—will not and cannot change, even when the leaves stop. Despite their new growth, the branches are the very ones there yesterday. If there is a student (or car) on some spot at this moment, then even though the student moves, at every other moment, that there is no student on that spot at the initial moment is flatly false. Similarly, to characterize a rumbling sound as shrill even though the sound has gone would be incorrect and, hence, reality seems constrained by a sound that is no more, and though, as I write, the sense of frustration has passed, something remains unchanged, at least insofar as it must be true for evermore that a state of frustration precedes this state of relief. So even as one experiences an inconstant world, one experiences a constant one, a world in which how things are at any given moment seems unchangeable, complete. There are, then, these two indubitable phenomena—inconstancy and constancy—revealed in confronting the world.

I am considering inquiry that is supposed to begin without presupposition. Whether this putative shift in the world, and what I have just said about it, are compatible with such wholly critical inquiry is, then, worth examining. I suggest that these phenomena of inconstancy and constancy are patent. One might object that this is dogma, that I am just taking familiar features of the world at face-value and, hence, that this is not sufficiently critical for so-called original inquiry. This is mistaken. Regard the world merely as the impetus to inquiry, "it" presents as *thus*; regard it again, it is *as so*. (Perhaps, as one might say at some later point in inquiry, that the wind has let up or one has exhaled or one feels a heightened sense of suspense from one moment to the next.) To maintain that *all this* goes from *thus*... to *as so* is not merely to assert two claims; it is also to demonstrate twice the world, which differs from one demonstration to the next. This complex act and what it reveals are not to be an unquestioned starting point: question it. Again, the very effort to do so, even a struggle to understand what I am doing here or to see how best to challenge it, confirms the phenomena in question. The inconstancy in *all this* is perhaps more vivid; but the constancy is plain when one reflects that if *all this* is *thus*, to deny that it was as demonstrated is always incorrect. Note that I am not here taking for granted familiar notions of inconstancy and constancy; rather, I am providing one with the means to acquaint oneself with the relevant phenomena. Note, furthermore, that I am not presuming there is *change*. Change is a distinct phenomenon, one that must meet certain conditions that need not be present for the mere inconstancy confronted in *all this* going from *thus* to *as so*. So, again, I do not see how what I am doing could be dogmatic.

If one concedes there is, strictly speaking, no dogma here, someone dubious of original inquiry might nonetheless object that I am relying too much on *common sense*, and doing so is not sufficiently critical given my intentions. But "common sense," whatever it is exactly, uncritically accepts familiar concepts and presumes they are satisfied. This is no part of the inquiry I am proposing here, which begins by explicitly setting aside all concepts, familiar or unfamiliar. What I am trying to do is to direct one's attention to *all this*, stripped of any conceptualization, regarded merely as the impetus to inquiry, and to attach labels to phenomena that are *given* there (such as a lack of uniformity, that is, diversity and inconstancy and constancy). These phenomena are easily accessible—indeed, immediately verifiable—to anyone who might even try to contest them. So, again, I do not accept familiar notions of inconstancy and constancy, whatever these are supposed to be, and take them as applying to veridical phenomena. On the contrary, in light of *all this*, a shifting diverse array—on the basis of evident phenomena accessible to anyone, anywhere, anywhen—I introduce notions of inconstancy and constancy. One of the purposes of this book is to account consistently for both of these seemingly opposing phenomena in the context of a wholly critical account of what *all this* is.

These phenomena are no less manifest when one returns to a point of acute perplexity, questioning *all this*, erasing the outlines, as it were, of familiar things and confronting the—shifting—world as merely the impetus to inquiry. One must proceed from this terminus by answering appropriately some question, a question prompted by *all this*, the world. *All this* (now) presents as *thus* and not some other way. Therefore, not just any answer to some question will do. An appropriate answer must be consistent with the world presenting as *thus*. So there are, in fact, some constraints among *all this* even when one takes nothing for granted about anything, not even that *all this* is a thing itself. Yet if there are some constraints on inquiry, then there is some *thing* or other in the most general sense. A constraint cannot constrain if it does not exist and so any constraint is an existent, an entity, a being, that is, some thing or other. There is, then, a prior question to what *all this* is and this is the question of what a *thing* is. An answer to the latter, the primary ontological question, is, seemingly, where a wholly critical inquiry ought to begin. Hence, one needs a method of inquiry that enables one to explicate what a thing—*any thing whatsoever*—is.

Before continuing, pointing out that recognizing *some thing or other* is consistent with original inquiry as I propose it is worthwhile. There is no plausible common-sense notion of a thing, so I cannot be accused of merely accepting, uncritically, that notion. Moreover, I take nothing for granted about the category of thing there is, so there should not be additional concerns about dogma. I certainly am not, here at the outset, presuming that a thing is a substance, in some traditional sense (of this vexed notion), or a familiar concrete object. I presume nothing about what or how things are. A thing is just the basis of the diversity in *all this*, the basis of its presenting as *thus* and not some different way. Diversity requires distinctness. So the existence of thing*s* (plural)—the bases of the differences in *all this*—and not merely some thing (singular) is given. Therefore, I am not taking for granted things; I am not starting with the claim that there are things. Things are to be confronted and recognized in *all this*, more precisely, in *all this* presenting as *thus*.

Still, one might object, a *thoroughly* critical account of *all this* might—or should—start without things. In light of the foregoing, however, I do not see how it could. To confront the world and to refrain from acknowledging *any thing* or *every thing*, given that, in the context of original inquiry, the notion of a thing is initially entirely informed by *all this*, this diverse array, is, it seems to me, incoherent. Even if *all this* is—somehow—an utterly uniform static monolith, there still would be one thing, that monolithic whatnot. Again, a thing is nothing but an existent, a being, an entity; a thing-less world would be nothing at all, an account (presumably of something or other) that makes no recourse to things would be empty. A thing-less ontology, one without any existent, is no ontology.

If the method of original inquiry is to be wholly critical, it cannot presuppose at the outset, upon initial confrontation with *all this*, anything about things. Things in the most general sense are the focus and basis of any (constrained) inquiry and, as such, the means of any explanation. Understanding what a thing is, then, provides insight into the limits of inquiry and of explanation. Such understanding is, in part, the value of original inquiry. Understanding what a thing is, moreover, reveals how—again, in the most general sense—the world is structured, how things in *all this* stand with respect to one another. This, in turn, provides insight into, for instance, whether there are necessary connections among things themselves and whether some things are more or less fundamental than others. I believe that failing to begin inquiry with the primary ontological question, the answer to which provides an explication of what a thing is, can distort the world and obscure one's engagement with it. Consequently, many who have undertaken inquiry from other points have been burdened with specious concerns or theoretical objectives. I think it is such failure, then, that has led to confusion about the scope of explanation, thereby promoting acceptance of some mistaken version of a Principle of Sufficient Reason; that underlies the misguided reductionist ambitions of modern science and the hierarchical presumptions of most metaphysics; that hides the real bone of contention in discussions of the metaphysics of time; that promotes ill-founded views concerning the basis of modality (i.e., necessity and possibility); that makes it difficult to discern the appropriate account of the inconstancy and constancy in the world; and so has made elusive a satisfying account of *all this* and its boundaries.

Once one begins to reflect on things and can explicate what a thing (of any variety) is, one recognizes that the thing paramount to an account of *all this* is *time itself*. Time, I maintain, is indeed a thing, one crucial to the inconstancy in *all this* (as it shifts), yet just as important to illuminating its undeniable constancy. An account of time per se enables one to better understand the seemingly irresolvable controversies in discussions of the metaphysics of time and even to resolve these satisfactorily. The corollary accounts of the things dependent on time and those independent of it reveal the boundaries of reality in a (or the) vital dimension. I argue that all familiar things that exist in time exist now (and so propound a view that shares certain features with so-called *presentism*). This moment, now, is not after another moment nor before one; it is the only moment that exists, and so bears no relation to any other. Paradoxically, then, there never was anything prior to this moment and there never will be anything subsequent to it. Yet there *could be* more than there now is . . . and now there is. In addition to all those things in time that exist now, there are also the things in the world that stand in no significant relation to what now is, for they exist without, i.e., independently of, time. The account of how *all this*, temporal and atemporal things alike, evolves—the manners in which things come to be, how they change, how they cease to be—is the sought-after account of every thing and then some.

§1.1. How This Inquiry Is Different

I wrote this book because I have undergone a process of continuous questioning that led me to ask what any of this is. The process began when I was an inquisitive child and was accelerated when, as a philosophy undergraduate and then graduate student, I was repeatedly bewildered by problems I was supposed to find compelling, but were simply alien to me. The problems seemed to have little to do with what I found—and find—so fascinating, namely, *all this*. When considering such problems, I would often ask myself, *why would anyone say that*? In many cases, I could see that the philosopher making the statement was responding to some odd dilemma or claim made by a predecessor, who was responding to some more distant antecedent. This led me to wonder about the sources of the problems I was expected to inherit, and about a different course for inquiry.

Once I gained sufficient facility to examine philosophical problems themselves, I found most based on assumptions, some plausible, others not, that were rarely supported (and were usually unstated). Some of the problems were taken to be motivated by common sense, but in light of such rife disagreement I was (and remain) dubious of "common sense," whatever it is taken to be. I wondered how untutored, unreflective claims could provide insight into any matter, let alone one that were elusive. And I wondered whose claims were deemed common enough to matter, and under which circumstances. All these misgivings prompted me, as a junior professor, to undertake, with new determination, a process of questioning—unlearning—what I had had to accept about the world and inquiry in order to be initiated as an academic philosopher. The present work is, after some years, the culmination of this process.

My discussion here is, therefore, prompted by and guided by the world, not the literature. I begin, without ontological or epistemological prejudice, with nothing but *all this*. Throughout, I try to preserve contact with *all this*, by frequently regarding (and demonstrating) it. The accounts and theories I propound are informed by *all this* and illuminate it and, at each step, are justified by it. Hence, again and again through these chapters, I direct the reader to consider *all this*. I do, nonetheless, consider a good deal of what other philosophers have said. I certainly do not mean to suggest that by questioning everything and everybody one ought to be dismissive of anything or anyone. There is, of course, much to be learned by considering, and vetting, the work of others who have examined the world or parts of it. I do, however, begin in a different place—at a point of acute perplexity where nothing is taken for granted about *all this*—and with idiosyncratic, yet universal, objectives. I am endeavoring to provide insight into literally everything, to provide the foundations of and framework for all inquiry and to do so in such a way that these structural details are compelling, if not unassailable.

Original inquiry, the method I use to attain the account of what a thing is and what the world is cannot, at the outset, be characterized by means of hoary philosophical distinctions, such as a priori versus a posteriori, analytic versus synthetic, internal versus external, subject versus object, appearance versus reality; nor in terms of familiar, though nebulous, doctrines like naturalism, empiricism, rationalism, etc. These distinctions and doctrines are based on all sorts of questionable assumptions—about what things are, how they are, how they can be engaged, how they are to be engaged—that are inimical to wholly critical inquiry. From the point of acute perplexity, where this inquiry begins, no such assumptions are made, and so neither these orthodox distinctions nor doctrinal criteria have any purchase. By a point at which one has acquired a better understanding of *all this* and of inquiry, most of these distinctions and criteria are obsolete or, at best, misleading.

Nevertheless, and obviously, some of what I say is reminiscent of other philosophers interested in the world at large who attempt to elucidate *all this* and how one knows it. Even the little I say above surely suggests some familiar outlooks from the history of Western philosophy. I consider some here in order to make plausible that the present perspective is rather different from these more familiar ones—perhaps even original—and to make clear why I develop my project as I do. Thus, I urge one to query relentlessly, to a point from which one might ask what any of this is, and this suggests an initial skeptical position and a Cartesian method of doubt. In Descartes's best-known work, his goal is to ascertain what can be known (with certainty) about the world. Since such knowledge was thought to come via one's senses, Descartes raises doubts about such faculties to indicate another, the pure intellect, that better reveals the world. With the pure intellect, Descartes holds, one is able to discern metaphysical first principles, which are the most general constraints on reality.

But this Cartesian project is different from my own. Whereas Descartes's is primarily epistemic, toward metaphysical ends, my project is primarily metaphysical (with epistemic consequences). Any epistemic project is ultimately about knower and known thing and the requisite relation between the two. Yet how anything is known is posterior to how or what a thing is such that it exists at all (and so may then know or be known). The latter is the key issue here. My primary objective, therefore, is an account of what knower and known entity and any relation between them are qua things. To attain this objective, one must begin prior to a point at which there could be skepticism, and so doubt is no part of my method. I begin with *all this* and what I demonstrate by 'all this' is just the whatnot amidst anyone—indeed, anything—is. *All this* is not taken to be sensed nor known in some other way; nor taken to be non-mental, nor mental; nor extended, nor not extended. It is not taken to be any particular way. *All this* is simply confronted, and such unqualified whatnot is beyond doubt. From this confrontation, I endeavor to provide an account of *all this*.

An upshot of this account is insight into the conditions such that *all this* is confrontable at all. Characterized in this way, the project sounds more Kantian than Cartesian. In Kant's critical work, his primary objective is to determine whether and how metaphysics is even possible, where Kant takes metaphysics to be a systematic account of the a priori—and, hence, necessary—constraints on one's experience of the world. This objective serves the ultimate purpose of showing that reason alone reveals that these constraints on one's experience are compatible with both modern mechanistic science and established moral and religious principles. To discern these necessary constraints, which Kant, with Hume, maintains cannot be simply sensed, Kant urges a "Copernican Revolution," whereby one changes one's focus from what one senses to the means by which one has any of the familiar sensible experiences one indubitably does. Via this stratagem, Kant provides a schedule of concepts, inherent to one's human mind, that he maintains are needed for such experience. By a distinctive style of reasoning, what has come to be called a *transcendental argument*, Kant purports to show how the employment of these concepts are required for one to have any experience of the world in the first place.

Kant's ultimate purpose, his primary objective, and even his starting point, are different from mine. He begins by questioning what, if anything, one can know about the world independently of sense experience. I begin with the question of what the world is, one that is prior to any question concerning how anything is or can be known. To meet his primary objective, Kant suggests a change of focus, from the things one senses to how one has the sensible experiences one does. My primary objective is an account of what a thing, *any* thing, is, for such an account is crucial to understanding *all this* and, consequently, inquiry in general. Whether a thing is sensed, or engaged in some other way, is irrelevant to my objective. My focus, therefore, is not in the first instance on one's subjective engagement with the world, but with the world itself, whatever it might be. Of course, this is still inquiry, and what the object of one's inquiry is is not independent of how that object is engaged.

Nonetheless, I am not seeking the conditions on knowing or experiencing *all this* or experiencing some thing, but rather the conditions on being, what must be so in order for a thing to exist. An account of the former conditions alone would ignore or take for granted what I am after. One might, I suppose, deem an account of the latter—the conditions on being—with a deduction showing their connection to *all this*, a sort of transcendental argument. Were one to do so, though, one must acknowledge that the upshot is very different from what Kant purports to present. Indeed, Kant's objective is to illuminate the constraints on a subject's experience; mine is to illuminate what any subject, experience, or experienced object must be. Moreover, whereas Kant's purpose is to reconcile scientific, moral, and religious doctrines presumed to be correct, my purpose is to discern the constraints on any appropriate account of anything. At the outset, then, I suspend judgment on all doctrines or theories.

My project begins innocently, starting with nothing but with what one must: what is given, *all this*. One cannot presuppose anything about any thing, lest one beg the question with respect to an account of *all this* or a thing in general. A *presuppositionless* approach of the kind I aspire to might bring to mind those who were impressed by Kant's project but objected to it for being insufficiently critical. Reinhold and Fichte endeavored to present systems that were supposed to be, in some sense, presuppositionless and, hence, as critical as could be. Their projects, however, whatever their disagreements with Kant, were certainly Kantian, whereas mine clearly is not. Hegel, too, exhorted a presuppositionless philosophy. In whatever way one interprets his philosophy, it is quite different from Kant's. More importantly for present purposes, regardless of how one interprets Hegel, his historicism is (perhaps) uncontroversial. To do philosophy—to engage critically the world in the effort to understand it—Hegel believes that one must consider what came before, and how history developed so as to yield *all this*. One must, as well (according to Hegel), consider how one's culture is a product of this history, and how one is a product of one's culture. Without awareness and appreciation of one's historical situation, one might take what is inconstant to be constant, what is collective to be individual or simply miss the norms that constrain one's project.

My project is in no way historical or cultural. In confronting *all this* as merely the impetus to inquiry, one engages a diverse array that is without qualification and so accessible to anyone in any age regardless of one's position or capabilities. With no presuppositions about any thing, the unqualified whatnot amid which a wholly critical inquiry begins is not relevantly different for one with no philosophical interests, floating in a sensory deprivation tank, than it is for a professional philosopher looking out the window. Race or gender or socio-economic status or nationality, etc., are, given overt and insidious social forces, relevant to whether one is provided the means to undertake critical inquiry, but these aspects of one's identity cannot be relevant to what such inquiry discerns, if undertaken properly. I do not presume that what it is to be is different from age to age or culture to culture—but nor do I presume that it is not. To have any insight into whether existence per se does differ in these ways, one must have an account of what existence per se is and for this one must have an account of what a thing, *any* thing, is. That is my primary objective. Furthermore, history (or culture) requires the shift in *all this* that reveals the constancy and inconstancy in the world and time itself. An account of this thing and its relations to others, a further goal of this project, is needed to understand what history is and what its ambit could be. My objectives, therefore, are not determined or constrained by history or culture; rather, my objectives are to understand what the things necessary for either are.

Again, my project begins innocently, starting with nothing but the world, *all this*. This sort of inquiry requires one to look at the world anew, without prejudice, merely as the impetus to inquiry. For some, this might recall Husserl and the *epoché* instrumental to his phenomenological investigations. Husserl urges a method whereby one confronts the world "bracketing" the question of whether the things that appear actually exist independently of or external to one. The purpose is not to exclude the so-called objective world from scrutiny, but to gain a new perspective on it, by regarding how this world and the things in it appear subjectively, to one's consciousness. But Husserl's method is not mine. He begins with and relies crucially on a distinction between internal versus external or subjective versus objective that I do not. Although it is part of Husserl's method to ignore, to a certain extent, this distinction, it is not part of the inquiry I undertake. The qualifications the distinction requires apply to things, and my primary objective is an account of what a thing is prior to any qualification. Furthermore, Husserlian epoché, and the distinctions on which it depends, are appropriate only in a context that makes further assumptions, for example, about the importance of consciousness and about how a mind engages *all this* (viz., by representing it). I do not make these assumptions, for they are not apt at the outset of a wholly critical project regarding *all this*.

So my focus is on the world, whatever it is, and the things it comprises. Crucial to this project is understanding what a thing—a being—is, and this seems to require some insight into being per se. Considered in this way, the project might be redolent of Heidegger. Heidegger, though, is concerned primarily with the meaning of being or Being or 'being.' I am not concerned directly with the meaning of anything. Heidegger accepts that there are different modes of Being, yet this is a claim I explicitly reject and argue against (in due course). He thinks that crucial to understanding Being is *Dasein*, the peculiar mode of Being of human persons or, on another interpretation, the peculiar sort of being human persons are, and *things*, for Heidegger, are beings considered independently of their usual settings and so have a distinctive mode of Being, *presence-at-hand*. None of these notions, nor the distinctions they require contribute to my primary objective, an account of what a being is. Nor do they seem to have a place in the sort of wholly critical inquiry I propose to undertake, coming as they do from a hugely complex and eccentric historical and cultural project. The similarities between my project and Heidegger's seem, then, quite superficial, perhaps limited to the use of certain strings of symbols. Yet, despite their differences, there surely are many noteworthy connections between the two projects that would be revealed with more elaborate discussion. This is so not just with respect to Heidegger's project and my own, but with respect to all the projects considered so briefly above. My present concern here, though, is with the differences between my project and the others for, I submit, the approach I take to *all this* is original.

One might have reservations about any claim of originality in philosophy, suspecting that any approach presented as novel has already been taken by some figure in the canon, and so all one will see, via the putatively novel approach, is an unfamiliar reworking of a venerable view or a pastiche of venerable views more worthy of consideration. Hence, one might think I should defend my claim of originality by presenting, in great detail, the projects of others and contrasting theirs with my own. I do not proceed in this way, however. For any canonical figure whose work I would thoroughly contrast with my own, I would need a definitive statement of at least a significant portion of that figure's work. Such a statement would require the tremendous effort needed to see to the bottom of and digest the project of a canonical figure. My own interests, though, have never inclined me toward such a goal. I have always been much more concerned with *all this* than with what any particular person has maintained about it. So my attention has been on issues and problems that have kept me closer to the world than any historical-cum-literary investigation could. If I believed that some philosopher had provided an appropriate—or explicit—account of what the world is or what a thing in general is, then my attention would be on it. But I am unaware of any such account. More importantly, insofar as one seeks real insight into the world, the work of a canonical figure is worth considering only if it is true. To determine whether it is seems to require a wholly critical account of *all this*, in order to have the means of verifying the claims of that figure. The purpose of my project is to provide such a wholly critical account. Therefore, the completion of this project, I believe, is needed to know how best to interpret the work of a canonical figure or even how seriously to take it.

To begin with the work of others, then, will not do. Given my aim—insight into literally everything—I must begin with the world and the original approach I develop here. I should be clear that I am not trying to be original for the sake of novelty. Rather, I think a novel approach to *all this* is needed to understand it and to reveal the foundations of and framework for all inquiry. To vindicate this claim, I must demonstrate the approach and present its results. Thus, to both contrast conclusively my project with others, such as those of canonical figures, and to show its value, I need to execute *this* project. This book is the means of doing so. For these reasons, the views of others with sweeping metaphysical or epistemic projects do not appear on its pages as frequently as some might expect. To be unequivocal: it is not as if I believe that no one else has ever confronted *all this* with the hope of understanding it and how one engages it. I do, though, believe no one else has done it quite as I propose. Interesting subsequent projects would be to compare the accounts and theories propounded in this book with more esteemed ones. Such investigations would surely illuminate these accounts, the others, and the world. However, again, a prerequisite for such investigations is the present one, which begins with nothing but *all this* and ends with a wholly critical account of it.

This is, I must admit, an ambitious project and so an ambitious book. I make this admission with a mixture of pride and embarrassment. *Pride* because I offer herein a new way of looking at things, one that reveals the limits of inquiry and certain boundaries to *all this*, and this perspective might be, I hope, comforting or liberating or inspiring to some. *Embarrassment* because I have been in academic philosophy long enough to know that one ought not write books like this. Grand deliberations about *all this* and about novel methodology are liable to be regarded as naive or, worse, obnoxious.

Many seem to think that while such deliberations might once have been appropriate, when conducted by the great minds of earlier centuries, one ought to know enough about the world by now to restrict one's attention to narrow problems (or very narrow problems). These problems have been selected by a number of professional and social mechanisms, and there are plenty of them. To eschew these problems, then, in favor of one's own is often taken to be impolite, selfish, arrogant, pretentious. Hence, one risks offense with such a book.

Still, I think the approach I offer here is worth taking and the issues that arise therefrom deserving of consideration, so I present this project with confidence, but humbly, in an effort to challenge and provoke without offending. One need not have undergone a process of coming to question *all this* in order to appreciate the project. If one sees the value of wholly critical inquiry from a terminus of acute perplexity or if one is just curious as to the prospect from that point, one can get there directly, simply by regarding *all this* anew and taking no thing for granted.

§1.2. Overview of the Present Work

If one begins with nothing but the world and asks what *all this* is, one cannot take for granted the question has an answer. One must examine, then, the prospects of a wholly critical discipline capable of providing an account of the world from an original terminus at which no principle about *all this* is presumed. Call such a discipline *metaphysics*. In Part II of this work, Chapters 2–5, I consider this discipline, the methodology it requires, to wit, original inquiry, and the theoretical framework it provides. Doing so reveals the significance of time to an account of *all this*.

In Chapter 2, I characterize metaphysics as a wholly critical discipline whose chief objective is an account of *what the world is and what it comprises*. Some account of what the world comprises is needed, for reality is, if anything, *diverse*, and so, at least by this measure, complex. Consequently, a metaphysical account of the world, which, as an account of this encompassing totality, must be *all-inclusive*, must be *general*, as well. It must not only acknowledge differences, thereby indicating whence this diversity arises, but also overlook them, in order to provide some insight into what *anything whatsoever* is—including the world itself, if it be a thing. So metaphysics proceeds via the question of what a thing, of any variety, is.

If metaphysics is critical, if it is to provide understanding, rather than merely knowledge, any account it provides must itself be scrutinized and evaluated. This leads to a distinctive problem for the metaphysics I am pursuing: its objective is a wholly critical account of what the world is but, given the scope of the account, there appears to be neither independent phenomena with which to contrast it, nor salient means of evaluating it—yet understanding the world, the very purpose of this account, requires evaluation. Since the sought account of the world comes via the question of what a thing is, a different aspect of this problem is providing an apt account of what a thing is while assuming nothing about *all this*. In light of this distinctive problem, I critique alternative approaches to metaphysics in contemporary discussions. I do so for two purposes. First of all, in order to determine whether approaches that deflate metaphysics, such as ones on which there is no unity to the discipline or on which the objective of attaining insight into things themselves is chimerical or on which the discipline is to be naturalized, undermine the ambitious metaphysics I am pursuing. Secondly, in order to determine whether approaches that endorse ambitious metaphysics, such as ones on which the discipline is autonomous or foundational or on which it is to be regarded as "first philosophy," can contribute to resolving the distinctive problem of providing a wholly critical account of the world. I conclude that these traditional approaches neither undermine the ambitious discipline I am pursuing nor contribute to resolving its distinctive problem. This makes pressing the need for a novel methodology in metaphysics.

I introduce this methodology, *original inquiry*, above, and in Chapter 3 I develop it further. By taking up original inquiry, one is able to answer the question of what a thing *of any variety* is. One might have thought little hangs on such an indiscriminate question. But this is a mistake. Things in the most general sense are the focus and basis of any (constrained) inquiry and, as such, the means of any explanation. Thus, understanding what a thing is provides insight into the limits of inquiry and of explanation. Such understanding, moreover, reveals how—again, in the most general sense—the world is structured, how things are related so as to produce *all this*. What a thing is determines the extent of these relations and their force and complexity. An explicit account of what a thing is, therefore, is not only crucial to realizing the chief objective of ambitious metaphysics, namely, an account of the world (and what it comprises), it also provides the ground rules for any other inquiry.

Regardless of the putative significance of an account of what a thing is, some will be dubious of the possibility of such an account, for that there can be no *summum genus*, no class that includes each thing just in virtue of its existing, has long been maintained. If this were so, the question of what a thing is would be misguided, unanswerable—and the ambitious metaphysics I am pursuing would be futile. I defend the legitimacy of the question by considering, and dismissing, both the traditional reasons adduced for maintaining there can be no *summum genus*, as well as an additional concern, regarding the unavoidable circularity of any account of what a thing is. This concern is alleviated through original inquiry. This method begins by regarding the world as merely the *impetus to inquiry*, nothing but a diverse array that is *thus*. Here, as above, 'thus' demonstrates how *all this* presents to one, as a more or less determinate panoply. From this terminus, one descries therein what a thing must be if the world is *thus*, which, indeed, it is. A thing, it turns out, is an ontological locus, that is, a *natured entity*, something that is and is how it is and what it is just in itself. A thing is but a constraint in *all this*. The aptness of this account is recognized in the very confrontation that enables it. In defense of these claims, and the methodology itself, I discuss how exactly original inquiry resolves the distinctive problem of metaphysics.

How and what the *structure in the world* (or the *structure in reality*, I use these terms interchangeably) is are among the consequences of a thing being a natured entity. Descriptions of these consequences, each of which can be regarded as a principle, taken together provide a theoretical framework. A theoretical framework is a collection of principles, consistency with which constrains inquiry into some subject matter and its correct account. Because this theoretical framework pertaining to the structure in the world arises from an account of what a thing is, and every (constrained) inquiry is directed at some thing(s) or other, the framework provides foundational conditions on—the ground rules for—all inquiry. Call this account of the structure in the world and the theoretical framework it provides *radical ontology*. This metaphysical account is *radical* in that it arises from the roots of inquiry and *ontological* in that it begins, not specifically with impressions nor ideas nor concepts nor subjective phenomena, but with things in general, any one of them or all of them. Among its many uses, radical ontology enables one to move past stalemate in metaphysical discussions of the world by revealing the grounds of a principled choice between seemingly incommensurable worldviews.

In Chapter 4, I discuss how the account of a thing as a natured entity illuminates the structure in the world. In particular, I make clear the consequences of this account for the *integrity* of this structure, showing how natured entities require there to be necessary connections among things in themselves, and its consequences for the *intricacy* of this structure, revealing the apt notion of fundamentality that accompanies things as natured entities. I am then able to propound an account of what the world is, thereby meeting the chief objective of ambitious metaphysics. One might be surprised that this objective can be met relatively easily, and one might be disappointed by the answer: the world is not anything at all. The world is not a thing per se; it is not one thing itself, just the plurality of all things. Although such an account is the chief objective of metaphysics, it is not its main value. The main value of the discipline is the theoretical framework for all inquiry that it provides. Via this framework, this account of the world has ever so many applications. After enumerating the ontological categories, I present a number of the principles included in this framework, namely, ones regarding the uniformity, compulsoriness, determinacy, and non-fragmentariness of being a thing. I conclude by considering the means and extent of inquiry; how, in general, well-founded inquiry is to proceed. These considerations and the foregoing principles are useful in subsequent chapters, in the effort to understand the extent of the world and the irrefragable inconstancy and constancy herein.

As observed above, when one first considers the impetus to inquiry, it is *thus*. When one considers it again, it is *as so*. This phenomenon is patent; the very attempt to question it confirms the phenomenon. There are, therefore, two modes of differentiation in the world. There is the diversity one confronts when one first takes up original inquiry—apparent in the world as *thus*—that indicates complexity and the need for generality in metaphysics. But there is also the distinct mode of differentiation demonstrated and under consideration here: things going from *thus* to *as so*. A mode of differentiation, an arrangement of things whereby distinctions are apparent, is not a thing per se; it is, rather, some *structural phenomenon*, some multiplicity of things. The phenomenon being considered here, this second mode of differentiation, is as incontrovertible as the original diverse impetus to inquiry. Call whatever is the ultimate basis of this second mode of differentiation in the world *time*. The *metaphysics of time* is the discipline whose objective is a critical account of what time is and its role among *all this*, that is, an account of the metaphysics of time. Given the centrality of time to one's experience of the world, in any engagement with it, a further purpose of this work, whose main one is to provide a critical account of the world, is to propound a complete and satisfactory account of the metaphysics of time.

An answer to the question of what time is, if the metaphysics of time is to be appropriately critical, must take nothing for granted about time, not even that it is a thing. So this discipline, too, must begin from a point of original inquiry, though a point from which one may be guided by the principles of radical ontology. Thus, in Chapter 5, I first consider how elusive an explication of what time is has been, despite the great deal of attention given to the metaphysics of time. The phenomenon of *change* is key to an account of the metaphysics of time, so, after distinguishing change from differentiation, I elucidate the former. Although time and moments are essentially related, I show that they are distinct and quite different. I then argue that time is itself a thing, discussing some of its significant qualities. Finally, I propose a theoretical framework for the metaphysics of time. The explication of what time is that I provide summarily resolves several putative controversies that have, traditionally, been regarded as central to discussions of the metaphysics of time. This just reveals that the genuine controversies here are not about time per se, they are, rather, about *temporal reality*, the structure of things in the world given the existence of time.

I devote Part III of this work, Chapters 6–9, to characterizing the correct general account of temporal reality, that is, the world in time. Modern discussions of the metaphysics of time, from their outset, have been premised on an unchallenged divide, thus suggesting irresolvable tension at the heart of this field of inquiry. The divide arises from one's very engagement with *all this*. Confronting the world in original inquiry, one encounters the world going from *thus* to *as so*—*temporal differentiation*—the phenomenon that reveals time itself. In this confrontation, one can experience equally both *inconstancy* in the world and *constancy*: undeniably, things go from *thus* to *as so* and yet once they do, when things are *as so*, to accept that they were—or, in some sense, *are*—as they were when demonstrated by 'thus' is undeniably appropriate. What underlies all the perennial disputes in discussions of the metaphysics of time is the attempt to accommodate both this inconstancy and constancy in an account of time and the world. What leads to dispute is disagreement about the things needed to do so, and the corresponding controversy regarding which of these two phenomena, inconstancy and constancy, is primary in an account of the metaphysics of time.

There are two generic approaches to accounting for all temporal phenomena based on two general views of the structure in temporal reality. The main purpose of Chapter 6 is to make explicit these two views and their importance to the metaphysics of time. On one view, the world in time is *ontologically homogeneous*. There are (infinitely) many moments with no peculiarly temporal thing distinguishing any one of these from any other. Each thing in time has a permanent existence: each moment exists without ceasing to be and whatever exists at any moment exists ceaselessly at all moments it exists. Thus, all the many moments of time—and everything that exists at them—are equally real. The key feature of the opposing view of temporal reality is that according to it there are significant structural and, hence, ontological differences in the world when it goes from being *thus* to *as so*. Given that this general view is based on difference, it admits of much greater variation than does the view on which the world in time is ontologically homogeneous; the unifying feature of all these many versions is that the world in time is *ontologically heterogeneous*.

The general view one adopts determines the things available to explain any temporal phenomenon and, therefore, the pivotal dispute regarding the metaphysics of time is which of these two incompatible views of temporal reality is correct. In Chapter 7, I arbitrate this dispute, arguing that the world in time is not ontologically homogeneous. I do so by examining the very phenomenon that both reveals time in original inquiry and motivates the two general views of temporal reality, namely, temporal differentiation. The world going from *thus* to *as so*, like any phenomenon, must have a basis among the things there are. I examine this phenomenon to discern its complexity and for insight into what underlies it.

Temporal differentiation is indisputable. Indeed, no one disputes it. There is disagreement only regarding what things, what structure, in the world is needed to account for the phenomenon. I discuss the *passage of time* as it has traditionally been understood and maintain, as many have, that an account of temporal differentiation in terms of passage is misguided. I then reflect on what appears to be the minimal structure needed to account for temporal differentiation and one's experience of it, viz., distinct moments bearing temporal relations, to determine whether this is in fact a satisfactory basis. I show that it is not and, therefore, no account of the world in time on which it is ontologically homogeneous can be successful. This view of temporal reality is incompatible with one's experience of temporal differentiation and of the world in time more generally; moreover, it cannot account for a certain inconstancy in the world, namely, the crucial transition in temporal differentiation—how the world goes from *thus* to *as so*. I close the chapter by considering how these decisive shortcomings of the view that the world in time is ontologically homogeneous, which had been the predominant one for decades and remains quite popular, might have been overlooked in previous discussions of the metaphysics of time.

The world in time is, therefore, *ontologically heterogeneous*: at least one moment is unique, bearing a temporal property or having some distinction that separates it from any other moment. There are many specific accounts that elaborate this general view of the world in time. On some of these, the heterogeneity in temporal reality is supposed to be *merely qualitative*, a difference in the properties that moments or the things that exist at them bear. On other accounts, the heterogeneity is more profound, a difference in what *exists simpliciter* from one moment to the next. In Chapter 8, I argue against accounts on which there is merely qualitative heterogeneity in temporal reality. Each of these, in one way or another, is inconsistent. I begin by considering the most familiar account of mere qualitative heterogeneity in temporal reality, namely the *traditional passage view*. This sort of view is shown to be inconsistent by considerations arising from ones first proposed by McTaggart, so I examine McTaggart's (in)famous argument for the unreality of time. There are those who reject the traditional passage view, yet nevertheless accept views on which, like the former, all moments ever in the world exist eternally (and permanently). To avoid the sort of contradiction revealed in light of McTaggart's argument, these so-called *moving spotlight views* must include certain principles regarding change and things themselves that I maintain are untenable. Thus, moving spotlight views must be rejected.

On any account according to which the heterogeneity of the world in time is merely qualitative, there is a permanent array of moments and things existing at them, and so all temporal phenomena are supposed to be explicable in terms of this array and any qualitative differences among the things in it arising from the temporal property, *presentness*, that distinguishes a unique moment. It turns out that to avoid obvious inconsistency in one's account of temporal reality, one must accept some *ontological transience*: some things, including moments, come into being or cease to be simpliciter. Explanations of temporal phenomena, therefore, can be in terms of whether certain things exist at all. I present an argument that some things of which one is directly aware cease to be simpliciter and argue further that a tenable metaphysics of time must recognize significant ontological transience among temporal entities, including moments. Importantly, recognizing the scope of ontological transience provides one with key insight into the phenomenon of temporal differentiation. These considerations preclude yet more accounts of the structure in temporal reality, to wit, so-called *growing block views*. They thereby illuminate part of the structure of the world in time, revealing that there is nothing whatsoever prior to this moment, now.

This raises the question of how things are subsequent to this moment. I begin Chapter 9 by considering views of the world in time on which there are moments subsequent to this one, now. New applications of arguments from preceding chapters show that these views are incorrect, there are no later moments. That this moment, now, is the only one there is follows. Of course, there is more to the structure in temporal reality than a single moment, for one's experience of the world is not momentary. Not only does one experience the world as *thus* and then *as so*, one also experiences it *as such* and *such* and so forth. There must, then, be more to the basis of the experience, further things to account for this continuity. An account of what underlies this experience is given in terms of time itself and of *absolute becoming*, whereby moments come into being simpliciter. Reflecting on this continuous experience of temporal differentiation indicates that the world as it now is, although complete, is not exhausted: it remains latent. There *could be* more to the world.

What more there could be, however, would, seemingly, be different from what is or has been. Presumably, what is to be includes *contingency*, an openness such that incompatible alternatives are possible. I discuss the relation between the world in time and this contingency and consider, in particular, how such contingency is included among the things in temporal reality. Given the structure of the world in time, which does not include more than one moment, and the ontology underlying this inquiry, the only contingency in the world arises from what now is: although nothing could now be otherwise than it actually is—*so everything must be just as it is*—in some cases, a thing could be otherwise (than it now is) at some moment yet to be. Likewise, although all there now could be (in time) is what there is at this moment, there might be more (or less) at some moment yet to be. Contingency arises *through* a moment, with the actualization, at a distinct moment, of the potential of the things at the first. Contingency and, hence, incompatible alternatives are not present *at* any moment; there is no *synchronic possibility*, that is, the possibility of a thing being otherwise than it is at a moment at that very moment. There is, therefore, a crucial connection between contingency and temporal differentiation.

In Part IV, Chapters 10–11, I propound the correct specific account of the world in time—*transient presentism* (or *momentary transientism*)—and characterize its limitations, arguing that no account of temporal reality can itself be an account of the metaphysics of time. There is nothing that will be, that is, nothing that exists subsequent to this moment, now; nothing that was, that is, nothing that exists prior to this moment. What now is is wholly determinate and complete. It is complete yet not exhausted, for although there *will not be* more in time, there, of course, *could be* more. Not at this moment, nor at a subsequent one, for there are none, but at some novel moment that comes to be. This moment, now, exists but for an instant, and is replaced by another, which stands in no relation to the former. This account of the world in time, which surely seems meager to some, is suggestive of *presentism*, a somewhat notorious view (or number of views) regarding the metaphysics of time. In Chapter 10, I elaborate my account of temporal reality by examining it vis-à-vis presentism. I do so to determine whether my account can satisfactorily illuminate the indubitable inconstancy in the world—as evidenced by the coming to be of things, the multitudinous changes among them, and their ceasing to be—and whether it and its attendant explanation of temporal differentiation suffice as an account of the metaphysics of time.

To these ends, I discuss what presentism is supposed to be and consider to what extent the account of temporal reality I am propounding is appropriately regarded as presentist. This is worth considering because presentism is open to some obvious and formidable objections. Whether my account is presentist is a surprisingly nuanced issue, for presentism, it turns out, is neither a single view nor even a unified class of them. Although transient presentism rejects what is standardly the definitive ontological claim of presentism, that *only present things exist*, I believe regarding it as presentist is nonetheless appropriate. This account, which avoids all the objections usually directed at presentism, provides the optimum explanation of the inconstancy in the world. Nevertheless, it is open to a most pressing objection, one associated with several often leveled at presentism, concerning the indubitable constancy in the world. The objection, I acknowledge, is conclusive. This acknowledgment, however, does not present grounds for rejecting my account of the world in time; rather, it reveals that a complete and satisfactory account of the metaphysics of time includes more than merely an account of temporal reality.

There is, according to transient presentism, simply no thing in temporal reality and, a fortiori, no structure in temporal reality that is stable in the way that constancy demands. Yet an account of this constancy is needed, for it, no less than inconstancy, is undeniably in the world. The satisfactoriness of a complete and satisfactory account of the metaphysics of time depends on such an account being able to explain both the inconstancy and constancy in the world. Since this constancy cannot be explained in terms of transient moments or the dynamic entities existing at them—and there is little more to temporal reality according to transient presentism—to regard constancy as temporal at all is a mistake. Nevertheless, this phenomenon, like any other, must be accounted for in terms of some thing(s) or other in the world. What constancy reveals, then, is that there is more to *all this* than what exists in time. The ontological basis of inconstancy is among such things. Therefore, what is needed to provide a complete and satisfactory account of the metaphysics of time is a theory of the *world without time*, that is, an account of *atemporal reality*, one that comports with and complements the theory of temporal reality presented above.

In Chapter 11, I consider anew, from the point of original inquiry, the constancy in the world. These considerations indicate that constancy is not to be found among or based on anything significantly related to time and thereby reveal the importance of atemporal reality. So I examine *timelessness*, existence outside of—without—time. Some philosophers maintain that there is no feasible account of existing outside of time, others that nothing does so or could. The account I provide of time per se, however, enables me to provide a straightforward and non-metaphorical account of timelessness. I maintain that there are indeed things that exist without, that is, outside of time. Although some of these atemporal entities exist without origin and, as such, did not come into existence, not all lack an origin. Thus, some things come into existence, but outside of time. This phenomenon of *atemporal becoming* might initially seem incoherent, but it is not, and is of the utmost importance to the correct theory of the metaphysics of time and to understanding *all this*. In conclusion, I propound an account of the constancy in the world. The ontological basis of this constancy is *simple facts*, static entities that come into existence outside of time and exist permanently atemporally.

I take up again, in Chapter 12, the question with which I began, concluding that what *all this* is, in its entirety, are the things inside and outside of time.

The insightfulness of this answer turns on the account of what a thing is, and so I consider again, from the perspective afforded by the preceding discussion, the method of original inquiry and the discipline of metaphysics. Metaphysics is inquiry that reveals there can be successful inquiry at all. The discipline is definitive, it can be undertaken once and for all, because it is pre-conceptual and pre-theoretical. Nevertheless, it produces a universal theory that constrains all other inquiry. The generality of the discipline is the basis of its significance, but also its limitations. Metaphysics is not entirely general, though, for original inquiry does reveal the existence of certain substances, most importantly, time. Time is crucial to any and every inquiry and plays a distinct and central role in structuring *all this*. Metaphysics and the metaphysics of time begin at the same point and are dependent upon each other. The former reveals the ontological structure in reality, the latter its temporal and modal structure. Together, the two define the means and limits of inquiry. Given the limitations of metaphysical inquiry, it cannot itself be ameliorative—but it is not idle if one aspires to positive change. If, in understanding what *all this* is, one wants to make a better world, the present inquiry shows how improvement must begin.

PART II
METAPHYSICS, ONTOLOGY, AND TIME

The Significance of Time

2
Metaphysics and Its Distinctive Problem

Original inquiry begins with nothing but *all this*. One might ask, from this terminus at which everything is questioned, what any of this is. An answer to this question that takes nothing for granted about the world would begin to provide insight into the ultimate constraints on inquiry, those that enable inquiry to go in the first place. An account of these constraints would reveal what underlies any phenomenon, the fundamental bases of explanation. However, whether such an account is forthcoming is not obvious, for whether original inquiry is feasible is dubious. I exhibit its feasibility in Chapter 3, where I undertake such inquiry and discuss further its method. In this chapter, though, I show the significance of original inquiry by first considering the sort of very broad, very abstract investigation of the world that has been associated traditionally with *metaphysics*. I maintain that one needs original inquiry to resolve a distinctive problem for the ambitious, wholly critical metaphysics I propose.

§2.1. Metaphysics vis-à-vis *All This*

Despite common roots, there has not been, in Western philosophy, a unique enterprise that is metaphysics. In two and a half millennia, philosophers with different motivations and adopting incompatible bases have undertaken many projects as metaphysics. These projects, of course, have some similarities, sharing a concern with formal or general features of the world or questions of perennial interest to creatures such as we are, but these similarities do not suffice to characterize a *discipline*, a focused domain of inquiry with a method. There is, therefore, no one activity that metaphysics has been.

I propose to regard metaphysics as the discipline with the greatest ambit, one that can provide insight into, literally, every thing, and so constrain all other disciplines. As the discipline with the greatest ambit, metaphysics begins (and ends) with *reality*. Reality, that is, the world, *all this*—whatever "it" is—is undeniable. (Try to deny it. Whatever one tries to withhold assent from, the very effort to do so, affirms what one is supposed to be denying.) *All this* is no claim, hence, no assumption; 'all this' demonstrates the whatnot, in "its" entirety, that is. If one takes the world to be merely *all this*, *that* it is is obvious.

Much less obvious, though, is *what* the world is or what "its" basic features are. Whether the world is itself a thing, that is, a being, an existent, an entity, is questionable; if it is a thing, whether the world is an instance of some kind or sui generis is unclear; if the world is not a thing, whether "it" is a harmonious collection of dependent entities or a mere collection of dependent entities or a mere collection of disparate entities or some mix of disparate and dependent entities or something else entirely is also unclear. To the extent that whether the world is even a thing is uncertain, whether the world itself has features, basic or otherwise, is as well. Metaphysics is the discipline whose chief objective is an account of *what the world is and what it comprises*. As a term of art, 'metaphysics' can be, and has been, used as one chooses; I use it with the sense just defined.

One needs some account of what the world comprises, for reality is, if anything, *diverse*, lacking uniformity, and so, at least by this measure, complex. Consequently, a metaphysical account of the world, which, as an account of this encompassing totality, must be *all-inclusive*, must be *general*, as well. It must not only acknowledge differences, thereby indicating whence this diversity arises, but also overlook them, in order to provide some insight into what *anything whatsoever* is—including the world itself, if it be a thing. The account needs to provide insight into how exactly these things exist together as the world or so as to make it up. Therefore, the primary question of a discipline directed at an account of what the world is and what it comprises is: *what is a thing?* This understanding of metaphysics is meant to be consonant with platitudes, like metaphysics is "inquiry into the most basic and general features of reality"[1] and the "systematic study of the most fundamental structure of reality."[2] Yet it is also meant to suggest the means of illuminating such claims, which though very familiar are nonetheless elusive. An account of what a thing is illuminates the pivotal notions of being basic, that is, *fundamentality*, and of *structure* (as I argue in the next two chapters). Without

---

[1] Kim and Sosa 1999: ix.
[2] Lowe 1998: 2.

a clear understanding of these notions, one is in no position to evaluate the upshot of metaphysical inquiry that begins with *all this*.

So echt metaphysics, as I take the discipline, is directed at an account of what the world is via the question of what a thing is. There are also investigations that are *metaphysical*, though not metaphysics per se. Such investigations are directed at obtaining a suitably general account of something (or some kind of thing) in the world, rather than reality at large, and provide insight into what that thing is, what its capacities are, what it does, and, hence, how it interacts with other things. There are projects in, for example, the metaphysics of persons, the metaphysics of value, the metaphysics of mind, the metaphysics of modality, and, like the present one, the metaphysics of time. Perhaps *every* field of inquiry is metaphysical in this sense, and so biology can be understood as the metaphysics of living things, physics the metaphysics of matter, economics the metaphysics of markets, sociology the metaphysics of institutions. All these specific projects and fields must be consistent with each other, for insofar as each is directed at something real, their objects co-exist and contribute to *all this*. Moreover, and importantly, since each is directed at something—some *thing*—in the world, the theories these projects and fields yield must comport with metaphysics, the metaphysical account of reality, because this account, being all-inclusive and general, is supposed to elucidate what a thing of any variety is and how things, in general, relate. Hence, metaphysics is foundational, providing the ground rules for any investigation, insofar as any investigation is directed at some thing or other.

Inquiry is activity directed at acquiring *awareness*. Mundane inquiry, in the first instance, is directed at non-representational things in the world, to wit, whatever is the basis of a correct account of the object of that inquiry. However, to the extent that one aspires to such an account—an expressible *theory*—of the object(s) of one's inquiry, this inquiry must also be directed at true claims about its object(s). The mental states associated with these true claims, appropriately arrived at and accepted, are *knowledge*. So inquiry is epistemic, but also significantly ontological, in that it initially engages with and is based on what is so, the things in the world.

The purpose of *critical inquiry*, unlike inquiry more generally, is to attain *understanding* of a certain object of inquiry, rather than merely some awareness of or knowledge pertaining to it. Understanding some thing requires having insight into it. One might attain this understanding by recognizing *what* that thing is—how it must be, how it could be otherwise, what it does, how it interacts with other things—and, consequently, *how* that thing is as it is. One might attain further understanding of an object of inquiry by recognizing why true claims about it are to be accepted and on what basis. Such understanding seems to require, then, an appreciation of the grounds of such truths. One can, perhaps, attain deeper understanding of some object with accounts of how the grounds of true claims pertinent to that object relate to other, ostensibly unrelated ones and whether they must. If a *theoretical framework* is a collection of *principles*, that is, claims consistency with which constrains inquiry with respect to some object of inquiry, then inquiry can take place by means of an unexamined theoretical framework. Critical inquiry, however, cannot. Simply taking claims for granted—even one's principles—failing to examine why or how they are true or true together (and whether they must be) is incompatible with the understanding that is the goal of critical inquiry.

Given that there is indeed a world, "it" is either a thing or not. There must be, then, some account of what the world is, or why reality is not a thing, and so there must be a sort of inquiry whose chief objective is this account (regardless of whether it has ever been undertaken). In other words, there must be the discipline that I characterize above as metaphysics. Merely a true account of what the world is—in the absence of some further account of why or how these claims about the world are true, why they are true together, and whether they must be—would be incomplete, missing crucial details about what the world, *all this*, is. Metaphysics, therefore, must be a form of critical inquiry. Moreover, given that metaphysics is to provide insight into all things, any thing whatsoever, it must be free of any presuppositions regarding things, lest it distort what it is to reveal with what it takes for granted. Metaphysics must be, then, not just critical inquiry, but *wholly critical inquiry*, inquiry without presumption. Note there are no presuppositions here about how the account of what the world is that metaphysics is to provide can or must be obtained, nor any conditions on this account, beyond its conditionlessness, its all-inclusive generality. This characterization of metaphysics is minimal, motivated simply by the world, this indisputable datum, and defined only by its objective—an account of what *all this* is (and what it comprises)—yet is nevertheless substantial.

This minimal, yet substantial account of metaphysics seems to me uncontroversial. One might have no interest in such metaphysics or have a dim view of its prospects (though at the outset such pessimism can hardly be justified), but there is no denying there is this discipline. Given that it is uniquely foundational, insofar as one has an interest in *any thing*—hence, in any subject or any field—one has a reason to pursue this discipline. However, if this is what metaphysics is, it has a distinctive problem.

§2.2. The Distinctive Problem of Metaphysics

Metaphysics, as I characterize the discipline, begins with the world, *all this*. It does not begin, then, with any tradition, school, text, figure, science, theory, or claim. Its impetus is immediately accessible to any inquirer, in any circumstance, for at the outset of wholly critical inquiry, no way to *all this* is relevantly different from any other. Hence, metaphysics is distinct among fields of inquiry in that at any point in pursuing it, one can, whenever lost, begin anew, simply by looking up, with the focus of inquiry, via the world before one, no less clear or further away. As wholly critical inquiry, metaphysics is incompatible with presumption, which in this context is any claim about anything that does not obviously arise (from *all this*). Given the breadth of its focus, and its stricture against presumption, that metaphysics has a distinctive problem is not surprising. The chief objective of metaphysics as a discipline is a comprehensively general account of what the world is (and what it comprises); as a form of critical inquiry, metaphysics is to provide understanding and not merely knowledge. This objective with this critical requirement presents a formidable problem.

Successful inquiry yields an account, a true theory. In the case of metaphysics, this would be a comprehensively general account of what the world is and what it comprises. Since metaphysics is critical, however, its principles, the claims that make up the theoretical framework for this account (such as, perhaps, *that there is a diverse world* and *that something exists*) cannot be taken for granted; the metaphysician must assess the grounds of each. With respect to any theory, it seems one needs some vantage outside that theory, that is, a position graspable in a way that does not involve the theory, in order to assess whether its claims are correct—not just with respect to the principles and terms of that theory itself, but in light of what it is supposed to be a theory of. This sort of vantage, however, is precluded by a comprehensively general account of what the world is and what it comprises: there is no vantage beyond *all this*, the world. Consequently, there is nothing to which the theory does not apply by means of which one can apprehend, independently of the theory, its principles or even its terms. Without such independent apprehension, there seems to be no way of assessing the aptness of the theory (by any standard other than mere consistency). Such a comprehensively general account, therefore, seems unevaluable. Yet no theory that is to provide understanding can be unevaluable. If one cannot see why a theory is apt, through some sort of evaluation, it cannot provide the insight necessary for understanding, which is the goal of critical inquiry. The problem here, which arises from its generality, further distinguishes metaphysics from all other inquiry.

To illustrate this important point, and illuminate the distinctive problem to which it gives rise, consider some theory, T, which results from inquiry in some limited domain. Suppose, according to T, that e is Q, where e is some entity and Q some quality. If one has a grasp of Q independent of T—and given that T arises from inquiry in some limited domain, one can legitimately assume that one can acquire such independent grasp—then one is in a position to assess the aptness of T. If e is indeed Q, then T is apt (at least in this case). Or suppose according to some theory, T', which arises from inquiry in some limited domain, that e is a K, where K is some kind. If one has a grasp of K independent of T', then one is in a position to assess the aptness of T'. If e is indeed an instance of K, then T' is apt (again, at least in this case).

But suppose M is some comprehensively general account of what the world is and what it comprises. M is to explicate, without presupposition, what the world is, what being is or what a thing is. As such, pivotal to M would be some terms expressing being or being a thing and claims elucidating what it is to be or what it is to be a thing. Say, according to M, e has being or e is a thing. In this case, it seems one cannot have a grasp of having being or of being a thing independent of M. M is supposed to be the very means of explicating what it is to be (or what a thing is)! Moreover, to grasp any theoretical claim, one must take that claim to be characterizing something or other in some way. To grasp any (theoretical) claim at all, then, one must either take some thing for granted or have some prior understanding of some thing and, hence, what it is to be. Yet, again, M is supposed to be the very means of explicating—without presupposition—what it is to be (or what a thing is)! In order to comprehend the pivotal claims of M, one must already presuppose or have the comprehension it is supposed to provide. M, therefore, seems incomprehensible and so unevaluable.

Likewise, one cannot accept M, if one is inquiring earnestly, without first assessing its claims. To assess, say, the claim that e has being, one must have some prior grasp of what it is to have being, in order to determine whether *e* does indeed have being (just as above, one must have a grasp of Q, independent of T, in order to assess the T-theoretical claim that e is Q). But, yet again, M is supposed to be the means of explicating what it is to be! One cannot have, then, a prior grasp of what it is to have being, that is, a grasp independent of M. Thus, one cannot assess M without already accepting the theory. Again, M seems unevaluable (if one is inquiring earnestly). It seems, therefore, that one cannot evaluate—or even comprehend—a comprehensively general account of what the world is and what it comprises; if the theory cannot be evaluated, it cannot provide the understanding that is the goal of critical inquiry.

The distinctive problem of metaphysics, therefore, is this: the objective of metaphysics is a wholly critical account of what the world is and what it comprises, but, given the scope of this account, there is nothing not subsumed by the account by which to evaluate it—yet understanding the world, the very purpose of this account, seems to require evaluation. The problem is unique to metaphysics because for every other field of inquiry producing a true theory, there is some true theory more general than the initial one—or in some way independent of it—that can serve as a check on the initial, circumscribed one. Moreover, every field of inquiry other than metaphysics restricts its claims to specific things in the world; the theories produced by such fields can then be assessed by whether these restricted claims are true. Yet this is not the case for metaphysics, which makes general claims about each and every thing: anything and everything confirms the correct account of *all this*. This distinctive problem is adumbrated above, when it is noted that metaphysics, properly executed, would reveal the ground rules for any inquiry and, hence, is crucial to inquiry per se. Metaphysics is itself a form of inquiry, however, and so it follows that it, somehow, informs itself. This suggests—misleadingly, as I argue—that the discipline really has no principles, for if a discipline informs itself, by providing its own principles, these principles seem arbitrary (or otherwise unconstrained in an appropriately independent way). A wholly critical metaphysics seems no more than a game.

Reflecting on the preceding discussion, any wholly critical, comprehensively general account of what the world is and what it comprises, that is, any putatively true theory of metaphysics, seems open to the charge of arbitrariness. If there are no means of evaluating such theories, and each is arbitrary, there is no (probative) basis to choose among them. (The principles of any given theory cannot even be evaluated for *plausibility* without the presupposition of other principles which themselves would require evaluation, for whatever standard of being plausible one presupposes is itself open to question. And what the basis of this further evaluation might be is not at all clear.) Insofar as the basic features of reality are supposed to be reflected in the theoretical framework of a true theory of metaphysics, there seems to be no means to settle disagreement between metaphysicians who accept different features and, hence, different principles. A theory of metaphysics can perhaps be evaluated on the basis of its internal coherence, but this does not provide the means for choosing among incompatible yet internally coherent theories. Worse, evaluating a theory of metaphysics merely on the basis of its coherence cuts it off from what the theory is supposed to be a theory of, namely, *all this*. It appears, then, there cannot be the discipline of metaphysics as I characterize it, wholly critical inquiry that provides a comprehensively general account of the world and what it comprises while also permitting understanding of this account and of the world. If one begins at a point of acute perplexity, questioning everything—*all this*—one seems marooned there.

§2.3. A Critique of Contemporary Metaphysical Inquiry

I do believe that there is a way forward, that metaphysics, as characterized here—as a wholly critical discipline directed at a comprehensively general account of what the world is and what it comprises—is not only possible but deliverable. Thus, one can have an account of *all this* that permits understanding and thereby illuminates all inquiry. In order to make good on this wholly critical discipline and to deliver such a comprehensively general account, I must devise a method that addresses the distinctive problem of metaphysics. The better to do this, I first discuss several alternative approaches to investigating formal or general features of reality, approaches called "metaphysics" by their proponents and that I call versions of *traditional metaphysics*. I discuss these for two purposes: firstly, in order to determine whether those that would deflate any investigation of the world at large undermine the vision of metaphysics I propose and, hence, even if its distinctive problem can be resolved, there are reasons for abandoning metaphysics; and, secondly, to determine whether those philosophers who also endorse an ambitious discipline investigating reality can contribute to resolving the distinctive problem for a wholly critical inquiry into *all this* that I have articulated. I conclude that neither is the case. This makes pressing the need for a novel method for the metaphysics I propose.

§2.3.1. Deflationary views of metaphysics

A true theory of metaphysics, as I have characterized it, would provide insight into what anything whatsoever is and thereby inform every (true) claim about the world. Such a discipline is clearly ambitious. Many philosophers, however, reject any ambitiousness in an investigation of the world at large, holding it merely reveals naivete or pretension. Their motivation for doing so differs. Some maintain that (any version of) traditional metaphysics is no discipline at all; others recognize some such discipline, but deny metaphysics any exceptional status, acknowledging it as merely one discipline among many and, hence, limited in scope, or as playing only a subsidiary role to some other philosophical discipline or to properly "scientific" investigation.

§2.3.1.1. Metaphysics as a hodgepodge

The metaphysics I am pursuing is directed at discerning what the world is and what it comprises; it has, then, a unitary focus. I maintain that understanding what the world comprises reveals what a thing in general is and, hence, provides insight into any phenomenon. There are philosophers who, although they acknowledge a host of legitimate metaphysical projects, ones that investigate general features of reality or seek answers to questions of perennial interest, deny that there is any one issue that underlies these projects. Consequently, there is insufficient unity among them for there to be a discipline of metaphysics with a unitary focus examination of which could bear illuminatingly on all such metaphysical projects. Trenton Merricks, for one, denies there is a significantly unified discipline of metaphysics (of course, one could stipulate any arbitrary list of projects to be "metaphysics").[3] Karen Bennett recognizes what she takes to be metaphysics, but only as one discipline among many that contribute to philosophical inquiry; metaphysics per se, as she understands it, cannot provide insight into every phenomenon.[4] Both Merricks and Bennett are critical of systematic metaphysics as it has traditionally been understood and so are not arguing explicitly against the wholly critical metaphysics I propound. Nevertheless, there is genuine disagreement between us, because what they argue cannot underlie a unified discipline of metaphysics I hold does, in fact, underlie it. (Our disagreement, then, is not merely a verbal dispute about how to use the word 'metaphysics').

---

[3] See Merricks 2013.
[4] See Bennett 2016.

Merricks regards traditional metaphysics as inquiry into a mere hodgepodge of issues. After listing a number of claims pertaining to freedom, causation, determinism, truth, ontological categories, persistence, material objects, composition, truthmaking, modality, and essence, he asserts: "It is... false that there is some... single unified topic that every one of these claims is about."[5] Merricks seems to be relying on the ostensible heterogeneity of his examples to justify this conclusion. Bennett likewise views metaphysics as lacking unity, as being a disjunctive enterprise, one part focused on the sort of hodgepodge of traditional metaphysical issues that Merricks lists, the other focused on "maintaining the toolbox,"[6] that is, determining what it is in the world that underlies "pervasive philosophical vocabulary," the terms that express the notions that philosophers rely on in their investigations (of value, mind, language, knowledge, science, etc.). Bennett admits to being unable to see any way of unifying either the hodgepodge of traditional issues or her disjunctive account of metaphysics.[7] Thus, she shares Merricks's view regarding the irremediable disunity of metaphysics.

I characterize wholly critical metaphysics as the discipline directed at an account of what the world is and what it comprises (via the question of what a thing is). Such an account would be elaborated in terms of the *structure* in reality: how the things there are, including any relations, are related. In light of this, one response to claims about the disunity of (traditional) metaphysics is that there is indeed a discipline bearing illuminatingly on the world, everything there is, including the hodgepodge of traditional metaphysical issues. This discipline is focused on the most basic or general or *fundamental* structure in reality and is unified by being about how this structure yields *all this* and so underlies any phenomenon to be inquired about.

Both Merricks and Bennett, however, explicitly deny that traditional metaphysics has this focus on fundamental structure, implying that no systematic discipline could. Merricks maintains that the hodgepodge of metaphysical issues is "not all about the fundamental structure of reality."[8] Although he has a particular view of structure in mind,[9] that he intends the claim to apply to any view of structure is clear. However, he provides no argument for this claim; he seems to regard it as simply obvious. Bennett gives three constraints

---

[5] Merricks 2013: 722.
[6] Bennett 2016: §4.
[7] Bennett 2016: 33.
[8] Merricks 2013: 723.
[9] He is critiquing here Theodore Sider's position from Sider 2011.

on what (traditional) metaphysics is, maintaining that each rules out that it is about fundamental reality.[10] If these constraints are apt, and so apply to any discipline that would account for *all this* and thereby elucidate the traditional metaphysical issues, this would show that metaphysics, as I understand it, should be rejected. In her discussion, though, Bennett takes for granted a certain notion of fundamentality, one on which to be fundamental is to be simple, to have no (material) proper parts. Yet the notion of fundamentality is multifarious. It is, for example, widely regarded as the correlate of the notion of ontological dependence: to be fundamental is to *not* be ontologically dependent (and, note, this need not have anything to do with mereological simplicity). Moreover, since there are many varieties of ontological dependence, there are many notions of fundamentality. Bennett's claim that metaphysics is not unified by being about how the world comprises things, that is, by being about the (fundamental) structure in reality is, therefore, premised on an account of fundamentality that one might reject. Indeed, which is the pivotal notion of fundamentality in this context, Bennett's or some other, depends on what a thing is (as I argue in Chapter 3) and so is posterior to a theory of metaphysics as I characterize it.

Hence, neither Bennett nor Merricks gives conclusive reason to reject an ambitious, wholly critical (systematic) discipline of metaphysics. Pursuing such metaphysics presents an account of things and the structure in reality that unifies the metaphysical issues that Merricks lists, one that turns on a different notion of fundamentality than the one Bennett presumes. Of course, all this needs to be shown. (Support for these claims comes in the following chapters of Part II.)

§2.3.1.2. Deflationary views that are based on substantive assumptions
Merricks dismisses a unified discipline of metaphysics because he assumes there is no account of structure that underlies all traditional metaphysical issues. Bennett dismisses a unified discipline on the grounds of a certain notion of fundamentality with which it seems incompatible. Both, then, reject the ambitious, wholly critical metaphysics I propose on the basis of

---

[10] She holds that metaphysics must be distinguished from science and since a part of science, viz., physics, is about fundamental reality, metaphysics cannot also be. Moreover, she holds that metaphysics would still be a discipline even if there were no fundamental reality—if "some or all dependence chains fail to terminate in something fundamental"—and hence it cannot be just about fundamental reality, because there might not be such. Finally, she holds that metaphysics must account for what practicing metaphysicians do (as metaphysicians), and not all of what they do is concerned with fundamental reality. See Bennett 2016: §4.

metaphysical assumptions that, I eventually argue—from a neutral, universal starting point—are incorrect. Their positions, in a way, underscore the need for such wholly critical inquiry. Other philosophers, too, hold deflationary views of (traditional) metaphysics on the basis of assumptions about the world that are incompatible with a wholly critical account of *all this*, one that takes nothing for granted about its object of inquiry at the outset.

Such deflationary views are objectionable in the present context. The reason is parochial, but of the utmost importance here. These views begin with principles that are incompatible with the sort of ambitious, wholly critical metaphysics that I propound, a discipline that purports to confront *all this* taking nothing for granted about what is confronted. Insofar as one is undertaking this discipline, one has reason to set these views aside. The views, moreover, should be reassessed in light of the metaphysics I deliver. If this metaphysics does indeed, as I contend, illuminate the ground rules for inquiry, then these incompatible metaphysical views might include principles inconsistent with inquiry itself, in which case the views should be abandoned. However, in this context, I am not trying to refute these views; rather, I am simply trying to show they do not undermine the ambitious metaphysics I propound.

Consider, then, the many philosophers who hold that inquiry into the world per se or things in themselves is misguided. The world itself, so they hold, is without structure—differentiated but amorphous—the things in it indeterminate. The appropriate focus of inquiry, therefore, insofar as one is interested in the formal features of a structured reality, are the means conscious beings use to conceptualize, classify, or otherwise organize what they experience. It is the capacities of mind or the nature of language that one should investigate for insight into the world, and such investigations supersede any other metaphysical ones. The sort of ambitious metaphysics that I am proposing is idle because its objectives are chimerical and so its methods, whatever they are supposed to be, are futile.

This (anti-)metaphysical perspective is closely associated with—indeed, usually rests on—epistemological views regarding the access to the world that human persons are supposed to have. The world is accessible only to the extent that it is experienced, where such experience is primarily, if not entirely, sensory. The roots of this perspective in modern philosophy are in Hume, and it is developed through his work and, in different ways, in Kant's. The influence of these two philosophers has been hegemonic, if not definitive, in the analytic tradition. Through the Logical Positivists and the lingering dominance of Carnap and Quine, it remains potent in contemporary discussions of metaphysics.[11] For present purposes, I need only observe that to the extent that this metaphysical perspective, in all its varieties, begins with epistemic assumptions, it cannot challenge a wholly critical discipline whose purpose it is to question *all this* without ontological or epistemological prejudice.

As becomes clear through subsequent discussion, I reject the accounts of the world—and the accompanying epistemologies and methodologies—put forth in the work of Hume, Kant, and their contemporary heirs. There are compelling reasons to do so, ones revealed via the pursuit of ambitious, wholly critical metaphysics and by resolving its distinctive problem. Such metaphysics is a discipline that provides the means of determining which of profoundly different accounts of the world is correct. So, rather than showing that such metaphysics is idle, the (anti-)metaphysical perspective broached here makes pressing the need for pursuing it.

§2.3.1.3. Naturalized metaphysics
One sees a similarly ironic move—rejecting ambitious metaphysics on presumptuously metaphysical grounds—from those who would "naturalize" metaphysics. Some of these naturalists deny that there is any discipline of metaphysics at all. They accept, of course, that there are questions that need to be answered regarding many of the same conspicuous phenomena that exercise the ambitious metaphysician, they just presume that these questions are to be answered by natural scientists, ultimately by physicists. There is, therefore, nothing for the metaphysician to do. Moreover, because the only valid method of inquiry is that of natural science, and this is not the method of metaphysics, even if the metaphysician persists in their efforts, any results they obtain would be nugatory.

Modern physics has no doubt been successful, by some measure, but to think it provides the means of answering every question about the world is mistaken. There is, first of all, the question of what the world is. There is also the related question of what a thing is. One might have no interest in answering these questions, one might have no idea how to answer them, but there is no denying that they are legitimate questions. The "serious" physicist, one not misled by sentimentality or superstition and who believes that physics is the only means of insight into fundamental reality, merely takes for

---

[11] See, for example, Chalmers 2009; Hofweber 2009; Thomasson 2009, 2007; Yablo 2009.

granted their answers and, in so doing, apes the metaphysician: the world is (something along the lines of) a closed, law-governed system of causally related or relatable spatio-temporal entities; a thing just is something with causal capacities and a spatio-temporal location. But certainly one might wonder whether these answers are correct—perhaps the world is not a thing at all; perhaps "it" is not unified as a system; perhaps there are no governing laws; perhaps there are things that are not in space or not in time. In other words, one might at the outset of inquiry want to question the answers that the "serious" physicist takes for granted.

If one does, however, physics itself does not provide the means. That the world is a closed, law-governed system of causally related, spatio-temporal entities—and the empiricist assumptions about how one can come to know about this system and these entities—are constitutive of the enterprise of physics. These ontological (and epistemological) assumptions are the principles, the theoretical framework, of physics. Taken for granted, the constraints they impose, with the empirical method they prescribe, lead one to overlook, dismiss, or deflate any phenomenon that might tell against them. To question the principles themselves, to go beyond physics in this way, is ipso facto to take up a different enterprise. Yet surely these principles can and should be examined critically.

The naturalist, therefore, simply presumes a circumscribed account of what the world is, how it is composed, and what the things are that compose it, but does not have the means, qua naturalist (or physicist), to examine these tendentious basic ontological assumptions. The metaphysician does, though, if metaphysics is the (ambitious, wholly critical) discipline whose chief objective is an account of what the world is and what it comprises. Thus, I propose to begin at a point that forgoes such assumptions. To reject outright such inquiry by presuming naturalistic answers to the questions that motivate it is just to dismiss ambitious, wholly critical metaphysics without providing a reason for thinking its objectives unattainable to one who questions and, hence, is not committed to naturalism or physicalism. Physics certainly has its place—as the discipline whose objective is a systematic account of the interactions of spatio-temporal entities—but there is more to inquiry than physics. Metaphysics is crucial to an incisive account of *all this*.

Nonetheless, proponents of naturalized metaphysics reject traditional metaphysics in general, and so would reject the ambitious, wholly critical metaphysics I propound. Considering some of their criticisms of the former is worthwhile, for doing so shows that these criticisms do not undermine the

METAPHYSICS AND ITS DISTINCTIVE PROBLEM   47

latter. Consider, then, Ladyman, Ross, and Spurrett, hereafter "LRS," who are not only naturalistic, but avowedly scientistic,[12] and defend a "radically naturalistic metaphysics" by which they mean a metaphysics "motivated exclusively by attempts to unify hypotheses and theories that are taken seriously by contemporary science."[13] They reject traditional metaphysics, maintaining that it is directed at the "domestication"[14] of science, that is, at making scientific discoveries "compatible with intuitive or 'folk' pictures of structural composition and causation"[15] and that its purpose is to "reassure the metaphysician that what they already believe is true."[16] Regardless of whether this is an accurate portrayal of traditional metaphysics, I can concede to LRS that an activity with such purposes has no clear value. These purposes, however, are obviously not those of the ambitious metaphysics that I propound. The latter is a wholly critical discipline; domestication and reassurance have no roles to play in it. So there is here no challenge to the metaphysics I am pursuing.

Still, LRS's "core complaint" concerning (traditional) metaphysics is that since the fall of logical empiricism it "has proceeded without the proper regard for science."[17] This criticism does apply to metaphysics as I characterize it, if the proper regard for science requires one to view it as prior to metaphysics. LRS maintain that any metaphysical account of the world must be constrained by one's best scientific theories, that "no other sort of metaphysics counts as inquiry into the objective nature of the world."[18] This is a very strong claim. LRS, however, merely assert that fundamental physics has "maximum scope," that there is nothing beyond fundamental physics to investigate.[19] This is not so. As discussed above, there are (at least) the crucial ontological questions of what the world is and what a thing is, while assuming nothing about *all this*.

Not surprisingly, LRS overlook these questions. At the outset of their discussion, they tacitly assume something like the familiar physicalist picture of the world. In the end, though, they maintain that proper naturalism leads one to abandon "the image of the world as composed of little things, and

---

[12] The title of Chapter 1 of Ladyman and Ross 2007 is "In Defence of Scientism."
[13] Ladyman and Ross 2007: 1.
[14] Ibid.
[15] Ibid.
[16] Ladyman and Ross 2007: 12.
[17] Ladyman and Ross 2007: 7.
[18] Ibid.
[19] See their Primacy of Physics Constraint on page 44.

indeed of the more basic intuition that there must be something of which the world is made."[20] At both points—hence, throughout their discussion—they take for granted some account of what the world is and what things are.

In their naturalized metaphysics, LRS accept uncritically a certain metaphysical account of reality, one that might very well be wrong. LRS are not unaware of this sort of criticism. Their response, though, is dismissive. They maintain that the "naturalist can argue that the metaphysical assumptions in question are vindicated by the success of science, by contrast with the metaphysical assumptions on which [metaphysics that is not appropriately naturalized] is based which are not vindicated by the success of metaphysics since it can claim no such success."[21] This is hardly an adequate response. Success depends on one's objectives. The objective of the metaphysician, as I understand them, is a wholly critical account of what the world is and what it comprises. Such an objective is beyond the purview of physics and, indeed, prior to it (to the extent that the physicist and naturalist rely on some account of the world and of things in formulating their theories). The point remains that the basis of physical theory and naturalized metaphysics are ontological theses, accepted uncritically (and perhaps false).

LRS would, presumably, remain unmoved by the foregoing considerations. They state: "it seems to us to be just ridiculous when philosophers look up from their desks and tell us that while sitting there concentrating they've discovered (usually all by themselves) facts about the nature of the world that compete with the fruits of ingenious experimentation conducted under competitive pressure and organized by complex institutional processes."[22] What this rhetoric indicates, however, is not some problem with metaphysics, but its authors' failure to recognize the scope of the ambitious discipline that I have characterized, and the insight it might provide into inquiry itself. One's desk is just as good a place as any to confront *all this* wholly critically, as merely the impetus to inquiry.

There are many stripes of naturalist. Their reservations about traditional metaphysics and their critiques of it differ, yet similar assumptions underlie each of these critiques, rendering them simply incompatible with the sort of wholly critical, ambitious metaphysics I am pursuing without really challenging such a discipline. Given the prevalence of naturalism and the dismissive attitude toward metaphysics in general it encourages, reinforcing this

---

[20] Ladyman and Ross 2007: 12.
[21] Ladyman and Ross 2007: 7.
[22] Ladyman and Ross 2007: 57.

point by considering the position of another naturalist opponent of metaphysics is worthwhile.

Penelope Maddy urges exclusively naturalistic inquiry into the world. She is moved by "the fundamental naturalistic impulse: a resolute skepticism in the face of any 'higher level' of inquiry that purports to stand above the level of ordinary science. The naturalistic philosopher is a member of the scientific community; she regards the methods of science as her own. . . ."[23] Thus, "[n]ot on principle, but relentlessly in practice, her investigations are pursued on one level, as part and parcel of the single mosaic of natural science."[24] Maddy develops this sort of naturalism via the character of the Second Philosopher, an inquirer "born native to our contemporary scientific world-view."[25] She does not attempt to undermine directly traditional metaphysics, as do Ladyman, Ross, and Spurrett; rather, she maintains there is simply nothing for the metaphysician to do.

Maddy bases her claims about the superfluousness of "higher level" ambitious metaphysics on the futility of certain attempts, by "proto-naturalists," to extend the methods employed by natural scientists. Thus, Maddy considers, for example, the efforts of Hans Reichenbach and Rudolf Carnap in the first decades of the 20th century to respond to developments in physics that seemed incompatible with the views of Kant. Kant is central to Maddy's discussion because she regards him as the paradigm of a philosopher who tries to expand naturalistic, empirical inquiry into an ideal, transcendental realm.[26] His objective in doing so is to obtain a priori insight into the structure of—the apparent necessary connections within—the world as experienced. Thus, Kant tries to go beyond, with an additional level of inquiry, the empiricism of Hume. Maddy is concerned that such transcendental inquiry differs markedly from appropriately naturalistic inquiry and that "it is not so clear what tools or methods or principles are involved, or what justifies them."[27] As neo-Kantians, Reichenbach and Carnap try in different ways to preserve something of the Kantian account of necessary structure in reality; however, it is generally agreed, their efforts to do so are unsuccessful. It is

---

[23] Maddy 2001: 39.
[24] Maddy 2007: 47.
[25] Maddy 2007: 14.
[26] Maddy also develops (in the first three chapters of Maddy 2007) the views of the Second Philosopher by beginning with Descartes and considering the issue of radical skepticism. My concerns about Second Philosophy would be the same were they articulated via consideration of this epistemological thread of Maddy's discussion.
[27] Maddy 2001: 38. Emphasis removed.

these failures to extend empirical inquiry, to add a "supra-scientific" level, that Maddy takes as evidence that any attempt to do so is misguided.

I can concede every criticism that Maddy makes of Kant's efforts, and those of his followers, to go beyond the sensible to discern the structure in reality. This is because to begin, as Maddy does, with the views of Kant (or Hume or indeed any philosopher) is contrary to the critical attitude that motivates the ambitious discipline of metaphysics I am pursuing. Kant works in a tradition that leads him to begin with epistemic assumptions that redirect his focus from the world to one's experience of it; his ultimate purpose is to reconcile certain scientific principles with moral and religious ones, all of which are just taken for granted. Maddy is sufficiently critical of Kant, his tools, methods, and principles, but uncritically accepting—and explicitly so—of a certain worldview: "[T]he naturalist begins her inquiry from a perspective inside our scientific practice, which is, in turn, an extension of common sense.... From this perspective, she pursues a scientific study of science."[28] Thus, she adopts the theoretical framework of physics, and its accompanying accounts of what the world is, how it is composed, and what the things are that compose it. Whereas her view, in the end, is a familiar one of material things causally interacting in a law-governed system, as opposed to the world bereft of "things" endorsed by LRS, the same empiricist, naturalistic tenets underlie both views. Maddy begins with ontological presuppositions that are incompatible with the ambitious, wholly critical metaphysics that I propound. So her Second Philosophy is no more of a challenge to this metaphysics than is LRS's scientism.

Maddy asserts that if the metaphysician is "to remove the empirical blinders from the Second Philosopher's eyes, he must explain to her why extra-empirical investigation is needed, what purposes it will serve."[29] But in light of the foregoing, there is here an explanation: one needs a different mode of inquiry to provide an apt account of what the world is and what it comprises, when one is unwilling merely to accept such an account as an article of (scientific) faith. A wholly critical account of *all this*, which would illuminate the fundamental structure in reality without presuming anything about this structure, would reveal the ground rules for any further investigation into anything whatsoever. The purposes of an ambitious discipline of metaphysics are, then, quite significant.

---

[28] Maddy 2001: 50.
[29] Maddy 2007: 63.

§2.3.2. Metaphysics as autonomous

Though not complicated, this criticism of deflationary, naturalized metaphysics is keen. One should not underappreciate it because of its lack of complication. The "hard-headed" scientist and the naturalist simply take for granted ontological claims about what the world is and what a thing is and, consequently, the means available to know about the structure in reality. If, however, one seeks to understand *all this*, taking nothing for granted about "it," one needs to take up a different enterprise. Empirical science has not the scope to provide what is being sought. Ambitious metaphysics does and is, therefore, neither superfluous nor without value. Nor is it challenged by the criticisms that those who would deflate or naturalize metaphysics direct at traditional metaphysics.

Given its scope and objectives, ambitious, wholly critical metaphysics must have a different method than that of the empirical sciences. It must address the distinctive problem of metaphysics—thereby providing a critical account of what the world is and what it comprises, an overarching theory of reality that provides some insight into what anything whatsoever is—and so illuminate the things that are both the focus, for example, the stars, the organisms, the molecules, the atoms, the fundamental particles, and the means, for example, the telescopes, the microscopes, the particle accelerators, the eyes, the brains, of empirical inquiry. In this way, metaphysics is prior to physics and so autonomous in the sense George Bealer employs:[30] it can be pursued "without relying substantively on the sciences."[31] Metaphysics is autonomous yet continuous with science in that it provides the ground rules for any discipline that has a basis in the structure in reality (thus, *every* discipline). Still, the question remains of what the method of metaphysics, as I characterize it, is and how the metaphysician is to resolve its distinctive problem.

§2.3.2.1. Autonomy and aprioricity
There are many philosophers who are sympathetic to some version of autonomous, ambitious metaphysics and would resist, presumably on similar grounds, the portrayals of metaphysics criticized above. Nevertheless, those who object to attempts to dismiss or deflate metaphysics might have different

---

[30] See Bealer 2002, 1998, 1996. Bealer writes about "philosophy" in general, but that his discussion also applies to metaphysics more specifically is clear.
[31] Bealer 1998: 201.

goals than I, and so make assumptions that render their approaches incompatible with the wholly critical metaphysics I am pursuing. As a result, such approaches do not engage the distinctive problem for this metaphysics.

Thus, for example, a common assumption among those who take (traditional) metaphysics seriously is that it must be an *a priori* discipline. Insight into the formal features of the world is to be obtained by reflecting on the means one uses to organize or represent "it," to wit, one's concepts, or by some other method that eschews sensory experience. I reject this assumption, not because I think metaphysics is an a posteriori discipline, but because the epistemological distinction between a priori and a posteriori is not applicable at the outset of inquiry, where ambitious, wholly critical metaphysical theorizing takes root. The very distinction presumes too much about the world, its structure, and the cognitive capacities of human persons by assuming a crucial difference between perceiving the world with one's senses and engaging it—in some way or other—by a different faculty. Metaphysics as I characterize it cannot be this presumptuous.

Bealer himself argues that (traditional) metaphysics is a priori because the justification for its claims derives from a necessary connection between one's intuitions regarding certain possibilities, prompted via reflection, and the truth. This necessary connection, according to Bealer, is a consequence of what it is to possess determinately the concepts relevant to those metaphysical claims. Bealer maintains that these concepts, the ones pertinent to claims concerning, for example, "the nature of substance, mind, intelligence, consciousness, sensation, perception, knowledge, wisdom, truth, identity, infinity, divinity, time, explanation, causation, freedom, purpose, goodness, duty, the virtues, love, life, happiness"[32] are independent of how things in the mind-independent world are—how they apply would not differ, even if the world one experiences were quite different.[33] The employment of these concepts is supposed to place necessary constraints on the world one confronts; more specifically, it is supposed to constrain those parts of *all this* relevant to (traditional) metaphysical issues. Bealer holds, then, that some of reality must be as it is ultimately because of the means conscious beings use to organize or represent it. Perhaps this is so. But merely to presume it is or to hold it, as Bealer and other like-minded metaphysicians—such as Frank Jackson, David Chalmers, and Eli Hirsch[34]—do, on the basis of received

---

[32] Bealer 1998: 203.
[33] They are "semantically stable". See Bealer 2002: 72; 1998: 228; 1996: 134.
[34] See Jackson 1998; Chalmers 2012, 2009; Hirsch 1986.

problems arising from considering rationalism versus empiricism, is incompatible with ambitious, wholly critical metaphysics. This sort of autonomous metaphysics is, therefore, different from the metaphysics I am pursuing and provides no insight into its distinctive problem.

Kit Fine, too, accepts that metaphysics is autonomous. He, too, believes the source of this autonomy is the distinctive character of the concepts one employs when doing metaphysics, and claims that his position is very similar to Bealer's.[35] Nevertheless, the positions of these two metaphysicians seem to me quite different. Fine states that his conception of metaphysics is "broadly Aristotelian"[36]—whereas Bealer's seems to me clearly Kantian— and, more explicitly, that "metaphysics is concerned, first and foremost, with the nature of reality."[37] This latter claim might sound consistent with the metaphysics I propound, yet it is not. In claiming that (his or traditional) metaphysics is about the nature of reality, Fine presumes that reality itself has a nature; in so doing, he takes for granted some account of what the world is, presuming, at least, that it is a thing with a nature (or involves things with natures). However, the purpose of metaphysics, as I characterize the discipline, is to provide an apt account of what the world is and thereby determine whether "it" is indeed a thing at all (and to determine whether and in what sense things have natures). Fine's substantive theoretical assumption is, then, inconsistent with the metaphysics I am pursuing. Moreover, to take for granted Aristotelian principles at the outset of inquiry into *all this* is no less inconsistent with the wholly critical inquiry I am pursuing than is taking for granted Kantian principles (or, obviously, any others). A wholly critical metaphysics, which begins at a neutral, universal point, would provide the means of arbitrating among such incompatible worldviews and the traditions they have inspired.

Despite these differences between the metaphysics he and I are proposing, I do agree with Fine that metaphysics is "not merely one form of enquiry among others but one that is capable of providing some kind of basis or underpinning for other forms of enquiry."[38] Were Fine to articulate how metaphysics is able to do this, he might contribute to resolving the distinctive problem of metaphysics, but, unfortunately, he does not. Even with the assumptions he makes, Fine never really answers his titular question ("what

---

[35] Fine 2012a: Footnote 1.
[36] Ibid.
[37] Fine 2012a: 8.
[38] Fine 2012a: 9.

is metaphysics?"). Rather he asserts five main features of (his conception of) metaphysics—derived, presumably, from Fine's knowledge of the history of metaphysical inquiry—that he maintains distinguish it from other forms of inquiry, namely, "the aprioricity of its methods; the generality of its subject-matter; the transparency or 'non-opacity' of its concepts; its eidicity or concern with the nature of things; and its role as a foundation for what there is."[39]

Each of Fine's features requires extensive comment and clarification. Comment and clarification that cannot be provided without many further assumptions about the world, what a thing is, and one's cognitive engagement with the world and things. Insofar as one's objective is a wholly critical account of *all this* and what it comprises, such assumptions are only obfuscatory. Although Fine appreciates the importance of (traditional) metaphysics, and its autonomy, he presupposes as much about the world—what it is and how best to engage it so as to reveal its nature—as any dismissive naturalist (though, of course, his presuppositions are quite different). Consequently, his approach sheds no light on an appropriate method for a wholly critical metaphysics, and so does not contribute to resolving the distinctive problem of such a discipline.

Timothy Williamson has given much consideration to methodology in philosophy. Williamson is no "crude empiricist."[40] He maintains that there is scientific inquiry that is not entirely empirical and, thus, there are "armchair sciences," mathematics for one, adding: "If mathematics is an armchair science, why not philosophy too?"[41] So, like Bealer and Fine, he seems to recognize the importance of particularly philosophical inquiry. Still, if philosophy in general and so, presumably, metaphysics in particular has an "armchair" method, Williamson does not think metaphysics is an a priori discipline. On this he and I agree (though whereas Williamson maintains that the a priori/a posteriori distinction is "too crude"[42] in the context of a basic investigation of philosophical methodology, I believe it is too theoretically loaded).

Williamson and I also agree that metaphysics is not primarily linguistic nor conceptual, not dependent on intuitions (whatever these are taken to be), nor about reflective equilibrium. Rather its goal is "to discover what fundamental kinds of things there are and what properties and relations they have, not to study the structure of our thought about them."[43] However,

[39] Fine 2012a: 8.
[40] Williamson 2007: 2.
[41] Williamson 2007: 4.
[42] Williamson 2007: 169. See, as well, page 3.
[43] Williamson 2007: 19.

precisely because it has this goal and, thus, there is no "special domain for philosophical investigation,"[44] metaphysics has its distinctive problem. The generality of its subject matter requires that the discipline provide some insight into what anything whatsoever is, and so there are no means beyond metaphysics by which to evaluate this insight—yet, as a critical enterprise, it requires evaluation.

The resolution of this distinctive problem requires a singular method. But Williamson maintains that there is nothing exceptional about metaphysical inquiry. Such inquiry is really just non-philosophical inquiry: "much past and present philosophy consists in just the unusually systematic and unrelenting application of ways of thinking required over a vast range of non-philosophical inquiry. The philosophical applications inherit a moderate degree of reliability from the more general cognitive patterns they instantiate."[45] If this were so, there could be no wholly critical discipline of metaphysics. Williamson does not consider the prospects of such an ambitious metaphysics, presumably because he does not see the need for it. If one does, though, then one would recognize the especial difficulties of a wholly critical metaphysics and, hence, of devising the appropriate method for it. Williamson exhorts his readers to *do better* when inquiring philosophically, yet I do not believe he has provided the means to do so.[46] By attending to the fruits and difficulties of a discipline that confronts the world without taking anything for granted about "it," and then discerning the method that resolves its distinctive problem, one *can* do better. For doing so would enable one to understand *all this* and gain insight into the ground rules of inquiry.

§2.3.2.2. Metaphysics as first philosophy

If the ambitious metaphysics I envision is unified, not naturalistic (in a rigidly empiricist sense), autonomous yet not a priori; if this wholly critical discipline is prior to others, providing a basis for empirical science and inquiry more generally, then all this suggests a quite traditional, Aristotelian view of the discipline: metaphysics as *first philosophy*. To say exactly what the subject matter of Aristotle's *Metaphysics* is is hard to do and, thus, to say exactly what first philosophy is supposed to be is, as well; but at some points, Aristotle characterizes it as the study of *being qua being*. The characterization assumes

---

[44] Williamson 2007: 5.
[45] Williamson 2007: 3.
[46] Here I allude to the Afterword of Williamson 2007.

that something or other exists and that it, whatever it is, can be studied simply as an existent.

This is eminently plausible. So this approach seems conducive to the chief objective of the ambitious discipline of metaphysics I am undertaking, namely, a comprehensive general account of what the world is (and what it comprises) pursued via the question of what a thing, a being, an existent is. However, whatever Aristotle took first philosophy to be, it is not the wholly critical discipline I envision. He explicitly argues that being is not a genus, that there is no class that includes all things as things, and, hence, that there is no insightful answer to the question of what a thing—in the most general sense—is.[47] Nonetheless, given the clear affinities between first philosophy and the ambitious metaphysics I am undertaking, considering the views of some metaphysicians working in an Aristotelian fashion is worthwhile, in order to see how these views compare to those criticized above and whether they can contribute to resolving the distinctive problem for this wholly critical metaphysics.

Few recent philosophers have done more to promote traditional metaphysics—more specifically, metaphysics as a sort of first philosophy— than E.J. Lowe. His expansive body of work is rich, important, often incisive, and his *The Possibility of Metaphysics* was, I believe, largely successful in achieving its objective of making robust metaphysics a central part of contemporary philosophy.[48] Throughout his work, Lowe develops a neo-Aristotelian ontology (one based on the Aristotle of the *Categories* and inimical to hylomorphism), taking metaphysics as "'first philosophy', a discipline that is conceptually and epistemologically prior to any of the empirical sciences and an intellectual prerequisite of their pursuit of truth concerning the natural world and the human mind."[49] This is indeed an ambitious discipline, foundational and directed at the world. Still, Lowe's approach, given my objectives, is not sufficiently critical.

Lowe assumes, pace Aristotle, that being is a genus and, thus, that there is an absolutely general class of entities (i.e., existents, beings, things),[50] yet Lowe provides no account of what a thing is. Without such an account, the ontological basis of one's metaphysics is obscure and, worse, from my perspective, based on presumption. Furthermore, on Lowe's approach to

---

[47] I recur to this point in §3.2.1.
[48] See Lowe 1998: 1 and the Preface to the book.
[49] Lowe 2013b: 196.
[50] Lowe 2006: 7–8, 39.

metaphysics, one has not the means to determine whether the world is a thing. If the chief objective of ambitious, wholly critical metaphysics is an account of what the world is, one cannot meet this objective with a discipline that provides no insight into what a thing is. Lowe takes for granted some inexplicit and, hence, undefended notion of a thing. Indeed, Lowe's metaphysical framework includes four categories of thing. Although Lowe is quite clear about the distinctions among these categories, he provides no account of whence they are derived or why one should accept them. Of course, they come from Aristotle (though Aristotle presumed several more), but locating this historical source is not satisfactory from a critical perspective. Nor are the copious demonstrations of the theoretical utility of a four-category ontology provided in Lowe's many papers and books: usefulness is not necessarily an indication of what is so. Thus, Lowe simply takes for granted Aristotelian principles and problematics. His metaphysics, as a result, is incompatible with my own account of the discipline, and so cannot contribute to resolving the distinctive problem of the latter.[51]

Working in the same vein, Tuomas Tahko defends a view of metaphysics as first philosophy. He argues that metaphysics is not about what is, as Quine and his followers believe, but about how these things are.[52] This leads to his view, similar in many respects to Lowe's, that metaphysics is the science of essence.[53] Suppose, then, that first philosophy is indeed, as Lowe and Tahko would have it, the science of essence. The first question this raises is what an essence is. However, one cannot answer this question (or argue that an essence is not a thing, as Lowe does[54]) without an account of what a thing is. Although Tahko provides a theoretical account of essence,[55] this account is articulated within a framework of Aristotelian priority and forms. Such an account, like Lowe's four-category ontology, just raises the question of whether—and why—such a framework should be adopted in the first place. To answer this question requires a wholly critical account of *all this*.

Ultimately, an Aristotelian approach to metaphysics and to inquiry more generally might be insightful, but the metaphysician who takes for granted the framework of such an approach is no different—and so no less objectionable from the perspective of one who would like a wholly critical

---

[51] Moreover, Lowe takes metaphysics to be an a priori discipline. See Lowe 2014.
[52] Tahko 2012b: 30.
[53] See Tahko 2013. For a significant difference between Tahko's and Lowe's positions, see page 58.
[54] Lowe 2013a, 2008.
[55] Tahko 2013: 54, 55.

account of *all this*—than the strident naturalist who just takes for granted the "modern scientific worldview." The uncritical adoption of Aristotelian principles, distinctions, and apparatus is precisely what gave rise to the (eventual) uncritical adoption of the world as a closed, law-governed system of causally related spatio-temporal entities. What is needed is a steadfastly and wholly critical discipline that does not presume some worldview, but rather is directed at providing an account of what the world is in the first place; a discipline that presumes at its outset no tendentious principle about *all this*. This is precisely what ambitious metaphysics, as I am pursuing it, is.

§2.4. Metaphysics and the Need for a Novel Method

The ambitious discipline of metaphysics that I am pursuing is one directed at an account of *all this* and what it comprises via the question of what a thing is. This is a wholly critical discipline and so it is directed at understanding rather than merely at truth. The purpose of the foregoing survey of traditional metaphysical inquiry is twofold: to determine whether there is any reason, in light of various critiques of ambitious metaphysics, to reject the discipline as I understand it, and to determine whether the views of those who recognize the value and need of an ambitious discipline can contribute to the distinctive problem of a wholly critical metaphysics.

The survey shows that the discipline I am pursuing is neither undermined by the critics of traditional metaphysics, nor aided by any of the proponents of an ambitious discipline. It is not challenged by the former nor aided by the latter because both critics and proponents of traditional metaphysics are insufficiently critical in their positions (and *of* their positions): they make assumptions about *all this*, and take things for granted, that an ambitious, wholly critical metaphysics does not. They begin with different purposes at points that are neither neutral nor universal, and so are just incompatible with a mode of inquiry that aspires to begin with nothing but *all this*.

As a discipline that could illuminate all inquiry, every principle of metaphysics, as I envision it, must be grounded in some way. This, however, leads directly to its distinctive problem, which in light of the foregoing should now be urgent: the objective of such metaphysics is a wholly critical account of what the world is and what it comprises, but, given the scope of this account, there is nothing not subsumed by the account by which to evaluate it—yet understanding the world, the very purpose of this account, seems to require evaluation. The account of the world I seek comes via the question of what a thing is, so a different aspect of this distinctive problem of metaphysics is the problem of providing an apt account of what a thing is while assuming nothing about *all this*. If wholly critical metaphysics as a discipline is feasible, developing an insightful, practicable, grounded account of a thing from seemingly nothing at all must be possible! Such an account is crucial to inquiry itself, providing the ground rules for every investigation, given that every investigation is directed at and constrained by some thing or other.

Therefore, insofar as one would understand the ultimate bases of one's inquiry and resulting theory, solving the distinctive problem of metaphysics is of central importance to any theoretical endeavor. Its solution requires a novel method, one not taken up in any of the traditional approaches to metaphysics considered above.

3
The Method of Original Inquiry

Return to questioning *all this*, to the terminus at which one takes nothing for granted about what one is engaging. In doing so, one confronts a diverse array. With one's senses open or stopped, one confronts an array of what, ordinarily, in a less critical context, one might say includes, inter alia, colors, shapes, phenomenal feels, moods, textures, familiar objects, emotional states, sounds, thoughts, smells, mental images. That one confronts a diverse array should not be taken for granted here. Question it. The questioning, the effort to hold some whatnot at critical distance to assess "it," demonstrates the lack of uniformity that is the diverse array. This diversity reveals complexity and so multiplicity; it also reveals some of the constraints on any account of *all this*, the world. There exist constraints, the basis of this diversity—there must be, then, some thing or other, in the most general sense of *thing*. If the ambitious metaphysics I propound in Chapter 2 is to be vindicated, it must provide an account of what such a thing is consistent with the unremittingly critical nature of the discipline. Showing how this is to be done is the primary purpose of this chapter.

Again, in the present context, *thing* should be construed as having the utmost generality. In the relevant sense, a *thing* just is an *entity*, an *existent*, a *being* (I make no distinction among these). What is at issue here is an account of the members of the *summum genus*, the all-inclusive category. Language can mislead, suggesting the presence of some thing when, in fact, none is there, but anything in the world is a thing. If there be material objects, substances, mental entities, essences, forms, kinds, properties, relations, modes, tropes, events, processes, stuff, forces, laws, states of affairs, facts, propositions, moments, points, collections, sets, numbers, holes, privations, fusions, aggregates—what have you—each example of any of these varieties is a thing. The present task is to say what a thing *of any variety* is.

One might have thought little hangs on such an indiscriminate question. But in light of the foregoing, that this is a mistake should be clear. Things in the most general sense are the focus and basis of every (constrained) inquiry and, as such, the means of any explanation of any phenomenon. Thus, understanding what a thing is provides insight into the limits of inquiry and of explanation. Such understanding, moreover, reveals how—again, in the most general sense—the world is structured, how things in *all this* are related. What a thing is determines the extent of these relations and their force and complexity. An explicit account of what a thing is, therefore, is not only crucial to realizing the chief objective of the ambitious, wholly critical metaphysics I am pursuing, namely, an account of the world (and what it comprises), it also provides the ground rules for any subsequent inquiry.

I develop these claims below. Regardless of the putative significance of an account of what a thing is, some will be dubious of the possibility of such, for some philosophers, most notably Aristotle, have long maintained that there can be no *summum genus*, no class that includes each thing just in virtue of its existing. If this were so, the question of what a thing is would be misguided, unanswerable, and metaphysics, as I am pursuing it, would be futile. I defend the legitimacy of the question by considering—and dismissing—the reasons adduced for maintaining there can be no *summum genus*, as well as an additional concern that a satisfactory answer to the question cannot be given. Addressing these reasons and this concern, however, brings to light again the singular difficulties in obtaining such an account, difficulties that are just marks of the distinctive problem of metaphysics. So I take up again *original inquiry*, the method needed to resolve this problem. I discuss this method in detail, and articulate the answer to the question of what a thing is that it provides. I conclude by examining how exactly original inquiry resolves the unique problem challenging a wholly critical account of *all this*.

§3.1. What Hangs on the Question of What a Thing Is?

An answer to the question of what an existent is provides the grounds for a principled account of the scope of reality, what exists and what does not, and, hence, what must be included in an account of the world. To be clear, a totally general account of what a thing is does not directly answer the question of whether some particular thing exists or whether some kind of thing does. So such an account does not itself reveal whether the number 2 or God exists, or whether there are numbers or deities in general. Rather an account of *thing* would provide insight into what, if it (or They) exists, the number 2 or God is qua thing—how that thing (or any other) must be simply by existing. (To determine whether, say, the number 2 exists requires a different mode of investigation, one posterior to original inquiry and with specifically numerical considerations.) A general account of *thing* provides, then, the means of fully understanding the claim that some particular thing (or kind) exists. If one holds that Santa Claus exists or that witches, minds, or black holes do, one holds that there is a certain (kind of) thing in the world. Without some account of what a thing is, one is no position to appreciate the ontological import of what is being held or what its consequences are.

Each thing is related to myriad others. The relatedness of things is evident from the very diversity and complexity of the array one confronts when one turns to *all this*. If this array were somehow illusionary, so that what underlies one's confrontation is not in fact how it appears to be, the experienced diversity itself, it seems to me, cannot be illusory and, hence, neither can the relatedness of things. Even if this were incorrect, so that an experience as of diversity could fail to include in itself any genuine diversity, if the experience is an illusion, there is some difference between how (or what) things are presented to a conscious subject and how (or what) the basis of this presentation actually is. Thus, in any illusion, there is diversity, a lack of uniformity—between, for example, the subject and their experience or this experience and its basis—and so related things. Whether related things are so related by standing in relations, or by merely being related simpliciter, is not important here. (But if there be relations, each is a thing.)[1] Regardless, this diverse array, a complex of related things, is the *structure in reality*, i.e., the *structure in the world*.

There are two axes of disagreement regarding the structure in reality that are the mainsprings of much, if not most, of the dispute in the history of Western metaphysics. One axis turns primarily on an issue concerning the relatedness of the things in this structure, the other on one concerning the things so related. I maintain that an answer to the question of what a thing is resolves the issues along both axes. Therefore, given its role in both circumscribing reality and resolving pivotal disagreement about the structure in it, this answer is the key to an account of the world.

Consider, then, these two axes of disagreement regarding the structure in reality. The first concerns the *integrity*—the source and force—of the relatedness among things that yield the structure. Certain philosophers maintain that some things are themselves necessarily related (or that there are necessary relations among things themselves), that is, that some things,

---

[1] I argue, in §4.3.1., that there are indeed relations in addition to related things, i.e., relata.

independently of how they are thought of or described, *must* be related as they are. Thus, certain things—substances, for example—are supposed to be necessarily related, given what or how they are, to other things—the kinds they instantiate or some of the properties they exemplify or other substances. Or, for another example, certain things—states of affairs, facts, or events— are supposed to be necessarily related to others—distinct states of affairs, facts, or events. Other philosophers deny that any things are themselves necessarily related, maintaining that any one thing can be related anyhow to any other and, hence, any relatedness that in fact obtains could fail to. Those in this latter camp hold that any necessity among things arises not from those things per se, but from some other source, such as the capacities of minds or the activities of conscious beings engaging what is real.

Such disagreement about the provenance of necessity raises the grand question of what role minds play in constructing mundane reality, as well as associated ones regarding the appropriate accounts of contingency, causation, the laws of nature, and explanation and its limits. These issues are at the heart of the early modern rejection of Scholasticism, and from that juncture have largely directed the narrative of Western philosophy (though disagreement surrounding them goes back much further, at least to Protagoras). Contentious assumptions regarding the issues underlie empiricism (and positivism) and so inspired Kant and the legion of idealists, of various stripes, that followed him and all the realists, of various stripes, that have objected to their views. Basic disagreement about the integrity of structure remains central in contemporary debates between the heirs of Hume and Kant and neo-Aristotelians.

What is crucial, for present purposes, is recognizing that this disagreement about the necessity of the structure in reality turns on whether (and how) *things* are necessarily related. It can be resolved, therefore, with an account of what a thing is. If anything, just by being, must be related to some other thing(s), then the very existence of a thing would require necessary structure in reality. Existence and necessity would be concomitant. Given such necessary relatedness, to some extent the world would be ready-made; there would be, prior to the engagement of any mind, joints to carve, that is, things related to others in set ways. On the other hand, if each thing could exist without being necessarily related to another, then there would be in the world per se—reality consisting only of every thing as it is independently of any mental engagement with it—no necessity. To the extent that things appear to be necessarily related or indeed are, the necessary relatedness must arise from a source other than those related things themselves (presumably via the activity of some mind). Hence, this long-standing disagreement about the integrity of structure depends on what a thing is.

The other axis of perennial disagreement regarding the structure in reality concerns its *intricacy*, the ontological complexity and bases of the relata that are supposed to yield it. Consider some relatum that related to other, ostensibly independent things contributes to the structure in reality. Some philosophers maintain that such a thing can be dependent upon—in the sense of *made up of* or *based on*—others;[2] thus, the very being of the former is derived from the latter. Certain things—a wooden table or a statue or a mental property, for example—are supposed to be derived from others—cellulose molecules, a lump of clay, a physical property, respectively. Therefore, the existence of one thing (or that thing being what it is or its having its distinguishing features) is explicable in terms of some other thing(s). There is a variety of putative relations here—composition, constitution, grounding, realization, emergence, etc.[3]—so there is a good deal of contention. This contention lacks any obvious unity. Some deny that composition ever occurs, some maintain constitution is identity, some repudiate grounding altogether, etc., with one's position regarding one relation not clearly determinative of one's position regarding another. Most philosophers, however, take for granted that there are at least some such *constitutive dependence relations*. Whether indeed there are is a point worth examining.

Such disagreement about whether (or under what conditions) one thing can *make another be* raises the profound question of ontological status, whether there are *levels* in being. If the structure in reality were hierarchical, there would be something distinctive about those things that make others yet are themselves not made to be, for these would be the ultimate grounds of an explanation for what or how the world is. Whereas necessity is crucial to an account of the integrity of structure, it is *fundamentality* that is key to an account of its intricacy. Philosophers often construe fundamentality—mistakenly, as I argue—as the contradictory of *ontological dependence*, whereby what is fundamental is not ontologically dependent. The fundamental is supposed to be what builds, but is not built; what is simple or not

---

[2] These are metaphors. In this connection, see Karen Bennett: "One theme that cuts a surprisingly large swath through philosophy is that of *building up* or *generating* or *constructing* or *giving rise to* or *getting out of*... and there are many other metaphors that could continue that list" (Bennett 2011b: 79–80). Bennett calls all these "building relations."

[3] Other putative examples of such relations include, microbased determination, truthmaking, singleton formation, bundling. See Bennett 2011b: §2.

constituted or ungrounded. Such issues have been contentious from the beginning of Western philosophy, at least since Aristotle's critique of the atomism of Democritus. This critique motivated Epicurus and his followers, leading to modern corpuscularianism and contemporary physicalist materialism. Controversy has been compounded in recent decades by various reductive and non-reductive hierarchical views, involving a host of putative constitutive dependence relations, and remains central to much contemporary metaphysical discussion.

What is crucial, for present purposes, is recognizing that this disagreement concerning fundamentality turns on whether one *thing* can be made to be by *another*. Like the foregoing disagreement regarding necessity in the relatedness of things, disagreement here can be resolved with an account of what a thing is. If a thing, by its very existence, precludes being made to be by some other, then there would be no constitutive dependence relations, no relations in which existence is derived or transferred. Consequently, there would be no hierarchical structure in reality—no levels of being—and one would be misguided in characterizing the fundamental in terms of what builds, but is not built. No thing would be (ontologically) built. On the other hand, if the very existence of one thing can be derived from another, then there could be building relations, i.e., relations of constitutive dependence, perhaps even the variety widely presumed to be. However, an account of what a thing is might nonetheless provide some insight into which building relations actually hold and the connections among them.

Thus, disagreement about both the integrity and the intricacy of the structure in reality—whether its connections are necessary and what is fundamental in it—turns on the question of what a thing is. Determining its answer is crucial to the wholly critical, ambitious metaphysics I am pursuing.

§3.2. Can This Question Be Answered?

The question here is not what *being* is. This presumes that being is itself a thing, one to be explicated. Prior to this question is the one of what it is to be or, what I take to be tantamount, what a thing of any variety is. This is the one I am asking here. Once this question is answered, one can consider, if one chooses, the question of whether being is a thing.

If indeed answering the question of what a thing is is crucial to the metaphysics I am pursuing, some might conclude from this alone that such metaphysics is futile. From near the outset of traditional metaphysical inquiry, this question has been regarded as fruitless. Aristotle argues in Book *B* of *Metaphysics* that *being* is not a genus, that there is no class that includes all things as things.[4] Of course, each thing *is*, but there is no basis here on which to expound what it is to be something. Were this so, there would be nothing informative to be said about a being considered simply as a being and, thus, no answer to the question of what a thing is.

§3.2.1. Aristotle's argument that *being* is not a genus

Aristotle's argument that *being* is not a genus occurs in the context of his efforts to provide an account of what makes a familiar concrete object be what it is (and do the things characteristic of that object). The argument rests on several assumptions regarding how such objects are differentiated from others. In particular, Aristotle assumes that an object is first differentiated as being of a certain kind and that a kind is characterized by means of a *real definition*. A real definition is a set of conditions determining what that kind is in terms of a general class (that subsumes that kind) and a specific difference that distinguishes that kind of thing, i.e., that species, from others in the general class. Thus, a given man is differentiated as a human being, a certain kind of animal, by exhibiting general features characteristic of animals and by exhibiting rationality, a specific capacity that distinguishes human beings from all other animals.

This account of the differentiation of objects requires certain constraints. Thus, for a genus itself to apply to the specific difference that distinguishes a species of that genus is supposed to be impossible. To illustrate: *Being an animal* cannot apply to *rationality*, for, first of all, rationality is itself not an animal. Furthermore, if *being an animal* were to apply to *rationality*, any rational thing would be an animal, so 'rational animal' would be redundant and would not characterize a specific kind of animal. *Being*, however, were it a genus, would apply to any specific difference, because every specific difference has being, that is, exists. (For example, rationality must exist if it is being rational that distinguishes humans from other animals.) Therefore, *being* violates the supposed constraint and so cannot be a genus.

---

[4] 998b21–27.

This argument is not convincing. Even if one accepts that objects are differentiated by real definitions, the putative constraints on such an account are not well justified. In particular, the constraint on which the above argument rests, namely, that it is impossible for a genus itself to apply to a specific difference (of that genus), is merely presumed. This constraint is plausible enough when considered in light of certain examples (like *being an animal* and *rationality*) but there is no reason to think that it generalizes to most or all cases, including the pertinent one of *being*. Of course, as just observed, *being*, as a genus, would apply to any specific difference, but whether the resulting definition is redundant or otherwise unacceptable cannot be evaluated in the absence of any particular proposal. (A related concern about circularity is addressed in the next section.)

Although some support is offered for the key constraint in the *Topics*, this support is also based on example rather than general principle.[5] I believe it is misguided, then, to think that a sweeping and all-important question regarding existence—what each thing is—is settled by a brief argument resting on a constraint concerning, in particular, the differentiation of familiar concrete objects that is just taken for granted.[6] Relatedly, and more significantly, this argument from differentiation via real definition includes a number of quite precise presuppositions about things (like that a genus cannot apply to a specific difference of that very genus) that are unacceptable in the context of trying to explicate, in a wholly critical way, what a thing—anything whatsoever—is in the first place.

Therefore, I conclude that that *being* cannot be a genus and that there is no *summum genus* of all things are by no means obvious. This is corroborated in contemporary discussion of this issue: Some take it for granted that there is a *summum genus*;[7] others take pains to leave open the question of whether there is;[8] yet others, for reasons that seem problematic, deny that there is.[9]

---

[5] See *Top.* VI. 6, 144^{a}31-^{b}3 and Madigan's commentary, page 74, on *Metaphysics*, Book B and Book K 1–2.

[6] Alexander of Aphrodisias seems to have criticized Aristotle on similar grounds, see Madigan's commentary (Aristotle 2000: 74).

[7] See, for example, Hoffman and Rosenkrantz 1994: 17–18 and Lowe 2006: 7–8, 39.

[8] See, for example, van Inwagen 2013: 15–16, especially Note 8.

[9] Thus, Amie Thomasson (2007: 113–114), following David Wiggins (2001: 69), maintains that being is not a kind because 'being' (or 'thing') is not a sortal—since the term does not bring with it definite persistence conditions. Setting aside concerns about the conflation of linguistic or conceptual issues with ontological ones, this argument presumes that all things must conform to persistence conditions and so exist in time. This is a controversial presumption for which no argument is given. David Oderberg (2007: 37, §5.3, especially 106–107) denies that being is a genus, but does so because he accepts the Scholastic doctrine of the Analogy of Being. This doctrine, however, has its roots in

§3.2.2. The circularity of any explicative account of *thing*

If one rejects doctrinal Aristotelian (and other supposed) reasons for maintaining there is no *summum genus*, and takes whether *thing* is a kind to be an open question, one might nevertheless be pessimistic regarding an insightful answer to the question of what a thing is given its utter generality. With some reflection, that there can be no real definition of *thing* along the lines offered for other kinds is clear. These definitions are provided by citing some general class and then distinguishing the *definiendum* from among that class by its peculiar properties; in this case, however, one is seeking illumination of the general class, the all-inclusive *summum genus*. Moreover, if a real definition requires a genus and a specific difference, and any specific difference exists, then *being* will be distinguished by itself, and so the resulting definition, if not redundant (as considered above), would be objectionably circular. (Indeed, this sort of consideration is what, in part, leads some to deny that *being* is a genus.)[10]

These concerns about the form of a real definition and its circularity are misplaced. A real definition or an explicative account more generally is meant to illuminate what some kind is essentially; it makes perspicuous what it is to be something (of that kind). A traditional sort of real definition—an analytic definition, a definition *ad genus per differentiam*—might provide the means of doing this for some kinds, while incapable of doing so for others, such as *thing* (i.e., *being*). Failure in the latter case does not show that there can be no explicative account at all, for there is no reason to think that every such account must have the form of a (traditional) real definition. There can be other manners of providing an explicative account of what something is. The success of a proposed account needs to be assessed on the basis of the insight it provides, not whether it has any particular form. Still, what a thing is cannot be given in terms of anything but some thing—there can be no other means to articulate the account. Furthermore, *every* definition or explication is of one thing in terms of another (or others). The explication of *thing* can be no different. If one is trying to illuminate what a thing—anything at all—is via an explicative account, and that account must be in terms of a thing (or things), such an account is bound to be, in some way, circular.

---

the work of Aristotle considered above, where the claims on which it is based are found to lack appropriate justification.

[10] See Oderberg 2007: 107.

Fortunately, not every circular account is inappropriate or unilluminating. An impredicative account, which in a sense is circular, is one that provides insight into some particular thing or kind by means of a plurality that includes that thing (or instances of that kind).[11] Consideration of such accounts has been undertaken in several contexts, for example, in attempts to address the semantic paradoxes and to provide criteria of identity for various kinds. There seems to be consensus among those who have considered impredicative accounts—contra Russell[12]—that there is nothing about impredicativity per se that makes it problematic.[13] To paraphrase E.J. Lowe: impredicativity is only problematic in the absence of an appropriate supporting framework concerning the entities that one is trying to define.[14] Thus, each explicative account—impredicative or not—should be evaluated on its own terms given one's theoretical objectives.

§3.3. The Means of Resolving the Distinctive Problem

The question then arises of what supporting framework would be fruitful for illuminating what something—any thing—is. In order to appreciate an explicative account of *thing*, which must be in terms of something or other, one must have some wider perspective on the *explanandum*. Here the prevalence of things seems to present an obstacle. What is required is some feasible origin that is not explicitly or obviously about things yet nevertheless has purchase on them. Such an origin needs to be entirely inclusive, so that it may bear on all things, otherwise its limited scope would render it unsuitable to provide the means of illuminating what each and every thing is. Despite its inclusivity, the origin needs to be telling enough to provide a context in which to understand what a thing is, yet not so telling as to preclude implausibly any particular claim about the world. The purpose here, after all, is to provide an uncontroversial account of *thing* that anyone would have to accept in light of *all this*, and then show how this account constrains, even settles, more controversial metaphysical issues. Finally, the key origin needs

---

[11] Such an account of impredicativity, which comes from the work of Russell and Whitehead, can be found in Gödel 1944; Quine 1985: 166; and Lowe 1989.

[12] Russell 1908: 63.

[13] See, for example, the papers by Gödel, Quine, and Lowe cited above. Indeed, Gödel argues that impredicative definitions are acceptable whenever the objects being defined exist independently of one's definitions.

[14] See the concluding paragraph of Lowe 1989.

to be plausible; if it were implausible it would undermine, rather than augment, an account of *thing* that accorded with it.

§3.3.1. The world as impetus to inquiry

What is needed to appreciate an explicative account of *thing*, an account that cannot be but circular, is a contextualizing origin that has unlimited scope, is substantive without being tendentious, and is plausible. The stringency of these criteria is daunting. Yet there is a source that meets them, one that is so obvious that it goes unremarked in any but the most rarefied investigations, a source that one has already confronted and can easily confront again: *the world at large—all this*.

Accepting *all this* is, of course, not to accept that there is a *material* world or an *external* one. As plausible as these claims might be, in the present context, in which one seeks an account of what a thing is, they are too controversial, presupposing too much about what exists or how it does. Rather, *all this*, the contextualizing origin I am demonstrating, is not in the least controversial. So confront "it" anew, without presupposition and eschewing any familiar discrimination, as the whatnot that can induce perplexity and move one to inquire; in other words, confront the world merely as the *impetus to inquiry*. This impetus, so engaged—without presupposition and, hence, unconceptualized—is unconditioned, unrestricted. Engaged as the impetus to inquiry, the world inspires a sense of the "great blooming, buzzing confusion," in William James's famous phrase,[15] that James supposes is presented to an infant before a mind discriminates a tractable array.

What is engaged is not presumed to be what one perceives. What is engaged is *whatever* one encounters in confronting *all this*, and so includes not only what, if anything, one perceives, but whatever one is conscious of, be it near or far, internal or external, subjective or objective. Such engagement confirms that *the world is not monolithic*. It is, on the contrary, lacking uniformity: it is *diverse*. Any inquiry, in any circumstance, from the humblest—a child examining a flower, a person looking to the sky—to the

---

[15] See Chapter 13 of James's *The Principles of Psychology*. The reference here to James is not merely casual. The ontological project in the present work is closely related to James's in empirical psychology. In fact, this project seems to me to be a necessary precursor to James's, insofar as ontology has a certain primacy in inquiry concerning the mind, and intentionality more specifically. In this connection, see Fiocco 2015.

most sophisticated or grand, begins with diversity. There can be no inquiry, no querying of what, how, or why, if there is no distinction between *inquirer* and *object of inquiry*, the whatnot that piques and provides the focus of one's query. This distinction and, hence, diversity is a formal constraint on, that is, a necessary condition of inquiry. This is so even if one's object of inquiry is itself simple or uniform, which the world, this diverse array, is patently not.

When one confronts the world as merely the impetus to inquiry, renouncing assumptions and discriminating concepts, one engages bare diversity; not the diversity of flower and stem or moon and star, but simply lack of uniformity in whatnot. What one confronts, without ontological or epistemological prejudice, as the impetus to inquiry, here, from the "armchair," is undiscriminated, yet formally no different than what one confronts when undertaking more theoretical inquiry in any laboratory, observatory, data center, etc. In each case, one has diversity, at least of inquirer and object—if not further diversity in the object itself. What one can learn about inquiry and its object(s) from this point can, then, because of its formal, general perspective, illuminate inquiry per se.

The generality and immediacy of the world when confronted as merely the impetus to inquiry makes *all this* an apt contextualizing origin for appreciating an explicative account of *thing*. This origin, one will recall, must have unlimited scope, be substantive without being tendentious and be plausible. *All this* confronted as merely the impetus to inquiry is unconditioned and, hence, unlimited. As discussed below, *all this* cannot fail to have a basis, so "it" is substantive. 'All this,' nota bene, is not a claim, it is an (unconditioned) referential expression; and *all this* is no claim either, "it" is, then, no assumption and so cannot be tendentious. *All this* is the whatnot immediately confronted by one insofar as one is conscious. Any inquirer, in any context can engage and examine it. The diversity herein is likewise immediately engageable. However, in wholly critical inquiry, such as this one directed at an explicative account of any thing at all, even the impetus to inquiry and its diversity ought to be questioned. Question them then. The very effort to question something—anything—demonstrates the impetus to inquiry; the very effort to hold some whatnot at critical distance to assess "it" demonstrates the lack of uniformity that is diversity. So *all this*, this diverse array, may be questioned, "it" is, nevertheless, indisputable. Still, because there is here no assumption, no claim even, there can be no dogma. (Consider, again, the related discussion opening Chapter 1.) *All this* with its diversity is, therefore, inescapably plausible.

Indeed, not even the most enthusiastic skeptic could deny that there is *all this*, the impetus to inquiry, a prompt to ontological (and epistemological) investigation. Because one can immediately engage the lack of uniformity in *all this*, there can or should be no doubt about the diversity in the world either. Given that there is no claim and no thing posited when confronting the world as merely the impetus to inquiry, there is just nothing about *all this* to doubt when beginning inquiry at this point. There is, then, no toehold here for the skeptic. Consequently, because nothing—no thing—is being presumed, there can be at this point no distinction between what is and what can be known; there is no defined subject, no discriminated object, nothing internal, nothing external. Inquiry from confronting *all this* as merely the impetus to inquiry—*original inquiry*—does not even permit a distinction between *appearance* and *reality* and so at this point ontology and epistemology converge. Neither, if one is wholly critical, can begin with less.

All this, engaged as the impetus to inquiry, provides a neutral, universal starting point for any inquiry that is to be wholly critical. With such original inquiry, one can confront the world, yet eschew any supposition about the nature and, at this point, explanatory basis of what is thereby engaged, even that what is engaged is a thing. One can, I maintain, discern from here what a thing, any thing at all, is and thereby resolve the distinctive problem of metaphysics. I maintain that the elusive and unfamiliar, an explicative account of *thing*, can be appreciated in the context of the overwhelmingly familiar, the world at large, and that the aptness of the former can be evaluated by how well it can elucidate what, even when questioned, is indisputable, to wit, this diverse array. This is, admittedly, an extraordinary gambit—recognizing the world, this encompassing array, yet not ipso facto supposing that any *thing* exists—but such a move should not seem out of place in a wholly critical, ambitious metaphysics, a rudimentary investigation of *everything*. In fact, such an unsettling opening should not be entirely unfamiliar. As noted in Chapter 1, it is reminiscent of, though different from, the preliminary stances of others: consider Descartes *dans le poêle* and Husserlian *epoché*.

Original inquiry begins here, then, within the contextualizing origin of the world at large, whatever "it" is. Confronting *all this* as merely the impetus to inquiry, one engages an incontrovertible diverse array. To discern what a thing is, one proceeds from this point by descrying the conditions of being in or of this diverse array. There must be such conditions, for there must be some basis for the diversity in *all this*. This is because diversity is difference, and there is no difference simpliciter, there is only difference in or between some thing(s). To see why, assume there is difference, but in nothing or nothing at all. Nothing does not differ from "itself" or anything else (just as nothing is not identical to "itself") and nothing does not differ. Nothing is no way at all, a fortiori "it" is not and cannot be diverse. Therefore, if there is diversity, there is something. Furthermore, diversity and distinctness require more than a unique thing. No thing can be distinct from itself; for there to be distinctness and, hence, diversity, there must be some thing, in the totally general sense of 'thing,' and another related to the original. Diversity requires things, even if they are not independent or wholly distinct, and so diversity requires *structure*: some whatnot related to some other whatnot. Therefore, given that there is diversity in *all this*, there are things.

This conclusion can hardly be surprising. Even assuming nothing about *all this*, one cannot intelligibly assume there is nothing at all. For one to assume or even entertain that nothing whatsoever exists is incoherent! So there are some things (beings, entities, etc.). Accepting this, however, does not itself provide any insight into what a thing is. Since the existence of things is discernible by engaging the diversity in the world, things obviously contribute in a crucial way to *all this*. Without things—were there nothing at all—there would not be *all this*. Things are, then, the ontological basis of an explanation for *all this*.

An *explanation* is an epistemological-cum-ontological thing: some act or object that illuminates some phenomenon by presenting some thing(s) vis-à-vis another (or others). Explanation works by indicating some relation between the *explanandum*, the phenomenon to be explained to an inquirer, and some thing or things (the *explanans*), whereby how the former is depends on or is determined by the latter. So a genuine explanation, one that succeeds in illuminating some object of inquiry, must be underlain by a determinative relation among things in the world.[16] The *ontological basis* of an explanation is the thing (or those things) in the world that account(s) for the explanandum.

So far, original inquiry reveals that there are things and that these are the ontological bases of any explanation for the diversity in *all this*. One might grant this much, if only because the claims are so exceedingly plausible that they seem hardly worth doubting. One might be dubious, though, that further investigation—from the point of engaging the world as merely the

---

[16] For this sort of realist view of explanation, see Ruben 1990, especially Chapter 7. See, as well, Kim 1994: 67–68.

impetus to inquiry—can provide more penetrating insight into *all this* via an explicative account of *thing*. Such qualms are misplaced. Worthwhile inquiry is inquiry that need not be futile because it does indeed have an object: there is some thing in the world that constrains that inquiry, providing a criterion of success or failure with respect to the undertaking. Successful inquiry, by any suitably high standard, cannot be guaranteed; however, worthwhile inquiry can, by a demonstration that the object of that inquiry is real. Given that there must be an ontological basis of an explanation for the diversity in *all this*, one can be assured that original inquiry is worthwhile, even if, for some reason, it cannot ultimately be successful. One can learn something about the bases of *all this*, even if it is just that one cannot ever learn as much as one wishes (and why one cannot learn as much about things as one wishes would surely reveal much about what or how things are). Note, though, any pessimism regarding what one might be able to learn about the world is misguided when pursuing original inquiry. Although there might be, eventually, compelling reasons to deny or, more cautiously, to be skeptical of the possibility of successful inquiry given certain conclusions about the world or limitations in the capacities of inquirers, at the outset of original inquiry, there are no assumptions made about *all this* and no recognized limitations on minds (nor inquirers). Thus, if one is so inclined, one may begin wholly critical inquiry into *all this*, confronting it merely as the impetus to inquiry, with optimism or, at least, without skepticism or pessimism.

In general, there is an ontological basis of an explanation for diversity and, thus, there is a basis of an explanation for the diversity in *all this*. Of crucial importance to present purposes is that there must also be an ontological basis of an explanation for a more specific phenomenon. In confronting *all this* as merely the impetus to inquiry, one engages a world that is diverse; more specifically, one engages a world that is *thus*—here 'thus' demonstrates the more or less determinate panoply (of whatnot) immediately present upon engaging *all this*. Some such more or less determinate panoply is available to *any* inquirer in *any* circumstance. The world presents, when engaged, in a particular way; "it" is *thus* and not some other way. (In a less austerely critical context, one might say the world now presents to one as being, among other ways, brownish and shiny over there, smooth here, itchy there; and as including, among other things, a blue cylindrical bit next to a pink rectangular one, a picture on top of a bookcase, an aroma of coffee, a pang of hunger, a low-level whoosh and some tick-tocking, a memory of green hills, a mental image of a bridge over a river; with a twinge of anxiety, a hint of wonder, and all suffused with a sense of determination, etc.) In other words, in confronting *all this*, one engages a world that is diverse precisely *thusly*. Given that there must be an ontological basis of an explanation for the diversity in *all this* and *all this* cannot fail to be diverse in some particular way and is in fact *thus*—"it" is diverse precisely *thusly*—the ontological basis of an explanation for the diversity in *all this* is the basis of an explanation for how the world is *thus*. In light of this ontological basis, how the world is *thus* is an object of worthwhile inquiry.

I should be clear about what exactly is in need of explanation. What needs to be explained is how the impetus to inquiry is currently as it is rather than some other way. Such an explanation cannot be causal, if causal explanations are what they are usually taken to be. These explanations are supposed to account for how events occur in space over time in terms of the laws of nature or the powers of the constituents of those events. In the present context, a causal explanation would presuppose too much about what things exist and how they interact. Furthermore, not only does it seem that the *explanandum*, an impetus to inquiry that is *thus*, is not even susceptible to a causal explanation—it is all-encompassing and no mere event—but even if it were, such an explanation would not illuminate the object of inquiry. What requires explanation is not how the impetus to inquiry *arose* or *how it came to be* thus; what is needed in the first instance is, again, some explanation for how the impetus to inquiry *is* (now) as it is. Such an explanation cannot be causal, it would be more generally *ontological*, even *transcendental* (to use a provocative notion) in that it would rely on certain background conditions having to be met in order that more obvious ones be accounted for. One might think a sort of *metaphysical explanation*, one on which something exists at all or is what it is or as it constitutively is because of some other thing, is relevant here. However, as I argue below, such metaphysical explanations are precluded by what a thing is.[17]

The world as the impetus to inquiry is not presumed to be a thing. Yet, regardless of the sort of explanation needed, for the reasons given above, there is an ontological basis for how the world is *thus*. This basis is those existing constraints that make the world *thus* (rather than some other way). Whatever a thing is, then, it must be able to provide the basis of an explanation, at least in part, for how the world is as it is. So applying the method of original

---

[17] For recent seminal discussion of metaphysical explanation in the sense characterized above—also known as *grounding explanation*—see Fine 2012b, 2001; Rosen 2010; Schaffer 2009.

inquiry as initiated above, one obtains a preliminary answer to the question of what a thing is: it is something that provides the basis of an explanation for how the world is as it is. Though this is circular—*thing* is characterized in terms of some thing—it is not vacuous, *the world*, this encompassing diverse array, provides context and gives it heft. One begins with an incontrovertible contextualizing origin, *all this* taken merely as the impetus to inquiry, and by engaging "it" is able to discern that there must be related things that make "it" so, that make "it" *thus*. But this account of a thing as something that provides the basis of an explanation for how *all this* is *thus* is not a real definition nor a satisfying explication, for it merely says what a thing *does*, not what it *is*. What is still needed is an account of what it is to be something capable of providing the basis of an explanation for how the world is *thus*.

From confronting the world as merely the impetus to inquiry, original inquiry reveals that a thing is an ontological basis of an explanation for how *all this* is as it is. One will notice, however, that the preceding discussion, a demonstration of the method of original inquiry, is not without assumptions. There are, for example, assumptions about apt explanation and, more subtly, assumption pertaining to logic and inference that underlie the argumentation within the discussion. There are indeed these assumptions. Nevertheless, their presence is consistent with original inquiry being wholly critical and, importantly, with the value of inquiry that is presuppositionless in the relevant way. I take up these issues when I consider how exactly original inquiry is able to resolve the distinctive problem of metaphysics. Before doing so, though, I continue with original inquiry in order to provide the needed explicative account of *thing*.

§3.4. What a Thing Must Be: A Natured Entity

Original inquiry reveals that a thing is an ontological basis of an explanation for how *all this* is as it is, how the world is *thus*. That explanation must end at some point is a truism; a thing is whereby an explanation *can* end. The question of what a thing is, then, becomes the question of what an entity must be in order to play this determinative role. A thing, at least in part, makes the world as it is; so that the world is *thus* is (again, at least in part) in virtue of some thing.

Since it is a thing that provides the basis of at least a partial explanation for how the world is as it is, for the following reasons, *there can be nothing further that determines how a thing in its entirety is.* Every thing is included in *all this*—the world, this encompassing diverse array—and so must make some contribution to it. If how an entity, *e*, were (in its entirety) explicable in terms of some other thing, *e* itself would be ontologically idle, making no contribution per se to how the world is; such an "entity" would, if anything, merely be a manifestation of the latter, that genuine existent. Hence, if there were something that made *e* how "it" is, *e*'s contribution to how the world is would be made by that thing that wholly determines or makes *e* how *e* is. Yet if *e* "itself" were not capable of contributing to a partial explanation for how *all this* is as it is, if "it" per se were insufficient to do at least this, *e* would be no thing at all. "It" could in principle make no contribution to the world and, therefore, is, literally, nothing.

This conclusion is corroborated by a more straightforward argument that shows that no thing can explain the very existence of another and so account for the latter's presence in *all this*; in other words, no thing can be *made to be* by something else. Suppose that x makes to be y, in the sense that y is *grounded by* or is "latent" in x and so y derives its very existence from x.[18] *Makes to be* is, if anything, a relation (and if it is not anything at all, it cannot contribute to the structure in the world); as such, it relates things. If *makes to be* relates distinct things, if $x \neq y$, then both x and y must exist in order to stand in this relation, in which case, the existence of y is a precondition of its standing in the relation. Consequently, it cannot be by standing in this relation that y exists. The very existence of y is, therefore, not attributable to or determined by x: it is not the case that x makes to be y. If $x = y$, then 'x' and 'y' are merely co-referential terms and so y is merely a guise of x (and vice versa): it is not the case that x makes to be some other thing.

One might challenge this argument by maintaining that it shows merely that if x makes to be y, then the two things must co-exist. It does not follow from their necessary co-existence, one might contend, that x is not in some sense *prior* to y. If it is, x is—in some way—more fundamental than y, and so can ground or otherwise determine the being, the existence of the latter. However, what this sort of response overlooks is that the relation of priority employed here is supposed to be explanatory. As such, it is constrained by the norms of explanation. No genuine explanation can require that the explanandum play an instrumental role in permitting the dependence relation

---

[18] This is how many, including Jonathan Schaffer, understand the relation of *grounding*. See Schaffer 2009: 378, 379.

on which that explanation is based to hold at all. Were an "explanation" to require this, its underlying dependence relation would rely crucially on what it is supposed to be realizing in the first place. Yet if x were to explain the very being of y, y must exist in order for x to stand in a determinative relation to y. The holding of this determinative relation would rely crucially on the existence of y, which is precisely what the relation is supposed to be realizing. Thus, the argument does not overlook putative relations of grounding or ontological priority and is not undermined by them; rather, it shows why there can be no such relations.

If one thing cannot be made to be by something else, it follows that one thing cannot make another thing be *what* it is. This is because no thing can exist without being the kind of thing it is, i.e., what it is. (Though some things might change *how* they are in certain respects, this does not change, in the relevant sense, *what* they are.) That one thing cannot make another be what it is stands to reason in light of the foregoing conclusion, to wit, one thing cannot make another how it is (in its entirety), for, presumably, how a thing is is not independent of what it is. Similar reasoning also shows that the *individuation* of a thing, i.e., its being the very thing it is (and so distinct from any other); its *unity*, i.e., its being one thing despite having many parts; and its *identity*, i.e., its being itself, rather than some other thing, cannot be explicable in terms of some other thing. For any such explanation would require some relation between a thing and the thing(s) supposed to make the former the very thing it is—or to unify it or make it itself—but anything, if it is to stand in any relation whatsoever, must be the very thing it is (or be a unit, if it is indeed one, or be itself), so it cannot be by standing in any such relation that a thing is individuated (or unified or made to be itself).

Therefore, each thing is an *ontological locus* in the sense that (i) its being and its being the very thing it is (as distinct from others) and its being itself are not determined (by anything beyond itself) and so are not explicable; (ii) its being how it is (in its entirety) is not determined by some other thing and, hence, is not explicable; (iii) its being what it is, the kind of thing it is and whether it is a unity, is not determined by some other thing and, hence, is not explicable; and (iv) the existence of that thing is the basis of at least a partial explanation for how the world is as it is. As the basis of an (at least partial) explanation for how the world is *thus*, a thing is some ways or others. Given that at least some of the ways a thing is are not explicable in terms of anything else and so are attendant upon its being (and, thus, being what it is), as an ontological locus, a thing is these ways simply because it is. Such a thing is *natured* insofar as it must be certain ways just in existing; the explanation for its being *as* it is, with respect to these ways, is simply its being *what* it is (and this is no real explanation). One might say that such a thing *has* a nature or *has* an essence, namely those ways it must be merely in existing. Such locutions should be avoided, however, for they are misleading. They suggest that a nature (or essence) is itself some variety of thing—some thing to be had by another—and this might suggest further that a thing is what it is because of its nature (or essence). But, again, there is nothing that makes a thing what it is or as it is essentially.[19] So a thing is not an entity *with* a nature or *with* an essence, albeit *natured* and *essentially certain ways*.[20]

In light of these considerations, I can now answer the key question: What is a thing? *A thing is a natured entity.* This is the sought-after explicative account of *thing*, an illuminating descriptive statement of what a thing is corroborated by anything and everything. The account is, as was to be expected, circular—a thing is a natured thing—nevertheless, it is not vacuous, for it reveals what is underlying *all this*. For there to be this encompassing diverse array, there must be natured entities. This account in terms of being natured[21] captures an important insight: each thing is constrained and, hence, a constraint, yet there is nothing to explain how it itself is constrained and constrains. This does not mean that each thing is an explanandum lacking an explanans; rather, no thing is amenable to explanation. Things are the bases of explanations, they are themselves not to be explained. Each thing—of any variety whatsoever—is fundamental, ontological bedrock, as it were.[22] A natured entity just is, just is what it is; it is nothing but a constraint on *all this*. Being so is what makes a thing a suitable basis of an (at least partial) explanation for how the world is as it is, and of any other explicable phenomenon.

---

[19] Hence, what is being espoused here is a sort of *real essentialism*, not the *contemporary essentialism* made familiar by Hilary Putnam and Saul Kripke, according to which an essence is a set of properties a thing must have because it is these properties that make that thing what it is. See Oderberg 2007: Chapter 1, for this distinction and a convincing critique of contemporary essentialism. The real essentialism that I am propounding here is quite different from Oderberg's, for my account of a thing leads me to reject Aristotelian forms and hylomorphism in general.

[20] It is important to not reify essences. E.J. Lowe also stresses this point (2013a, 2008). The real essentialism propounded here is more similar to Lowe's than Oderberg's (see previous note). However, my overall project is quite different from Lowe's. I am attempting to justify and thereby provide adequate foundation for a systematic metaphysics by asking the primary ontological question, viz., what is a thing? Lowe simply adopts an Aristotelian framework, and takes for granted a notion of an entity in the most general sense, never articulating this notion. See Lowe 1998: 180–181; 2006: 7.

[21] One should not be misled by language here: *being natured* is not a property, i.e., a thing.

[22] See Fiocco 2019a. I say more about fundamentality in Chapter 4.

With this insight and the irrefragable need of some explanation for how the world is *thus*, one has a robust account of what it is to be.

Therefore, every explicable phenomenon has an ontological basis in *all this*, the world (if there were nothing to the phenomenon, it would not be anything whatsoever). A thing itself, however, is beyond explanation—*inexplicable*—not merely in that it is apt for explanation, yet none is available, but in *not even being susceptible to explanation*. No thing can stand in a determinative relation to a thing per se. Things are the bases, the means of explanation, and not themselves appropriate targets of explanation. What *is* (and must be) explicable are particular structures, that is, certain *pluralities*, related things among *all this*. For what can be explained, then, there is an ontological basis in *all this*, but not everything whatsoever can be explained. What is not even open to explanation is not brute or arbitrary, it just is.

In light of this, I accept a principle according to which any object of inquiry that is a structural phenomenon (and, hence, not a thing), can be explained on the basis of the things in the world, though each of these is itself inexplicable.[23] Here, the notion of explanation is general, subsuming any suitably realist account that turns ultimately on what is in the world and the determinative relations among *all this*. This principle might suggest the circumscribed Principle of Sufficient Reason proposed and discussed by Shamik Dasgupta.[24] The two, however, are actually quite dissimilar. The differences are illuminating and help clarify important features of the view of *all this* to which original inquiry commits one.

Dasgupta articulates a principle according to which: "For every substantive fact Y there are some facts, the Xs, such that (i) the X's ground Y and (ii) each one of the Xs is autonomous."[25] A substantive fact is one that is "apt for being grounded" and an autonomous fact is one that is "not apt for being grounded in the first place."[26] Obviously, then, of central importance to this principle are the putative phenomena of grounding, an associated one of metaphysical (i.e., grounding) explanation and of being autonomous in the relevant sense. As stated above, one thing is supposed to ground another when the former makes the latter exist or to be how constitutively it is. A metaphysical explanation is one whereby some phenomenon is accounted for in virtue of some other in which the former is grounded. Dasgupta illustrates this with the toy

---

[23] For discussion of this principle, see §5.2.1.
[24] See Dasgupta 2016.
[25] Dasgupta 2016: 390.
[26] Dasgupta 2016: 383.

example of explaining the existence of a conference in terms of "how various people are acting, e.g. that some are giving talks, others are asking questions, etc."[27] and by suggesting "that a set exists *because* its members exist, and that there is a table here *because* some particles are arranged here in a certain way."[28] An autonomous fact is one not fit for grounding (and, hence, unfit for a metaphysical explanation). Dasgupta takes the notion of autonomy here as primitive, but tries to illuminate it. Just as a mathematical fact, such as that 1 + 2 = 3 is not fit for a causal explanation—the question of what *causes* this fact is misguided given what causation and what abstract entities, such as numbers, are supposed to be—there are, Dasgupta maintains, some facts that are not fit for a metaphysical explanation. He suggests that essentialist facts are among the autonomous ones. As (toy) examples of essentialist truths, he uses that water is composed of H_2O and that knowledge is true and justified belief; corresponding to these truths are the putative autonomous facts that it is essential to water that it is composed of H_2O and that it is essential to knowledge that it is true and justified belief. One who asks in virtue of what is it part of what water is that it is composed of H_2O reveals confusion similar to that revealed by one who ask what causes 1 + 2 = 3. The only apt answer to the former question seems to be that that is just what water is, and this seems more a dismissal of the question as misguided than a genuine answer to it.[29]

In Dasgupta's discussion, he takes facts to be the relata of the grounding relation and, consequently, states his Principle of Sufficient Reason in terms of facts. Whatever a fact is supposed to be, though, it ultimately concerns things, referring to or being composed of them. Moreover, as noted above, explanation ultimately turns on determinative relations among things. Dasgupta's principle, then, can be construed in the following way: all metaphysically explicable phenomena have explanations in terms of what itself is not apt to be metaphysically explained, for instance, how things essentially or constitutively are.

Put this way, Dasgupta's principle might appear to be similar to my own. The two, however, reflect very different views of reality. A view consistent with Dasgupta's principle is committed to a hierarchical ontological structure in the world: some things are ontologically prior to, more fundamental than, others, in that the former ground—give rise to or give being to—the

---

[27] Dasgupta 2016: 381.
[28] Ibid.
[29] See Dasgupta 2016: 386.

latter. This hierarchical ontology of things is reflected in a hierarchy of facts, with facts about more fundamental things grounding ones about less fundamental things and the autonomous facts the inexplicable ones about things somewhere in this hierarchy. Such ontological structure is, however, incompatible with the account of things provided by original inquiry. On this account, no thing makes another be; each thing is fundamental. Thus, the structure in *all this* is, ontologically, flat. There can be no grounding and, hence, no metaphysical explanation of the sort central to Dasgupta's position. The basis of any phenomenon that can be explained is some things or other, with the explanation provided by how those things interact as they do, given what they (just) are. Moreover, not only is the view of reality reflected by the two principles very different, their scope is as well. Dasgupta's principle is limited to a certain range of facts, "substantive ones," and so applies exclusively to grounded phenomena; only metaphysical (or grounding) explanation is, then, relevant to the principle. In contrast, any feasible account of explanation, that is, any suitably realist one turning ultimately on determinative relations among *all this*, is relevant to the principle revealed by original inquiry. Any phenomenon that can be explained *at all* has an explanation with an ontological basis in the world.

That the two principles are so dissimilar is not surprising given that they arise in the contexts of radically different inquiries. Dasgupta's inquiry presumes much, for the sake of exploration, and is not critical in the way my own is. He takes certain things, such as essences, the grounding relation, and grounds, for granted (and takes the notion of autonomy as primitive) in order to see what sort of explanatory principle can be articulated in terms of them. On the contrary, original inquiry takes no thing with respect to *all this* for granted and proceeds from this wholly critical point to an account of *thing*, one that reveals the fundamentality of each thing and the crucial foundational role that such (inexplicable) things play in accounting for any (explicable) phenomenon.

As fundamental, what a thing, a natured entity, is is not determined by the ways it is; rather, the ways it is—specifically how it is essentially[30]—are determined simply by its being (and, thus, being what it is). Better purchase

---

[30] This qualification is needed because some things can be, in addition to the ways they are essentially, ways that they need not be. Call these ways how a thing is *accidentally*. How a thing is accidentally—some way it does not have to be merely in existing (and, hence, being what it is)— might be amenable to an explanation. But set such considerations aside for the present. In this chapter, I am addressing *all* things and all things are some ways essentially, even if they are not, in addition, certain ways merely accidentally.

on this claim can be obtained by considering a different and perhaps more familiar one: Suppose, contrary to this account of *thing*, that a thing is what it is because of how it is. That is, suppose a thing is made to be what it is because of the ways it is. This is not far-fetched; in fact, I suspect such an account is presumed by many philosophers. On this alternative account, a thing is an apple *because* it is round, red, organic, grows on certain trees, has certain DNA, etc., or is a sample of water *because* it is liquid (at room temperature), potable, odorless, is of the same stuff that fills rivers and lakes, is composed mostly of H_2O molecules, etc. Under scrutiny, however, this alternative account of what makes a thing what it is is problematic. First of all, such an account must apply to *all* things, not merely familiar concrete objects. But then one must give an account of the ways that make, say, a red trope be what it is or the ways that make the property of being potable what it is (and so exist at all). These consequences indicate that the alternative account is misguided. Worse, though, this account of what makes a thing what it is seems incoherent, for an explanation of a thing's being *what* it is cannot be based on its being *as* it is, for it must first be in order to be as it is, and it cannot be without being what it is.[31]

Hence, by being as it is, a natured entity contributes to the world by being the basis of an (at least partial) explanation for how the world is *thus*. Every thing together provides a complete explanation for how *all this* is as it is. A thing is as it is, the ways it is (essentially), because of what it is, and it is what it is simply in existing. So if there is a (general, instantiable) property, say *redness*, there is no thing that makes *redness redness* or makes *redness* a property. If there is a red mode (a particular instance of redness), there is no thing that makes that red mode a red mode or a mode. This is so even if there is some other thing—to wit, this apple—that must exist in order for that very red mode to be identified as the mode it is (i.e., the particular redness of this apple) or something else—to wit, the property *redness*—that the red mode could not exist in the absence of. If there is a (general, instantiable) kind, say *apple*, there is no thing that makes *apple apple* or makes *apple* a kind. If there is a particular apple, there is no thing that makes that apple an apple. If there is a state of affairs of this apple's being red, there is nothing that makes this a state of affairs or makes it the state of affairs it is—and to the extent that there is reason to think that the apple and its redness make this state of

---

[31] Though, presumably, in many cases, a thing can persist as what it is without being precisely as it is.

affairs be the state of affairs it is, there is reason to think there is no state of affairs (rather than just an apple and its redness). Similar claims can be made about a putative natured entity of any other variety whatsoever. (I say more about the relations of ontological dependence adverted to in this paragraph in §4.1.)

§3.5. Original Inquiry as Wholly Critical

The distinctive problem of the ambitious metaphysics I am pursuing, one will recall, is that the objective of such a discipline is a wholly critical account of what the world is and what it comprises, but, given the scope of this account, there is nothing not subsumed by the account by which to evaluate it—yet understanding the world, the very purpose of attaining this account, requires its evaluation. The world comprises things, so, as observed above, one aspect of this problem is providing an apt account of what a thing is while assuming nothing whatsoever about the world. I have now shown how one can attain such an account via original inquiry. Here I want to make clear how this method is indeed wholly critical and so does, in fact, resolve the distinctive problem of metaphysics.

With an account of *thing*, one has the means both to say what anything in the world is—what *all this* is composed of—and to ascertain whether the world is itself a thing (if it is, one might then go about determining what it is like). Original inquiry provides such an account: a thing is a natured entity. If one is to understand this account, to not only accept it on appropriate grounds, but to appreciate why it is apt (and has to be), one must evaluate the account in light of its grounds. The problem is, though, that there seems to be no vantage from which to evaluate it. Since the account has absolute generality—applying to literally everything—there is nothing independent of it by which to verify it. In order to have any means by which to evaluate the account, one must, it seems, first take something or other for granted and, hence, presuppose the very account one is trying to evaluate. Such "evaluation" is not illuminating and cannot provide understanding.

Resolving this distinctive problem, therefore, requires one to provide an account of what a thing is that is wholly critical, that is, that takes nothing for granted about the world, yet nonetheless can be evaluated without presupposing that very account. Resolution comes by recognizing there are distinct forms of inquiry and, hence, different ways of producing an account (or theory). Consequently, there are different ways of evaluating such an account.

The more familiar form and, perhaps, standard way of attempting to illuminate some object of inquiry is by means of a *criterion*. Such *illumination via criterion* is constitutively comparative, whereby one thing, the object of inquiry, is considered vis-à-vis another, a criterion; whether the object is judged to be a certain way (or of a certain kind) turns on whether it stands in a given relation to the criterion. Thus, for example, one might have a simple account of red things as those entities that are *this color* (as one demonstrates a fire engine); a thing is red if it exemplifies that color. Or, for another, more complex, example: one might have an account according to which a mental state is knowledge if, and only if, that state meets certain conditions taken to be criterial of knowledge. Whether the account that results from this sort of inquiry is apt depends crucially on the relevant criterion. If that is the (or a) correct criterion for the object one is attempting to illuminate, and one has chosen correctly the relation in which a thing must stand to that criterion, then one has an apt account of that object. One's object of inquiry is indeed as or what that account characterizes it as being.

This way of attempting to illuminate some object of inquiry is, in the end, deeply problematic. Whether one can demonstrate, without stultifying regress or circularity, that one's adopted criterion for that object is correct is dubious.[32] More important for present purposes, however, is recognizing that such illumination via criterion cannot be wholly critical. This way of attempting to illuminate some object depends on previously accepting some standard—a criterion—by which to judge other things, as well as the means needed to deploy that standard. Thus, in regard to the first example above, one must accept the color (of that fire engine) as the criterion by which to evaluate one's objects and, moreover, also have the conceptual means of discerning the color of a thing from, say, its shape. In regard to the second example, one must accept certain conditions as criterial of knowledge and also have the conceptual means not only to discern mental states, but to comprehend and apply the definitive conditions. This form of inquiry is, then, inherently theoretical, relying on prior assumptions about what is in the world and how these things, in specific ways, are (including how they are related).

---

[32] For a sense of the looming difficulties, in one specific case, see Roderick Chisholm's classic discussion of "the problem of the criterion" (Chisholm 1973).

There is, though, I submit, a distinct form of inquiry and so another way to produce an account of some object of inquiry, an account that can be evaluated without recourse to some further thing. This way of attempting to illuminate some object—call it *illumination via engagement*—is not constitutively comparative; it does not take for granted some criterion to which a thing is compared and assessed with respect to its relations to that other thing. Rather, on this way, one engages one's object of inquiry, by attending to it, and simply tries to characterize it. The only thing requisite to producing the account is, then, the object of inquiry itself, an instance of the very kind (or quality) the account is supposed to be an account of. Consequently, what determines the aptness of the account is not the correctness, by some measure, of a criterion (or the correctness of the choice of the relation in which a thing must stand to the criterion), but simply whether its object is as the account characterizes it to be.

Because the aptness of the account turns ultimately on but one thing—the object of that account itself—this form of inquiry is not inherently theoretical. It need not take for granted some criterion, conceptualized in a certain way, nor other assumptions about what is in the world and how these things are and are related. Therefore, this way of attempting to illuminate something can be wholly critical. When undertaking it, an inquirer need engage and, hence, acknowledge, only the object of inquiry. This form of inquiry can, then, be theoretically originary or foundational as illumination via criterion cannot be. I believe there must be this way of attempting to illuminate an object of inquiry, and that it is sometime successful, if any account illuminates, in a well-founded way, something in the world.

Of course, when expressing an account in some language, one must make assumptions, pertaining to the semantic and heuristic features of the terms one chooses. But the aptness of these choices turns on what and how the object of inquiry is—not vice versa. Such instrumental assumptions are, then, ancillary in the inquiry. The relevance of these assumptions can be mitigated at the outset of inquiry by starting with a term that is purely demonstrative and, hence, non-conceptual (such as 'this' or 'thus') and then, once the object of inquiry is thereby set, proceeding by introducing terms exclusively for that (kind of) phenomenon or for some other in the context so created. (This is the strategy I adopt in the principal, foundational discussions of this book.)

So when producing an account via this form of inquiry, one does not begin with some criterion and with assumptions that require evaluation insofar as one wants assurance that one's account is apt. Rather, one begins with some phenomenon that is not, in itself, right or wrong—it just *is*—and so does not require evaluation. One tries to characterize that whatnot, not in terms of previously accepted theory or standard, but simply in terms of the phenomenon itself. Thus, the only thing relevant, in the end, to the aptness of one's account of the object of inquiry is that object itself. In other words, whereas an attempt to illuminate via criterion begins with what is correct or incorrect, with respect to one's object of inquiry, an attempt to illuminate via engagement does not. The latter begins with simply what is so, namely, one's object of inquiry. Because original inquiry is an attempt to illuminate *all this* and the things it comprises via engagement, the method is able to resolve the distinctive problem of metaphysics.

In original inquiry, one does not begin with nothing, with nihility—that is incoherent—one begins, rather, with the world. One confronts *all this*, taking nothing for granted about "it," not even that "it" is a thing. In doing so, one apprehends that *all this* includes things, thereby engaging one's object(s) of inquiry, and discerns structure, relations among these things. These things so related are the ontological basis of how the world is diverse in the particular way it is, how it is *thus*. Each thing is certain ways, contributing those ways to *all this*, and reflection reveals that no other thing can make a thing be or be as it is just in existing. A thing, therefore, is a natured entity. One gets an account of something from nothing, as it were, by confronting the world and descrying therein what a thing must be—a constraint per se—given that *all this* is just as it is (namely, *thus*). One evaluates this account, not in terms of some previously accepted criterion of being, itself some thing, or claims about existents, but in light of the object of inquiry itself, some thing or other one has engaged amid *all this*. One then considers whether that thing is indeed a natured entity, an ontological locus, that in relation to other things provides the basis of a complete explanation for *all this*. Upon consideration of the account and its provenance, I accept it as apt; appreciating why it must be so provides, I contend, understanding of what it is to be in the world.

So original inquiry is practicable; the distinctive problem of metaphysics can be resolved by means of this method and the wholly critical account of what a thing is and, consequently, what *all this* is that it provides. (I answer the question of what *all this*, the world, is in the next chapter.) Still, the notion of a wholly critical method is so controversial that further defense of original inquiry as wholly critical seems worthwhile. Thus, one might object that at the outset of original inquiry I move unjustifiably—and, hence, with self-defeating prejudice—from the diversity in *all this* to *things*, rather than to *stuff* or some more unitary whatnot. This objection, however, misunderstands the generality of *thing* in the present discussion. Even if the world were stuff, or some other unity, this would be a thing in the relevant sense (some existent, entity, being—what the world comprises). Importantly, this thing would exhibit diversity that demands explanation; explanation that, as argued above (§3.3.1.), requires distinctness. Whatever category (of thing) or kind (of thing) that ultimately accounts for this distinctness, that whatnot or, better, those whatnots are things in the relevant sense.

Even if it is unobjectionable that original inquiry illuminates things (or attempts to) some might remain dubious that the method is indeed wholly critical. After all, I myself recognize above (in §3.3.1.) that there are assumptions involved in presenting and executing original inquiry. Some might worry that these assumptions ineluctably render the method biased, tendentious, question begging, or in some other way not wholly critical. There are indeed assumptions operative, and necessarily so, when undertaking original inquiry; nevertheless, these assumptions do not undermine original inquiry as a wholly critical method and so do not compromise its purpose and value as such.

The purpose of original inquiry is to gain insight into the world without prejudice, that is, to gain insight that does not rely on any doctrine or theory being taken for granted. Such insight would provide a general basis on which anyone who would inquire into the world would have to agree. One can gain this ecumenical insight and, hence, this general basis by ascertaining, in a wholly critical way, what a thing is, how these things are ultimately related so that the world is *thus* and, to anticipate subsequent discussion, how the world *becomes* so that anything, including inquiry, can happen at all. This general basis could serve not only as the means to arbitrate disagreement concerning worldviews or large-scale features of reality—any theory of any phenomenon must be consistent with this basis—but also to illuminate the more particular considerations that must be introduced to theorize about specific things amid *all this*. Illuminating the context in which these more particular considerations are introduced could reveal the need and justification for doing so, and help one understand which ought to be accepted (and which rejected). Thus, the value of original inquiry is that it can reveal the form of inquiry and, hence, the constraints on any inquiry whatsoever; in other words, it can provide the ground rules for inquiry (which themselves might be useful in more substantive inquiry).

Given this purpose and (potential) value, what is crucial to the method of original inquiry is the purity of its starting point. This must be a point that is given, not assumed; one that is not taken to be certain ways or conceptualized at all, but, rather, is just accepted and is in such a manifest way that even if questionable (and questioned) is incontrovertible. In confronting *all this* without presupposition—without even presuming "it" is a thing—confronting the world, then, as merely the impetus to inquiry, one engages a diverse array. This diverse array is a neutral, universal starting point for an examination of inquiry per se, what any inquirer must recognize and what any successful inquiry, to some extent, illuminates. Original inquiry has, therefore, a primary source with the requisite purity to meet its objectives.

But, of course, inquiry is a circumscribed activity. To perform original inquiry is to *inquire*; it is not to dance nor to listen to music nor to play baseball nor to stand on one's head. To engage in a particular activity is to abide by the specific norms that determine whether the activity is being pursued correctly—or at all. Thus, inquiry must begin in a certain way, with some phenomenon, the object of inquiry, and must proceed in a certain way, namely, by pursuing means that would feasibly illuminate that object. Even this simple characterization shows that inquiry involves assumptions, for example, that when inquiring one's end is to illuminate one's object rather than, say, to venerate it or to eat it. Any specified pursuit, that is, any activity has norms, and these must be adopted explicitly or taken for granted if one is to participate in that activity. So original inquiry involves, at least, those assumptions one must make to perform inquiry.

Original inquiry, though, involves more than merely these assumptions. Crucial to inquiry itself is engaging some thing—the object of one's inquiry—and then reflecting, in that context, on the object in order to make inferences and draw conclusions, informed by one's engagement with it, about that object. One cannot reflect and reason in this way without presuming some principles of logic. Thus, certainly, in propounding above the account of a thing as a natured entity, I avail myself, at least, of modus ponens and of a principle of non-contradiction. Any such principle adopted in original inquiry, so as to conduct this inquiry, must be plausible—if not compelling—in light of *all this*, lest one thwart the inquiry before it can begin by raising questions that cannot be answered by the world regarded merely as the impetus to inquiry (such as, *where does that principle come from?* or *why accept it here?*). The principles I adopt are compelling given the world. (One can confirm this oneself simply by considering these principles in light of *all this*.)

Therefore there are, I concede, assumptions made in original inquiry. These are essential to it in that original inquiry cannot be undertaken without them. However, and this is the key to understanding how original inquiry can be a wholly critical method despite these assumptions: *the assumptions do not bear on* all this *and so cannot distort it*. The essential assumptions are only instrumental, arising, innocently enough, in one's response to *all this*— in the effort to illuminate whatever this whatnot is—rather than in one's very engagement with "it." As such, they do not compromise the engagement with the world regarded merely as the impetus to inquiry in a way that would defeat the purpose of original inquiry, namely, to illuminate the ontological bases of *all this* and so the constraints on inquiry per se. The assumptions, then, do not taint the primary source of original inquiry with tendentious traditional conceptualizations of what is or how it is related. The source remains pure, an incontrovertible origin that can provide insight into every thing (and one's means of acquiring it).

There are yet more assumptions that arise when performing original inquiry, at least in certain contexts. These assumptions, though, are inessential to the method itself, and so should raise no further concerns about it being wholly critical (in the requisite way). My project here involves not only undertaking original inquiry, but also writing a book about it, so that others, too, might consider the method and its results. As part of this public project, I describe original inquiry and express the account of what a thing is that results from it. There are, then, conceptualizations of the phenomena and issues that I presume in order to do so. Moreover, I must make assumptions about the meaning of English words and further assumptions about my readers as I anticipate objections and try to forestall them in a way that is both perspicuous and persuasive. These assumptions inform my choices, as I try to argue—to impartial readers and ones who are skeptical—that the distinctive problem of metaphysics can be resolved and must be resolved in the way I describe, with the account of *thing* I propound. As just noted, however, any of these assumptions arise because of my particular ends. Original inquiry itself is a private process, one that anyone can take up in isolation, and so does not need to be described to be undertaken, nor do its results have to be expressed to be apt. Description and expression are posterior to the method. Hence, the assumptions required for these ends, or similarly auxiliary ones, are not pertinent to original inquiry per se being wholly critical—and so the appropriateness of any of these presuppositions can always be evaluated in light of one's presuppositionless engagement with *all this*.

In this chapter, I have propounded an account of what a thing—any thing at all—is. I have done so by undertaking original inquiry, and I have argued that this method is indeed wholly critical. Via original inquiry, then, with its presuppositionless (in the requisite sense) account of thing, I have resolved the distinctive problem of metaphysics. A thing is a natured entity, one that provides at least a partial explanation of *all this* being as it is, being *thus*. The discussion herein yields the means of answering the question of what the world is and of discerning some of the theoretical principles of inquiry per se. Thus, in the next chapter, I answer this question and present some of the ontological upshots of original inquiry that provide the framework for all inquiry.

4
Radical Ontology and Its Principles

All this, a complex of relations and relata—each relation[1] and each relatum likewise a thing—is the structure in the world, i.e., the structure in reality. There are two salient axes of disagreement regarding this structure. One concerns its integrity, the source and force of the relations that yield the structure. The other concerns the intricacy of this structure, the ontological complexity and bases of the relata that yield it. (See §3.1.) The account of a thing as a natured entity illuminates this structure, resolving disagreement along both axes.

How, and what, the structure in the world is are among the consequences of each thing being a natured entity. There are others. Descriptions of these consequences, each of which can be regarded as a principle, taken together provide a general theoretical framework for inquiry itself. A theoretical framework is a collection of principles, consistency with which constrains inquiry with respect to some object of inquiry. (See §2.1.) Because this general theoretical framework arises from an account of what a thing is, and every genuine inquiry is constrained by some thing(s) or other, this framework provides foundational conditions on—the ground rules for—all inquiry. In other words, every inquiry, be it empirical or a priori, scientific, mathematical, logical, social, etc., must conform to these principles, lest it fail to engage anything in the world and ultimately be vacuous.

Call this account of the structure in the world with the theoretical framework it yields *radical ontology*. This metaphysical account is *radical* in that it arises, via original inquiry, from the roots of inquiry and *ontological* in that it begins, not specifically with impressions nor ideas nor concepts nor subjective phenomena, but with things in general, any one of them or all of them. Among its uses, radical ontology enables one to move past stalemate in metaphysical discussions of the world by revealing the grounds of a principled choice between seemingly incommensurable worldviews.

---

[1] I argue below, in §4.3.1., that there are indeed relations in addition to related things, i.e., relata.

In this chapter, I discuss how the account of a thing as a natured entity illuminates the structure in the world. In particular, I make clear the consequences of this account for the integrity of this structure, showing how natured entities require there to be necessary relations among things in themselves, and its consequences for the intricacy of this structure, given the fundamentality of things as natured entities. I am then able to propound an account of what the world is, thereby meeting the chief objective of the ambitious, wholly critical metaphysics I am pursuing. One might be surprised that this objective can be met relatively easily, and one might be disappointed by the answer: *the world is not anything at all*. However, although such an account is the chief objective of the metaphysics pursued here, it is not its main value. The main value of the discipline is the theoretical framework for all inquiry that it provides—radical ontology, this theory of every thing—and how this framework can be employed to reveal, in more specific detail, the extent of *all this* and the structure therein. With its principles, radical ontology constrains and, hence, guides inquiry into any phenomenon. After enumerating the ontological categories, I articulate principles pertaining to the uniformity, compulsoriness, determinacy and non-fragmentariness of being a thing. I conclude by considering the means and limits of inquiry; how, in general, well-founded inquiry is to proceed. These considerations and the foregoing principles are useful in subsequent chapters, in the effort to understand the structure in the world with regard to its compelling inconstancy and constancy.

§4.1. The Structure in the World

The account of a thing as a natured entity has clear implications for the two axes of perennial disagreement regarding the structure in the world. So consider again disagreement regarding the integrity of this structure. The controversy here turns on whether some things, independently of how they are thought of or referred to or otherwise interacted with, *must* be related as they are. The upshot for the integrity of structure given that each thing is a natured entity is obvious. As the basis of an (at least partial) explanation for how the world is *thus*—the precise way *all this* is diverse—each thing is, in itself, some ways or other; a thing could not contribute to *all this* being the very way it is, if that thing were no way at all. Each way of being, that is, each quality, particular or universal, is a thing. As a natured entity, an ontological locus, some of the ways a thing is, such as those associated with its being what it is (i.e., those ways it is essentially), are attendant upon its existence. A thing must be these certain ways just in existing. Therefore, there are necessary relations among things. That there are follows simply from the existence of any natured entity.

Hume declared: "There is no object, which implies the existence of any other if we consider these objects in themselves."[2] and this has come to be known as Hume's Dictum.[3] Many philosophers have accepted this dictum; it underlies their view of the world and so plays a crucial role in their inquiries. Although there has been discussion about the scope of Hume's Dictum, concerning whether it applies to all entities or to only those that are "wholly distinct"[4] and so do not, say, stand in the relation of part to whole or share parts, some very influential philosophers appear to accept the dictum in full generality.[5] Arguably, Hume himself does, and W.V.O. Quine and David Lewis appear to, as well. Clearly, Hume accepts the dictum with respect to any thing that can stand in causal relations to others; for him also to countenance necessary relations among other things is of questionable coherence, and seems implausible given Hume's outlook and method. Consider Quine's derisive attitude to what he calls "Aristotelian essentialism," which takes there to be necessary relations among things independently of language.[6] Consider Lewis's "Humean supervenience," a doctrine named "in honor of the greater denier of necessary connections," according to which "the world is a vast mosaic of local matters of particular fact, just one little thing and then another . . . an arrangement of qualities. And that is all"; as well as his criticisms of others who concede *any* necessary connections among things.[7] Hume's Dictum, as applying to all things, is shown to be false by the account of a thing as a natured entity. This result constrains inquiry into any thing among *all this*. One of the principles of radical ontology, then, is that there are necessary relations among the structure in the world—a good deal of this structure must be as it is merely given the things it comprises.

[2] Hume 1739: Book I, Part III, §VI.
[3] For an intricate discussion of the dictum, see Wilson 2010.
[4] See Armstrong 1997: 18 and Wilson 2010: §1.4.
[5] Wilson recognizes that some philosophers accept Hume's Dictum in its full generality (Wilson 2010: 600). She regards this interpretation of the dictum (and another version) as "implausibly strong." See Wilson 2010: §1.3.
[6] See Quine 1953a: 155–156; 1953b: 175–176.
[7] See Lewis's manifesto for Humean supervenience in the introduction to the second volume of his collected papers (Lewis 1986b), part of which is quoted above, and, for example, his criticisms of David Armstrong (in Lewis 1992, 1983).

Reflecting on this controversy regarding the integrity of the structure in the world seems to corroborate this important result. If there is to be a genuine issue here, that there be absolutely no necessary relations among things as they are in themselves must be possible. Hence, there would have to be a thing, some entity that serves as the basis of an (at least partial) explanation for how the world is *thus*, that could be any way whatsoever, interacting with any other thing anyhow. But such a "thing," one of boundless potentiality, so uninhibited in its own being, is incoherent. A "thing" of boundless potentiality need not be any particular way—not even of boundless potentiality!—such a thing might, then, be bounded and, consequently, incapable of being some way or other; it would be a bounded boundless thing. Such a "thing" is impossible and so not feasible as the basis of an account of anything, let alone a systematic metaphysics that would provide insight into *all this*. This sort of "thing," with its corresponding account of the integrity of the structure in the world, is precisely what is precluded by a thing's being a natured entity.

Now consider again disagreement regarding the intricacy of the structure in reality. The controversy here turns on whether one thing can be made to be by or derived from another or, conversely, whether one thing (or things) can make another be in the sense of providing the being through which the other exists. This matter has been settled by discussion above. (See §3.4.) Everything is fundamental in that no thing can be made to be by another—each thing is such that its being, its being the very thing it is, its being itself, and its being how it is (in its entirety) and what it is, the kind of thing it is and whether it is a unity, are inexplicable, that is, not even susceptible to explanation.[8] There are, then, no building relations, no relations of constitutive dependence, that would give rise to a hierarchy of things. Consequently, there is no such thing as an "ontological free lunch," in David Armstrong's sense (where, if one thing supervenes on another, it need not be accorded the same ontological status as the latter) and, pace David Wiggins, each thing is indeed something "over and above" any other.[9] Regardless of its complexity, each and every thing is fundamental, in that it must be included on an inventory of the world. To use a trite locution: if God were to make the world just as it

---

[8] Of course, in other senses, one thing can be made (to be) by other things: a carpenter can make (or build) a table, a tree can make fruit, parents can make a child. But this *causal* and *diachronic* sense of making differs from the *ontological* and *synchronic* one pertinent here. In none of these cases does one thing provide the very *being*—rather than merely the materials, the nutrients, the genetic material—that determines and, hence, explains the phenomenon of the coming to be of another thing (at a particular moment).

[9] See Armstrong 1989: 55–56 and Wiggins 1968: 91–92.

is, They would have to make *every thing*—not merely some of the things (the putative subvenient basis or "building blocks"), but all of them. Therefore, a further principle of radical ontology is that there is no hierarchical structure in reality—no ontological priority, no levels of being—and it is misguided to characterize the fundamental in terms of what builds, but is not built.[10] Every thing among *all this* is existentially on par; the world is ontologically "flat."[11]

Although no thing is built from another, not everything is simple. A thing can have parts. The parts of a whole, a complex thing, however, do not make up that whole in the sense of *making it be*. In other words, a whole does not constitutively depend on its parts; the whole and (each of) its parts are equally fundamental. Nevertheless, a whole might be ontologically dependent on its parts or on some other thing(s) entirely; being fundamental is, then, not only consistent with being complex, it is consistent with being ontologically dependent. The notion of *ontological dependence* is multifarious, though.[12] The egalitarian notion of fundamentality in light of radical ontology provides constraints on any tenable account of ontological dependence. Whereas there are (and must be) relations of ontological dependence in the *jointly existing* sense—whereby the existence of one natured entity, given what it is, requires the existence of another—there is no relation of ontological dependence in the *constitutive* sense—whereby one thing makes another be. Such considerations are among the more subtle upshots of the principles of radical ontology for the intricacy of the structure in reality.

Yet there are cases where many philosophers maintain that one thing exists *because* of another (and, hence, that the former is made to be by the latter) is plausible, even "intuitively obvious." The most familiar of these cases involve a singleton and its sole member. Singleton Socrates, for example, is widely held to exist because of Socrates. But given the argument above (§3.4.), no thing exists because of any other. Were the existence of singleton Socrates to come from Socrates, the two things must stand in some relation (say, the *making be* relation). However, in order for anything,

---

[10] See Fiocco 2019a.

[11] This notion of a "flat" world comes from Karen Bennett. (See Bennett 2011a: 27, 28 and Bennett 2011b: 88.) She is somewhat dismissive of such a view, assuming it to be false (2011b) and calling it "crazypants" (2011a). I believe this unfavorable assessment is a result of failing to begin with the primary ontological question of what a thing is and subsequent oversight of the ontological difficulties attendant on the claim, crucial to positions like Bennett's, that one thing's very being can come from another.

[12] For instructive discussion of the varieties of ontological dependence, see Koslicki 2012 and Lowe and Tahko 2015.

including singleton Socrates, to stand in a relation, that thing must first exist; therefore, that another exists in virtue of standing in a relation to some thing (including Socrates) cannot be. Any sense of Socrates, or anything else for that matter, grounding or otherwise explaining the existence of singleton Socrates, or anything else, is illusory. A singleton, given what it is, requires the existence of its sole member; and any thing, given that it, arguably, must be collectible in the abstract way pertinent here, cannot exist in the absence of its singleton. What, if anything, is illuminated by this misleading example is *what* these things are, not *that* one of them exists. Singleton Socrates is a collection whose sole member is Socrates and so could not exist without him; Socrates is a necessarily (even essentially) collectible thing and so could not exist without singleton Socrates. There is here, then, mutual ontological dependence—one thing cannot exist in the absence of the other—and so nothing to indicate a hierarchy in the structure in the world.

A more interesting putative example of one thing making another be, for it involves a clear asymmetry between the relevant things, is the example of a mode and the thing it qualifies. Consider the red mode—the particular redness—of this apple, which is widely held to exist because of the apple. But, again, no thing exists because of any other. A mode, nevertheless, as a mode, requires the existence of the unique substance it qualifies; the redness of this very apple could not exist in the absence of this apple. The apple, however, could exist in the absence of that red mode. The apple is capable of taking on different colors (it might rot and turn brown or it might be painted blue). So the apple could exist without that red mode, but the mode could not exist without that apple. The same holds for any number of substances and modes (but not for all, since any thing is some ways essentially). What such examples indicate is an ontological asymmetry between entities. There is, then, a notion of ontological dependence that is asymmetric.

An asymmetric relation, though, does not indicate that either relata is more or less fundamental than the other. In some cases, an asymmetry necessitates nothing distinctive about either relata per se; for example, when one thing is to the left of another or one thing is taller than another. In other cases, an asymmetry does necessitate something distinctive: when two things, e_1 and e_2, stand in, say, the asymmetric *is the father of* relation, such that e_1 is the father of e_2, e_1 must be older than e_2. But this does not suggest that e_1 is, ontologically speaking, *more* than e_2 (or vice versa) or that e_2 is, ontologically speaking, *less* than e_1 (or vice versa); e_1 and e_2 are merely different in ways requisite to stand in the *is the father of* relation. Likewise, if o_1 can exist in the absence of o_2, but o_2 cannot exist without o_1; this just provides insight into the sort of thing o_1 is or o_2 is; it does not show that o_1 is ontologically superior, in some sense, to o_2 (or that o_2 is ontologically inferior, in some sense) and so does not support the claim that o_1 is somehow more fundamental than o_2 or, in any other way, indicate an ontological hierarchy. If one insists that it does, one must defend this claim in light of the argument above, according to which fundamentality cannot involve one thing making another be, and the present considerations, which show that an asymmetric relation is not, in itself, ontologically significant. Of course, one can stipulate that when one thing can exist in the absence of another, though the latter cannot exist without the former, then the former is more fundamental. This would be misleading, however: not only does such a notion of fundamentality not correspond to a substantive ontological distinction between the relata per se, but moreover—and because of this—the relation of asymmetric ontological dependence on which the notion is based does not show, despite its asymmetry, a hierarchy in the structure in the world (and is incompatible with those who presume that what is more fundamental gives being to what is less fundamental).

Thus, the stock (supposed) examples of one thing being grounded in another, of the latter making the former be, give no reason to recognize a hierarchy in the structure in reality. They show, at most, an asymmetric relation between distinct, equally fundamental, entities. The principles of radical ontology, emerging from original inquiry, indicate structure in the world that is necessary and in which each and every thing is fundamental. This structure arises merely from the existence of things and so is there independently of the workings of any mind (but not independently of minds, per se, for the structure includes many minds). The view of the world revealed by original inquiry is, therefore, quite different from those commonly taken for granted in modern and contemporary discussions of metaphysics. Much more familiar are views on which the structure in the world arises from features of the mind or the linguistic activities of conscious beings, and a host of reductionist or constructivist views on which there is hierarchical structure in reality with the very existence and natures of most things explicable in terms of the existence and natures of a select class of entities. Most commonly, those things in this select class of privileged, "fundamental" entities are material and tiny.

These more familiar views are the heritage of a too-strict empiricism—a fetishism of the senses that overlooks more basic questions of intentionality, of how mind and the world engage[13]—and an associated (and laudable) maxim to be properly scientific, one that nonetheless has a parochial conception of science. The views were developed by the giants of modern philosophy and were refined and perpetuated by the giants of 20th-century analytic philosophy, until now when they have become hegemonic. Their progenitors were reacting to the dogma and hegemony of Aristotelian Scholasticism. In recent years, though, some have recognized the need, in order to address seemingly intractable problems, to reexamine and adopt Aristotelian views that were long ago discarded.[14] The basic, guiding principles—and, hence, the theoretical frameworks—adopted by proponents of standard, "modern scientific" metaphysical views and those working in a neo-Aristotelian vein differ profoundly. Yet metaphysicians on neither side present reasons (other than, perhaps, pragmatic considerations or "intuitive" ones) for adopting the principles they do. In other words, partisans do not give (insightful) reasons for starting in the camps they do. One might wonder, then, given these seemingly incommensurable approaches, yielding incompatible pictures of the underlying structure in the world, how to arbitrate between them or whether either should be accepted.

The essentialism and the rejection of any ontological hierarchy that come with radical ontology arise from original inquiry; they are consequences of a wholly critical metaphysics that furnishes an account of what a thing is. These principles are, therefore, constraints on any inquiry. The theoretical framework of radical ontology is clearly incompatible with the "modern" view of the world. Although the worldview these principles inform share some features with the older tradition, which accepts necessary relations among things in themselves, these principles are antithetical to familiar Aristotelian doctrines, such as *hylomorphism* (according to which something, viz., a *form*, makes a thing be what it is or makes it be essentially as it is[15]). Therefore, one of the upshots of this ambitious, wholly critical metaphysics, which begins by confronting the world and asking the primary ontological question of what a thing is, is that one ought to eschew both a broadly reductionist, modern view of the world that most never question and a venerable tradition that some have found promising. By questioning *all this*—by

---

[13] See, in this connection, Fiocco 2019b.
[14] See, for example, the work of the late E.J. Lowe, Kit Fine, Kathrin Koslicki, David Oderberg, Tuomas Tahko, and the work of those authors collected in Tahko 2012a; Novák and Novotný 2014; and Novák, Novotný, Sousedík, and Svoboda 2013.
[15] See, again, Fiocco 2019a.

starting at the origin of inquiry, at a point prior to disagreement and, a fortiori, perennial disagreement regarding necessity and fundamentality—I argue that one discovers grounds for adopting novel or, at least, unfamiliar views of inquiry (and science more particularly) and of the world.

§4.2. What the World Is

The chief objective of the ambitious, wholly critical metaphysics I am pursuing is an account of what the world—*all this*—is and what it comprises. Part of this objective has been met: the world comprises natured entities. To complete this (initial) project, I need to provide an account of what the world is. Whatever *all this* is, it must be intimately related to the structure herein. For insight into the world, then, one might examine this structure in more detail.

§4.2.1. The structure in the world is not a thing

The structure in the world is a myriad of fundamental things standing in countless (fundamental) relations. The structure includes both relata and relations. (Again, I argue in §4.3.1. that relations are indeed things.) Some of the relations are essential and, hence, necessary, holding concomitantly with the existence of their relata; other relations are not essential to anything (though perhaps still necessary). A natured entity, as an ontological locus, is something whose being how it is (in its entirety) and what it is is not determined by any other thing. In light of this, the structure in the world is clearly not a natured entity. This structure is not just what "it" is because "it" is. On the contrary, this structure is what it is—a complex of relations and relata—because of these things, these relations and relata. Any difference in being with respect to a relation or relatum, any addition or loss of such, is ipso facto a difference in the structure in the world—not merely in *how* it is, but in *which* structure it is. The structure is not merely ontologically dependent on all these things, in the sense that "it" could not exist in their absence, it is straightforwardly just how it is because all the relations and relata that make it up are just as they are.[16] This structure is, therefore, no thing. "It" is, rather, just a plurality of things: many without unity.

---

[16] Note the clear disanalogy with singleton Socrates and Socrates: singleton Socrates is not just how it is because Socrates is just as he is. Consequently, the slightest difference with respect to

Denying that the structure in the world is a thing is not to deny that there are or could be *structures* in the sense of principles of arrangement, that is, things that organize other things to function in a certain way.[17] It is just to deny that the structure in the world is such a principle of arrangement. Everything together is not organized in such a way that there are particular positions or roles that can be played by one thing (or another) toward achieving some particular purpose, in the way that, say, a team of horses or baseball players is organized to move a load or win a game. Everything together just does what each thing does; each thing occupying its own position, playing a unique role, viz., its own. One might hold there is (or could be) some particular purpose to which everything together is working. Such a purpose, however, would have to involve all things and so include the patent independence one witnesses, as well as the tremendous competition and cross purposes to which many things, including oneself, contribute. Given these considerations, the claim that everything together is working toward some purpose seems just a way of acquiescing to all things being and doing as they are.

So the structure in the world is not a thing, despite the definite description, "the structure in the world," that seems to function as a singular term. (As noted in the prologue to Chapter 3, the grammar of natural language is no guide to what exists.) The structure in the world is the most inclusive of what can be called a *structural phenomenon*, an object of inquiry that involves many things standing in relations. Every inquiry has an object—not every object of inquiry is a thing, however. Some, of course, are; others are mere pluralities. One might regard a structural phenomenon as a thing provisionally as one investigates it to determine whether it is indeed one thing or many of them. But if the phenomenon is the latter, "it" is nothing itself. Investigating such a phenomenon can, nevertheless, provide insight into the world, insofar as it reveals how some things relate to others. Thus, if an object of inquiry is a thing, the purpose of that inquiry is an explicative account of what and qualitatively how that thing is (including how it relates to certain other things). If the object is merely a structural phenomenon, the purpose of

---

Socrates does not thereby produce a genuine difference in singleton Socrates. Differences in Socrates that do not alter his identity, such as growing taller, getting older, becoming a husband, produce no difference in singleton Socrates, the set whose sole member is Socrates—whereas any difference in any thing yields a difference in the structure in reality.

[17] Structures in this sense are recognized and employed in the work of many philosophers. See, for a couple of prominent examples, Koslicki 2008: 252–254 and Ritchie 2020.

such inquiry is an account of those things that together prompt the inquiry, that is, an account of the delimited plurality that makes up the phenomenon. In either case, inquiry has an ontological basis in some thing(s) or other. The structure in the world is the most conspicuous structural phenomenon. There are others. Some of these—change, inconstancy, constancy—are central to subsequent discussion.

§4.2.2. The world just is the plurality of all things

A thing provides the basis of an (at least partial) explanation for the world, *all this*. Providing such a basis suffices to be a thing. Obviously, nothing at all cannot make an explanatory contribution to the world; anything that does make such a contribution must be some entity (i.e., existent, thing) among *all this*. Providing the basis of an (at least partial) explanation for *all this*, however, is also necessary for being a thing. Some "thing" that did not provide, at least in part, an explanation for the world would make no contribution to *all this*—but *all this* is an encompassing totality. Thus, what provides no basis of an (at least partial) explanation for this encompassing totality is nil, not anything at all. Were this not so, a thing could be in the world, making its unique, distinctive contribution to *all this*, and yet not be the basis of an (at least partial) explanation for how the world is the precise way it is. This is incoherent.

If the world were itself a thing, it would have to make, by existing, some unique contribution to *all this*. *All this*, however, just is the world. So were the world itself a thing, it would have to make some unique ontological contribution to itself. Nothing could make such a contribution. For something to make an ontological contribution to itself, it must exist, in which case there is no further (ontological) contribution to be made. Likewise, since each thing makes a distinctive contribution to *all this*, the world itself would be a thing only if every thing in the world were insufficient to account for *all this* (or some thing(s) or other amid this encompassing totality). But, of course, the plurality of all things that are not the world per se can account for *all this* (and each thing therein). If the world were itself a thing, rather than merely many things, there would have to be some phenomenon that it accounts for that could not be accounted for by any one thing or by some independent things. (Just as if there is indeed a team of horses, it is because there is some phenomenon, such as the movement of a cart, that cannot be accounted for by any one thing or by some independent things.) There is, however, no phenomenon in the world for which each thing individually or some independent things—including everything together—could not account. Nor is there any phenomenon beyond *all this* for which the world itself to account, because there is nothing beyond *all this*. Therefore, the world itself is not a thing.

Perhaps, by this point, this conclusion is obvious, but it can be corroborated by considerations similar to those presented when examining whether the structure in the world is a thing. As natured, a thing is constrained by *its* very existence in what it is and, hence, to this extent, in being as it is. Nothing makes that thing be what it is or the ways it must be (given what it is). However, the world—this encompassing totality—is made to be what it is, a totality, by other things, namely, those things it comprises. Its being is the being of these things: if one of these ceases to be, or even changes in the slightest, the world as the totality of things is a distinct totality. The world's being as it is, moreover, is determined entirely by what and the ways the things it comprises are. There is no feature of "it" that is not the feature of something else. One might suggest that the world has an all-inclusiveness that no other thing has. But *all-inclusivity* is not a feature of any thing; it is, rather, a notion that applies to many things, to wit, every thing together. Similarly, *totality* is not a kind of thing, but also a notion that applies to many things (more or fewer, depending on the context). There are, then, no constraints imposed by "its" own existence on the world being as it is. Therefore, *all this* is not natured and so is not a thing. The world just is the plurality of each thing.

Indeed, these considerations regarding the world and the foregoing ones regarding the structure herein indicate that the world just is this structure. One can speak of "the world" or "the structure in the world," but these are merely different, and equally misleading, ways of speaking not of something, but of all things. One is taking or speaking of all things together. Nevertheless, these things are not one, not a unity; they are only represented as such. Independently of such representation, all things are many, a plurality. Each and every thing in this structure, that is, in the world makes an ineliminable contribution to it. This array of fundamental natured entities, each related—essentially, necessarily or otherwise—to everything else in one way or another is the basis of a full explanation for how the world is *thus*, i.e., the precise way *all this* is diverse.

So the world is nothing itself, "it" is just all things, a plurality comprising every existent, every natured entity. With this account of the world, and the account of a thing as a natured entity on which it crucially relies, one has accomplished the chief objective of the ambitious, wholly critical metaphysics I am pursuing. One might be surprised that this objective can be met. The relative ease with which it has been met might make one suspicious; indeed, so suspicious that one might be more inclined to dismiss these accounts than entertain them. There is, I have found, a certain pessimism among those who engage in grand inquiry of this sort that leads them to think that no substantive or profound question about reality can have a definitive answer, certainly not a perspicuous one. Such pessimism leads some to disdain both the thought of progress in metaphysics and especially the effort to provide such. Yet here I submit such answers in an effort to make genuine progress with respect to the question of what *all this* is (and what might be done with it). These answers come via original inquiry, a method propounded precisely as a means of settling, once and for all, perennial ontological and more specific metaphysical questions. If one is suspicious, then, of this account of the world or of a thing or of the further principles of radical ontology that have so far emerged, one should not simply dismiss them, but should engage critically original inquiry itself to locate where this method goes astray.

One should not view the accomplishment of the chief objective of this ambitious, wholly critical metaphysics as the end of the discipline, for the accounts of what the world is and what a thing is are not its main value. The discipline indeed reveals what the world is; however, one might want to know more about *all this* than that "it" is the plurality of every natured entity, no thing itself. One might want to know, or understand, what original inquiry can reveal about how exactly the world is or must be—whether this method can reveal the formal structure of *all this*, that is, what relations and relata it must include so that the world can be as it is at all. More generally, though, the main value of this metaphysics comes from the theoretical framework it provides. This framework, radical ontology, constrains all genuine inquiry, any inquiry directed at some thing(s) or other. One's account of any object of inquiry must be consistent with radical ontology. So, in a sense, all apt inquiry is metaphysical, applications of this framework in specific domains. To discern as many principles of radical ontology as one can is, therefore, insightful and useful.

Before articulating several of these principles, however, it is important first to note a couple significant consequences of the foregoing account of the world. If *all this* is not itself a thing, the world per se has no features—"it" does not and cannot bear any property, nor stand in any relation. (This is no mere assertion, but a special case of two principles—one pertaining to the uniformity of being a thing and the other to its compulsoriness—that I develop below. [§4.3.2., §4.3.3.]) There are, then, in particular, no *worldly* or *global* properties; only things themselves are various ways. Furthermore, the world at large can play no theoretical role in inquiry. Any account of any phenomenon that attributes such a role to the world, which, again, is no thing at all, is misguided.

This second consequence might seem trivial, but it is not. There are points in many inquiries, of general and specific issues, where that the world itself can be and is certain ways is taken for granted. Sometimes this presumption plays merely a background role, furthering some discussion that might be furthered by other means; in other cases, it serves a crucial theoretical purpose. Thus, people consider whether the world were created, whether it has a beginning or will end, whether it is a good place or a bad one—whether it is the best of all possible worlds. Others consider how the world changes or evolves or whether it is deterministic or indeterministic or whether it is entirely material, natural or physical. None of these considerations, taken literally, is appropriate given that the world is not a thing. For specific theoretical ends, some identify possible worlds with *ways things might have been*, where such ways are properties of the world.[18] If the world is not a thing, there is not only no way "it" is, there is no way it might have been; pluralities do not instantiate single ways. Moreover, Jonathan Schaffer maintains there are "physical and modal considerations that favor the priority of the whole,"[19] where "the whole" in this context is the "entire cosmos." If the "entire cosmos" is supposed to be the world—*all this*—"it" is neither prior nor posterior to anything, since the world is no thing at all. "It" stands in no relations.[20]

Another example of this presumption that the world itself can be certain ways, one important to what comes below, is from discussions of the metaphysics of time. The putative temporal features of the world per se are sometimes taken to be an object of inquiry or are sometimes presented as a means of resolving some problem. Hence, many take it to be a desideratum of an

---

[18] See, for the classic example of this sort of view, Stalnaker 1976.
[19] Schaffer 2010: 32.
[20] If by "entire cosmos" Schaffer is referring only to physical things, then this criticism might not be apt. If the physical cosmos is merely a plurality and, hence, not a thing, the criticism holds; if the physical cosmos is indeed a thing, the criticism does not. Either way, referring to the physical cosmos as "the whole" is misleading without explicit argument that there are no things that are not physical.

adequate theory of the metaphysics of time that it account for the dynamic—or static—nature of the world. Yet the world is not a thing and has no nature in itself. (To hold that the world "itself" is neither dynamic nor static is, however, certainly not to deny the irrefragable inconstancy and constancy of the structure in the world.) Relatedly, some who maintain that there is but a single moment of time hold that the grounds of the truth of past- and future-tensed claims are properties of the world such as *having been such that Napoleon is emperor* or *going to be such that there are lunar colonies*.[21] But, again, *all this* "itself" bears no properties and, a fortiori, is not such that it is or was or will be any particular way.

One should not be misled by these theoretical uses of the world to think that it might, after all, be some thing. One might suggest that were the world a thing, it could, say, provide an account of what possible worlds are or of the basis on which all else is "grounded" or of the truth of past- (or future-) tensed claims, thereby accounting for some phenomenon that nothing else can. However, original inquiry reveals what a thing is, a natured entity, and, consequently, that the world is not a thing. This account of a thing is a formal constraint on inquiry: since the account is wholly critical, attained by confronting *all this* without presupposition about it—beginning with bare diversity, the least with which any inquiry could begin—any inquiry directed at some thing or other (as any genuine inquiry is) must comport with the account. A theory that takes the world to be a thing does not, and so this is sufficient grounds for rejecting such a theory. No consideration, then, regardless of how useful, can challenge the corollary, derived from the account of what a thing is, that the world is no thing at all.

§4.3. Further Principles of Radical Ontology

Because they derive, via original inquiry, from the very roots of inquiry, the principles of radical ontology—beginning with that a thing is a natured entity—have a foundational epistemic standing that claims that do not have this origin could not have. Therefore, they are crucial to our consideration and understanding of the world and to the development of an apt theory of any phenomenon. There is no set number of these principles. Different ones are central or salient depending on one's object of inquiry. Any inquiry,

---

[21] See Bigelow 1996 for this "Lucretian" strategy.

however, if it is to be well-founded, must comport with all of them. Here I present several principles of radical ontology, ground rules of inquiry, that seem to me to be the most significant given the pursuits of contemporary metaphysicians. One of my goals in this book is to give an illuminating answer to the question of what *all this*, the world, is; another is to provide a substantive account of what a thing is. These aims have already been met. A further goal, for reasons that become apparent in Chapter 5, is to give an account of the extent of the world in light of its irrefragable inconstancy and constancy. I intend to give an account of *all this* that illuminates how anything, including inquiry, can happen at all. Such an account of this structure would reveal further formal constraints on inquiry—and every other process. To meet this goal, I articulate some principles of radical ontology that prove useful.

§4.3.1. The categories of *thing*

A thing is a natured entity, a constraint per se, that underlies a partial explanation for how the world is *thus*, the precise way *all this* is diverse. I argue below (§5.1.1.) that there is change and that this is apparent when confronting the world merely as the impetus to inquiry. Consequently, change must be considered when taking up wholly critical inquiry from a neutral, universal starting point and the means to account for it must be amid *all this*. As the preceding discussion illustrates, attaining an account of what a thing is requires some effort. With this account, though, and in light of change, it is relatively easy to distinguish sorts of thing. The most general sorts may be regarded as *ontological categories*. Things are of different ontological categories when they make distinct—in manner—contributions to an explanation for how the world is as it is. Obviously, a great deal could be said about these categories and their derivation; however, for present purposes, the discussion in this section suffices.

The existence of change, a structural phenomenon rather than thing itself, reveals that there are distinct aspects of *all this* that require different means to explain. There are things that change and others, significantly different, but no less things, by which they do so. Thus, there is a category of things that can undergo change and a category of things by which they change. Call an instance of the former category a *substance* and one of the latter a *mode*. These terms have associated with them long traditions. I choose the terms only to evoke these traditions, not to endorse any particular theses or views from them regarding what substances or modes are. What I say here exhausts my accounts of the different categories of thing.

Without there being both substances and modes, there could be no account of change as one and the same thing being one way, i.e., having one mode, and then being an incompatible way, i.e., having a distinct mode. A mode is *qualitative*, and so qualifies a thing, that is, imposes a constraint upon it without effecting what it is, thereby limiting and characterizing how that thing is. In some instances, distinct things are constrained and, hence, qualified, with respect to each other. Certain modes are, then, relational. (Modes, as natured entities, are essentially certain ways. Thus, modes have modes.) Substances are not qualitative; a substance does not itself qualify how a thing is. Although a mode qualifies a thing and might be essentially related to that thing, the mode does not make a thing what it is. Nor does it contribute to an account of what makes a thing what it is—there is no such account. A mode can, though, contribute to an explicative account of what a thing is, for this is merely a description that illuminates what it is to be that thing. Nevertheless, each thing, substance or mode or instance of any ontological category, just is what it is.

Still, two things being natured in exactly the same way and, hence, being appropriately classified together is a phenomenon that demands explanation. One might deny this, but the need for explanation is so plain in just confronting *all this* that such a denial can only be motivated by presumptions about what is in the world or the limits of explanation that are inappropriate in original inquiry. A *kind* is, then, a category of thing, one that accounts for how distinct substances go together. Two such substances are both related to that one kind. Call this relation *instantiation*. Likewise, a *quality* (or *property*, I use these terms interchangeably) is a category of thing, one that accounts for how distinct modes, exactly similarly natured, go together. (The qualities that account for how distinct modes that qualify things jointly, exactly similarly natured, go together are *relations*.) Two such modes are both related to that one quality. A thing is a *universal* if it has instances. Exactly similarly natured particular substances are instances of the same kind and, hence, the kind is a *substantial* or *non-qualitative universal*. Exactly similarly natured particular qualities, i.e., modes, are instances of the same quality and so the latter is a *qualitative universal*.

These categories—*substance, kind, mode, quality*—can be discerned through original inquiry, by engaging the world as merely the impetus to inquiry and then reflecting on it, making inferences and drawing conclusions using only means compelling in light of *all this*. Via this method, one confronts the world and comes to recognize what it is with which one is engaged that accounts for *all this* and how it is *thus*, the precise way *all this* is diverse. No other categories are apparent in engaging the world in this way. Therefore, original inquiry reveals a four-category ontology. Each thing is of one of these four categories. Such an ontological schedule is first described in Aristotle's *Categories* and has been defended and put to many uses in the work of E.J. Lowe.[22] Given that there are *minds*, i.e., things that present other things for consideration, and that each thing is fundamental, there is reason to accept that the things with which one is ordinarily presented exist and are largely as they seem. So there is *this*, which for convenience one may call *a (human) body*, and *this*, which one may call *a chair*, and *that, a leaf*, and *that*, the particular *greenness* of the leaf, etc. From this point on, I take it that the world includes most of the familiar things one encounters in one's mundane affairs, including other instances of *natural kinds*, such as this human person, that tree, that sample of water, and the kinds themselves; other instances of *social kinds*, *artifactual* and *institutional*, like this computer, that clock, this university, and the kinds themselves; as well as the multifarious modes and qualities one encounters.

As a natured entity, each thing is ontologically dependent on others; not, of course, in a way that gives rise to an ontological hierarchy, but insofar as no thing can exist without some other. Regardless of its category, a thing is essentially some ways and is—usually, if not in every case—an instance of some universal, substantial or qualitative, and so is necessarily related to other things. There is, then, no category of thing and, a fortiori, no thing that is wholly independent of other things. In other words, no thing can exist alone; indeed, no thing can exist without many other things. This is worth noting because, traditionally, substances were supposed to have a special status among existents in light of their putative capacity to exist independently of other things in certain ways.[23] None of these ways, even if actual, is ontologically significant. Things of different categories make distinct, in manner, contributions to *all this*, but no contribution is separable from

---

[22] See Lowe 2009, 2006, 1998.
[23] For contemporary discussions of substance that contribute to this tradition, see Lowe 1998 and Hoffman and Rosenkranz 1997, 1994. For critical discussion of independence criteria of substancehood, see Koslicki 2018.

others or ontologically more important than another. Thus, no thing or category has (ontological) pride of place among what exists.

§4.3.2. Being a thing is uniform (and so there are no non-existent beings)

Reflecting on *all this*, this structure of things of different categories, reveals further principles of radical ontology. In original inquiry, one confronts the world as nothing but the impetus to inquiry. Doing so reveals that *all this* is a plurality of natured entities, each one the ontological basis of a partial explanation for how the world is *thus*, the precise way *all this* is diverse. This method could not indicate a thing that does not exist. One cannot be moved to inquire by something that is not; nor is nothing an apt basis for an explanation. Given that original inquiry reveals what the world is, and its limits, by enabling one to determine what any thing at all is, that there are only existent things follows. Thus, if one is to be constrained by this wholly critical method, grounded in a bare confrontation with the world, and thereby held by the framework of radical ontology, one must eschew any putative "thing" that is supposed not to exist.

Original inquiry reveals, moreover, each thing simply existing. The method provides no motivation to recognize multiplicity in being simpliciter, that is, different ways of *being*, as opposed to different ways *qualitatively to be*. This is confirmed by the consonance in the impetus to inquiry. *All this* is, indeed, diverse—but uniformly so. No thing in it is distinctive peculiarly in its being. In particular, then, there is no *subsistence* or *having being* while lacking existence, where these are supposed to be intermediate ways of being in the world, a subsistent "thing" (or one that has being, but does not exist) supposed not to be a full existent, yet not nothing either. Nor are there *degrees of existence* simpliciter, ways of being more or less real. Nor are there existents that are *merely possible*, though not actual, that is, "things" that merely could be in the world but in fact are not. 'Being' is univocal and being a thing uniform. This is, therefore, another way of arriving at the conclusion that each thing contributes to the structure in the world. There is nothing more in or to the world. Contributing to *all this* is not only necessary and sufficient for existing, it is constitutive of *existing, being, being real, being actual*. I make no distinction among these, for I think none is intelligible—let alone, tenable—in light of the foregoing considerations.

A thing either exists, contributing to the world to the same extent and in the same way—qua being—as every other thing, or "it" is not there at all. Given this ontological uniformity, alleged multiplicity in being simpliciter is no basis for explaining any phenomenon. I emphasize this uniformity of being a thing for there are certain contexts of inquiry in which philosophers, in more or less subtle ways, deny it. One of these contexts is the metaphysics of mind, when considering the capacity of a mind to think about—to state the point paradoxically—things that do not exist.[24] Another of these contexts is the metaphysics of time. Some philosophers, in considering temporal reality, distinguish degrees of existence.[25] Others distinguish things that *were*, yet *are not* or things that *will be*, yet *are not*, distinctions that are more subtle than explicit degrees of existence, but nonetheless incompatible with the uniformity of being a thing. I believe that in most cases in which one denies that being a thing is uniform,[26] one is merely misled by mental or semantic considerations. However, insofar as the phenomena at which these considerations are directed are actual, one's theorizing about them must be constrained by the framework of radical ontology.

§4.3.3. Being a thing is compulsory (to bearing any property or standing in any relation)

The contexts in which philosophers complicate what should be straightforward, to wit, the uniformity, with respect to existence, of the structure in the world and this structure as the sole basis of *all this*, are many. Consequently, articulating further principles of radical ontology regarding being a thing is helpful. Some accept that there are no non-existing things in the world and, hence, that being a thing is uniform, but maintain nevertheless that "things" that *are not* can contribute to the world. Such "things" are in no sense in the world—they are not non-existent things, they are nothing at all!—yet can be certain ways, stand in certain relations and so serve as the explanatory bases of phenomena.

However, again, what original inquiry reveals is a world of natured entities, existents that are constrained by their very being and, by being,

---

[24] Consider Meinong 1904 and Twardowski 1894, who notoriously posited non-existent things to which one can be cognitively related.
[25] See Smith 2002.
[26] As Aristotle did. For a contemporary discussion of ways of being, see McDaniel 2009.

constrain other things. Original inquiry cannot reveal what is not there at all. The certain ways that nothing at all is supposed to be, according to some philosophers, and the specific relations in which nothing is supposed to stand are themselves natured entities. To be constrained by them—by having them, by standing in them—is to be in the world, that is, to exist. So to be any way or to stand in any relation is to contribute to the world in exactly the same way as any thing does and, therefore, is to exist.

Any putative reason one might have for denying these considerations cannot arise from original inquiry. To maintain that *nothing* can be certain ways (or stand in relations) is to make assumptions, presumably in light of some worldly phenomenon, that are incompatible with a wholly critical account of the world or the things it comprises. Such assumptions are, then, inconsistent with principles with which any genuine inquiry must comport and so can have no purchase on *all this*. Therefore, only by existing can a thing be constrained by properties or relations and so be the basis of an explanation. What fails to exist is no way whatsoever. Being a thing is not only uniform, it is compulsory for having any property or standing in any relation.

Given the uniformity and compulsoriness of being a thing, there are no non-existent things and what is not a thing at all is no way, stands in no relations. Thus, if one assumes—as is exceedingly plausible—that it is true that Aristotle was a philosopher, that Nathan admires John Lennon, and that Santa Claus is a jolly elf, this cannot be because Aristotle, John Lennon, and Santa Claus fail to exist and yet are certain ways and stand in certain relations. Either these things exist in the same way as any other or, if not, the world must include other things that are the basis of an explanation for the truth of these (and similar) claims.

§4.3.4. Being a thing is determinate (so there is no ontological indeterminacy)

There has been much recent discussion of *ontic vagueness*, that is, indeterminacy in the world, an unsettledness in what or how things are in themselves. Such indeterminacy is contrasted with *semantic vagueness*, indeterminacy of the truth-value of claims about some thing(s) or other that arises from imprecision in the representational means one employs in making the claims. Some reject the notion of ontological indeterminacy as unintelligible[27] or

---

[27] See Dummett 1975: 314.

unclear;[28] others defend it in general[29] or even rely on ontological indeterminacy to account for some phenomenon, such as the open future[30] or the materiality of things.[31]

I reject ontic vagueness, not because I cannot make sense of the notion of the putative phenomenon, nor because it cannot be clearly distinguished from semantic vagueness, but because there could be no such indeterminacy. For there to be ontological indeterminacy, either there would have to be a thing that existed indeterminately—and so neither existed nor failed to—or a thing that determinately existed, yet were indeterminately some way—and so neither bore some property (or stood in some relation), nor failed to. Neither case is possible. This is a consequence of the uniformity (and compulsoriness) of being a thing.

To see this, consider some thing that is supposed to exist only indeterminately. Such a thing is either no way at all or some way or other. If an indeterminately existing thing is no way at all, it is no thing; "it" is nothing and, as such, could make no contribution, determinate or indeterminate, to the world. If, on the other hand, an indeterminately existing thing is some way—bears some property, stands in some relation—given the compulsoriness of being a thing, it must be some thing. If it is, then, given the uniformity of being a thing, it exists in the same way, as fully, as any other: so that thing could not exist only indeterminately. Either way, therefore, there could be no indeterminately existing thing. This stands to reason: an indeterminately existing thing would exist differently than any thing—but, given the uniformity of being a thing, there is only one way to be simpliciter. Via existing in that one way, a thing just is what it is. If it exists, it is, thereby, what it is no less than any other thing, and so makes as full a contribution to *all this*, qua thing, as any other. Thus, moreover, there could be no determinately existing thing that is indeterminately what it is.[32]

Many who accept ontic vagueness concede that there are no indeterminate things, that no thing is not fully existent or fully what it is. Nevertheless,

---

[28] See Sainsbury 1994 and Lewis 1993, 1986a: 212.
[29] See Barnes 2010.
[30] See Barnes and Cameron 2009.
[31] See van Inwagen 1990.
[32] In Evans 1978, Gareth Evans argues, persuasively, that there can be no identity statements—statements of the form $e_1 = e_2$, where 'e_1' and 'e_2' are singular terms—with indeterminate truth value. This indicates that to what some thing is identical cannot be indeterminate. This is consistent with there being indeterminately existing things. The argument above is meant to show that there could be no such thing. Evan's position, however, does comport with my conclusion that there is no worldly indeterminacy.

they maintain the world is indeterminate with respect to how some of these determinate things are. These proponents of ontic vagueness maintain, then, that for some (determinately) existing thing, whether that thing bears a certain property or stands in some relation is indeterminate: that that (determinate) thing bears that property or stands in that relation is neither so nor not so. However, this, too, is not possible. If a thing is determinately a certain way, that way it is exists; so if it bears a property, that particular instance of the property exists and, likewise, if that thing stands in a certain relation—be it instantiation or exemplification or the parthood relation or any other—that instance of the relation exists. If a thing is determinately not a certain way, there is no relevant instance of the property or relation in question. Every property (instance) and relation (instance) is itself a thing and so either exists, fully and as what it is, or does not exist, making no contribution to the world. Obviously, if a certain way, some instance of a property or relation, that qualifies a thing exists, that thing is determinately that way (and if there is no such way, that thing is determinately not that way). If a thing is supposed to be indeterminately some way, then, how it is—that way—can neither exist, lest that thing determinately be that way, nor fail to, lest it determinately not be that way. That way it is would have to exist only indeterminately. Given the uniformity of existence, however, which is conceded by proponents of this account of ontic vagueness, there could be no thing that exists indeterminately. Therefore, a thing cannot bear a property or stand in some relation indeterminately; for every way a thing is, it either is determinately that way or it determinately is not. Not only does nothing exist indeterminately, there is no thing that is indeterminate with respect to how it is.

One might defend ontic vagueness in light of the foregoing considerations by maintaining there can be vagueness in the world because there can be indeterminacy with respect to some way without there being some thing such that it is indeterminate with respect to that way.[33] Such a position, though, is incompatible with radical ontology. The world itself is not a thing, so "it" cannot be the source of or otherwise support ontic vagueness among *all this*. Given radical ontology, every phenomenon, including indeterminacy, must have a basis in some thing(s). There is nothing more—or less—to *all this*. So if there is ontic vagueness, either some thing, a way or entity of another category, exists indeterminately or some determinately existing thing is indeterminate with respect to some way. As just argued, both cases are impossible.

---

[33] See Hawley 2002: 129, 130 for discussion and defense of such a position.

Therefore, the uniformity of being a thing and the (full) contribution that each thing makes to the world is incompatible with any indeterminacy in what or how things are in themselves. Since each thing is determinate, any vagueness with respect to some thing or other, comes from how that thing is being represented. In other words, all vagueness is semantic. Those who defend ontological indeterminacy make assumptions, presumably in light of some worldly phenomenon, that contravene the framework of radical ontology. Their positions are inconsistent with the principles with which any genuine inquiry must comport, and so are insupportable. Whatever phenomena are supposed to justify accepting worldly indeterminacy, then, must be accounted for in other ways, in particular, by means of the determinate things in this determinate structure.

§4.3.5. Being a thing is not fragmentary (so the world is complete)

Each thing, as a natured entity, given what it is, must exist with certain other things. Likewise, each thing precludes the existence of certain things, to wit, anything that would make an incompatible contribution to the world. If it did not, if a thing were able to exist with some other that made an incompatible contribution to *all this*, the former could not—as each thing must—be the basis of a partial explanation for how the world is *thus*, for any such explanation would be undermined by the latter. Therefore, if there is only one way for a thing to exist and each thing that exists is determinate, making its own full contribution to the world, one that is compatible with the contributions of every other thing, then *all this* is uniquely settled. The world is complete and consistently so.

This principle of radical ontology is of profound importance. Given that the structure in the world is complete and consistent, any true account of any phenomenon is compatible with any other true account of any other phenomenon. There are different ways of characterizing *relativism*. Some varieties are superficial and, hence, not that interesting. The most provocative varieties of relativism are those that maintain there are or could be literally distinct worlds. One way of illuminating this paradoxical notion is in terms of truth. There would be distinct worlds if there were truths, correct claims about reality or correct theories of phenomena herein, that are ultimately discrepant. Because of how things in the world are, the truths cannot go together.[34] Such relativism, however, cannot be so. Things as natured entities ensure that, in one way or another, all truths are reconcilable.

Any putative disagreement with respect to true accounts of some phenomenon actually involves distinct phenomena or turns on how exactly a phenomenon is being represented and, hence, is not a genuine disagreement, that is, a context in which incompatible claims are being asserted about a single subject. Given the completeness of the world and the compatibility of all truths, there might be one—infinitely complex—true representation of the structure in the world. However, that there is (or could be) a unique feasible representation of *all this* or even an optimum one certainly does not follow from this principle of radical ontology. Any (tractable) representation—even one via reproduction—must be incomplete. What is left out might matter with respect to some project. So there are ever so many different yet correct ways of representing the world and all these things it comprises. Just as there are innumerable ways to connect a bunch of dots to make a picture. Some of these pictures might appeal to certain viewers more than other pictures or be more useful given their interests or needs. Still, there is one complete arrangement of bases from which to work.

What follows from the completeness of *all this* is simply that there is some perspective from which all disagreement could disappear. Whether that perspective is attainable or effable or otherwise communicable is not clear. Nothing follows about the resolution of disagreement or about the superiority of any one view of things. The principle here, derived from confronting *all this* as merely the impetus to inquiry and reflecting on the world from that critical point, is that every inquirer engages the same totality of fundamental, determinate, compatible things.[35]

§4.4. The Means and Limits of Inquiry

The foregoing principles of radical ontology provide some of the ground rules of inquiry. Insofar as inquiry is genuine, it is directed at some thing(s) or other. Inquiry is, consequently, constrained by natured entities and so must be conducted in accordance to these principles, which arise via reflecting

---

[34] For insightful discussion of relativism in these terms, see Rovane 2013, 2012.
[35] That the method of this book and the conclusions it provides repudiate most, if not all, of the ontologically relativistic theses (regarding foundationalism, historicism, absolutism, realism, etc.) propounded in Rorty 1979 is perhaps worth noting.

on the world of things—natured entities—making inferences and drawing conclusions using only means compelling in light of *all this*. There are four categories of fundamental things, each thing related to every other by more or less interesting relations, some of which are essential, some otherwise necessary. Everything exists in the same way and must exist in this way if it is to make any contribution to *all this*. Each thing makes a full, determinate contribution to the structure in the world and this structure is complete and consistent.

If one is investigating a certain thing, one is seeking an explicative account of what that thing is. Such an account would provide insight into how that thing is in existing at all, that is, into how it is natured, and would include some insight into how that thing relates to others. Given that each thing is fundamental, an explicative account of what a thing is is simply an illuminating description of that initial thing—rather than a relational account of what that thing is in terms of other things that make it be or that determine how it is. No thing per se is amenable to explanation in this latter sense: not its being, its being what it is, its being as it is essentially, its being the very thing it is or its being itself. One thing cannot explain another. A thing is what makes an explanation possible; things are only the means of explanation and are themselves inexplicable in that they are not even susceptible to determinative explanation. What is explicable, therefore, is only the distribution of things in the world, a bit of this diverse array, some structural phenomenon. If one is investigating some such phenomenon, a successful account is one that characterizes what things are included in that plurality, what they are and how they relate among themselves and, perhaps, how they relate to other things. Acquiring insight into what a thing is or into why some structural phenomenon is as it is and why it must be so in virtue of the things it comprises is to achieve understanding regarding that object and to discharge the task of critical inquiry with respect to it.

The world, this panoply of things, includes the objects of inquiry (of any sort), the inquirers and the ontological bases of understanding anything. There are only things and so these are the limits of successful inquiry. Everything about which one could inquire is among *all this*, as is any means of accounting for any thing and any phenomenon. These observations illustrate the principle of the *primacy of ontology*—inquiry begins and ends with things—and indicate an important methodological point that comes to the fore in subsequent discussion. One must seek an account of any phenomenon in terms of things: what they are and what they do, i.e., how they are constrained per se and how they constrain and are constrained by others. Appropriate investigation, inquiry consistent with the framework of radical ontology, might reveal unfamiliar things in the world; the initial strangeness of some thing in an otherwise compelling account of a phenomenon encountered in original inquiry or in the course of wholly critical metaphysics must be preferred to any more familiar account involving nonexistent entities or levels of reality or other such notions that do not comport with radical ontology. Any account that fails to comport with this theory of everything is ultimately ungrounded and incoherent.

I think many of the problems taken seriously by philosophers, now and historically, are intractable because they are not pursued in light of an account of what a thing in general is and the theoretical framework—radical ontology—that this account provides. Philosophers often begin with a host of unexamined yet sacrosanct assumptions that actually preclude a true account of their object of inquiry. Such an approach usually comes from a parochial view of science, a stringent physicalism and corollary reductionism (or similarly hierarchical view of reality) or an obstinate reliance on one's senses to the exclusion of any other capacity one might have to engage *all this*. Thus, one might assume that each thing is "categorical" and then try to account for modal or dispositional phenomena. Or one might assume that the only acceptable bases of explanation are things that are not colored and then try to account for one's indubitable and undisputed experiences of color. Or one might assume that there are no values—just non-normative facts—and then try to account for one's indubitable and undisputed experiences of normativity. Or one might assume that the only acceptable bases of explanation are things that have no intentional or conscious qualities and then try to account for one's indubitable and undisputed mental experiences.

A good deal, if not most, of modern philosophical inquiry, especially "analytic" inquiry, proceeds in this way. Not by beginning with *all this*—or with *this thing*, whatever it is—but with an orthodoxy antithetical to the structure in reality. One presumes how things must be, confronts things that are manifestly not like that, then tries to give an account of these things in terms of others that are explicitly taken to be unlike the former in the crucial respects. The methodology, when considered critically, is bizarre. Yet all such reductive or nonreductive, hierarchical projects, based on supervenience or grounding or other constitutive dependence relations whereby one thing makes another be, proceed in this way. Such projects are misguided. The framework of radical ontology, based on the account, extracted from *all this* via original inquiry, of a thing as a fundamental, natured entity shows why. Thus, how one ought to proceed instead is by confronting critically the world in order to acquire insight into one's object of inquiry by engaging it amongst the structure in reality, all the other things there are. Doing so usually dissolves problems regarding that object that were supposed to be intractable, while leaving the means to resolve the tractable problems that remain. These solutions are not in terms of some ontologically privileged class of thing, but in terms of what is clearly there, those things that prompt one's inquiry in the first place (or the things requisite for the structural phenomenon that prompts inquiry).

So one has now an account of the world (and what it comprises), as well as a theoretical framework for conducting further inquiry. If one takes up again original inquiry to check one's work, so to speak, or to see what more one can learn about the world from a wholly critical origin, one finds that *all this* is different. This reveals some thing of the utmost importance to understanding the world.

5
The Metaphysics of Time

When one confronts the world in original inquiry, one finds a diverse array of whatnot, an array that, in a less critical context, one might say includes, inter alia, colors, shapes, phenomenal feels, moods, textures, familiar objects, emotional states, sounds, thoughts, smells, mental images. This array is diverse in a precise way: it is exactly *thus*. (With 'thus' I refer to *all this*, but in a way intended to draw attention to the precise arrangement of "it," i.e., the world.) If one takes up original inquiry again, one finds *all this* diverse in a distinct precise way: it is exactly *as so*. And if one takes it up yet again, one finds the world differently diverse: *as such*. In fact, whenever one takes up original inquiry, one confronts a unique diverse array. This phenomenon seems indubitable. In this wholly critical context, however, one should try to doubt it. So, then, confront the world merely as the impetus to inquiry; confront it again, trying to discern whether *all this* remains diverse in precisely the same way. One's new attention to the details of the world, one's fresh scrutiny indicates that it is not (as would merely a novel intention to find *all this* diverse in precisely the same way). Thus, one's very effort to doubt this phenomenon demonstrates it. The phenomenon is indeed indubitable—but, more, it is central to one's experience of the world. As such, it is an imperative object of inquiry insofar as one seeks to understand *all this*.

Reflect, then, on this crucial experience: When one initially considers the impetus to inquiry, it is *thus*. When one considers it again, it is *as so*. A *mode of differentiation* is an arrangement of things whereby distinctions are apparent. There appear to be, therefore, at least two modes of differentiation in the world. There is the diversity one confronts when initially taking up original inquiry, apparent in *all this*, that indicates complexity, by some measure, and the need for generality in a wholly critical metaphysics. But there is also this distinct mode of differentiation under consideration here: the difference in the world going from *thus*... to *as so*. The latter is not in the world as *thus*— only in *all this* going from *thus* to *as so*.

A mode of differentiation, as an arrangement of things, is not itself a thing; rather, it is a multiplicity of things and so a structural phenomenon. The

Time and the World. M. Oreste Fiocco, Oxford University Press. © Oxford University Press 2024.
DOI: 10.1093/oso/9780197777107.003.0005

phenomenon being considered here, this second mode of differentiation, is, as demonstrated above, as incontrovertible as the diversity engaged when initially confronting *all this* as merely the impetus to inquiry. It is real—in the world—and so this phenomenon, like every other, has an ontological basis among *all this*. The phenomenon has, then, some account in terms of the things in the world.

Call whatever is ultimately the key to this second mode of differentiation in the world *time*. To name this key, I could have used any term. I choose 'time' because of its association with a number of obvious phenomena involving change and process, such as growing old. Despite this association, and the familiarity of the term itself, it has no standard—or even obvious—meaning. 'Time,' then, is a particularly felicitous term for present purposes. As subsequent discussion reveals, time, the key to the second mode of differentiation in the world, illuminates the obvious phenomena associated with the familiar term, 'time,' making clear how these phenomena could exist at all; yet, insofar as 'time' has no standard meaning, my novel use of this term, to refer to whatever is the key to the second mode of differentiation in the world, need not compete with some entrenched usage with which it might be confused. Since time is the key to this second mode of differentiation, it may be aptly called *temporal differentiation*.

From a point of original inquiry, temporal differentiation and, hence, time are as apparent as the diversity in *all this*. Time, then, be it a thing or structural phenomenon, is, like temporal differentiation itself, an imperative object of inquiry if one seeks to understand the world. The metaphysics of time, as I pursue it, is the discipline whose objective is a wholly critical account of what time is and its place among *all this*. Given the centrality of time to one's experience of the world—in any engagement with it—a further purpose of this work, whose primary one is to provide a wholly critical account of *all this*, is to present a comprehensive and satisfactory account of the metaphysics of time. Such a theory would not only provide an account of what time is, it would also illuminate all peculiarly temporal things and phenomena in the world, doing so in a way consistent with one's experience of *all this* from a point of original inquiry. This experience, as I discuss below (in Chapter 6), is confounding in that it indicates both inconstancy and constancy.

An answer to the question of what time is, if the metaphysics of time is to be wholly critical, must take nothing for granted about time, not even that it is a thing. So this discipline, too, must begin from a point of original inquiry, though a point from which one may now be guided by the principles of radical ontology. Thus, in this chapter, I first consider how elusive an explicative account of what time is has been, despite the great deal of attention given to the phenomena it enables, such as, change, process, and a host of common happenings. This phenomenon of change is crucial to an account of the metaphysics of time, so, after distinguishing change from differentiation, I elucidate the former. Change requires *moments*, temporal entities of a certain kind. Although time and moments are essentially related, I show that they are clearly quite different. I then argue that time is itself a thing, discussing some of its significant qualities. Finally, I provide a theoretical framework for the metaphysics of time. The account of time that I propound summarily resolves several putative controversies that have, traditionally, been regarded as of principal importance to philosophical discussions of (what has been taken to be) time. This just reveals that the genuine controversies here are not about time per se; they are, rather, about *temporal reality*, the structure of things in the world given the existence of time.

§5.1. Confronting Time

Although other philosophers have adopted approaches to metaphysics different from the one I introduce and develop in this work, it is nonetheless surprising, given the metaphysical attention shown, in recent decades, to the phenomena associated with time, how little consideration has been directed at time per se.

This claim might be perplexing, for certainly, one might think, many philosophers in the course of Western philosophy have devoted a great deal of attention to time. Indeed, over the last few decades, there has been a tremendous amount written ostensibly about time. Still, examination of this literature, historical and contemporary, reveals that most (if not all) discussions in what is traditionally regarded as the metaphysics of *time* focus on phenomena *attendant upon time*—like existence in time, i.e. persistence; the gain or loss of properties over time, i.e. change; coming to be in time, i.e. becoming; one's experience of time; the linguistic means to characterize the world in time, i.e., tense; dependence relations among things over time, i.e., causation—rather than time itself. All these phenomena depend on time and those that consider them merely take time, whatever is ultimately the key to *all this* going from *thus* to *as so*, for granted. Consideration of these phenomena, moreover, usually occurs in a context in which it is presumed that there are two competing "views of time."

There is some dialectical difficulty in presenting a wholly critical metaphysics of time, for issues that are supposed to be of principal importance to the discipline—and which are likely at the forefront of the mind of anyone who engages in philosophical investigations of time—are, I maintain, posterior to the foundational issues that enable one to clarify the former and to arbitrate the familiar disputes in the traditional discipline. My discussion, therefore, cannot be linear from the point of original inquiry; some anticipation of issues discussed much more thoroughly in chapters below, in what seems to me their proper context, is necessary here. Thus, as is familiar to one with any acquaintance with modern investigations of time, the competing "views of time" that standardly provide the context of these investigations are called variously, the *A-theory* and the *B-theory* or the *tense* and *tenseless* theories or the *passage* and *block* theories. The first member of these pairs is supposed to be the view that time is objectively, that is, independently of any experience of it, in some sense dynamic; the second, that time is objectively static (in some sense).

I discuss these views—and there are a few conflated here—in more detail below. At this point, I just want to observe that even if there were here useful views as easily characterizable as these are supposed to be, and even if they were relevant to a comprehensive metaphysics of time (two claims I challenge below) what exactly they are views *of* is not clear. Although, say, the A-theory and B-theory are often presented as theories of *time*, a bit of reflection indicates that they are, rather, views of how things *in time* are (viz., bearing the monadic temporal properties of *pastness, presentness*, and *futurity* or standing only in temporal relations of *earlier than, later than*, or *simultaneous with*). But then neither view provides any insight into what time is, and without some account of what it is per se, one can have no insightful account or real understanding of what it is to exist *in* time. I maintain that a distinction between existing inside and outside of time is crucial for a satisfactory metaphysics of time and, relatedly, an illuminating account of *all this*. Hence, an account of what it is to exist in time is of the utmost importance, and so some account of what time is is required.

More generally, if these familiar pairs of views are supposed to present opposing accounts of something, they raise the question of what exactly that thing (or phenomenon) is. If it is supposed to be *time*, some account of time itself should be given so that one is in a position to appreciate the contrasting approaches illustrated by these pairs of views. In a wholly critical metaphysics of time, like the one I am pursuing here, such an account cannot just be presumed. The account must be based on the incontrovertible phenomenon of temporal differentiation, which prompts inquiry into time in the first place. An account that elucidates this basis would reveal the common ground from which any dispute concerning time arises. This account would be, therefore, ecumenical, acceptable to anyone investigating the metaphysics of *time*.

§5.1.1. Differentiation and change

Original inquiry reveals temporal differentiation—*all this* going from *thus* to *as so*—a phenomenon distinct from the differentiation in the world when one initially regards it merely as the impetus to inquiry. Differentiation, the phenomenon whereby distinctions are apparent, can be *variance*, where variance is explicable in terms of sheer distinctness. Any array of things whatsoever, then, can account for variance. The diversity of the impetus to inquiry illustrates variance. *Change*, however, is a distinct phenomenon, one that is more strict. Change occurs only under certain conditions, when there is differentiation of a precise sort, namely, when, in the world going from *thus* to *as so*, a single thing is one way and (then) an incompatible way.

The very apprehension of temporal differentiation demonstrates the existence of change. One, whatever one is, is aware of the world as *thus* ... and one is aware of the world *as so*. Being aware of the world as *thus* and being aware of the world *as so* are incompatible—one cannot be aware of the world both as thus *and* as so. So, in engaging the world in original inquiry, there is change in or to one: one engages the world as *thus* and (then) engages it *as so*. Consequently, there is change in the world, at least in some inquirer, the thing prompted by *all this* to inquire. Note that the world, which is not a thing itself, does not and cannot change; "it" is not one way, and then another. Rather, there is some thing in the world—in this case, an inquirer—who changes.

Anyone who confronts the world and appreciates the distinct modes of differentiation herein can accept the phenomenon just described and so accept the reality of change. Such change arises in original inquiry. Just as, as I demonstrated above, the diversity in *all this* and *all this* going from *thus* to *as so* are literally incontestable without demonstrating the phenomena in question, so, too, seems this change. Try to contest it. Make no assumptions about the world, confront it merely as the impetus to inquiry—"it" is *thus*; do so again—*all this* is *as so*. Now try to contest that one and the same inquirer engages the world as *thus* and *as so*. The very effort to do this—to attend to the complex situation, to consider whether one can legitimately contest change therein, to try to formulate some objection—demonstrates the phenomenon in question, to wit, change in an inquirer. Therefore, change is a conspicuous and incontrovertible phenomenon amid *all this*.

Yet some philosophers, for example, Parmenides and other Eleatics, deny change. I maintain, in light of patent demonstration, that there is both temporal differentiation and change. These demonstrations make no assumptions about *all this*. Without presupposition, one confronts the world (finding it *thus*) and confronts the world again (finding it *as so*). In these experiences of original inquiry, I hold, one can apprehend the indisputable existence of the two phenomena. Thus, if one were to dispute the existence of change, one must reject these experiences as illusory. Any grounds for doing so must come from presuming that the world is not, in fact, as it appears when confronted merely as the impetus to inquiry, that is, confronted without making any assumptions about *all this*; or from presuming, at the outset of inquiry, that the capacities an inquirer has to engage the world distort or otherwise fail to reveal *all this* or the things herein. However, at the very outset of inquiry, simply confronting the world, such assumptions can have no basis and so adopting them is entirely arbitrary. Of course, one must start somewhere, by some means. Starting with (arbitrary) assumptions, though, rather than what is not assumed, but is just there—namely, *all this*—seems not only unpromising, but perverse. There is, then, in the structure in reality, no basis to deny the existence of change.

This conclusion is confirmed by recognizing that even if one grants arbitrary assumptions at the outset of inquiry, since confronting the world merely as the impetus to inquiry certainly seems to present one with change, the rejection of change would require some *argument* that this phenomenon is in fact illusory and could not exist. But any argument, as a dialectical epistemic tool, itself requires change (and, a fortiori, distinct modes of differentiation): as one considers different premises and then comes to a conclusion, there is, with respect to the inquirer, both change in regard to what is being considered, and some further change from one mental state to another via inference. Therefore, not only could no innocent engagement with all this support the denial of change, no argument—from any premises—could undermine the claim that it exists either.

A Parmenidean, one who denies change, might respond to this by conceding that their position is so outré—yet nonetheless penetrating—that it cannot be stated or even contemplated without undermining itself. The Parmenidean argues and provides insight by self-defeating means; but once this insight is attained, one ignores these means and the doubt they themselves cast on one's newfound position. (In a Wittgensteinian spirit, one climbs the ladder, then kicks it away.) I do not see how this sort of response could be plausible, for the insight that is supposed to be provided, by inquiry employing self-defeating means, is into *all this*, the world. However, engaging the world innocently, that is, without assumption about "it," in order to even consider how to pursue inquiry, presents one with what seems to be change. To accept, with the Parmenidean, that there is actually no change calls into question what one is engaging, casting doubt on the world itself and the very possibility of inquiry—or anything for that matter! This position, then, does not hint at profound esoteric insight, but rather seems to promise stultification. The same is true for any other that would deny, from a position of original inquiry, diversity in *all this* or distinct modes of differentiation.

Therefore, at least some things, though perhaps not all, can and do change. This raises the question of what change is, whether it is a thing per se or a plurality of things, i.e., a structural phenomenon. Change, as defined above, occurs when a single thing is one way and (then) an incompatible way. To appreciate what this object of inquiry is, or to understand it, one must show how change is in the world consistent with the framework of radical ontology, the basis of which is only natured entities (some of which are relations, others only relata). A further question that needs to be addressed, by a comprehensive account of the metaphysics of time, is how exactly change is related to time, to whatever it is that accounts for a second mode of differentiation in the world. An answer to the latter question can be pursued by answering the first.

Although one can speak of this or that "change," as if referring to a particular thing, change is not a thing per se. Change occurs when a single thing is one way and an incompatible way. Crucial, then, to the phenomenon is incompatibility. Given that being a thing is not fragmentary (§4.3.5.), incompatible things cannot co-exist; a fortiori, a thing itself cannot realize incompatibility. Consequently, change must be some plurality of things, a structural phenomenon. As a structural phenomenon, an explicative account of what change is would provide insight into the delimited plurality that makes up the phenomenon, with some further account of how these things relate to others—especially any things on which these ontologically depend.

If a thing changes, that thing is incompatible ways. No thing, however, can in itself—*via its own being*—realize incompatible ways; such a "thing" would be incoherent, impossible. Thus, there must be some means to account for this incompatibility with respect to that thing. In other words, a single thing can be incompatible ways only in relation to some other thing. Call whatever it is that accounts for how a single thing can realize incompatible ways through temporal differentiation a *moment*. Again, like with my choice of name, viz., 'time,' for whatever is the key to the second mode of differentiation in the world, I choose a word here—'moment'—to name this thing that is indispensable to change because it is familiar, associated with a number of obvious temporal phenomena, yet has no standard, precise meaning. I intend here to exploit the familiarity of the word while introducing an exact meaning as the name of this thing indispensable to change.

When a thing changes, it is one way in relation to—*at*—one moment and an incompatible way at a distinct moment. So there is a kind of thing, *moment*, and change requires distinct instances of this kind, that is, change requires distinct particular moments. The ontological bases of the phenomenon of change are, therefore, (at least) one thing capable of existing at distinct moments, distinct incompatible qualities, and distinct moments (appropriately related).

§5.2. Moments and Time

Time is whatever is ultimately the key to the second mode of differentiation in the world—*all this* going from *thus* to *as so*—the mode that enables change. Change is a structural phenomenon whereby one and the same thing is incompatible ways. What enables a single thing to be incompatible ways is a moment. Moments are, then, part of the ontological basis of change and so necessary to an explicative account of what this phenomenon is. If time enables change and change requires moments, this raises the questions of how time is related to moments and what, if anything, can both be key to temporal differentiation and be so related to moments. Answering these questions can make much clearer how exactly change and time are related.

§5.2.1. Moments do not suffice to account for temporal differentiation

Temporal differentiation, the second mode of differentiation revealed through original inquiry, is, as demonstrated above, a genuine—indeed, incontestable—phenomenon. Like every genuine phenomenon, the world going from *thus* to *as so* must have an account with an ontological basis amid *all this*. This ontological basis, like any other, is some thing (or things). Time is supposed to be whatever is ultimately the key to temporal differentiation. Because this mode of differentiation enables change, which requires distinct moments, temporal differentiation involves distinct moments. Distinct moments themselves are not some thing, but a plurality of things. Hence, if time is itself a thing, it cannot, as the ontological basis of and key to an account of temporal differentiation, be but a single moment (for at least two are needed), nor can it be a plurality of moments, which is not a thing at all.

Nevertheless, it is an open question what exactly time is, whether it is a thing per se or a structural phenomenon, that is, a plurality of things. If there are distinct moments, one might think that temporal differentiation can be accounted for on the basis of these alone. There would be no need, then, to recognize some additional thing to account for how *all this* goes from *thus* to *as so*. In which case, time would not be a natured entity, but merely a plurality of moments—just as the world is not a natured entity itself, but a plurality of (all) things. As a matter of fact, the B-theory, mentioned above, is sometimes characterized as the view on which time is nothing but all moments—and the things existing at them—together in their permanent relations.[1]

This line of thought is mistaken. More is needed to account for temporal differentiation and change than simply distinct moments (and the things existing at them). Any thing that can be incompatible ways has the capacity for both of the mutually exclusive ways; yet, as noted above, it cannot itself realize both. Its capacity for incompatible ways must be constrained to one or the other of the ways, if that thing is to make (as it must) a coherent contribution to *all this*. A moment is the thing that so constrains it. Thus, a thing cannot be incompatible ways at the same moment. A consequence of this is that one moment cannot exist at another. If one moment, m_1, were to exist at another, m_2, then a thing that is one way at m_1 and an incompatible way at m_2

---

[1] See, for example, Tallant 2013: 372 for the claim that, on the B-theory, the "reality of time consists in nothing more than various objects standing in the 'fixed and permanent' relations earlier than and later than."

would be incompatible ways at the same moment, viz., m_2. It would be both of the mutually exclusive ways at m_2, because it is one of the ways at m_1 yet m_1 exists at m_2 when it is the other way. Distinct moments, therefore, exclude one another. (I examine this point in greater detail in §8.1.1.2.) Nothing further follows regarding one moment vis-à-vis another considering only moments themselves.

However, the structural phenomena of change and temporal differentiation, which involve distinct moments, both require that moments be in the world in a systematic or, at least, orderly way. *All this* is *thus* . . . and *as so* . . . and *as such* and so forth. Given that no moment itself requires such orderly being, some further thing is needed to account for it. According to one explicative account of change, this phenomenon occurs when a thing is one way, that is, has a quality or stands in some relation, at one moment and is an incompatible way at another moment that *is later than* the first (or, conversely, a thing is one way at a moment that *is earlier than* a distinct moment at which it is an incompatible way).[2] A plurality of a mutable thing, two moments, incompatible properties, and the relation of, say, *later than*, though, do not themselves account for change. A moment is the thing in relation to which a single entity can be incompatible ways. There is nothing about such an entity to suggest that it is, much less, must be related to another moment. If change requires that some moment be later than another, then, when change occurs, some thing must account for why these moments are so related when they themselves do not necessitate this. The relation *later than* presumably does not necessitate that particular moments be related by it. Moreover, if *later than* is asymmetric, some thing must account for why any moments that stand in this relation are related as they are—why one is later than the other rather than vice versa. Some further thing, therefore, is still needed to account for change—even granting the relation *later than*—and, more generally, for the orderly being in temporal differentiation.[3]

---

[2] I argue in Chapter 8 this account of change—despite its great plausibility—is in fact incorrect.
[3] Note that if a state of affairs or an event is merely a complex of one or more substances, one or more qualities or relations, and a moment, such pluralities could not account for change or the orderly being in temporal differentiation, for a state of affairs or an event would just be a plurality of things that themselves do not account for change or the orderly being in temporal differentiation. Even if a state of affairs or an event were not a plurality, but a unit—a thing itself—there is nothing about such an entity to suggest that it must be related to any other in a way that would explicate change or temporal differentiation in general. Furthermore, states of affairs or events, on any plausible account of such phenomena, cannot address the forthcoming problem regarding the source of moments.

There is a further consideration that undermines the line of thought that distinct moments (and the things existing at them) suffice to account for change and, hence, temporal differentiation. Arguably, some things must exist per se. Such things could not come to be, nor could they cease existing. They have to be amid *all this* simply given what they are. Other things, however, do not have to exist in themselves. These things are in the world although they need not be considering only what they are. Take some such thing, *e*. Any plurality of things that includes *e* is a structural phenomenon; any such phenomenon demands an explanation. What is needed is an account of how *e* stands in relations to other things—is amid *all this*—in the first place, that is, an account of whence, ontologically speaking, it exists at all (given that it need not, considering only what *e* is). Nota bene: What is not needed is an account of how *e* exists as it is existing, for this sort of account, one that would explicate the very being of an existing thing, is impossible, since each thing is fundamental.

A thing itself is not even susceptible to explanation. But every structural phenomenon is. The right thing, one that given what it is requires that the things constituting the relevant structural phenomenon be arranged as they are—or be arranged at all—would be the ontological basis of an explanation for that phenomenon. Consider again *e*, some entity that does not have to exist per se. The *source* of *e* is some thing (or plurality of them) that necessitates the initial existence of *e*; the source yields *e* in that, given what the source is (or what and how it is), *e* comes to be in the world even though it does not have to exist in itself. The source of *e*, therefore, is the ontological basis of an explanation for any (initial) structural phenomenon involving *e*.

The observation that every structural phenomenon is susceptible to explanation raises the question of whether every structural phenomenon in fact has one. If so, then every thing that does not have to exist per se has a source. (If such a thing did not have a source, there would be a structural phenomenon that did not have an explanation, namely, some arrangement involving that thing.) Suppose a thing that does not have to exist per se exists but indeed has no source. There would be, then, a sort of *bruteness* in the world: some phenomenon that is explicable yet not explained. Such bruteness in a world of things is implausibly incongruous. At a point of original inquiry, one confronts *all this*, a diverse array of whatnot, and comes to recognize things as the ontological basis of and means to an explanation for this diversity. Thus, from the outset of inquiry, one encounters things and explicable phenomena. Subsequent inquiry reveals other phenomena, such as temporal differentiation, the world going from *thus* to *as so*. These phenomena either have explanations (and, hence, ontological bases thereof) or lack them. If a phenomenon has an explanation, then insight might be needed to apprehend it and its ontological basis, which might be some thing quite unfamiliar, but no motivation is needed for accepting that there is some explanation at all. On the other hand, if a phenomenon has no explanation, motivation for accepting such unintelligible arrangements of things is required. None seems possible. The most that might be proffered is that were there an explanation for some seemingly recalcitrant phenomenon, its ontological basis would be exotic. However, in a world of fundamental things and explicable phenomena—and fallible inquirers—exotic things are less incongruous than brute phenomena. Therefore, I accept the principle, noted in passing above (§3.4.), that every structural phenomenon has an account in some thing(s) or other. This principle guides me in my efforts to illuminate *all this*.

A moment, again, is the entity that accounts for how a single thing can realize incompatible ways through temporal differentiation. There is nothing about a moment, understood in this way, to suggest that such a thing must in itself exist. Indeed, one's engagement of the world demonstrates that each moment ceases to be entirely (§8.2.). Nevertheless, there are and must be moments, for there is—incontestably—change and change requires distinct moments. The presence in the world of some moment(s)—though no particular moment must exist and ceases to once it does—is a structural phenomenon that demands explanation. What is needed is some account of how any moment is amid *all this* in the first place, that is, an account of the (ontological) source of any moment.

Thus, moments per se are insufficient to account for temporal differentiation: They cannot account for the orderly arrangement of moments in the world required by change and, hence, by temporal differentiation; nor can moments account for why there is temporal differentiation in the first place, given that no moment in itself need exist. What is needed is some thing to account for the orderly arrangement of moments in *all this* and some thing that is the source of moments. Precisely how a source yields what it does can account for the orderly arrangement of the latter in the world. This indicates one thing can do both, that is, account for the orderly arrangement of moments as their source. Whatever did do both would certainly be aptly regarded as the ultimate (ontological) key to temporal differentiation. As noted at the outset, time is supposed to be whatever is ultimately the key to temporal differentiation. Time, therefore, is the thing that yields moments and, in so doing, accounts for their orderly arrangement in the world—whatever this arrangement turns out to be.

§5.3. Time Is a Thing

The world comprises things standing in constraining relations. Time makes a unique contribution to *all this* and, hence, is a thing rather than merely a structural phenomenon. Time both yields moments and is the basis of an account of their orderly arrangement. As such, it is the ontological basis of the second mode of differentiation encountered in original inquiry, the world going from *thus* to *as so*. Time is, consequently, the natured entity that enables change.

As a thing, time is subsumed by one of the four categories. It is not qualitative, it does not qualify a thing, thereby itself constraining how that thing is (without effecting what it is). Thus, time is neither a mode nor a quality, that is, property. Nor is it the sort of thing that has instances. It is not, then, a substantial universal, i.e., a kind. So time is a substance. Given what time is, to wit, the thing that is the basis of an account of the orderly arrangement of moments, there cannot be distinct times—lest there be competing accounts of this orderly arrangement and, hence, no account at all. This point is corroborated by recognizing that there is no need for more than a single source of moments and seemingly no phenomenon amid *all this* that might motivate such redundancy. I conclude, therefore, that time is not an instance of some kind; there are not times. (Of course, I do not here mean by 'times,' *moments*, for there are distinct moments.) As a thing, then, time is sui generis, a substance of its own sort.

Time, the natural source—and thereby regulator—of moments, as a thing, is not even susceptible to explanation; there is no explaining its existence. However, if time, like any moment, is a thing that need not exist per se, then time itself requires a source, some thing that necessitates its initial existence, that is the basis of an account of how it stands in any relations at all. Time, though, unlike a moment, is a necessary existent; it must exist given what it is. Consequently, insofar as there is any explanation for how time stands in relations to other things at all, the basis of this account is time itself.

That time must exist can be seen in light of the following considerations: As I demonstrate above, there is (incontestably) change. Without time, there could not be. Change requires moments and time is the source of any moment. So time is the thing that enables change by yielding the moments that make it possible; were time not to exist, change would not merely fail to be actual, it would be impossible. But change is not impossible, indeed, it is actual. Time, therefore, as necessary for change, must exist.

Of course, this argument only shows that time must exist if change does. This is consistent with time not being a necessary existent. If there had been no change, then perhaps there would have been no time. Or if there were to be no change, then perhaps there would be no time (as I discuss below, this is a position many philosophers accept). Or perhaps time provided all the moments ever needed for any change—and then ceased to be! Such observations notwithstanding, there is change and so there are moments. Time is the source of these moments. If time does not exist per se, time itself has a source. Time, however, could not have a source. Consider: A thing with a source comes to be, that is, it is not amid *all this* ... and (then) it is. Thus, coming to be is a phenomenon that depends on temporal differentiation. Temporal differentiation involves moments, which themselves require time; any coming to be is posterior to time itself. Time, then, cannot have a source. This is confirmed by recognizing that if, *per impossibile*, time had a source, that source would have to undergo some change—so that it can go from not yielding time, to yielding it. Change, however, requires moments; thus, there could be no change prior to the existence of time, the source of any moment. Given that there is change in the world and, hence, moments, there is time; since time exists and yet can have no source, time exists necessarily, i.e., it exists given what it is.

One might object to the characterization of time as *the* thing that enables change, for there are many things requisite for change, e.g., some thing that can exist through temporal differentiation (realizing incompatible properties), incompatible properties themselves and distinct moments. Although no change could occur without these things, and so they are necessary for the phenomenon, no specific moment, property, or mutable thing is requisite for change. However, without time—this very thing—there would be no moments and so there could be no change. Even if a thing, given what it is, has the capacity to change, without time itself, and the moments it yields, it could not do so. In this sense, time is the ultimate (ontological) key to change, just as it is the key to temporal differentiation. Regarding time as the enabler of change is, therefore, appropriate.

That there could not be change without time is wholly uncontroversial. However, from the earliest metaphysical considerations of the phenomena associated with temporal differentiation, philosophers have considered the question of whether there could be time without change. Aristotle maintains unequivocally that there could not be.[4] In a famous paper, Sidney Shoemaker denies this,[5] but nearly all philosophers endorse the Aristotelian position.[6] Nevertheless, according to the account of time propounded here, time can exist without change.

Time is a thing, a necessarily existent substance. It does not comprise other things. The structural phenomenon of change, though, is composed of certain things; in particular, some mutable entity, that is, a thing that can exist through temporal differentiation and has the capacities to be incompatible ways (at distinct moments). If there were no mutable things, which seems possible, there would be no change—and yet time, as a necessary existent, would exist. Even if some mutable things must exist, they need not, presumably, change at every moment. If none were to bear incompatible properties from one moment to another, there would be no change and yet time, the source of these moments, would nonetheless exist. Hence, there can be time without change.

In light of the traditional Aristotelian position that there cannot be time without change, this conclusion might be regarded as contentious. My goal in this chapter, however, is to present an ecumenical account of time, one that everyone should and can accept. Thus, to forestall contention, I note the questionable foundations of the Aristotelian position. Aristotle presents no explicit account of time. He seems to offer no better reason for holding that there could not be time without change than that this is a plausible assumption with which to begin an inquiry into time.[7] Without any account of time per se, though, this assertion regarding plausibility has no basis. One might, then, claim in support of the Aristotelian position that one is unable to conceive of time without change. Again, without any account of time per se, this

---

[4] *Physics* IV 11, 218b21–219a10.

[5] See Shoemaker 1969. Shoemaker only attempts to show, with a whimsical thought-experiment, that there can be some reason for thinking time and change can be independent. This, of course, does not show that they are.

[6] See, for just one example among many, Lowe 1998: 86. Lowe's endorsement is somewhat qualified. He maintains that change is conceptually prior to time, yet acknowledges that time might be ontologically prior to change. For his dissent to Shoemaker, see Lowe 2002: 247–249.

[7] Ursula Coope argues that this is Aristotle's reason. See Coope 2001: 360.

claim is without basis; moreover, it is belied, on any plausible account of conception, by the present discussion. This discussion, in contrast to Aristotle's, begins with original inquiry and proceeds by reflecting on the indubitable phenomenon of temporal differentiation. An account of time is derived from this secure basis, one according to which there can indeed be time without change.

§5.4. Time in the World

In this chapter, I present a framework for a critical metaphysics of time, one that is based on the method of original inquiry and extends the ontological commitments of radical ontology to include the means of inquiring into time. In conformity with this method, nothing about time is assumed at the outset of the metaphysics of time. One begins this inquiry by engaging the indubitable phenomenon of temporal differentiation and by appreciating that this phenomenon must have an ontological basis among *all this*. Time is whatever this basis is. By reflecting on this mode of differentiation—the world going from *thus* to *as so*—one recognizes change (in oneself, if nothing else). Considering this phenomenon, one recognizes moments and through these comes to see some of the features of time.

Time is a thing in the world, the necessarily existing substance that enables change by yielding the moments it requires. Time is also the basis of the orderly arrangement of any moments there are and, hence, what ultimately accounts for the relations holding between moments (and of any peculiarly temporal features they might have, insofar as these turn on the relations among moments) (§6.1.1.). This is the crux of the account of time I propound in this chapter. The account can be enhanced slightly with a couple further principles.

As discussed above (§5.2.1.), time itself is not composed of moments. In engaging the world as it goes from *thus* to *as so*, and reflecting on associated phenomena, there is nothing to indicate time is (or could be) composed of anything else. Hence, it is *simple*. The source of moments is no particular place—or any place at all—so time itself is not in space. It is, then, an *abstract* entity, rather than a concrete one (on one understanding of this distinction). One might here expect or hope for some principle illuminating *how* time yields moments or one regarding *how* it orders them. How exactly moments are ordered in the world and the role of time in this order are, in a sense, the central issues of Parts III and IV of the present work. With respect to how time yields moments, there is just nothing illuminating to be said.

To expect illumination on how time yields moments is like expecting insight into how—precisely—the number 2 yields 4 when squared or a set contains its members or a proposition represents or the color green appears as it does (to wit, green) or the disposition of fragility makes something fragile. Or how—precisely—a given particle spins as it does or a body wields the gravitational force it does. Assuming there are numbers, sets, propositions, colors, dispositions, elementary particles, material bodies, each instance of any of these is fundamental; there is no explaining how it is essentially, nor how it does what it does given what it is. Time is no different. One might insist, though, that time *is* different: it is supposed to *produce* things (i.e., moments).[8] In response, I concede that time is indeed different, it is a sui generis entity that does what no other thing can; however, qua *thing* time is merely a fundamental natured entity like any other. Furthermore the production of moments is not a process, it is a phenomenon that is a condition of any process; and, of course, this phenomenon involves no mechanism and requires no assembly. Producing, that is, yielding moments is simply what time does. There is no mystery here—no more than with any other thing.

To this point, nothing I have said about time per se, even if unfamiliar, should be contentious. The claims can be verified by any (open-minded, critical) inquirer who undertakes original inquiry and, guided by the principles of radical ontology and what is plausible in light of *all this*, tries to develop an account of the world going from *thus* to *as so*. The account of time I propound, and the accounts of a moment and of change, are, I believe, entirely ecumenical. With these accounts, a framework is now in place to address the controversial issues in the metaphysics of time.

However, as soon as one begins to consider some of the perennial questions and traditional controversies associated with the phenomenon of temporal differentiation, one sees that many are summarily resolved by the account of time provided here. First of all, time is real, it is part of the world. Yet some philosophers maintain that time is unreal. If a mind is simply a thing with intentionality, the capacity to present a thing for consideration, there is nothing in original inquiry that suggests that time cannot exist in the absence of any mind. As the necessary substance that enables change by yielding (and ordering) moments, time is quite unlike a mind.

---

[8] Note that material bodies are supposed to *produce* gravitational forces.

These considerations strongly suggest that time is not a thing that is mind-dependent. Yet some philosophers hold that time does depend for existence on some mind or, at least, the phenomena crucially associated with time do.

More specifically, time, like every other thing, is fundamental, it is not reducible to or grounded in anything; so there is no question of reductionism or relationalism about time.[9] If time is simple, furthermore, there is no question of the structure or topology of time per se. Time itself is not linear, nor does it branch. Given that time is a necessary existent, it has no beginning and it could have no end. There is, then, no first moment, no last. Consequently, there is no beginning to the world, no end. Even if there is a beginning to all the physical, material processes, some thing—time—had to exist in order for the realization of any such process. As the source of any moment, time must exist in order for any moment to. Hence, time itself does not exist *at* some moment that it yields and so time itself cannot change. There is, therefore, no direction to time, no arrow of time. Significantly, time per se does not pass, whatever passage is supposed to be.

But, of course, there are legitimate controversies pertaining to time and the world. Just as meeting the primary objective of a wholly critical metaphysics, viz., an account of what the world is (via an account of *thing*), leaves many issues regarding *all this* unresolved, attaining an account of what time is, the primary objective of the metaphysics of time, leaves unresolved many issues regarding time and the world. Some philosophers might hold that the account of time I propound here stultifies the metaphysics of time by making the perennial questions associated with it too easy or flatly unintelligible. This is not so. Rather, this account of time as a substance motivates reexamining, from a new perspective, the issues that give rise to these familiar questions, and from a basis—a theory of time per se—that can be accepted by all. This account is central to a framework for the metaphysics of time that provides the means to formulate every question about time and any temporal phenomenon more perspicuously, stripped of metaphor, so that it can be answered literally.

What these easy answers to perennial questions about time show is that the issues prompting them are not about time per se, but about *the world in*

---

[9] The context and purpose of my discussion of time differ so greatly from those of Newton's discussion that I doubt there are more than merely superficial connections between his account of *absolute time* and my account of time as a necessarily existing substance—especially given the account of temporal reality I present in Parts III and IV. Certainly nothing I say about time directly supports any conclusion about space.

time. The world in time—*temporal reality*—is those things in the world that are ontologically dependent on time, to wit, those that are able to stand in certain relations via time and cannot, given what they are, exist in the absence of it. These questions, therefore, are better understood as being about things in the world and their standing with respect to time, rather than about time itself.

An account of time per se is necessary in order to distinguish time from temporal reality. The real bone of contention concerning the metaphysics of time is what there is, and how these things must be, in order to account for temporal differentiation, the world going from *thus* to *as so*. Seemingly all contemporary discussions of temporal phenomena turn on these particular ontological questions, which pertain to temporal reality (and not time itself). There are two generic ways of answering them associated with two general views of the world in time. In the next four chapters, Part III of this book, I characterize these competing views and demonstrate which one is correct. Doing so contributes to the overarching objective of the present work, which is to acquire a better understanding of *all this*. Such an understanding provides insight into how the world goes from *thus* to *as so* and, hence, into how anything, including inquiry, can *happen* at all.

PART III
A GENERAL ACCOUNT OF TEMPORAL REALITY

The Heterogeneity of the World in Time

6
Two General Views of Temporal Reality

In Part II of this book, I present a method, original inquiry, capable of solving the distinctive problem of metaphysics. Solving this problem provides both an account of what a thing is—a natured entity—and what the world is, to wit, no thing itself, but rather all the natured entities there are (including the relations in which these things stand). This account of what a thing is provides principles that are the guidelines for all inquiry into any thing or into any structural phenomenon, that is, arrangement of things. In taking up original inquiry, one confronts a diverse array of things, an array that is *thus*; in taking up original inquiry again, one confronts a distinct diverse array, one that is *as so*. There are, then, distinct modes of differentiation in the world: the one apparent in the diverse array that is *thus* and the one apparent in the world going from *thus* to *as so*. The first mode is accounted for merely by the many things there are. The second, temporal differentiation, is ultimately accounted for by time itself and the moments it yields and orders. Time, therefore, is a thing; more specifically, a substance, i.e., a non-qualitative particular, one that, as I argue above, is necessarily existent, simple, and abstract. It is this substance, time, that must be the initial focus of a critical metaphysics of time.

This plain theory of time arises via original inquiry and so is supposed to be ecumenical. Any inquirer must accept temporal differentiation—the world going from *thus* to *as so*—and that this phenomenon must be explained by means of some thing(s) or other in the world. Time is just the thing that ultimately accounts for this phenomenon. As discussed above, however, this ecumenical theory seems to resolve summarily many of the disputes traditionally associated with the metaphysics of time. The ease with which it resolves these perennial disputes might raise doubts about the theory. The problem here, though, is not with this account of time, which is minimal and should not be controversial; it is, rather, with how these disputes have been conceived.

The perennial disputes regarding the metaphysics of time are universally characterized in terms of time per se and whether it has or lacks certain

Time and the World. M. Oreste Fiocco, Oxford University Press. © Oxford University Press 2024.
DOI: 10.1093/oso/9780197777107.003.0006

features. The actual bases of these disputes are more complicated, pertaining to how things in the world relate to and because of time, rather than to time itself. The disputes concern those things whose existence depends on time, what I call *temporal reality*. More exactly, they concern the *structure in temporal reality*: the extent of these things whose existence depends on time and the relations among them. When characterized in terms of time itself, not only is the content of these disputes distorted, what in the world incites them is lost, leaving one with no guide to their resolution. As a result, the disputes seem intractable, forcing a choice between two appealing sorts of view. The theory of time I propound in Chapter 5 does not in itself resolve any of these perennial disputes. It does, however, provide the means of revealing what they really are about and common ground from which to approach them.

This chapter begins with an account of temporal reality, an ecumenical one that is the natural accompaniment to the account of time itself presented above. With these two accounts, there is a foundation for widespread agreement regarding the metaphysics of time. Yet modern discussions of the metaphysics of time, from their outset, have been premised on an unchallenged divide, thus suggesting irresolvable tension at the heart of this field of inquiry. I canvass the different ways this divide is presented, ways that give rise to the familiar lines of division among those who engage in such inquiry. This canvass reveals a number of seemingly disparate issues underlying the perennial disputes in the field. No one of these issues is principal. Nonetheless, there is a single incitement for these disputes. It comes from one's very engagement with *all this*. Confronting the world in original inquiry, one encounters temporal differentiation, the world going from *thus* to *as so*. In this confrontation, one can experience equally both inconstancy in the world and constancy: it is given that things go from *thus* to *as so* and yet, once they do, when things are *as so*, that it is appropriate to accept that they were—or, in some sense, *are*—as they were when demonstrated by 'thus' is undeniable.

What underlies all the perennial disputes in discussions of the metaphysics of time is the attempt to accommodate both this inconstancy and constancy in an account of time and the world. What leads to dispute is disagreement about the things or structure needed to do so, and the corresponding controversy regarding which of these two phenomena, inconstancy and constancy, is primary in an account of the metaphysics of time. This disagreement is what gives rise to the proliferation of issues mentioned above, and examining these enables one to discern two generic approaches to accounting for temporal phenomena based on two general views of the structure in temporal reality. The opposition between these two views is the basis of the overarching dialectic in discussions of the metaphysics of time. The real bone of contention in this field, the one that informs the key disputes herein, is which of these two incompatible general views of the world in time is the correct one. The main purpose of this chapter is to make explicit the two views and their importance in modern discussions of the metaphysics of time.

§6.1. Time in the World, the World in Time

The world is not a thing, but rather a plurality of them. Indeed, the world comprises all the things there are. In the world, this all-encompassing structure, every thing is natured, constrained in its being and, through this being, interacting with other things in prescribed ways, thereby constraining these others. Each of these natured entities provides the ontological basis of a partial explanation for how the world is as it is. Time underlies an explanation for how the world is differentiated in going from *thus* to *as so*. Time is, therefore, in the world.

§6.1.1. What temporal reality is

Each thing is related to every other, at least to the extent that each is among *all this*; everything in the world co-exists. As natured, however, each thing is related to certain others more intimately than merely existing with it. One thing, given what it is, might require the existence of some unique distinct thing or the existence of some instance(s) or other of some kind of thing. This family of relations, whereby one thing, natured as it is, must exist with some other(s) are relations of *ontological dependence*. These relations are crucial to the essential and necessary connections among things in the world and, hence, to the integrity of the structure in reality.[1]

Since time is a necessary existent, there is nothing that could exist in its absence—nothing can exist without what must be. Nonetheless, there are some things that must exist in the presence of time, not merely because time cannot fail to exist, but because what these things are requires the existence of time. The connection between them and time is not merely incidental, but

---

[1] See Tahko and Lowe 2015 for a useful overview of this family of relations.

determined by their being natured as they are. Such things are, then, ontologically (or existentially) dependent on time. Consideration of what time itself is indicates what these ontologically dependent entities are.

Time is the thing that underlies an account of how the world is differentiated in going from *thus*, at one moment, to *as so*, at another. By being the source of each moment and, hence, the thing that determines the order of any moments, time enables things to go from *thus* to *as so*. Merely being the source of a thing is not sufficient for the latter to be ontologically dependent on the former (thus, for example, each human person can exist in the absence of one or both parents). What makes one thing ontologically dependent on another is the one being so natured as to be incapable of existing without the other. A moment is the thing crucial to an account both of how a thing that could be ever so many ways—many of them mutually exclusive—is actually only some consistent group of these and of how that thing can then be ways incompatible with that. What a moment is, then, is the thing that enables certain entities to exist in a world with time and also enables such an entity to undergo change. In light of this, the most obvious example of a thing ontologically dependent on time is a moment. Each moment is rigidly existentially dependent on time itself, that is, no moment, given what it is, could exist in the absence of the unique thing that time is.

Considering moments, there are supposed to be relations that, ultimately, hold only between such things, namely, the putative converse dyadic relations, *earlier than* and *later than*. These relations, with time, are presumed to order any moments that exist. There is supposed to be, as well, the relation that, ultimately, holds only between a moment and those things constrained to be the consistent group of ways they are, among all the incompatible ways they could be, by that moment, that is, the relation that holds between a moment and each thing that exists *at* it. This is the indeterminately polyadic relation, *simultaneous with*. None of these relations could have instances without moments and although each might, perhaps, exist without instances, what each is is still, in the first place, a relation involving moments. Since there could be no moments without time, the relations are associated closely enough with time that it is quite plausible that they are rigidly ontologically dependent on it. Each is, then, a *temporal relation*.

Moreover, there are putative properties that are supposed to be borne, ultimately, only by moments. There is the property *presentness* (or *being present*), which is supposed to be had by this moment, now. There is, as well, *pastness* (or *being past*) and *futurity* (or *being future*). These are properties supposed to be had by moments that are, respectively, earlier than and later than now. There is much debate as to whether these properties are absolute, that is, monadic—and so a moment would be future, present, or past simpliciter—or whether they are relative—and so a moment would be only future-at-*m*, present-at-m, past-at-*m* (where *m* is some moment). Setting this debate aside, as with temporal relations, none of these properties could have instances without moments and although each might, perhaps, exist without instances, each is still a property of a moment. Since there could be no moments without time, the putative properties are associated closely enough with time that it is quite plausible that they are rigidly ontologically dependent on it. For this reason, each is a *temporal property*.

Another class of things ontologically dependent on time are those that change (or could). A *mutable thing* can change from being one way to a contradictory way and so has, per se, the capacity to be contradictory ways. In itself, such a thing is neither of two contradictory ways (with respect to all the ways it might be); it could be both. A mutable thing has to be one way or the other, though, to make a determinate contribution to the world, as each thing must. Hence, there has to be some other entity that constrains that mutable thing to make it be, for every contradictory pair of ways it might be, one of those two ways. The entity that provides this constraint is a moment. So each mutable thing must be significantly related to a moment—it must exist *at* one—if it is to be in the world at all. By constraining mutable entities to be but some of the ways they are capable of being, moments enable change. This is why a mutable thing can go from being one way at one moment to an incompatible way at a distinct moment.

Consider an apple. It can change from being red to being not-red, e.g., brown. The apple, per se, has the capacity to be both ways, but is (in itself) neither. An apple at no moment, *per impossibile*, would be neither red nor not-red. Since any apple must make a determinate contribution to the world—and, hence, must be red or not-red—it must be constrained by something in order to do so. What constrains it is a moment, and so any apple must exist at a moment. By being red *at* m_1 and being not-red *at* m_2, the apple changes. The same holds for any mutable thing. Therefore, a mutable thing must exist *at* and, thus, *with* some moment or other; a mutable thing is generically ontologically dependent on moments. Consequently, a mutable thing cannot exist without time itself, for any moment ontologically depends on it, and so a mutable entity is, too, rigidly ontologically dependent on time. Furthermore, the particular ways a mutable thing is, the modes of that thing, are ontologically dependent on what they qualify. Since what they qualify, a mutable thing, is ontologically dependent on time, then so, too, are these modes.

Temporal reality is all that is ontologically dependent on time: moments, any temporal relations that exist, any temporal properties that exist, all mutable things and the modes of these things. This structure is the *world in time*. Temporal reality is not itself a thing, but rather a plurality of them, namely, all those that, given what they are, must exist in this significant association with time. Call these things *temporal entities*. Time, given what it is, could not exist in the absence of time and so, in this uninteresting way, is ontologically dependent on itself. Therefore, it, too, is a temporal entity and among the things in temporal reality.

§6.1.2. Ecumenical accounts of time and temporal reality

Time is in the world, it is one of the things amid *all this*. Temporal reality is also in the world; the things it comprises, temporal entities, are subsumed by the structure in reality. (There is also atemporal reality, comprising those things that exist without time. As I discuss in Part IV, atemporal reality is crucial to a comprehensive and satisfactory account of the metaphysics of time.) The account of time I propound above and the account of temporal reality that accompanies it are supposed to be ecumenical—indeed, they should be uncontroversial. The world goes from *thus* to *as so*. This phenomenon is incontestable from original inquiry. Like any phenomenon, the world going from *thus* to *as so* must have an ontological basis among the things in the world. This is one of the principles of radical ontology. Time is simply the thing that is the ultimate basis of an account of this phenomenon. The world is *thus* at one moment and *as so* at a distinct one and time is the thing that yields (and orders) these moments. This account of time, then, arises through original inquiry and so anyone who seeks insight into the world from a point that is wholly critical can and should accept the account. If one were to deny it, one's grounds would have to be metaphysical or epistemological considerations far less secure than the account itself.

The account of temporal reality provided here is similarly uncontroversial and, hence, ecumenical. There is time. I also argue above that there is, undoubtedly, change, and so there is at least one moment and at least one mutable thing (and the ways it is). Thus, temporal reality comprises at least these things. This account of temporal reality is not committed to there being singular relations between the moments whereby the world goes from *thus* to *as so*, nor to these moments bearing distinctively temporal properties. If there are such temporal relations or properties, these would be included in temporal reality—but if there are not, temporal reality, as characterized here, nonetheless exists. Any controversy, then, regarding specifically the existence of such temporal entities (i.e., temporal relations or temporal properties) does not impugn this ecumenical account of the world in time.

Anyone concerned with the metaphysics of time, therefore, can and should recognize both time and temporal reality as characterized here. Moreover, everyone does accept temporal differentiation—the world going from *thus* to *as so*—and should accept the plain account of change presented above, according to which a thing changes when it is one way at one moment and an incompatible way at a distinct one. There is much common ground here: when considering the metaphysics of time, everyone can accept the proposed account of time, the proposed account of the world in time, that is, temporal reality; as well as temporal differentiation and the proposed account of change, two key temporal phenomena. So there is a rather extensive ecumenical basis for a comprehensive and satisfactory account of the metaphysics of time. Nevertheless, despite the potential of this shared basis, there is concerning the metaphysics of time a tremendous amount of contention. This raises two prodding questions: *why there is such controversy regarding the metaphysics of time when there is a basis of universal agreement for so much concerning time* and *how this controversy is to be resolved by means of this basis*. Answering the first of these questions is the goal of this chapter; the second motivates the discussion throughout the rest of the book.

§6.2. Controversy Regarding the Metaphysics of Time

Like with anything, questions arise about time. Attempts to answer these, however, rather than begin by recognizing a wide foundation of common ground—shared accounts of time, temporal reality, temporal differentiation, and change—most often (if not always) begin with a sort of preamble that introduces immediately division. Some of these preambles are as short as could be, a single sentence. Thus:

Metaphysical theories of time divide into *A-theories* and *B-theories*.[2]

and

Contemporary metaphysics of time is shaped by the opposition between A-theorists and B-theorists.[3]

There is no straightforward way of characterizing the views supposed to be on the opposite sides of this divide. Locating the source of the nomenclature here, though, is easy enough. It comes from the font of modern metaphysics of time, J.M.E. McTaggart's seminal 1908 paper, "The Unreality of Time."[4] In this paper, McTaggart observes that:

> Positions in time, as time appears to us prima facie, are distinguished in two ways.... I shall give the name of the *A* series to that series of positions which runs from the far past through the near past to the present, and then from the present through the near future to the far future, or conversely. The series of positions which runs from earlier to later, or conversely, I shall call the *B* series.[5]

Hence, A-theories are supposed to be those that, in some way, prioritize the temporal properties of *pastness*, *presentness*, and *futurity*; B-theories are supposed to be those that, in some way, prioritize the temporal relations of *earlier than* or *later than*.

The crucial difference between temporal properties and relations is taken to be that any moment (and, hence, the things that exist thereat) that bears such a property does so only temporarily, whereas any two moments (and, hence, the things that exist at them) that stand in a temporal relation do so permanently. So a moment that is future is supposed to be so only temporarily. Eventually, it is supposed to become present (and, hence, cease being future) and then past (and, hence, cease being present); whereas a moment that is earlier (later) than another is supposed never to fail to stand in this relation. This difference has led those who consider the metaphysics of time

---

[2] Deasy 2018: 270.
[3] Deng 2013a: 19.
[4] The contents of McTaggart's 1908 paper are largely restated in Chapter 33 of the posthumous second volume of his magnum opus *The Nature of Existence*. It is this later chapter that is often reprinted and which I cite.
[5] McTaggart 1927: 24. This page number refers to the 1993 reprint in Le Poidevin and MacBeath.

to associate some sort of inconstancy with A-theories and some sort of constancy with B-theories. Thus, a typical longer factious preambles states:

> Debate in the philosophy of time is primarily between A-theorists, who think there is an ontological distinction between past, present and future, and that time is dynamic in some sense, and B-theorists, who deny both of these claims.[6]

This "ontological distinction" between past, present, and future is accounted for in terms of different moments bearing the different temporal properties or in terms of differences in *being* simpliciter (because of or in association with the bearing of these different temporal properties). So that, perhaps, what is past is less real than what is going to be or what is present. The connection between these two features of the A-theorist's view are not merely coincidental: the dynamism in time is supposed to be accounted for in terms of the possession of these different temporal properties or ways of being simpliciter. The B-theorist eschews these (non-relational) temporal properties and the sort of dynamism that is supposed to require them for its explanation.

Thus, a long-standing way of accounting for a basic divide in the metaphysics of time is in terms of the priority of temporal properties over temporal relations, or vice versa, in characterizing "time." However, in an era in which ontological issues were often conflated with linguistic ones, this basic disagreement regarding temporal properties and relations was transposed into debate about the sentences most appropriately used to talk about time or the things therein. The inconstancy of moments having temporal properties was equated with the use of sentences with verbs inflected to indicate a perspective required to evaluate their truth, that is, sentences with *tensed* verbs. Sentence types with tensed verbs, for example, "I am typing," have some tokens that are true, some that are false, and such variation was supposed to indicate an inconstant world. Sentence types with tenseless verbs[7] or that are dated, for example, "I am typing at 9:32 AM on October 18, 2016," have tokens that do not vary in truth-value. The aptness of such sentences was supposed to indicate a constant world. Consideration of time and the world was supplanted by consideration of how one thinks or speaks about time and

---

[6] Dyke 2003: 380.
[7] I say more about tenseless verbs in §6.3.2.1.

the world. More specifically, the focus on "positions in time" was replaced with the descriptions of such, and debate about the priority of temporal properties over relations (or vice versa) was replaced with debate about reducibility or translatability of tensed sentences to tenseless ones (or vice versa). This change in focus is illustrated in the following claim:

> [There are] two fundamentally different ways in which we conceive of and talk about time. On the one hand, we conceive of time in a dynamic or tensed way, as being the very quintessence of flux and transiency.... [On the other hand,] is the static or tenseless way of conceiving time, in which the history of the world is viewed in a God-like manner, all events being given at once in a *nunc stans*.[8]

Tense is a feature of language or, more generously, of representations. Nothing in the world that is not representational is or could be tensed. Nevertheless, a conflation of the worldly, i.e., the ontological, and linguistic, i.e., the representational, is codified in D.H. Mellor's influential 1981 book, *Real Time*. On the first page of the book, Mellor states:

> One way and another, tense [i.e., "the distinctions we draw between past, present and future"] covers most of time's metaphysics, for its status is itself the main and most contentious metaphysical question about time.[9]

Mellor soon adds his account of what is supposed to be the basic divide in discussions of the metaphysics of time:

> Distinctions and transitions of tense, between what has been, is and will be past, present and future, divide philosophers into two fundamentally opposed camps. The one, 'tensed', camp takes these distinctions to reflect real nonrelational differences between past, present and future things (events, facts, etc.) ... that is what [those] in the 'tenseless' camp deny.[10]

This idiosyncratic usage of 'tense' became entrenched, to the point where it continued to be used even in an era more hospitable to examining the world itself, an era in which not every metaphysical problem was viewed as a

---

[8] Gale 1967: 65–66.
[9] Mellor 1981: 1.
[10] Mellor 1981: 4.

problem of linguistic representation or conceptualization. Thus, those who clearly distinguish ontological and representational issues still characterize a basic divide in the metaphysics of time in terms of tense:

> An important issue discussed by tensers [i.e., tensed theorists] and detensers [i.e., tenseless theorists] concerns whether temporal properties of a certain sort are exemplified. Some philosophers characterize the debate between tensers and detensers in terms of whether events have monadic temporal properties of presentness, pastness, or futurity (A-properties) or whether the only temporal properties of events are the polyadic properties (relations) of earlier than, later than, and simultaneity (B-relations).[11]

and

> One of the central and most rapidly developing debates in contemporary metaphysics concerns the status of our ordinary division of time into past, present, and future. On one side of the debate stand the *tensed theorists*, who take seriously our intuitive conception of time, expressed metaphorically (or perhaps not so metaphorically) by the picture of time 'flowing'. On the other side stand the *tenseless theorists*, who deny the reality of temporal passage, and take our intuitive conception simply to reflect our perspective on time rather than the nature of time itself.[12]

and more recently and succinctly:

> There are many different theories of time to be found in the literature, but they each fall into one of two broad categories: the *tenseless* theories, on the one hand; and the *tensed* theories on the other.[13]

For some, the terminology has come full circle. Ironically, in his 1998 sequel to *Real Time*, Mellor rejects the use of 'tense' he once promulgated, in favor of McTaggart's original terminology:

---

[11] Smith and Oaklander 1994: 1–2.
[12] LePoidevin 1998: 1.
[13] Bourne 2006b: 3.

In *Real Time* I followed the custom of calling temporal locations like past, present and future 'tenses', while distinguishing them of course from the corresponding forms of English verbs. However as failure to observe this distinction still vitiates much philosophy of time, I here call these locations 'A-times'.[14]

Although they are clearly closely related, focus on these so-called temporal locations—more specifically, on the moments in time that compose them—rather than on the temporal properties these moments are supposed to bear or the temporal relations in which they are supposed to stand, portrays the basic divide in the metaphysics of time in a different way. Thus:

> The following questions go to the heart of the deepest metaphysical disagreement about the nature of time: (1) Are there objective differences between what is past, present, and future? (2) Are present events and things somehow more "real" than those wholly in the past or future?[15]

Those who maintain an affirmative answer to the second question are often called *presentists*. Those who reject an affirmative answer to this question or the first one are called *eternalists* or, sometimes, *four-dimensionalists*.[16] Eternalists hold that what exists prior to this moment, at this moment, now, and subsequent to it all have the very same ontological status. Some, so-called *growing block theorists*, maintain that the past and the present have the same ontological status, one that the future lacks.[17] At least one metaphysician, a *shrinking tree theorist*, maintains that the future and present have the same ontological status, one the past lacks.[18] Some argue that presentists are committed to the (or an) A-theory;[19] some argue that any A-theorist must be a presentist.[20] Some maintain that disagreement regarding the A-theory and B-theory are independent of the issues dividing presentists and eternalists[21] and some do not distinguish the debates at all.[22]

---

[14] Mellor 1998: xi.
[15] Zimmerman 2008: 211.
[16] This use of "four-dimensionalism," which applies to a view of the ontological status of the past, present, and future, should not be confused with the view about the persistence of objects, namely that they exist in time by having distinct temporal parts, of the same name. For discussion and defense of the latter view, see, for example, Heller 1990 and Sider 2001.
[17] See for example Broad 1923 and Tooley 1997.
[18] See McCall 1994, 1976.
[19] See Sider 2001: 15.
[20] Zimmerman 2008: 213–216.
[21] See Rea 2003: 251.
[22] See, for example, Dyke 2003 and C. Williams 1996.

The terminology used in stating what is thought to be the basic divide in the metaphysics of time is even more varied than the foregoing indicates. Some who concentrate on the indubitable inconstancy of the world—as opposed to temporal properties and relations, tensed or tenseless language, or the ontological status of so-called temporal locations—talk of *dynamic theories of time*[23] or *passage theories*. These are set up against a *block theory* of time or a theory of the *manifold*,[24] which take the world to be fundamentally constant.

Surveying these various statements of what is taken to be the primary disagreement regarding the metaphysics of time is helpful propaedeutic because it makes vivid that there is a bewildering terminology employed in stating this disagreement. This terminology is, of course, also used to characterize the issues that exercise those who investigate time and the positions they adopt. Little of this terminology has become standardized, so there are here few terms whose meaning can be taken for granted. Thus, for example, one avowed A-theorist's view might be incompatible with another's and, importantly, there is just no saying, in general, what temporal passage or the relevant dynamism is supposed to be. Since there is this morass of terminology and its associated thicket of issues, the conscientious metaphysician concerned with time and temporal reality must define their terms before trying to make any point. The benefit of propounding a metaphysics of time that begins with original inquiry is that it provides a new perspective on this convolution, a perspective that enables one to extricate the key issues and to express them more perspicuously, in terms of things recognizable from a wholly critical confrontation with *all this*. This is, of course, the practice I adopt above in this work—providing explicit accounts of the world; a thing, in the most general sense; time itself; a moment; and temporal reality that arise from original inquiry—and is a practice I continue below. One upshot of this practice is that some of the most vexed terminology in traditional discussions of the metaphysics of time can be discarded.

This brief survey is also important for a more substantive reason. It seems to show that at the heart of the metaphysics of time is a basic divide between, perhaps, A-theorists and B-theorists or tensed and tenseless theorists or passage and manifold theorists, a divide based on considering the inconstancy and constancy of *time itself*. No thing, time included, could possibly be

---

[23] See, for just a single example, Olson 2009.
[24] See Williams 1951.

essentially both inconstant and constant. The survey suggests, then, an irreconcilable conflict inherent to the metaphysics of time: in providing a theory of time—or the world—it seems one must favor its inconstancy, thereby neglecting its constancy or its constancy, thereby neglecting its inconstancy. Were this so, one of the main objectives of the present work, which is to give a comprehensive and satisfactory account of the metaphysics of time, one that acknowledges both the indubitable inconstancy and the indubitable constancy in the world, would be chimerical.

Note, however, that there is nothing in this survey to indicate that any of these philosophers would deny that the world is *thus* and then *as so* and that there is an ontological basis in the world of this apparent phenomenon. Inspection of the survey, therefore, reveals that despite ostensible disagreement between "theories of *time*" or concerning the "nature of *time*," the issues that have traditionally divided these metaphysicians are not about time per se. They are about the properties that moments bear or the relations in which they stand or the ontological status of moments before or after this one, now, or the number of moments. In other words, the issues pertain to *things ontologically dependent on time and how they are arranged*. Therefore, any disagreement here is not about time itself, but about the extent of temporal reality and its structure. So the real question is not whether time itself can be both inconstant and constant, for obviously it cannot be; rather, the question is whether in *all this*, the world with its enormous complexity, there are the things to account consistently for the indubitable inconstancy and constancy in the world. Looking at the issues in this way, there is no reason to presume they arise from irremediable conflict, an unbridgeable divide. Recognizing this should make one more optimistic regarding the prospects of a comprehensive and satisfactory account of the metaphysics of time.

§6.3. The Real Bone of Contention Concerning the Metaphysics of Time

Even if it is not about time per se, there is a schism among those who investigate the metaphysics of time. The conflict between these metaphysicians might not be irremediable, but if it is to be overcome, a clearer view of it is needed. This raises the key question of what underlies all this controversy. In the survey above, several disputes emerge in connection to a primary divide that is taken for granted, ones regarding the properties that moments bear versus the relations in which they stand; the language one uses to talk about temporal reality; the number of moments; the ontological status of moments before or after this one, now; and the genuine dynamism—or lack thereof—in the world. One might think that one of these disputes has priority over the rest so that by resolving that dispute, the others are thereby settled. But this is not the case. Although there are some obvious connections between them, many of the connections between the disputes are not straightforward and certain of them are independent of each other. Thus, for example, if there is an A- or B-series (it does not matter which), then it clearly follows that there is not just a single moment, but many. However, if there is an A-series it does not follow, as many have presumed, that there is genuine dynamism in the world. If there is but a single moment, nothing at all follows about the appropriateness of tensed or tenseless language (or about dynamism in the world).

One does not find, then, a neat division of those investigating the metaphysics of time among these traditional disputes. The only point that seems uncontroversial, beyond that time (however it is regarded) is real, is that there is a basic divide among the philosophers who examine time or temporal reality. The divide has something to do with the inconstancy and constancy evident in one's engagement with the world—this much is clear—but what exactly the crucial problem is is not.

Perusing the foregoing short history of modern metaphysics of time in an effort to find this problem, the real bone of contention here, the traditional disputes might seem rather trivial. Why there is so much disagreement about whether moments or the things at them have temporal properties or just stand in temporal relations is perplexing, given that it is hardly obvious they could not have one without the other, as is why some disagree about whether there are many moments or just one. Likewise, what exactly is at stake among those who defend some sort of "dynamism" in the world—given that no one would deny that things are constantly changing—is difficult to see. How such arcane issues could provoke the discord they do is hard to fathom. What is missing is the incitement for taking up these issues in the first place. Perhaps the different disputes are incited differently. Still, there is supposed to be a single great divide among metaphysicians examining time. This suggests that there is a single source of all these disputes. Uncovering such a source would reveal the basis of all the controversy regarding the metaphysics of time.

To be the source of so many disputes and to lead to what is taken to be a basic divide among those who inquire into the metaphysics of time, whatever motivates these disputes must be closely related to time itself or to one's experience of it. This raises the question of what is so vexing about *all this* with respect to time. Whatever phenomenon underlies these disputes must be widely accepted—yet vexatious—if it is to be the basis of so much controversy.

§6.3.1. Experience of inconstancy and constancy

In confronting the world in original inquiry, one experiences it as being *thus*... and *as so*. *All this* is one way (at one moment) and then a different way (at another). This incontestable phenomenon—temporal differentiation—reveals time itself. Time is the thing that in the end underlies an account of temporal differentiation.

One can focus on distinct aspects of temporal differentiation. If one focuses on the differences among things when they go from *thus* to *as so*, one is struck by the inconstancy in the world. This inconstancy is universally acknowledged, embraced by proponents of all the competing views regarding the metaphysics of time. The awareness of this inconstancy has traditionally been characterized as a sense of *flow* or *passage*. Thus, D.C. Williams asserts we are "immediately and poignantly involved in the jerk and whoosh of process, the felt flow of one moment into the next"[25] and J.J.C. Smart maintains "certainly we *feel* that time flows."[26] Tim Maudlin states that there is a "manifest fact that the world is given to us as changing, and time as passing."[27] Bradford Skow characterizes the awareness by noting, "[o]f all the experiences I will ever have, some of them are special. Those are the ones that I am having NOW. All those others are ghostly and insubstantial,"[28] and Laurie Paul observes, "I . . . feel the cool breeze on my face. I feel the freshness of the cool breeze *now*, and, as the breeze dies down, I notice that time is passing."[29]

However, if one focuses on things being *thus* when they are *thus* or on how the world was, when demonstrated by 'thus,' when it is now *as so*, one is struck by the constancy in the world. For given that the world is now *thus*, to regard it as such at *this* moment, even once the world is *as so* is always

---

[25] Williams 1951: 465–466.
[26] Smart 1980: 3.
[27] Maudlin 2007: 135.
[28] Skow 2009: Section IV.
[29] Paul 2010: 333. For further acknowledgment of this experience of inconstancy, see, for example, Schlesinger 1982: 501, 515 and Mellor 1998: 66–67.

appropriate. Of course, this is not to say that the world does not cease to be *thus*—obviously it does, it is now *as so*. Nevertheless, to regard the world as *thus* when it is is always appropriate, and so that the world is as it is at this moment is always true. This constancy in the world is less celebrated, indeed, less discussed than the inconstancy, but is no less striking. It is less remarkable (or remarked upon) because it might seem trivial, and so is more taken for granted than examined. Surely the statement of it seems trivial: however a thing is now, at moment, m, that the thing is just as it is, at m, must always be true. But if this is so, then there must be some thing(s) in the world to account for this constancy.

Inconstancy and constancy are incompatible; what is constant is stable in a way that is antithetical to its being inconstant. The source of all the controversy, of each of the familiar disputes, regarding the metaphysics of time is, therefore, time itself, for time gives rise to equally compelling experiences of inconstancy and constancy. The awareness of these phenomena are indisputable and undisputed. Like any other phenomenon, they must have some basis in the world. Constancy, no less than inconstancy, must be explicable in terms of the things there are. The world is not itself a thing (it is a plurality of them), so there is no question of the world itself being inconstant or constant. Nor is the incisive question whether the things in the world are ultimately inconstant or constant, because some might be the former while others are the latter. The crucial problem is to provide an account of how things must be or be related—that is, how things must be structured—in order to explicate both the striking inconstancy and constancy in the world. In one way or another, this problem gives rise to the familiar disputes in discussions of the metaphysics of time. Which of two generic approaches to adopt in order to resolve the problem is the primary bone of contention in the metaphysics of time.

§6.3.2. Two general views regarding the world in time

The key question regarding the metaphysics of time, then, is what is needed, with respect to time and other things in relation to it, to account for the indubitable inconstancy in the world without neglecting the indubitable constancy. This question can be seen to underlie the introduction of the A-theory and the B-theory and to be a significant consideration motivating a distinction between tensed and tenseless theories and so called passage and block (or manifold) theories. Here, finally, is the means to reveal a basic divide between two approaches.

To characterize the one approach as providing "dynamic" theories of an inconstant world and the other as providing "static" theories of a constant one is tempting. But this is incorrect, for no metaphysician who considers time denies the inconstancy in *all this*, at least to the extent of recognizing that things change and come into and go out of existence (in some sense), and that these phenomena have a basis among the things there are. So constancy is compatible with change, and the inconstancy in the world, however it is best understood, is distinct from mere change. What proponents of the two approaches disagree about, then, is not there being inconstancy in the world, but what such inconstancy is, what things are needed to account for it. Therefore, from these two approaches emerge two general views of temporal reality, both of which are supposed to account for inconstancy and constancy and all corollary temporal phenomena. These general views include all the various positions considered above and divide them in a natural, plausible way.

§6.3.2.1. The ontological homogeneity of temporal reality
On one view, the world in time is *ontologically homogeneous*. There are (infinitely) many moments with no peculiarly temporal thing distinguishing any one of these from any other. Each thing in time has a permanent existence: each moment exists without ceasing to be and whatever exists at any moment exists ceaselessly at all moments it exists. On this view of temporal reality, all the many moments of time—and everything that exists at them—are equally real. So when the world is *thus* and then *as so*, what exists when it IS *thus*—that moment and everything thereat—IS just as real, just as much a part of *all this*, as the moment when the world IS *as so* (and everything thereat). Here I introduce a convention adopted by proponents of this view in their effort to make it more perspicuous.

Verbs in ALL CAPS are supposed to indicate a tenseless use of language, that is, one that does not require a certain perspective on the world in time for the proper evaluation of that language. Indeed, the convention is supposed to remove any suggestion that there is a privileged or even distinctive perspective on temporal reality. This is thought to be important because tensed language does require a certain perspective for its proper evaluation, and this need seems to indicate, misleadingly, according to the proponent of this view, not only a privileged perspective on the world in time but a certain sort of inconstancy in it. Thus, a sentence with a past-tensed verb (e.g., "I was sitting") is true only if it aptly characterizes the world prior to this moment, now, and one with a future-tensed verb (e.g., "I will be sitting") is true only if it aptly characterizes the world subsequent to this moment, now, and a sentence token with a present-tense verb (e.g., "I am sitting") is true only if it aptly characterizes things as they now are—yet a different token (referring to the same things) of the same type of any of these sentences might be false. A sentence with a tenseless verb—for example, I SIT (at some moment, m)—is true if it aptly characterizes me at m, regardless of when m occurs and if this sentence is ever true it always is. Such sentences, therefore, are supposed to capture the homogeneity and constancy of temporal reality. (In subsequent discussion, I sometimes use, for emphasis, ALL CAPS for tenseless verbs, but in most places, I let context indicate when the verbs are supposed to be tenseless.)

On this view of temporal reality, there is no distinctively temporal difference between the world when it is *thus* and the world when it is *as so*. There is, then, no temporal property that the world (or any thing in it) has when it is *as so* that distinguishes *all this* from when it was referred to with 'thus.' In particular, when the world is *thus*, this moment is not (simply) present and when it is *as so*, this moment, now, is not (simply) present with the former moment (simply) past. Consequently, one who holds this position denies that any special, that is, distinctively temporal, monadic properties are needed to provide a satisfactory account of any phenomenon. Rather, one maintains that temporal reality is just an array of equally real moments standing in permanent temporal relations. There are differences among moments, of course, in terms of the identities of those moments and exactly what entities exist at them and how those things are arranged at those moments. There is, though, no thing—no property of presentness or anything else—that in any way privileges one moment over another. The operative notion of *ontological*, therefore, in the ontological homogeneity of temporal reality pertains to the temporal entities, like moments, temporal properties, temporal relations, in the world and their status.

One who maintains that the world when *thus* has the same ontological status as the world when now *as so* denies that anything ever comes into or goes out of being simpliciter. One who denies this maintains, to the contrary, that at no moment does anything that exists in time (i.e., at any moment) absolutely fail to be part of the world. This is not to say that on this view each thing *always* exists, for there can indeed be moments at which a thing does not exist. For instance, neither Eleanor Roosevelt, nor any dinosaur exists *now*. Nevertheless, even now Eleanor Roosevelt and each dinosaur EXISTS (tenselessly) at other moments (ones prior to this one, now). So what is *thus* is no less real, and just as it is, even when things are *as so*—the world is unceasingly *thus* when it is *thus* and *as so* when it is *as so* (and likewise for every other moment). Temporal reality is also ontologically homogeneous in the sense that the past, the moments (and things at them) that exist earlier than the moment of this context; the present, the moment of this context and everything that exists at it; and the future, the moments (and things at them) that exist later than the moment of this context, all comprise the same sorts of things, to wit, moments and the temporal entities that exist at them. Although some maintain that on this view there is no change (as McTaggart himself did), this is clearly false. If change just is one thing being a certain way at one moment and being an incompatible way at a different one, then change—and to this extent inconstancy—can be fully accounted for even in a world in which temporal reality is ontologically homogeneous.

There are at least a couple specific versions of the general view on which temporal reality is ontologically homogeneous,[30] and proponents of this general view disagree regarding the best account of certain details of it. There are, for example, variants that disagree about how best to account for what makes true the true claims about the world in time; thus, there are so-called token-reflexive theories and date theories.[31] There are also variants that disagree about how things exist through time, that is, how things persist; thus, there are so-called endurantists, perdurantists, and exdurantists.[32] Such disagreements, however, are posterior to the basic divide in accounts of the metaphysics of time. Proponents of these specific versions and variants all accept the ontological homogeneity of the world in time, and all who adopt this generic view maintain that every temporal phenomenon, including the experiences of inconstancy and constancy, can be accounted for in terms of a homogeneous structure of temporal entities.

§6.3.2.2. The ontological heterogeneity of temporal reality
Proponents of the second general view of the world in time deny that a homogeneous structure of temporal entities is sufficient to account for all temporal phenomena. The paramount feature of this opposing view is that according

---

[30] For one that is rather outré, see Tallant 2015.
[31] See the papers in Part I of Oaklander and Smith 1994 for illustrations of these different theories.
[32] See Haslanger and Kurtz 2006 for illustrations of these different accounts of persistence.

to it there are significant structural and, hence, ontological differences in the world when it goes from being *thus* to *as so*. Given that this general view is based on difference, it admits of much greater variation than does the view on which the world in time is ontologically homogeneous; the unifying feature of all these many versions is that the world in time is *ontologically heterogeneous*.

Since this view is so multifarious, it is not amenable to pithy characterization (beyond a statement of its unifying feature). Some of its proponents maintain that things *exist* simpliciter in different ways, that what is prior (or subsequent) to this moment is real, yet has a different way of being than what now exists. Other proponents maintain that moments have different temporal properties; so this moment has a property—presentness—that it did not have prior to now and, momentarily, will lose this property and take on a different one, viz., pastness. Others maintain that the ontological differences among moments are more significant, holding that there are things that come into or go out of existence *simpliciter*, that is, absolutely, in the sense that something, which in no sense existed, can come into being at a moment or that a thing can cease to be in every way and, hence, bear no properties or stand in any relation to anything (including any moment). Yet others maintain that there is but one moment and nothing whatsoever before or after it or that this moment, now, and what is prior to it (including moments and the things existing at them) are equally real, and that there is nothing at all subsequent to this moment. All such views recognize differences in the extent of temporal reality or the structure among temporal entities when the world goes from *thus* to *as so* and, therefore, take the world in time to be ontologically heterogeneous.

§6.4. The Primary Issue Regarding the Metaphysics of Time

There is a great deal agreed upon (at least tacitly) by those who consider the metaphysics of time: there is time itself; there are things that, given what they are, cannot exist in the absence of time and so there is temporal reality; and, crucially, merely by engaging the world—*all thi*s—one can experience both inconstancy and constancy. These experiences of inconstancy and constancy are both indubitable. All this can (or should) be agreed upon. Indeed, both general views of the world in time, and all their many versions, are consistent with the ecumenical accounts of time and temporal reality presented above (§6.1.2.). Still, there is an enormous amount of contention among those who would provide an account of the world in time. The primary issue here, the one that constrains one's positions with respect to all other issues pertaining to time and temporal reality, concerns how to account for one's experience of inconstancy while not neglecting the experience of constancy (or vice versa). There are two approaches to doing so based on the two general views of temporal reality. So the real bone of contention concerning the metaphysics of time is which of these two is correct.

The two views regarding temporal reality are clearly incompatible. In light of their differences, what would motivate one to adopt the view that temporal reality is ontologically homogeneous is perhaps clear: one's experience of a constant world, in which how things are at any given permanent moment is unchangeable. Likewise, the motivation for the view that temporal reality is ontologically heterogeneous is one's experience of an inconstant world, one in which things are dynamic and any given moment appears to be transient. But if one accepts what is beyond dispute, that *the world is both inconstant and constant*, how to proceed might not be clear. One's starting point presumably turns on whether one decides to regard constancy or inconstancy as the fundamental or, at least, dominant feature of a world that includes time.

Since, however, one's experiences of constancy and of inconstancy are both beyond doubt, to neglect either when considering *all this* can lead only to an objectionable metaphysics of time and account of the world more generally. Fortunately, the appearance of a dilemma here is based on a false assumption. This is the assumption that how the world is, given that it includes time, must be accounted for entirely in terms of temporal reality, that is, time and the things ontologically dependent on it. This is false. There is more to the world than the world in time—what more there is must be included in a complete account of *all this*, a world that is genuinely constant and inconstant. One way of recognizing this complete account of the world is via a comprehensive and satisfactory account of the metaphysics of time. The first step toward attaining the latter is to determine which of the two general views of temporal reality is correct. This is the task of the next chapter.

7
Against the Ontological Homogeneity of Temporal Reality

There are two general views of the structure in temporal reality, that is, of the extent of those things ontologically dependent on time and the relations in which they stand. On one view, this structure is ontologically homogeneous in that there is a boundless array of equally real eternal moments, and the things existing at each, standing in permanent temporal relations (*earlier than* or *later than*) and nothing peculiarly temporal to distinguish any one moment from another. On the other view, this structure is ontologically heterogeneous. As noted in the previous chapter, and as becomes clearer in subsequent discussion, there is a great variety of specific versions of this generic view. The experience of temporal differentiation—*all this* going from *thus* to *as so*—reveals irrefragable inconstancy and constancy in the world. The primary issue regarding the metaphysics of time is how to account for both this inconstancy and constancy (without neglecting either). Since the general view of temporal reality one adopts determines the things available to explain all temporal phenomena, the first step toward resolving this issue is determining which of the two generic views of the world in time is correct.

In this chapter, I argue that the world in time is not ontologically homogeneous. I do so by examining the very phenomenon that both reveals time in original inquiry and motivates the two general views of temporal reality, namely, temporal differentiation. The world going from *thus* to *as so*, like any phenomenon, must have a basis among the things there are. I examine this phenomenon to discern its complexity and for insight into what underlies it. There are certain dialectical advantages to evaluating first the view that temporal reality is ontologically homogeneous, so I start with it. I discuss the *passage of time* as it has traditionally been understood and maintain, as many have, that an account of temporal differentiation in terms of passage is misguided. I then reflect on what appears to be the minimal structure needed to account for temporal differentiation and one's experience of it, viz., distinct moments bearing temporal relations, to determine whether this is indeed a satisfactory basis. I show that it is not and, therefore, no account of the world in time on which it is ontologically homogeneous can be successful. This view of temporal reality is incompatible with one's experience of temporal differentiation and the world in time more generally; moreover, it cannot account for a certain inconstancy in the world, namely, the crucial transition in temporal differentiation. I close the chapter by considering how these decisive shortcomings of the view that the world in time is ontologically homogeneous, which had been the predominant one for decades and remains quite popular, might have been overlooked in previous discussions of the metaphysics of time.

§7.1. Arbitrating the Pivotal Dispute

Dispute between proponents of the two opposing general views of the structure in temporal reality is the overarching dialectic in discussions of the metaphysics of time. Clearly, if one is going to propound a comprehensive and satisfactory account of the metaphysics of time, one must arbitrate this pivotal dispute. This raises the question of how to do so. There is really only one way to settle the dispute definitively, and that is by examining the phenomenon that motivates it in the first place. However, to make this apparent, I examine some other considerations that are supposed to tell in favor of one general view or against the other.

§7.1.1. One's position must have an appropriate basis

If one's main theoretical interest is not time per se or temporal reality, which of the two opposing views of the world in time is correct might be less important than one's presuppositions that lead one to choose between them. In the present context, however, one is not theorizing about some phenomenon that requires—as so many do—assumptions about how the world in time is structured. Here, the object is precisely this structure.

Thus, simply to accept that the world in time is ontologically homogeneous because one takes this view to follow from empirical science will not do. Although the view is certainly suggested by prevalent physical theories, viz., ones employing the notion of space-time, these theories do not require that temporal reality be ontologically homogeneous. Any empirical theory is open to different interpretations; an apt interpretation must be constrained by what is in the world as revealed by original inquiry, a wholly critical investigation. Similarly, to accept that temporal reality is ontologically heterogeneous because "common sense" demands one recognize that time passes or because it is "intuitive" that there is something distinctive about this moment, now, will not do. What, if anything, common sense is or that there are the probative seemings that would justify such talk of intuition is not at all clear. Invoking either, then, as a conclusive means of arbitrating this pivotal dispute is inapt, and certainly misguided in an investigation, such as this, that is supposed to be as critical as can be.

If one aspires to an entirely critical metaphysics of time, one's grounds for accepting one of the two opposing views of temporal reality must be of the right sort. Given that the objective here is insight into the structure of the world in time, one's justification for accepting one of these two views must come from engagement with time itself or the things ontologically dependent on it. If this is so, a good deal of modern philosophical discussion of time is of no help in arbitrating the pivotal dispute. Much of this discussion has focused on the linguistic means of representing temporal reality rather than the structure represented. This is clear from some of the best-known and influential work in the area.[1] Certain philosophers were explicit about the use of linguistic considerations in the effort to gain metaphysical insight. For example, A.N. Prior states: "I don't deny that there are genuine metaphysical problems, but I think you have to talk about grammar at least a little bit in order to solve most of them."[2] Decades later, Peter Ludlow claims: "[w]e can gain insight into the metaphysics of time by studying the semantics of natural language,"[3] and adds that the goal of his book is "to illustrate an approach to metaphysics in which semantical theory and the philosophy of language are central."[4] Most philosophers, though, took up this semantic methodology without acknowledging it.

Central to this semantic methodology is the issue of whether tensed sentences can be translated into tenseless ones or, in a later development of it,[5] whether tenseless truth-conditions can be given for tensed sentences.

---

[1] See, for example, Broad 1938; Gale 1967; Prior 1968/2003; Mellor 1981; Smith 1993; Oaklander and Smith 1994: Part I; Ludlow 1999. Some still take this approach when investigating the metaphysics of time. Thus, for more-recent examples, see Johnson 2013; Beer 2010; Torre 2009.
[2] Prior 1968: 11.
[3] Ludlow 1999: xvi.
[4] Ludlow 1999: xvii.
[5] See Oaklander and Smith 1994.

However, considerations of translatability or truth-conditions are idle with respect to the pivotal dispute concerning the metaphysics of time. The world of things constrains language, the means of representing *all this*—not vice versa. In order to interpret correctly the sentences representing some phenomenon (or thing), one must have a prior understanding of how that phenomenon is. One's account of it, therefore, must be based on and informed by one's engagement with the phenomenon itself, rather than the language used to represent it. These considerations apply to any representation of any thing(s) in the world. So no semantic issue can reveal how things in the world are; a fortiori, no such issue can be of use in settling which of the two general views of the world in time is correct.

If one is to settle whether temporal reality is ontologically homogeneous or heterogeneous, one must engage the things in the world. The relevant considerations, then, must be ontological, concerning time itself or the things ontologically dependent on it. A number of such considerations have traditionally been broached to refute (or demonstrate) one of the two general views of the world in time. There is, for example, McTaggart's Paradox (§8.1.1.1.), which is supposed to show that there is no A-series. Some take the paradox to demonstrate that the world in time must be ontologically homogeneous. Yet even if the paradox does show that there is no A-series, this merely tells against certain specific versions of the general view that temporal reality is ontologically heterogeneous—to wit, those committed to an A-series—not against the general view itself. Likewise with the chestnut about the rate of time's passage.[6] Many have argued that time cannot pass for there is no rate at which it might do so and, on this basis, have concluded that temporal reality must be ontologically homogeneous.[7] But even if time cannot pass, this only tells against those specific versions of the view that the world in time is ontologically heterogeneous on which time is supposed to pass. There are versions of this general view that reject the passage of time (in the relevant sense), so this concern about its rate does not refute the general view.[8]

---

[6] See Le Poidevin 2003: 125–126; Williams 1951: 106 (page number refers to the reprint in Gale 1967); Smart 1967; 1949: 485; Broad 1938: 124 (page number refers to the reprint in Gale 1967). For more-recent discussion, see Skow 2012a, 2012b; Raven 2011; Olson 2009; Phillips 2009.

[7] Some maintain there is no problem here, for time passes at one unit of time per unit of time. See, for example, Prior 1958: 244; 1968: 7; Markosian 1993: 843.

[8] For other considerations that might undermine specific versions of the view that the world in time is ontologically heterogeneous, but, even if they do, do not impugn the general view, see Fine 2005 and Deng 2013b. The arguments of McTaggart, Fine, and Deng are presented as "philosophical arguments against the A-theory" in Deasy 2018.

Unlike the preceding considerations, which are supposed to support the general view that temporal reality is ontologically homogeneous (by undermining views erroneously taken to be its contradictory), there is another consideration that is supposed to tell against the view that the world in time is ontologically homogeneous. This is A.N. Prior's famous "Thank goodness that's over!" argument.[9] Examination of this argument, however, reveals that it turns either on semantic considerations or on the emotional attitudes or affective states that often accompany one's experience of the world in time.[10] The former, I argue above, are idle in this context; the latter are representational and so require interpretation in a way that renders them similarly fruitless as a means of ontological insight. Hence, this sort of argument is of no help in arbitrating the pivotal dispute between the two general views of the world in time.

The traditional ontological considerations simply do not do justice to the generality of the dispute here. They presuppose too much about the structure of the world in time to undermine a general view that need not include that specific structure. The appropriate basis for arbitrating this pivotal dispute must come from general considerations arising immediately from one's experience of temporal reality, ones that, if they are to be compelling, proponents of both views of the world in time must accept. One should begin, therefore, with the very phenomenon that incites the dispute in the first place: the experience of the world going from *thus* to *as so*.

§7.2. The Experience of Temporal Differentiation

When one confronts *all this* in original inquiry, one is given a world differentiated in discrete ways. One is first given a diverse array, the world as *thus*; yet this diverse array is presently superseded by a different one, the world *as so*. Time is the thing that enables temporal differentiation, this second arrangement of things whereby distinctions in the world are apparent, the one made evident in *all this* going from *thus* to *as so*. Time does this by yielding moments: one at which the world is *thus*, another at which

---

[9] Prior 1959: 17. This brief argument has received much attention, generating a good deal of literature. See, for example, the papers collected in Part III of Oaklander and Smith 1994; Dyke and Maclaurin 2002; La Vine 2016.

[10] For the latter interpretation, see Dyke and Maclaurin 2002.

it is *as so*. To experience these two modes of differentiation is to engage directly with temporal reality. Doing so raises the question of how exactly the moments involved are related so as to give rise to this singular experience of temporal differentiation.

This singular experience is ever-present and inescapable and, hence, utterly familiar. In fact, as noted above (§6.3.1.), it is universally acknowledged by those who consider time. A customary account of the experience is in terms of the *passage of time*, which is taken to be the sequential change of (temporary) temporal properties by moments: a moment is future, becomes present, then becomes past. So, in experiencing temporal differentiation, one is supposed to experience this moment, now, when the world is *thus*, as present; then to experience the moment as past as one experiences a distinct moment—when the world is *as so*—as present. (This latter moment is supposed to have been future when the former was present.) This account, which entails a specific version of the view on which temporal reality is ontologically heterogeneous, is quite controversial. Since the phenomenon it is supposed to explain is not, the experience in question should not be characterized as the *experience of passage*. It is, though, sometimes called the experience *as of* passage.[11] This locution might mislead, given its suggestion of passage, so it is best to avoid it. Hence, one should just regard this singular and all-important experience of temporal reality as that of temporal differentiation.

This experience of temporal differentiation is complex and so is its ontological basis. Obviously, it involves (at least) two moments. Also, it gives rise to the pivotal dispute concerning the metaphysics of time because it has two aspects: one revealing the inconstancy in the world and one revealing constancy. The complexity of temporal differentiation is shown in other ways, too. At its simplest, the phenomenon is the world going from *thus* to *as so*. This is how one first encounters temporal differentiation and how I advert to it many times above, for considering just this much of it suffices to illuminate many of its features and its centrality to discussions of the metaphysics of time. But even at its simplest, temporal differentiation includes a vital feature—a transition—that indicates complexity, for it, too, requires explanation. This transition from thus *to* as so is in need of some account,

---

[11] See, for just one example, Frischhut 2015: 144.

no less than the world being *thus and* being *as so*. The full experience of temporal differentiation, moreover, involves the world being *thus* and then *as so*—then *as such* and *such* and *such*, and so forth. There is the phenomenon at its simplest and these ineluctable iterations of it, which introduce further complexity.

There is no plausibly denying temporal differentiation. To articulate an objection to it requires the phenomenon; reflecting in order even to consider denying the phenomenon requires temporal differentiation. Hence, disagreement regarding temporal differentiation per se is not what reflects the pivotal dispute concerning the metaphysics of time. Rather, disagreement about what is needed to explain this phenomenon is. As just discussed, temporal differentiation is complex; the correct account of it must recognize this complexity while illuminating one's singular experience of it. Everyone can agree that this moment, now, when the world is *thus* is different from this moment, when it is *as so*. Perhaps, however, this distinction between moments, insofar as it pertains to temporal reality, is merely numerical difference. Such difference and complexity is compatible with the world in time being ontologically homogeneous. Yet the transition of the world from *thus* to *as so* (to *as such*, etc.) does seem to reveal distinctions in the world that require, for an apt account of them, more than mere numerical difference among moments. Indeed, many maintain that to account for the inconstancy revealed by this transition, there must be peculiarly temporal distinctions or more general ontological ones between moments and, thus, that temporal reality is ontologically heterogeneous.

The two most familiar accounts of temporal differentiation are the traditional passage view, in terms of eternal moments changing with respect to (temporary) temporal properties, and one on which an array of equally real eternal moments standing in permanent temporal relations is supposed to account for the phenomenon. There are others—including the one I argue is correct (§8.2.)—but these two are sufficient to illustrate the two basic strategies to account for temporal differentiation (and thereby one's experience of it). The two strategies turn on what structure, what arrangement of things in the world, is posited to account for the phenomenon: whether it can be accounted for by a world in time that is ontologically homogeneous or whether it requires that temporal reality be ontologically heterogeneous. Since the pivotal dispute concerning the metaphysics of time is which of these two general views of the world in time is correct, by determining the appropriate account of temporal differentiation one can arbitrate this dispute.

§7.3. Temporal Differentiation and the Ontological Homogeneity of Temporal Reality

I begin by considering accounts of temporal differentiation on which the world in time is ontologically homogeneous. To begin here is best for two reasons. First of all, this view of the structure in temporal reality seems to be, by some measure, simpler than the one on which it is ontologically heterogeneous. It might require fewer sorts of things or have less to explain; it is certainly a more plain view. Thus, if it has the means to provide an entirely satisfactory account of temporal differentiation, it would, it seems, be preferable. However, and secondly, since every specific version of the view of the world in time on which it is ontologically homogeneous must account for temporal differentiation on the basis of temporally indistinguishable moments standing in permanent temporal relations, if this basis is inadequate, this is grounds for rejecting the general view. There is no such uniformity among the specific versions of the general view of temporal reality on which it is ontologically heterogeneous and, hence, no single lever that can overturn each one of these specific versions and thereby the general view itself.

§7.3.1. The myth of passage

The experience of temporal differentiation evokes to many flow or flight or some other sort of motion. Motion is change (with respect to location). Thus, many who consider temporal differentiation have proposed to account for the phenomenon in terms of change, namely, change in moments with respect to temporal properties. This putative change—the so-called *passage of time*—is vexed. The prevalent attitude toward it by proponents of the view that temporal reality is ontologically homogeneous is captured by D.C. Williams. In a classic paper,[12] Williams maintains that those who reject that the world in time is ontologically homogeneous seem to hold that "over and above the sheer spread of events, with their several qualities, along the time axis, which is analogous enough to the spread of space, there is something extra, something active and dynamic, which is often and perhaps

---

[12] Williams 1951. Page numbers refer to the reprint in Gale 1967.

best described as 'passage'. This something extra, I am going to plead, is a myth...."[13]

What Williams dubs the "myth of passage" is widely presumed to be sustained by an illusion. There is supposed to be something in one's experience of temporal differentiation that suggests change in temporal properties. Whatever this is is taken to be illusory. Hence, many of those dubious of passage adopt a similar strategy to destroy its myth. Their strategy is to dispel the presumed illusion in temporal experience that suggests passage by undercutting the motivation for thinking that such change in temporal properties is needed to account for any phenomenon associated with the experience. Doing so, proponents of this strategy claim, would show that whatever dynamic "something extra" (as Williams puts it) is thought to be revealed by this experience is superfluous. All that would be needed to account for any temporal phenomenon, therefore, would be the "sheer spread of events," (eternal) equally real moments standing in permanent temporal relations.

J.J.C. Smart provides a clear application of this strategy, one representative of the approach to metaphysics in a good deal of 20th-century analytic philosophy. Smart claims that confusion about language gives rise to illusory experience of the world in time. In considering temporal differentiation, one may say that some moment (or event) "is future," then "is present"—or "is present," then "is past"—and such locutions, given their grammar, seem to attribute temporary temporal properties to a moment. Smart contends, however, that to think these predicates attribute properties is to misunderstand their linguistic function. They are not used to attribute properties, but to refer to the utterance one is making and to assert that a temporal relation holds between that utterance and some other thing, to wit, the subject of the utterance. To say, for example, some moment "is past" is merely to assert that that moment precedes one's utterance.[14] Smart maintains that the thought that one's temporal language requires moments changing with respect to temporal properties is what gives rise to an illusory experience of passage, and so he provides an interpretation of this language that does not involve temporal properties.

Smart's proposal is far-fetched, for such linguistic considerations are posterior to one's experience of temporal differentiation and so are incapable of

[13] Williams 1951: 102.
[14] See Smart 1967: 126, 127.

making the latter seem as it does. Nothing hangs on this, though, for a more current and appropriately ontological strategy to destroy the myth of passage shows that examining temporal differentiation indicates nothing suggestive of changing temporal properties in the first place and, hence, this experience provides no motivation for positing passage. There is simply no illusion for which to account; in a sense, then, the appearance of passage is itself a myth, born of insufficient reflection on one's experience of the world in time.[15] There can be no *illusion* of an experience of passage because there could be no *experience* of passage whatsoever.

If one were to experience passage, one would have to experience a moment as future, that is, bearing the property of futurity, then as present (or as present, then as past). Yet one cannot experience a moment as future (or as past). That in order to experience a moment at all, one must exist at that moment is plausible. Yet if one exists at a moment, it is, to one at that moment, present. Assuming that futurity and presentness (and pastness) are incompatible properties, one could not also experience that moment—at which one exists—as future (or past). But perhaps one does not have to exist *at* a moment to experience it. Even so, one must have some experience of a moment to experience it as future or past. Consider, then, some moment that is supposed to bear the property of futurity (or pastness). No such moment exists now, at this one; were it to exist now, it would be present and so could not be future (or past). If one had any experience of this moment that is supposed to bear the property of futurity (or pastness), it could not be as it is at this moment, for that moment does not now exist. One must, therefore, experience it as it is when it does exist. However, to experience it as it is then, when it does exist, would be to experience it as present, not future (or past). Regardless, then, of whether one has to exist at a moment to experience it, one can only experience a moment as present. Hence, there is no way to experience a moment as future or past and so no way to experience passage.[16]

This argument is straightforward and seems conclusive. I think its conclusion would be more easily accepted if that to admit that one cannot experience the passage of time is certainly not to concede that the world in time is ontologically homogeneous were recognized. Nor is accepting the conclusion of this argument to deny the experience of temporal differentiation—no

---

[15] For different arguments that one does not experience passage, that is, moments changing with respect to (temporary) temporal properties, see Frischhut 2015 and Deng 2013a.

[16] For another argument that one cannot experience passage, though one that begins from more controversial premises, see Prosser 2007.

one would deny this—nor even to deny that one's experience of temporal differentiation indicates that temporal reality is ontologically heterogeneous. What the foregoing considerations undermine is the claim that one's experience of temporal differentiation and the inconstancy it reveals provide evidence for a certain account of the underlying phenomenon, to wit, an account of temporal differentiation in terms of moments changing with respect to temporal properties. I would even accept with Williams, for reasons I give below (§8.1.1.), that passage, in this sense, is "altogether a false start, deceiving us about the facts, and blocking our understanding of them."[17] However, at this point, even granting that passage fails as an account of temporal differentiation provides no insight into the crucial question of whether temporal reality is ontologically heterogeneous or homogeneous. There are many ways for the world in time to be ontologically heterogeneous. Even if there are no moments changing with respect to temporary temporal properties, the world in time might nonetheless fail to be ontologically homogeneous.

§7.3.2. The ostensible ontological basis of inconstancy

Still, if one admits there is nothing in one's experience of temporal differentiation that indicates passage, nothing suggesting that moments change with respect to temporary temporal properties, one might think there is little left to do to establish that the world in time is ontologically homogeneous. For if one denies that moments change temporal properties, that there is no other phenomenon, no alternative "something extra," to use Williams's phrase, to be included in the plainest account of the structure in temporal reality seems correct. If this were so, the correct account would need just the minimum of what appears to be obviously required for the world to go from *thus* to *as so*, namely, distinct moments—one at which the world is *thus* and another at which it is *as so*—standing in a (permanent) temporal relation of later than (or earlier than). Other iterations of this simplest part of temporal differentiation would be accounted for by more moments and additional instances of temporal relations. Any specific version of the general view of the world in time on which it is ontologically homogeneous accommodates this structure. So, one might think, any such view could account for temporal

[17] Williams 1951: 102.

differentiation, and this shows that this general view of the world in time is the correct one.

D.C. Williams believes this is indeed so, maintaining: "There is passage, but it is nothing extra. It is the mere happening of things, their existence strung along in the manifold [of equally real moments standing in permanent temporal relations],"[18] and "the theory of the manifold [i.e., the view that temporal reality is ontologically homogeneous] provides the true and literal description of what the enthusiastic metaphors of passage [as change of moments with respect to temporal properties] have deceptively garbled."[19] According to Frank Ramsey, in a world in which temporal reality is ontologically homogeneous, all "events are really in temporal order one before the other; each is present to or simultaneous with itself, future to the preceding ones past to the subsequent. The moving present is really the series of events themselves."[20] Much more recently, Nathan Oaklander writes: "temporal passage or the dynamic aspect of time is grounded in a temporal succession or transition from earlier to later temporal items ... Succession is not an A-relation [that is, one that involves a monadic, temporary temporal property such as pastness, presentness or futurity], but it is not a static relation either."[21] Joshua Mozersky maintains explicitly that a world in which temporal reality is ontologically homogeneous includes passage.[22] Steven Savitt also maintains that all there is to a dynamic world is a series of equally real moments standing in permanent temporal relations; moreover, such an ontological structure contains "absolute becoming," for this is "just the happening of events."[23]

Therefore, to claim, as many do, that the view of temporal reality on which it is ontologically homogeneous is one on which the world is constant (or should be taken to be) is a mistake.[24] No one denies that things in the world change. Change is a manifestation of inconstancy and one that is compatible with temporal reality being ontologically homogeneous. More importantly for present purposes, no one denies temporal differentiation, that is, that the world goes from being *thus* to being *as so*. To this extent, *everyone* maintains

---

[18] Williams 1951: 105.
[19] Williams 1951: 109.
[20] Ramsey 2006: 157.
[21] Oaklander 2012: 7.
[22] See Mozersky 2014: 109.
[23] Savitt 2002: 159.
[24] See for just one recent example of such a claim, Frischhut 2015: 144. Frischhut maintains that the "B-theory" is a "static account of time." This sort of claim can be traced back to McTaggart's seminal discussion of the world in time.

that the world is inconstant. Those who accept that temporal reality is ontologically homogeneous just deny that in order to account for the inconstancy in the world, one must include passage, moments changing with respect to temporal properties. They deny, furthermore, that any other sort of inconstancy is needed. Their position can be obscured when couched in terms of "passage," a "moving present," or "absolute becoming," as the preceding quotations illustrate it sometimes is. These terms have more familiar uses associated with views of the world in time on which it is ontologically heterogeneous. Thus, such equivocation can lead to the confusion of a plain account of temporal differentiation, in terms of equally real moments in permanent temporal relations, with a more complicated one, in terms of passage. Both of these accounts are misguided, as I argue below, but conflating them just confuses matters, making it more difficult to discern the correct account. The use of 'absolute becoming' is particularly infelicitous in connection to a view of the world in time on which it is ontologically homogeneous, for its original and more natural use[25] characterizes a certain phenomenon in a world in which temporal reality is ontologically heterogeneous. This phenomenon is, I argue, crucial to the correct account of temporal differentiation (see §9.2.) and to the metaphysics of time more generally.

At this point, what should be clear is that proponents of the view that the world in time is ontologically homogeneous accept that the world is inconstant and maintain this inconstancy is included in a world that contains a structure of equally real moments standing in permanent temporal relations. If one is considering merely the world being *thus*, on the one hand, *and* the world being *as so*, on the other, this general view is not implausible.

§7.3.3. Ontological homogeneity and the experience of temporal differentiation

The inconstancy in the experience of temporal differentiation evokes to many flow or flight or some other sort of motion and, hence, suggests change. However, as discussed above, there is nothing in this experience suggestive of passage, that is, the change of moments with respect to temporary temporal properties. There can be nothing suggestive of passage in one's experience of temporal reality because there could be no experience of passage.

[25] See Broad 1938.

Still, although the experience of temporal differentiation provides no evidence that passage is the ontological basis of this phenomenon, the correct account of it should nevertheless illuminate the inconstancy it reveals and what about the experience of temporal differentiation suggests change.

A view of the world in time on which it is ontologically homogeneous seems to have the means to do so. This general view includes a structure of distinct moments—the ontological basis of the world being *thus* and then *as so* and *as such* and so forth—and, given the things at these moments, there can be change. Such change does not involve moments and their temporal properties, but rather mundane changes of ordinary properties among the familiar things that exist at these moments. Thus, there is inconstancy—genuine change—in the world in time. Conscious beings notice many of the changes that occur and thereby have experiences grounded by them; consequently, a conscious being is often in different mental states at different moments. A prevalent suggestion, then, among those who maintain that temporal reality is ontologically homogeneous, is that what accounts for the inconstancy in one's experience of the world in time is simply one's different mental states at the distinct equally real moments (standing in permanent temporal relations) at which one exists. One's states change from one moment to the next. Here, then, is the crux of a putative explanation of the inconstancy in one's experience of temporal reality consistent with it being ontologically homogeneous.

Thus, J.J.C. Smart maintains that the inconstancy, the rush, of existing through time can be explained in terms of the accumulation of memories. One has (roughly) more—or at least different—memories at later moments (at which one exists) than one has at prior ones, and these changes in one's stock of memories account for the inconstancy in one's experience of temporal reality.[26] D.H. Mellor holds something similar in his influential books *Real Time* and its sequel:[27] Accompanying one's experience of temporal differentiation are certain changes. These changes are not in moments per se, but in one's mental states at different moments, and it is such changes that account for the inconstancy in one's experience of temporal reality. For example, one first believes that it is not yet one o'clock, then believes that it is (the former is true at any moment prior to one o'clock, the latter is true at one). These changes in one's mental states are, according to Mellor, the

---

[26] See Smart 1967: 126–127.
[27] Mellor 1981: 114–116 and Mellor 1998: 66–69.

"psychological reality behind the myth of tense, the myth of the flow of time."[28] Nathan Oaklander defends a similar position. What is supposed to account for the inconstancy in one's experience of an ontologically homogeneous temporal reality, however, is not change in beliefs. Rather, it is change in the "psychological attitudes" one adopts at different moments, for, with respect to some event, one typically experiences "first anticipation, then consciousness, then memory."[29]

More recently, others have tried to account for the inconstancy in one's experience of temporal reality in terms of more arcane mental (or physiological) processes. According to Robin LePoidevin, the inconstancy in one's experience can be accounted for in terms of changes, from moment to moment, in apparent temporal properties of things. However, these properties "are not in the world, but are *projected* on to the world in response to certain features of our experience."[30] Temporal reality is ontologically homogeneous, yet one's mind or brain responds to things at equally real moments (standing in permanent temporal relations) in such a way as to make them seem to have distinctive temporal features. Essentially the same view is expressed by Laurie Paul, who acknowledges that there is a "whoosh" in one's experience of the world in time, and proposes an account of this in "reductionist" terms, that is, in terms that do not make use of an irreducible temporal property of presentness.[31] According to Paul, each experience has a distinctively temporal subjective character, a felt quality of "nowness" that reflects the existence of that experience at a moment of time. This phenomenal quality is a feature of the experience, not of the moment at which it exists. The quality has a physical basis in the brain, which "responds to closely spaced inputs that have sufficient similarity (yet have qualitative contrasts of some sort) by accommodating and organizing the inputs. In doing so, our brains create the experiences we have as of change and as of temporal motion."[32]

Change naturally accompanies temporal differentiation and is required by any experience of it, for in any such experience one and the same subject goes from being in a certain mental state to another, incompatible one. Thus, the traditional strategy to account for the experience of the world in time by those who maintain that it is ontologically homogeneous is to find some changes

---

[28] Mellor 1981: 116.
[29] Oaklander 1993: 164.
[30] LePoidevin 2007: 95. Italics in original.
[31] See Paul 2010: 341–342.
[32] Paul 2010: 354.

that are obvious to conscious beings, and maintain that these changes are sufficient to account for one's experience of the world in time, including its peculiar inconstancy. On the view of temporal reality according to which it is ontologically homogeneous, its structure includes only moments—and the things that exist at them—in permanent temporal relations. The explanatory resources available to all proponents of this general view are more or less the same, and so these attempts to account for the singular experience of temporal differentiation are all in the end very similar. The only real difference among them is in what the salient changes are supposed to be, one's stock of memories, one's beliefs, one's psychological attitudes, one's brain states, etc. These actual, mundane changes are what is taken to suggest flow or flight in one's experience of temporal differentiation.

In light of such accounts, the proponent of the ontological homogeneity of temporal reality might seem able to provide a satisfactory explanation of one's experience of temporal differentiation. But this is not so; the strategy is irredeemably problematic. Not because it leaves something out—some special temporal property or any other thing—but because of what it presumes, to wit, that there is no ontological difference between moments. This, the definitive tenet of the view that temporal reality is ontologically homogeneous, is simply incompatible with the experience one has of the world.

§7.4. Why the World in Time Is Not Ontologically Homogeneous

If all there were to temporal differentiation were the world being *thus and* the world being *as so*, then all that would be required to account for the phenomenon would be distinct moments (standing in some relation): one moment at which it is *thus*, another at which it is *as so*. (Additional moments would be required for the world being *as such* and *as such* and so forth. This complication is irrelevant here.) Yet there is more to temporal differentiation than just distinct moments—there is the crucial transition from one to the next. This transition requires explanation. Moreover, an account of one's experience of temporal differentiation in terms of this moment, now (when the world is *thus*) *and* this moment (when it is *as so*) does not accurately characterize this experience. A basis of equally real moments that do not differ in a substantive ontological way is simply not adequate to account for one's experience of the world in time. This experience reveals, in *all this* going from *thus* to *as so*, that there must be some considerable difference between the world when demonstrated by 'thus' and now when it is *as so*. The two moments cannot be entirely ontologically on par, differing only numerically (or in terms of the mundane things existing at them). Showing this is sufficient to refute the general view that temporal reality is ontologically homogeneous and, hence, to settle the pivotal dispute regarding the metaphysics of time.

§7.4.1. An argument against the ontological homogeneity of the world in time: A farrago of experiences

The world goes from *thus* to *as so* (to *as such* and so forth). This is the phenomenon of temporal differentiation given in original inquiry, and it is incontrovertible. According to the view of the world in time on which it is ontologically homogeneous, all there is to the structure in temporal reality is many equally real (eternal) moments standing in permanent temporal relations (and the things existing at these moments). By simply confronting the world in original inquiry, that the experience of temporal differentiation is incompatible with this view of temporal reality is clear.

Consider, then, this experience. Suppose one experiences the world as *thus* at moment, m_1, and the world *as so* at moment, m_2. At m_1, the world is fully, vividly *thus*; even if there is some anticipation of it becoming otherwise (at m_2), this anticipation does nothing to diminish the vividness of the world as *thus* at m_1. At m_2, the world is fully, vividly *as so*; even if there is some recollection of its being as it is at m_1, this does not diminish the vividness of the world *as so* at m_2. One experiences both moments and so exists at both. Now assume, as the proponent of the view that temporal reality is ontologically homogeneous holds, that both moments—and everything that exists at them—are equally real. Hence, one is just as real at m_1 as one is at m_2. If one is *wholly* at both moments or if one has only a *distinct part* or *stage* at each makes no difference, if having a part (or stage) at a moment suffices for one to experience fully that moment (no one contests this point). So one's account of persistence (§6.3.2.1.), how things exist over time, is irrelevant to the present argument.

If one is at a moment, m_1, experiencing the world as *thus* and just as real at an equally real moment, m_2, experiencing the world *as so*, then one should be having—at both moments—an experience of the world as thus *and* as so. As *thus* because one is at m_1, experiencing the world, and it is *thus* at that moment; *as so* because one is at m_2, experiencing the world, and it is *as so* at that moment; and thus *and* as so *together* because both moments, both experiences and one, as subject, are all equally real. Therefore, were temporal reality ontologically homogeneous, there would be some conflation of the experiences one has at m_1 and m_2, along with the experiences one has at all the other equally real moments at which one exists. One would not experience m_1 as salient and then m_2 as salient; rather, one's experience would be some farrago of the things at both moments. What it would be like to experience this farrago, the world's being as it is at m_1 and as it is at m_2 together, is hard to say, for these ways are incompatible. Presumably it would not be like anything at all. Regardless, that such a contradictory experience is *not* the one one actually has of temporal differentiation or of temporal reality in general is clear. One just experiences the world as *thus*, limited and without interference of any other moment, then *as so*, limited and without interference, and this shows that the world in time is not ontologically homogeneous.

The immediate response here by a proponent of this view of temporal reality is likely to be that at m_1 one does not experience the world as it is now, at m_2, because at m_1 the world is not *as so*—it was as demonstrated by 'thus.' It is only *as so* at m_2 and m_1, though just as real as m_2, is distinct from it. Likewise, at m_2, one does not experience the world as it is at m_1 because at m_2 the world is *as so*. Although all moments are equally real, the world is not *always as so* (i.e., as it is at m_2); it is only *as so* at one moment, viz., m_2. So there are no grounds for claiming that one should experience the world as it was when demonstrated by 'thus' at m_2, when it is *as so* and, a fortiori, no grounds for claiming that the ontological homogeneity of the world in time entails some farrago of contradictory experiences of temporal reality.

The claim on which this response is premised, namely, that the world is not always a particular way, is obviously true; indeed, it is granted merely by recognizing temporal differentiation. This claim, however, does nothing to undermine the preceding argument. That argument is not based on the mistaken assumption that the world is always as it was when demonstrated by 'thus' (viz., as it is at m_1); that it is this way at every moment, including now, at m_2 (when the world is *as so*). Rather, the argument is based on the claim, definitive of the view that temporal reality is ontologically homogeneous, that the moment at which the world is demonstrated by 'thus,' m_1, and the moment at which it is *as so*, m_2, are equally real. As such, the contribution each makes to the world is ontologically on par. Given that one exists at both moments, one should have an experience of the world at one moment just as vividly as an experience of it at the other. Yet one does not experience such a farrago.

The force of the present argument—and the scarce means available to respond to it—can perhaps be underscored by considering experiences less grand and more mundane than the world as given in original inquiry. Suppose, then, that at some moment one is in Los Angeles eating a hot dog and at another moment in San Francisco eating cioppino. Consider the question of which gustatory experience is more vivid or more real for one. The mere (spatial) location of an experience neither enhances nor diminishes the vividness or existence of that experience; moreover, given that the world in time is supposed to be ontologically homogeneous, neither does the moment at which it occurs. The two experiences have, then, the same ontological standing. One, too, is equally real at both moments (or a part of one sufficient for having for oneself a full-fledged experience of that moment).[33] Therefore, one's experience of *all this*, ignoring for the sake of simplicity all the other moments at which one exists, would include an (unpleasant) farrago of mustard, wine, processed beef, clams, steamed bread, etc. One's experience of the world, however, would obviously not, under the conditions described, include that experience. The proponent of the ontological homogeneity of temporal reality does not have the means of explaining why it would not.[34]

This same conclusion can be reached from a different perspective, by reflecting on one's current engagement with *all this*. At any moment, one has many experiences. Right now, I am experiencing, among other things, the solidity of my desk beneath my arms, the trees and their particular shades of green as I gaze through my window, the familiar anxiety of an attempt to articulate adequately a point I am trying to make as I write. All of these experiences are equally real, and contribute to the comprehensive mental state I now enjoy. If the world in time were ontologically homogeneous, then *every* experience I ever have is just as real as the ones I have at this moment, and *I* am just as real (or the temporal parts or stages of me are), whenever I exist. These other experiences (and their subjects) are, of course, later or earlier than the ones I have now, at this moment, but this is just to say that

---

[33] Relativizing one's experience to moments is of no use in an attempt to undermine the present argument. See Fiocco 2009.

[34] This point could be made again via a different modality with something of a puzzle: Suppose one looks through a translucent yellow stained-glass window at one moment and a similar blue window at another. The proponent of the view that the world in time is ontologically homogeneous does not have the means to account consistently for why one does not have an experience of the world that includes looking through a green stained-glass window.

they do not exist at this moment. Not existing at this moment, however, does not diminish these experiences ontologically, qualitatively, or in any other sense. So my comprehensive mental state, the one comprising all the real experiences I have, that is, the one including all my existing experiences, would, were temporal reality ontologically homogeneous, include every experience I ever have. My experience of the world in time, however, is not like this at all. Such experience is circumscribed, delimited by how things are now, at this moment.

The limitation of one's experience of temporal reality to this moment cannot be accounted for in terms inherent to one. As an inquirer or, more generally, an agent, one has undeniably the capacity to engage *all this* at an existent moment and at a distinct, equally real moment. One's mind patently has the capacity to present to one the things that exist at a moment and at a distinct (equally real) moment. Things that exist at moments are as they are at those moments, regardless of which moment it is. Hence, the basis of any limitation in one's experience of the world in time must be the structure in temporal reality: some distinctively temporal thing(s) or some relation in which such things stand.

When the world goes from being *thus*, at m_1, to *as so*, at m_2, and one experiences this temporal differentiation, there is no interference of one's experience at m_1 with one's experience at m_2 (and vice versa); there is no competition between one's experiences of these moments. The moments at which it was demonstrated as 'thus' and now, when it is *as so*, are certainly distinct, but their mere numerical difference is not ontologically significant, for it does nothing to affect one's existence at either moment or one's experiences of both. Each moment is undoubtedly salient when it exists, to those who exist at that moment. On the view that temporal reality is ontologically homogeneous, though, all moments exist, so all are as salient as they ever will or could be. Still, the experience one actually has of temporal differentiation and of the world more generally is of one moment *to the exclusion of all others*—even if (as, obviously, is usually the case) that moment is not the only one at which one ever exists. The experiences one has at that one moment alone determine one's comprehensive mental state. The general view that the world in time is ontologically homogeneous is not compatible with one's experience because it lacks the means to privilege or otherwise distinguish one moment to the exclusion of others. On this view, any privilege one moment has in regard to being in temporal reality is one that *all* must have, and any such privilege is no privilege at all.

Any privilege more exclusive than this is inconsistent with the ontological homogeneity of temporal reality. Thus, suppose one maintains that what one experiences at m_2, the world *as so*, is all that one can experience (at m_2) and, hence, one does not experience the world as it was when demonstrated by 'thus,' because it was that way at m_1, and m_1 and m_2 are distinct moments. On this position, the world is partitioned into moments, such that what occurs at one, say, m_2, is *removed* from what occurs at another, say, m_1, to the extent that if one exists at both moments, there is no commingling or conflation of one's experiences. However, in being so removed, m_2 has a privilege that all other moments lack; it is distinctive in some way, be it by property or ontological status, that gives m_2 a salience that no other moment has. The relevant distinction cannot be, then, that of existing at itself or being present at itself, which all moments have. Although the mere distinctness of moments is what is supposed to make the crucial difference, more is needed. So the crucial difference must be in terms of some unique property or status—such as being (present) at m_2 per se—that distinguishes this moment, imparting to it a special salience. But to accept this is to recognize some sort of ontological heterogeneity in temporal reality, and doing so is antithetical to the world in time being ontologically homogeneous.

If one maintains that the world in time is ontologically homogeneous, one must concede that there is no unique property that qualifies a moment per se, making that moment or what exists thereat distinctively salient. Suppose, though, the things at some moment, m (rather than m itself), had a property that makes just those things, the ones at m, especially salient. If the things at *every* moment had such a property, it would indeed be compatible with temporal reality being ontologically homogeneous. However, a property that qualifies things in this way would not limit one's experience of temporal reality to, say, m, when one is at m, for the things at every moment would be no less enhanced then are those at m. If each moment is to be salient to the exclusion of all others, the things at that moment must be enhanced as those at all others are diminished. So suppose the things at some moment, m, had a property that makes just those things (at m) especially salient—precisely in a way that occludes other no-less-real moments and the things at them. Such a property, though, would be a temporal one, for how it qualifies the things at any given moment depends on other moments, viz., how things are at those moments; so this property would make each moment temporally distinctive. Hence, a view that includes this property would be one on which temporal reality is ontologically heterogeneous, not homogeneous.

There appears to be no other plausible means compatible with the ontological homogeneity of the world in time to limit one's experience at a moment to that very moment. Note that if there were, every version of this generic view of temporal reality ever proposed or adopted is incomplete, for none has made explicit these means. In the end, given this view of the world in time, one can only assert—in the face of all the foregoing considerations—that the experiences one has at other moments do not contribute to the comprehensive mental state one now enjoys because those experiences do not exist *at* this moment. But, obviously, if the world in time is ontologically homogeneous, this makes no difference: *when* a thing exists neither enhances nor diminishes that thing in any way. What makes the idea that one's experiences at other moments do not contribute to one's comprehensive mental state *now* so alluring is, I believe, a tendency to regard distinct moments—those prior to this one, those subsequent to it—as making less of a contribution to the world or, at least, a different kind of contribution to it. However, this tendency is just incompatible with the general view that temporal reality is ontologically homogeneous.

The claim that the world in time is ontologically homogeneous yet one's experience at a moment, m, is limited to the goings-on at m—and, hence, one does not experience the goings-on at any other moment at which one exists, even though all those moments are equally real—is inconsistent. There is no feature m per se could have, nor any feature the things at m could have consistent with the world in time being ontologically homogeneous that could limit one's experience when at m to just the goings-on at that moment. This view of temporal reality does not have the ontological means for such a limitation of one's experience; it commits one to a farrago of experiences at each moment one exists. Therefore, at every moment, by any actual experience, the view is demonstrated to be false.

§7.4.2. A further argument against the ontological homogeneity of the world in time: The crucial transition

This problem of a farrago of experiences with which the view that temporal reality is ontologically homogeneous is saddled arises despite the numerical distinctness of moments. The problem cannot be avoided by means of another feature of temporal differentiation beyond dispute, namely, that at m_1 one experiences the world as *thus* and *then*, at m_2, experiences it *as so*.

The experiences are not conflated, one might suggest, because these distinct moments stand in a temporal relation: m_1 is *earlier* than m_2 (or m_2 is *later* than m_1). Any attempt to resolve this seemingly decisive problem by means of a temporal relation is not only futile, reflecting on such relations brings to light a second problem for the general view that the world in time is ontologically homogeneous that is no less damning.

A relation, temporal or otherwise, can only relate things, and all things are equally real: they all exist and exist simpliciter in the very same way. So if m_1 is earlier than m_2, both moments are equally real. The relation itself can impart no difference to the intrinsic status of either and, thus, to how either is experienced. So although one experiences the world as *thus earlier* than one experiences it *as so*, this cannot account for why one does not experience some farrago of distinct but related moments. Both the experiences and the moments at which they exist are no less real for standing in a temporal relation. Again, one must avoid the tendency to regard what occurs at moments other than this one, now, as contributing less to what is in the world—to what EXISTS—for one is assuming here that the world in time is ontologically homogeneous and so everything, *whenever* it exists, is equally real, just as everything, *wherever* it exists, is. Hence, standing in a (permanent) temporal relation does not affect the ontological status of the relata of that relation or how these things are natured. Neither the relation *earlier than*, nor *later than*—nor any other—provides the means of addressing the problem of a farrago of experiences that is a consequence of this view of the world in time.

Rather, focusing on the relations between the moments involved in temporal differentiation reveals another damning problem for the general view that temporal reality is ontologically homogeneous. In original inquiry, one has an experience of the world being *thus* and then *as so*. That when the world is *thus*, *this* moment has a salience that all others lack is apparent; likewise, when the world is *as so*, *this* moment has a salience that all others lack. The experienced salience of these distinct moments—one in the absence of the other—is indisputable. What is also indisputable is that the salience of a unique moment is not permanent: the moment the world is *thus* is salient, then, as *all this* becomes *as so*, this other moment is salient. The experience of temporal differentiation, therefore, involves a transition in salience from one moment to another. The ontological basis of this experience, the things involved in the phenomenon of temporal differentiation, must account for this striking transition. An account of temporal differentiation must explicate the structure—the things in the world and the relations among them—the transition requires in a way consistent with one's indisputable experience of the world given in original inquiry. This explication is of key importance to a comprehensive and satisfactory account of the metaphysics of time because the transition of the world from *thus* to *as so* is precisely what reveals the distinct modes of differentiation in *all this* that enable one to recognize time in the first place.

Despite its importance, those who consider temporal differentiation and the experience of this phenomenon usually fail to address explicitly this crucial transition per se. On the contrary, they simply take it for granted. Thus, as discussed above, many hold—incorrectly as I maintain—that the experience of temporal differentiation involves an awareness of a change in temporary temporal properties of the moments when the world is *thus* and when it is *as so*. One is supposed to experience the world as *thus* as *present* (and the world to be demonstrated 'as so' as *future*), then the world *as so* as *present* (and the world that was demonstrated by 'thus' as *past*). Awareness of these putative changes is supposed to account for the inconstancy in one's experience of the world and to impart a sense of passage. Even were this account of the experience apt, some explanation of how the world goes from present at one moment, when it is *thus*, to present at a distinct moment, when it is *as so*, is needed. Yet not only is no such explanation available from those who take such "passage" seriously, this transition itself is not even recognized as a phenomenon in need of explanation. Similarly, the accounts of temporal differentiation proposed by those who take the world in time to be ontologically homogeneous all involve awareness of differences in one's mental states at distinct moments. One experiences a certain mental state when the world is *thus* and a different one when it is *as so*, and it is these differences that are supposed to be the ontological basis of one's experience of temporal differentiation. However, even granting such an account, it would be significantly incomplete, for it provides no explanation of the crucial transition from the moment at which one is in one mental state to the moment at which one is in the other.

This transition is vital to temporal differentiation and, hence, is no less incontrovertible than is the latter. Like any other phenomenon, it must have a basis among *all this*. So there must be some structure of things in temporal reality that accounts for the world going from *thus* to *as so* and illuminates one's singular experience of this phenomenon. There is no account of this transition compatible with the world being ontologically homogeneous, for the transition requires a difference between moments that is simply antithetical to this general view of temporal reality. An adequate account of *any* transition must recognize some ontological distinction between the things involved in that transition. This distinction, be it qualitative, indicating a difference in capacity, or more extreme, is required as the basis of an explanation for why there is any transition at all, as well as why the transition goes as it does, from the first thing to the second, rather than vice versa. In the case of the crucial transition pertinent here, there is a transition from one moment to another. The bare numerical distinctness of the two moments is incapable of accounting for the transition; merely being distinct necessitates no significant relation between the two moments. A temporal relation between the two is also incapable of accounting for the transition. The transition involves a difference in salience, yet no temporal relation itself necessitates such difference. Moreover, the structure of things in temporal reality must account for why, when the world goes from *thus* to *as so*, this transition is as it is, viz., from the moment when it is *thus* to the moment when it is *as so*, rather than some other way. Yet mere distinctness of moments could not do this, nor could any temporal relation. Therefore, given that there is temporal differentiation, there must be peculiarly temporal ontological differences in the structure in temporal reality that are incompatible with the world in time being ontologically homogeneous. These arguments, like those of the previous section, demonstrate—*at every (new) moment*—that this general view of temporal reality is incorrect.

§7.4.3. Why these compelling considerations have been overlooked in previous discussions

These two arguments against the ontological homogeneity of temporal reality, the first, from the farrago of experiences to which the view is committed—a farrago that, in fact, one does not experience—and the second, from the crucial transition from the world as *thus* to *as so*, show definitively that this view of the world in time is misguided. The first argument turns on one's indisputable experience of a unique moment as salient. The salience of but one moment is incompatible with a view of temporal reality on which it comprises an array of equally real moments, no one of which is distinguished in any peculiarly temporal way. The second argument turns on the irrefragable phenomenon that distinct moments are experienced as uniquely salient. There is, then, in this inconstant world, some crucial transition from one moment to another. Any feasible account of this transition requires some moment to be ontologically distinctive in a peculiarly temporal way, that is, in a way suitable to explaining this transition between moments, and so requires ontological heterogeneity in temporal reality. Therefore, on these grounds, I reject the general view that the world in time is ontologically homogeneous. In closing, I consider why these arguments and the considerations on which they are based, which I maintain are conclusive, might have been overlooked in previous discussions of the metaphysics of time.

I believe the main reason these arguments have been overlooked is that, in discussions of the metaphysics of time, the view that temporal reality is ontologically homogeneous is often taken to be the default—because the view is simpler or supposed to be obvious or properly "scientific," etc.—and so is merely defended, rather than established. The defense of the view consists in refuting (some of) its competitors. Consequently, the focus of such discussions has been on flawed or unmotivated specific views of the world in time that posit some sort of ontological heterogeneity, rather than on the view that temporal reality is ontologically homogeneous itself. In this context, however, the untenable commitments and insufficient explanatory resources of this general view per se are the bases of my arguments against it; its competitors are here irrelevant. With attention on the problems with its specific competitors, the shortcomings of the view of temporal reality on which it is ontologically homogeneous have gone unnoticed and, hence, neglected. That the pivotal dispute concerning the metaphysics of time is which of these two general views of temporal reality, one on which it is ontologically homogeneous, the other on which it is ontologically heterogeneous, is correct is worth reiterating at this juncture. Refuting some specific version of the latter view seems to support the former, only if one fails to recognize the generality of the dispute. The arguments I give, however, are directed at the general view that the world in time is ontologically homogeneous.

Another reason these arguments against this view of temporal reality have been overlooked is, I believe, that in defending the general view that the world in time is ontologically homogeneous, its proponents often attempt to show that it leaves nothing out of one's experience of any moment of time and, hence, of temporal reality. In doing so, they focus on the experience of some given moment, attempting to find thereat some feature that indicates that that moment is to be temporally distinguished or has some sort of privilege that other moments lack. Of course, there is nothing to be revealed by attending to a single moment that would call into doubt the ontological homogeneity of temporal reality. Anything special in one's experience of *any* particular moment can be held consistently by the proponent of this view of the world in time to be found at *every* moment. The problems for the view that the world in time is ontologically homogeneous emerge only when one considers distinct moments: how one would experience these if temporal reality were ontologically homogeneous, and what accounts for the incontestable transition from one moment to another in temporal differentiation.

Therefore, discussions of the ontological homogeneity of temporal reality tend to presume this view, taking it for granted in comparison to untenable rivals, and then failing to examine important phenomena because such examination has been diverted by the problems of these rivals. This approach to determining the correct general view of temporal reality does not examine the adequacy of the view that the world in time is ontologically homogeneous in light of temporal differentiation, the key phenomenon for which it must account. The arguments I present against this general view begin with this phenomenon and from this incontrovertible basis reveal its own insuperable problems. As becomes clear in subsequent discussion, the chief problem with the view that the world in time is ontologically homogeneous is not that it *leaves some thing out* of temporal reality, as has traditionally been held, but that it *requires too much structure*.

If the world in time is not ontologically homogeneous, it is heterogeneous. However, the structure of temporal reality can be heterogeneous in many different ways. Some of these ways can be precluded and so set aside given principles introduced above, but some cannot. The purpose of the next two chapters is to determine in what ways specifically the world in time is ontologically heterogeneous.

8
Against Mere Qualitative Heterogeneity in Temporal Reality

The discussion in the previous chapter demonstrates that the world in time is not ontologically homogeneous. It must, therefore, be *ontologically heterogeneous*: at least one moment is unique, bearing a temporal property or having some distinction that separates it from any other moment. There are many specific accounts that elaborate the general view that temporal reality is ontologically heterogeneous. On some of these, the heterogeneity is supposed to be *merely qualitative*, a difference in the properties that moments or the things that exist at them bear. (Note that this *qualitative* difference nevertheless introduces *ontological* heterogeneity into temporal reality because a property is a thing.) On other accounts, the heterogeneity is more stark, a difference in what *exists simpliciter* from one moment to the next. These latter accounts explicitly include *ontological transience*: some things, including moments, come into being or cease to be simpliciter.

The primary purpose of this chapter is to argue against accounts on which there is merely qualitative heterogeneity in temporal reality. Each of these, in one way or another, is inconsistent. I begin by considering the most familiar account of mere qualitative heterogeneity in temporal reality, namely the *traditional passage view*. This sort of view is shown to be inconsistent by considerations arising from ones first propounded by McTaggart, so I consider McTaggart's (in)famous argument for the unreality of time. There are philosophers who reject the traditional passage view, yet nevertheless accept views on which, like the former, all moments ever in the world exist eternally (and permanently). To avoid the sort of contradiction revealed in light of McTaggart's argument, these so-called *moving spotlight views* must include certain principles regarding change and things themselves that I maintain are untenable. Thus, moving spotlight views must be rejected. To avoid obvious inconsistency in one's account of the world in time, one must accept some ontological transience. I present an argument that some things of which one is directly aware cease to be simpliciter and argue further that a tenable metaphysics of time must recognize considerable ontological transience among temporal entities, including moments. Importantly, recognizing the scope of ontological transience provides one with key insight into the phenomenon of temporal differentiation. These considerations preclude yet more accounts of the structure in temporal reality, to wit, so-called *growing block views*. They thereby illuminate the structure of the world in time prior to this moment, now (raising the question of how things are subsequent to this moment).

§8.1. Qualitative Heterogeneity in Temporal Reality

As discussed above (§6.4.), the primary issue regarding the metaphysics of time is what is needed, in terms of peculiarly temporal entities and their relations, to account for the indubitable inconstancy in the world without neglecting the no-less-apparent constancy in it. The most straightforward way to account for this constancy is to maintain that all the moments that ever exist, and the things at those moments, are equally real and exist permanently, bearing all their (non-temporal) properties permanently. One response to the inadequacy of the general view that the world in time is ontologically homogeneous is to accept such structure, as the basis of the constancy in the world, yet posit further structure—additional things—to account for the inconstancy in it.

§8.1.1. The traditional passage view: Change in moments

The motivation for adopting the traditional passage view of the world in time is clear. To regard whatever happens in time as part of the world and, hence, to take what precedes this moment, now; what occurs at it; and what succeeds it, as equally real is not implausible. So underlying this traditional view is a structure of eternal moments, in permanent temporal relations, with qualitatively different things existing at these moments. However, although such structure can account for change among the things existing at moments, as argued above (§7.4.1.), it cannot account for one's experience of the world in time. One might posit, then, peculiarly temporal, monadic (i.e., non-relational) properties—*pastness, presentness, futurity*—to distinguish moments in an effort to account for temporal differentiation, as well as one's experience of *all this* going from *thus* to *as so*.

Positing such properties is also not implausible, for what precedes this moment is seemingly different from what is now so. One might account for this in terms of the temporal property of pastness. Any moment prior to now is no less real, it just is past. Likewise, what succeeds this moment seems different from what is now the case, and from what once was. One might account for this in terms of a different temporal property, to wit, futurity. Hence, any moment subsequent to now is no less real, it just is future. When the world is *thus* and then becomes *as so*, one does not experience the world both as *thus* and *as so*. Although on this traditional passage view, both the moment at which the world is *thus* and the one at which it is *as so* are equally real, there is nevertheless a distinctive temporal difference between them. When the world is *as so*, this is the unique moment bearing the property of presentness. It is vivid in a way that no other moment is, one might hold, precisely because it is the only moment with this property. When the world is *as so*, the moment at which it was demonstrated by 'thus' bears the property of pastness. One might hold that because the moment is past one does not experience it in the same way that one experiences this moment, now. Indeed, one might hold that because it is past one does not experience it at all.

These temporal properties are supposed to be temporary, in that no moment bears any one of them permanently. Moreover, on this passage view, only moments are supposed to change properties, specifically, these peculiarly temporal ones. The things permanently existing at some moment do not change (or, if they do, they change with respect to their temporal properties derivatively upon those changes in the moment at which they exist). Given that this view of the structure in temporal reality acknowledges both the inconstancy and constancy in the world and appears to provide an account of temporal differentiation consistent with one's experience, its durability and long-standing popularity are understandable. The view has often been regarded as the only feasible view of the world in time—or even the *only* view—in opposition to one on which temporal reality is ontologically homogeneous. Its promise, however, is specious.

The problem with the traditional passage view is insuperable and arises directly from its features that make it so enticing, namely, its straightforward combination of a structure of eternal moments in permanent relations with change in those moments themselves. A view on which moments change is simply incoherent. This can be seen with the help of considerations introduced by McTaggart over a century ago.

§8.1.1.1. McTaggart's Paradox

McTaggart's examination of time can be regarded as the fountainhead of modern investigations of the metaphysics of time. The terminology introduced by him and his key arguments are seminal, informing discussion of these issues ever since. McTaggart attempts to show that time itself is impossible and, thus, unreal. Consequently, no account of temporal reality is consistent and so nothing exists in time. No one accepts this conclusion, but a lemma of McTaggart's argument is taken by many to show something important about the structure in temporal reality. I believe that this lemma, which has come to be known as McTaggart's Paradox, shows that the traditional passage view is inconsistent.

In his discussion, McTaggart introduces the terms 'A-series' and 'B-series'.[1] This talk of series can be understood as two correct ways of characterizing the array of eternal moments in permanent relations. Since the A-series— that series of equally real moments taking on successively the temporary, monadic temporal properties of futurity, presentness, and pastness—includes all moments standing in the permanent temporal relations of earlier and later than, the A-series includes the structure of the B-series. To accept the A-series is, then, to accept the traditional passage view. McTaggart's lemma, his Paradox, is an argument that this series is impossible.

The argument begins with an assertion that most would accept, namely, that the monadic temporal properties are incompatible.[2] McTaggart then continues: "But every event has them all. If M is past, it has been present and future. If it is future, it will be present and past. If it is present, it has been future and will be past. Thus all the three characteristics belong to each event. How is this consistent with their being incompatible?"[3] McTaggart maintains that it is not.

There is, of course, a different and obvious, if ill-conceived, response to McTaggart's question: the monadic temporal properties are indeed incompatible, but no moment has more than one simultaneously. Each property

---

[1] McTaggart 1927: 24. McTaggart originally presents his famous argument for the unreality of time in McTaggart 1908. The discussion in this paper is included in the chapter titled "Time" in McTaggart 1927. Excerpts from this chapter are reprinted in LePoidevin and MacBeath 1993. Page numbers refer to this reprint.
[2] Tallant rejects this assertion in his 2015 paper.
[3] McTaggart 1927: 32.

is borne successively—that is, at different moments—and there is nothing contradictory about a thing, in this case a moment, bearing incompatible properties at different moments. McTaggart anticipates this response and argues that it is inadequate. Consider the present moment. If it were to be past, it must be so at some moment subsequent to it. Any such moment is future. So if the present moment were to become past, it would be past at a future moment. But no moment is or could be both past and future. The response that that future moment is no longer future when the present moment becomes past at it just leads to the same problem. That future moment, if it were to become past, would have to be past at some moment subsequent to it. Any such moment is future. So the future moment would become past at a future moment. But no moment is (or could be) both past and future. One might respond to the second iteration of the problem, but any response similar to the first yields the same incoherent result. McTaggart notes this impending regress and claims that it is vicious, never allowing inconsistency to be avoided. He concludes, therefore, that a series of equally real moments successively changing with respect to the monadic temporal properties is incoherent and so impossible.

Philosophers have responded to McTaggart's Paradox in different ways. Some take it to show conclusively that temporal reality does not include the A-series and, hence, that it demonstrates the falsity of the traditional passage view.[4] Others have resisted its conclusion. This resistance has sometimes come via responses to the argument that propose to deal with it linguistically, by introducing semantic considerations that purport to enable one to express its premises in ways that do not entail a contradiction.[5] These responses, though, do not articulate the underlying structure of things that must accompany the proposed semantic considerations, and so do not engage the argument in the appropriately ontological way. Those who do engage the Paradox by considering the things in the world (including the relations in which they stand) to which it commits one, often focus on the putative regress that McTaggart introduces. Thus, one's opinion of the argument often turns on whether one takes this regress to be vicious or benign.[6]

---

[4] See, for a few key examples, Dummett 1960; Mellor 1981, 1998; and Oaklander 2002.
[5] See Prior 1967: 4–7; Gale 1968: 30–31; Ludlow 1999: 133–135.
[6] See, for example, the essays in Part II of Oaklander and Smith 1994.

§8.1.1.2. The real problem: The view requires moments per se to both change and be immutable

I think the considerations underlying McTaggart's Paradox do show conclusively that there is no A-series and, hence, that the traditional passage view is incorrect. However, I think McTaggart's argument is not as perspicuous as it could be and, as a result, is misleading. The real problem here has nothing to do with regress. It has to do, rather, with the clear inconsistency that accepting the A-series presents. As noted above, all the things (including the relations in which they stand) in the B-series are included in the A-series.

What the B-series is supposed to be is an ontologically homogeneous structure of eternal moments standing in permanent temporal relations. *Pace* McTaggart, there is change *among* these moments—whenever one and the same thing exists at distinct moments bearing incompatible properties—yet, within the B-series, there is not supposed to be change *to* any moment or *in* any one moment itself. Any way a thing is at a moment is how that thing is permanently at that moment, i.e., how it IS (tenselessly) at that moment. Consequently, any way a moment is is how it is permanently, how it IS (tenselessly). One might be tempted to say "how that moment IS *at that moment*," but this does not add anything and, indeed, I argue below that the qualification is insidious. So, given the B-series, no moment itself changes. Yet what the A-series is supposed to be is a structure of moments in which each is as it is only temporarily; each moment is supposed to be different, incompatible ways: future, present, past. But no moment can be both permanently as it is and only temporarily those ways; no moment can be changing and changeless. The inconsistency is obvious and is presented as such by McTaggart. His jarring claim that, if there is both the A- and B-series, all moments of time bear the incompatible properties of pastness, presentness, and futurity is simply a circuitous way of expressing a direct consequence of what these structures of temporal entities are taken to be.

The immediate response that a moment does not bear these temporal properties simultaneously, but *changes* with respect to them is not apt. The putative change of some (temporary) property of an entity supposed to be permanently as it is is precisely the problem; trying to avoid the problem by invoking change is, then, misguided. The having of incompatible properties (specifically, temporary temporal ones) is a consequence of the prior and more general inconsistent commitment to moments that are both changing and changeless. Any change to a moment per se would be no less problematic.

Therefore, if the problem is a commitment to moments being both changing and changeless, the solution would seem to be (if one is moved by the inconstancy in the world) to deny that eternal moments standing in permanent temporal relations cannot change. This would require moments to be like any mutable temporal entity. But, as I now argue, they are not. Change requires one and the same thing realizing incompatible ways, and so change requires a thing with the capacity to be incompatible ways. Since no thing itself can realize incompatible ways, change requires some entity in addition to that thing with the capacity to be incompatible ways. A moment is that entity that constrains a thing with this capacity (§§5.1.1.; 6.1.1.), making that thing, for every contradictory pair of ways it could be, one of those two ways (thereby enabling that thing to make a determinate contribution to the world). Thus, change occurs when one and the same thing is a certain way at one moment and an incompatible way at a distinct moment. Given this plain account of what a moment is, that a moment itself does not have the capacity to be incompatible ways is apparent: there is no (genuine) property a moment has that it could lack. A moment is essentially each way it intrinsically is; it is, then, in terms I employ below (§10.2.3.) a *static* entity. A static entity cannot change, that is, it is immutable.

This conclusion that a moment is immutable is corroborated by the following considerations. A thing that changes exists in relation to a moment while bearing some property: the thing exists *at* that moment. Change occurs when that very thing exists in the same relation to a distinct moment bearing an incompatible property. Thus, were a moment to change, like any mutable temporal entity, one moment would have to exist *at* another. Yet it cannot; the assumption that it does leads to incoherence. Suppose that e, some entity, exists at moment, m_1, as a certain way, P. A moment just is the entity in relation to which one thing can be incompatible ways. So suppose e exists at m_2, a moment distinct from m_1, as *not-P*, a way incompatible with P. If m_1 were to exist in relation to m_2, that is, at m_2, whatever exists at m_1 would exist at m_2. Existing at a moment does not suppress what a thing is, or make it any less real; it merely relates one real thing (viz., some temporal entity) to another (viz., some moment). If m_1 is a thing at which others exist and m_1 exists at m_2, then, at m_2, m_1 is a thing at which others exist. Thus, since e exists, and is P, at m_1, and whatever exists at m_1 exists, and exists as it is at m_1, at m_2, then e exists and is P at m_2. If this were so, at m_2, e would be both P—because e is P at m_1, which is at m_2—and *not-P*—because e is *not-P* at m_2.

However, nothing can bear incompatible properties at the same moment (or in relation to anything else).

In light of this argument, the appropriate response is to deny that one moment can exist at another. Other responses are not feasible. Thus, one cannot deny that one and the same thing (e.g., *e* above) can exist at distinct moments with incompatible properties. To do so would be to deny any change in the world. I argue above (§5.1.1.) that there is manifestly change—there is undoubtedly inquiry, and inquiry requires it. Even if one were to hold that things persist and change by having distinct temporal parts at distinct moments, the foregoing argument indicates that if one moment were to exist at another, a thing might have two incompatible temporal parts at the same moment. Yet clearly it could not. Nor can one deny that *e* is *P* at m_1 merely because m_1 exists at m_2 (at which *e* is *not-P*), an instance of the principle articulated in the preceding paragraph. This principle is itself an instance of a more general and even more compelling one: A thing standing in a relation to another does not ipso facto suppress the (non-relational) ways either of those things is.

This last principle is important. Say one concedes the conclusion of the foregoing argument, granting that no moment can exist at a moment. One might then posit some other entity—call it, for lack of a better term, a *hypermoment*—at which a moment can exist in order to bear incompatible properties. So moment, m_1, might exist at hypermoment, M_1, bearing presentness and m_1 might exist at a distinct hypermoment, M_2, bearing, say, pastness. Even if there were such structure, it would not solve the problem revealed by the traditional passage view and for the A-series more generally, for m_1, that very thing exists (i.e., EXISTS) being both present and past. Of course, it is present in relation to M_1 and past in relation to M_2, but standing in these relations to these things, these two hypermoments, does not suppress the (non-relational) ways m_1 is. Therefore, m_1 is no less present for being related to M_1, nor is it any less past for being related to M_2. m_1 is a thing, real, in the world, and is itself supposed to be incompatible ways. Merely relating this very thing to other entities does not diminish the incompatibility of the ways it is. More generally, if all things are equally real, incoherent structure—things that cannot exist together—cannot be made consistent via addition: regardless of what were added, the incoherence would not go away. One would just be positing further things in relation to what cannot be together.

William Lane Craig has noticed that McTaggart's Paradox is, to put it anachronistically, a special case of the problem of temporary intrinsics.[7] The latter is the problem of accounting for how one and the same thing can bear incompatible properties at distinct moments, if those moments—and that one thing at those moments—are equally real.[8] The available ways of responding to the more general problem cannot resolve McTaggart's. Thus, taking recourse to temporal parts—so what is one way at one moment is not numerically identical to what is an incompatible way at a distinct moment—is not apt, for instantaneous moments do not have temporal parts. Nor can one deny that there are many equally real moments, for the existence of the B-series is a precondition of McTaggart's Paradox (and the traditional passage view). Finally, the point of the argument above involving hypermoments is that any attempt to resolve the problem here, via positing additional ontological structure, by relativizing the having of the incompatible properties to some thing or other, is futile.[9] These considerations further support the conclusion that McTaggart's Paradox is insoluble; there is no A-series and, hence, the traditional passage view is incorrect.

This discussion indicates a more general conclusion, namely, that any attempt to account for the inconstancy in the world by means of mere qualitative heterogeneity in temporal reality is fruitless. The inconstancy one experiences in the world going from *thus* to *as so* requires more than just changes among permanently existing things. To deny this leads, in one way or another, to incoherence.

§8.1.2. Moving spotlight views: Change in the things at a given moment

This last claim is by no means obvious, and the allure, when reflecting on the indubitable constancy in the world, to accept a structure of permanently existing things is strong, so there are other views that attempt to introduce inconstancy into such permanent structure. What the arguments in light of McTaggart's Paradox show is that it is incorrect to hold that moments per se change. Thus, there are those moved by some of the same considerations,

---

[7] See Craig 1998.
[8] The locus classicus of this problem is Lewis 1986: 202–204.
[9] I make essentially this point, in connection to the more general problem of temporary intrinsics, in Fiocco 2009.

regarding constancy and inconstancy, as those who adopt the traditional passage view, who propound similar views that, by various means, avoid the commitment of the passage view to moments themselves changing.

These philosophers defend accounts of temporal reality—so-called *moving spotlight views*—according to which all the many equally real moments of time exist eternally in permanent temporal relations. Moreover, all familiar, mundane objects that ever exist in time exist permanently at the moments at which they exist. To this extent, moving spotlight views are like the traditional passage view and any on which the world in time is ontologically homogeneous. Like the passage view, though, and unlike those on which temporal reality is ontologically homogeneous, on moving spotlight views, there are qualitative differences among moments that make the world in time ontologically heterogeneous. What distinguishes moving spotlight views from the traditional passage view is that whereas on the latter, the qualitative differences are differences in moments per se, on the former, these differences are among the things that exist at moments. No moment itself ever changes—no moment goes from future to present or from present to past—but the permanent things at eternal, unchanging moments do, and in a certain drastic way. Given that all the things existing at moments change in this way, proponents of moving spotlight views maintain that the inconstancy in the world can be appropriately accounted for among a structure of eternal immutable moments standing in permanent temporal relations.

The name of these so-called moving spotlight views is problematic. It comes from a metaphor first used by C.D. Broad to characterize the traditional passage view:

> We are naturally tempted to regard the history of the world as existing eternally in a certain order of events. Along this, and in a fixed direction, we imagine the characteristic of presentness as moving, somewhat like the spot of light from a policeman's bull's-eye traversing the fronts of the houses in a street. What is illuminated is the present, what has been illuminated is the past, and what has not yet been illuminated is the future.[10]

Bradford Skow's theory, which is presented as a moving spotlight view, is, it seems, just the traditional passage view.[11] Daniel Deasy defends what he

---

[10] See Broad 1923: 59.
[11] See Skow 2009.

calls "moving spotlight views," but seems not to recognize the basic ontological commitments of such views (and so does not provide a convincing defense).[12] One theory, Meghan Sullivan's *minimal A-theory*, considered below, is a moving spotlight view, but is not presented by its author as such.[13] However, the most developed account of what I characterize as a moving spotlight view, Ross Cameron's (also considered below) is presented by its author as such. In light of this, and because I do not want to introduce more new terminology, I take up the somewhat infelicitous name, having made clear how I am using it.

§8.1.2.1. Sullivan's minimal A-theory
Sullivan, inspired by views of Timothy Williamson,[14] accepts the principle that everything exists eternally, including each moment and all the things that exist at any moment. She also recognizes that many things change. Since she is committed to all moments being equally real, in order to avoid contradiction in connection to temporary intrinsics, Sullivan holds that things persist by having numerically distinct temporal parts at different moments or change only by standing in different relations to different moments.[15]

Crucially, Sullivan regards the apparent coming into being and ceasing to be of eternally existing things as change like any other. Thus, the ceramic owl on my desk, which I bought in Barcelona in 2011, has, like any other thing, always existed. For most of its existence, though, it has had no location. That very owl existed, but not anywhere and, hence, not as a material object. Then, in (say) 2010, it came to be a material thing with a given location in space (presumably somewhere in Spain). Since then, it has undergone the mundane changes of a memento, being moved from one place to another and subjected to the usual wear and tear of such a thing. At some unforeseeable moment subsequent to this one, now, the matter of the owl will be destroyed; the owl itself will remain in the world, though without any location. There is nothing remarkable about this knick-knack, all eternal permanently existing mutable temporal entities have similar careers: they come to

---

[12] See Deasy 2015.
[13] See Sullivan 2012. Others recognize Sullivan's theory as a moving spotlight view—see Deasy 2015: Note 7. Though Deasy, in the same note, also presents Skow's theory as a moving spotlight view (as just noted, I regard Skow's as the passage view).
[14] See, for example, Williamson 2002.
[15] For the problem of temporary intrinsics, see §8.1.1.2. For reasons expressed therein (and more fully in Fiocco 2009), I do not think relativizing properties to moments avoids contradiction.

have a location, undergo change from moment to moment, then cease to be located at all while continuing to exist.

Merely holding that all things are eternal, and so many familiar things exist at moments without any location, is consistent with the world in time being ontologically homogeneous. On Sullivan's view, however, temporal reality is ontologically heterogeneous. This is because one moment is distinguished from all others in being the unique moment at which anything has a spatial location and, consequently, at which there are any spatial relations. This moment, now, is that unique moment. It is so only temporarily, for in an instant, a different moment is the only one at which anything has a spatial location. There is not some inherent property of this moment, now that distinguishes it from all others; rather, how certain things at this moment are—viz., spatially located—makes the moment different from all others. Therefore, this moment per se does not change when it ceases to be the one at which things have spatial locations—what changes are all those spatially located things existing at it. For these reasons, Sullivan's is aptly characterized as a moving spotlight view.

In presenting her minimal A-theory, Sullivan does not consider McTaggart at all. However, since on her view moments themselves are not supposed to change, it avoids the exact problems brought to light via McTaggart's Paradox. Sullivan also does not consider one's experience of temporal differentiation nor of temporal reality more generally. But if one has a spatial location only at a single moment, this would account for the quite different experiences one has of the world when, at one moment, it is *thus* and then, at this moment, now, is *as so*. Sullivan's actual motivation for propounding the view is that it is better than others on which the world in time is ontologically heterogeneous in dealing with three issues, to wit, ones pertaining to tense logic, a theory of singular terms and theories of inertial motion and acceleration.[16] Even if one grants that the view is better than others in connection to these issues, it is problematic in ways that make it untenable. It shares these problems with a more elaborate moving spotlight view, so I first present this. Criticizing both versions together reveals that the problems for the moving spotlight view are general, arising from its definitive assumptions.

---

[16] See Sullivan 2012: 167.

§8.1.2.2. Cameron's moving spotlight theory

Cameron simply takes for granted that the world in time is ontologically heterogeneous.[17] His goal is to present a specific version of this general view that is no worse than any rival at providing responses to a list of outstanding problems concerning the metaphysics of time, and is better, in some respect, than any of these rivals. One of the problems he considers is the one presented by the argument in McTaggart's Paradox. Cameron must deal with this problem because he accepts both that temporal reality is ontologically heterogeneous—with different moments temporarily distinguished from all others—and that all moments and the things at them exist eternally (standing in permanent temporal relations). He accepts that all moments (and the things at them) exist eternally in order to avoid difficulties that he believes beset accounts of the world in time that forgo this commitment.

Cameron cautions in several places that although on his view all moments (and the things at them) exist eternally and a unique moment is temporarily distinguished (before another is and another is and another is and so forth), his view cannot be regarded as one on which the world in time is ontologically homogeneous with an added temporary temporal property of presentness. On the latter, essentially the traditional passage view, things change only from one moment to another; how a thing is at a moment is how it permanently is at that moment. On Cameron's moving spotlight theory, though, how a thing is at a moment is not permanent: a thing that is simpliciter a certain way at a given moment, m, is not always that very way at m (that same moment). Moments themselves do not ever change, only the things at them do. Cameron's theory is, therefore, clearly a moving spotlight view as I use the name.

What McTaggart's Paradox shows, according to Cameron, is that if one accepts that all moments exist eternally and unchangingly, and yet different moments are temporarily distinguished from all others by, say, the property of presentness, one seems to be committed to the following principle:

> *Past Record*: If something was the case, then it *is* [IS, tenselessly] the case in the past

Thus, if a particular moment was once present, it IS (tenselessly) present in the past. This is contradictory. So Cameron's objective, then, is to propound

---

[17] Cameron 2015: 1.

a theory of temporal reality that includes the ontological commitments he thinks are apt and yet excludes *Past Record*, thereby avoiding the inconsistency McTaggart brings to light.

On Cameron's theory, as noted above, all moments and all the things that exist at any moment exist eternally, standing in permanent temporal relations. However, one moment is distinguished from all others as the way the world *is* simpliciter. How the world is *at* a moment is derivative on how it is simpliciter. The world is a certain way *at* m if and only if *m* is the present, and the world is that way simpliciter or *m* is a past (or future) moment and the world was (or will be) that way when *m* was (or will be) present. Every temporal substance that is not a moment, that is, anything that exists at a moment has an *age*, a property that characterizes how far along in its career that thing is. The age of a thing is different at each moment. Each thing existing at a moment also has a unique *temporal distributional property*, the same such property at *every* moment. This property characterizes how a thing is intrinsically at every moment regardless of whether that thing exists at that moment. The age of a thing and its temporal distributional property together determine how a thing was, is, or will be at every moment, *m* (again, regardless of whether a thing exists at *m*).

Thus, Caesar, like anything that ever exists at any moment, exists (that is, EXISTS, tenselessly) eternally. Of course, Caesar does not exist *at* every moment, he exists only at some of the moments there are. Indeed, Caesar has not existed at any moment for some two thousand years. Nevertheless, according to Cameron, Caesar presently, now, at this moment, has a certain age. This age, with Caesar's temporal distributional property determines how Caesar is at this moment (at which he does not exist). At this moment, he has simpliciter a certain location in space-time (one that does not overlap with this moment, now) and is essentially, at least, concrete and human. He also is simpliciter at this moment without height, mass, or an ordinary three-dimensional shape; though his temporal distributional property determines that at the moments at which Caesar had other ages, he had a certain height, mass, and build. Similarly, all things that ever exist are presently, at this moment, now, certain ways, and this is how the world is simpliciter.

Despite things existing (EXISTING) at other moments than this one, now, how they are at other moments, that is, how they were at those moments when those moments were present is now, at this moment, no part of reality. This follows from the rejection of *Past Record*. By eschewing this principle, Cameron's theory is supposed to avoid any problem with one and the same thing being equally real at distinct moments with incompatible temporary intrinsic properties. Consider a person who as a boy, at moment, m_1, is five feet tall and then, subsequently, as a man at moment, m_2, is six feet tall. If m_2 is the present moment, given his age at m_2 and his temporal distributional property, the person is six feet tall simpliciter. Given this age and temporal distributional property, that the person was five feet tall at m_1 must be the case. But his being five feet tall is not part of the world; at no moment is (or IS) this person five feet tall. He just *was* five feet tall at m_1, and this is because of how he now *is* (at m_2).

On Cameron's theory, there is a unique moment that is present. This moment, now, is that moment, not because it bears some fundamental peculiarly temporal property, but rather because it is the moment at which each thing is as it is simpliciter. In an instant, a distinct moment is present. The moment that just was present is no longer so; it merely was present. Because Cameron rejects *Past Record*, though, it does not follow from that moment having been present that it is (IS, tenselessly) present. Its being present is no part of reality. Thus, by rejecting *Past Record*, Cameron's moving spotlight theory avoids the problem brought to light via McTaggart's Paradox. By the same means, it seems to be able to account for one's experience of the world in time: the world is presently *thus*, and one experiences it as *thus*. Yet, in an instant, the world is *as so*, and one experiences it *as so*. When one is experiencing this, one has no experience of the world as *thus*. One merely *had* that experience and one's having that experience is now no part of reality. (One's having had that experience is determined by the age of things now and all their temporal distributional properties.) Cameron's theory, therefore, might seem promising as the apt specific account of the heterogeneity of the world in time. However, I think the theory is, like the traditional passage view, inconsistent. Its inconsistency just manifests in different ways.

§8.1.2.3. Problems with moving spotlight views
On the traditional passage view, all moments (and the things at them) exist eternally, so whatever happened, is happening, or will happen is equally part of the world. Nonetheless, one moment is special, temporarily distinguished from all others. McTaggart noticed that if an eternal moment is supposed to be temporarily distinguished from all others by a peculiarly temporal property, then, unless a moment itself changes, a moment must be incompatible ways. Yet, as I argue, moments themselves do not and cannot change. So the

underlying ontological commitments of such an attempt to account for the indisputable constancy and inconstancy of the world are incoherent.

Moving spotlight views attempt to account for this constancy and inconstancy in essentially the same way. But whereas on the traditional passage view, a moment itself is supposed to be temporarily distinguished from all others (by a peculiarly temporal property), on moving spotlight views, the mutable things at a given moment are supposed to be temporarily distinguished. These views, however, are also incoherent. How things at the temporarily distinguished moment are supposed to change is incompatible with what change is. Moreover, how certain things are supposed to be on these views is incompatible with what a thing is. What this shows is that the traditional passage view and moving spotlight views are untenable for ultimately the same reason: any attempt to account for the inconstancy in the world in terms of mere qualitative heterogeneity in a permanent array of eternal moments (and the things at these moments) leads to inconsistency.

Change is a structural phenomenon, that is, not a thing itself, but a plurality of things standing in relations. Change occurs when one and the same thing bears incompatible properties at distinct moments. A moment is needed for change because although some things, viz., any mutable entities, have the capacity to be incompatible ways, no thing itself can realize incompatible ways. A mutable entity is constrained to be, for every contradictory pair of ways it could be, one of those two ways by standing in a relation to some other thing, to wit, a moment (thereby enabling that mutable entity to make a determinate contribution to the world). A distinct moment is needed for the mutable entity to be an incompatible way. No thing can be incompatible ways in relation to the same thing, moment or otherwise.

This is what change is. Moving spotlight views, however, are committed to a sort of drastic "change" whereby a thing is first one way at a moment, then an incompatible way *at that same moment*. The very characterization of such *synchronic change* casts doubt on its coherence. Nevertheless, on Sullivan's minimal A-theory, if it is now, presently, m_1, a mundane thing, such as this ceramic owl, has simpliciter a spatial location at m_1. In an instant, when m_2 is the unique moment at which anything has (simpliciter) a spatial location, the ceramic owl no longer has a spatial location *at* m_1. It *had* a spatial location at that moment, but it is a key feature of the theory that it no longer has simpliciter one then. Thus, how the ceramic owl is at m_1 changes: it goes from having (simpliciter) a spatial location at that moment to not having (simpliciter) a spatial location at that very moment. Cameron's moving spotlight theory also includes synchronic change. If it is now, presently, m_1, I have simpliciter many intrinsic properties, say a certain shape, S. In an instant, when m_2 is the unique moment at which anything has (simpliciter) intrinsic properties, I might have at m_2 the same shape or a different one, but at m_1 I no longer have (simpliciter) S. I merely *had* S at m_1. And so how I am at m_1 changes: I go from having (simpliciter) S at that moment to not having (simpliciter) S at that very moment. Moreover, I change with respect to the basis of the features I have at m_1. First, I am as I am at m_1 because that is how I am simpliciter, then I am no longer as I am at m_1, but merely was as I was because of my new age and how I am simpliciter at m_2.

This commitment to synchronic change is not merely a feature of Sullivan's and Cameron's theories, it is a definitive feature of any moving spotlight view. If all moments (and the things at them) exist permanently and yet the things at some moment, m, are temporarily distinguished in some respect from those at any other, given temporal differentiation, those things must cease to be distinguished in that respect. They cannot remain so distinguished at m when the things at some other moment are supposed to be the only things to be so distinguished. Therefore, those things distinguished at m must cease to be so distinguished at that very moment, m. This requires synchronic change.

I do not think synchronic change is coherent, let alone possible. Given what change is, it requires one and the same thing to bear incompatible properties at distinct moments. Were there synchronic change, one and the same thing would have incompatible properties at the same moment. Of course, the incompatible properties are not supposed to be borne simultaneously at the same moment, but successively at the same moment. Yet nothing occurs *successively* at the *same moment*. Nothing could occur successively at the same moment unless that moment itself were to change. However, as I argue above, moments do not and cannot change. Besides, what differentiates moving spotlight views from the traditional passage view, despite their similar ontologies and strategies for accounting for the inconstancy and constancy in the world, is precisely the rejection by the former of the tenet that moments themselves change.

Neither Sullivan nor Cameron explicitly acknowledge the synchronic change to which their views commit them. The two, however, do characterize change in idiosyncratic ways so as to accommodate it. Sullivan asserts: "All that matters for property change is that there be an object that has a certain property and that object either lacked or will lack it."[18] Cameron

---

[18] Sullivan 2012: 168.

asserts: "Change is a matter of something being true at one time and not at another."[19] Both of these characterizations are initially plausible. But only, I submit, because both can be read as being consistent with the obvious and familiar account of change I hold. They are much less plausible—and, indeed, are untenable—when construed as characterizing synchronic change.

Despite their commitment to synchronic change and their similarly vague characterizations of change in general, Sullivan and Cameron actually have quite different views of how change underlies the inconstancy in the world. Sullivan maintains that all change, even putative change in existence, is property change of the sort I—and the proponent of the ontological homogeneity of the world in time—accept. She is just committed to such change in some instances occurring at a single moment. Cameron, on the other hand, denies that change such as this, "mere variation in how things are from one time to another,"[20] suffices to account for the inconstancy in the world. In order to account for this inconstancy, Cameron believes one must maintain "the *whole* of reality changes from moment to moment."[21] Everything has a different age at each moment at which that thing is simpliciter as it is; it has this age only for an instant before it has a new one. This permits the sort of "genuine" change that one who denies that temporal reality is ontologically homogeneous is thought to be seeking.[22] Since the theories of both Sullivan and Cameron rely on synchronic change and such "change" is incoherent, neither theory is tenable. The inconsistency of these moving spotlight views indicates that to attempt to account for the indisputable inconstancy in *all this* in terms of change at all is misguided. Before considering how this inconstancy is to be accounted for, I consider a further problem for moving spotlight views that corroborates their inconsistency.

As I argue above (§3.4.), a thing is a natured entity. As such, it is constrained by its very existence to be what it is and, hence, to be certain ways (and to interact with other things in accordance to those ways). Each thing is fundamental in that it is not made to be what it is or how it is essentially by any other thing: each thing simply is what it is and as it is essentially because of itself. This robust view of things arises via original inquiry, a wholly critical method whereby one endeavors to understand *all this* without making any assumptions about it. Consequently, the method is general—or pure—in

[19] Cameron 2015: 163.
[20] Cameron 2015: 111.
[21] Cameron 2015: 49. Italics in original.
[22] See Cameron 2015: 111.

such a way that what it reveals about the world and the things comprising it are constraints on any inquiry, for any inquiry is directed at some thing(s) or other amid *all this*. Any theory incompatible with this account of things, then, is ultimately inconsistent, accepting things in the service of theorizing about (some part of) the world, yet maintaining that a thing is otherwise than what it must be.

Both Sullivan's minimal A-theory and Cameron's moving spotlight theory require meager "things" that are not robustly natured—or, at least, are natured in fantastic ways incompatible with an understanding of what those things are acquired through regular interaction with them. This commitment to such meager "things" is a consequence of the way any given moment is supposed to be temporarily distinguished from all others and so, presumably, a commitment to similarly (wildly) adaptable "things" arises on any moving spotlight view. On Sullivan's theory, a human person who has a spatial location at this moment, now, eventually has no spatial location (that person has no temporal parts with a spatial location) and no property that depends on having a location. That human person, however, exists in the same way as any person at this moment, now; they are no less real than any human person that presently exists. On this view, then, there are human persons who have no height nor weight nor shape; they have no bodily processes and so cannot respire nor eat—nor do they have even the capacity for thought, if this capacity depends on undergoing brain processes. Likewise, on Cameron's view, it is presently, at this moment, true of Caesar that he has no height nor weight nor shape; that he has no bodily processes (and so cannot respire nor eat nor think). If that he lacks all these properties is true of Caesar himself, it follows that for a human person to exist and yet fail to be these ways, ways a human person seems to be essentially, is possible.

Sullivan acknowledges that her view is susceptible to objection in light of concerns regarding essentialism.[23] Cameron likely thinks his view is immune to such objections because he attributes essential properties to things. Caesar, for instance, is supposed to have, even at moments at which he does not exist, "his essential properties such as being concrete, being human, etc."[24] In her discussion of essentialism, Sullivan indicates that she understands the doctrine in the same way as Cameron (as revealed in the foregoing brief quotation): the essential properties of a thing make that thing both what it is and

---

[23] Sullivan 2012: 168–170.
[24] Cameron 2015: 149.

how it necessarily must be. Thus, a cluster of undifferentiated cells is supposed to be made what it is (say, a dog) by the property *is a canine*, and being human is supposed to make a thing essentially human.

This contemporary understanding of essentialism, familiar to anyone who has considered late 20th-century discussions of metaphysics,[25] is in fact incompatible with a thing being natured. Nothing and, a fortiori, no property makes a thing what it is. Were it otherwise, a thing would have to stand in a relation (say, instantiation) to a property to be made what it is. Yet in order to stand in any relation whatsoever, a thing must first exist as the very thing it is—thus, as what it is (§3.4.). A natured entity is not some meager thing, like a bare particular, that is made to be of a kind in relation to some property (or kind). Rather it is, in its very existence, an instance of a kind. Consequently, any human person or dog or other natural kind necessarily and essentially is many ways, to wit, those ways that a thing must be by being an instance of that kind. Of course, what all these properties are for any given kind is not clear; nonetheless, for, say, human persons, they certainly include some mundane properties involving an organic body (and, thus, require a location). Therefore, no thing is or could be barely a member of its kind, in that it has the property of being of that kind—or is of that kind or is what it is—in the absence of many of the other properties characteristic of that kind. Sullivan's and Cameron's views require such meager "things" and so are incoherent, incompatible with what a thing is. Since this appears to be a commitment of moving spotlight views in general, this is another manifestation of the underlying ontological inconsistency of such views, and a further reason for regarding them as untenable.

Cameron's theory is confronted by a further daunting problem, one that is yet another manifestation of the underlying ontological inconsistency of this sort of view. On his theory, a thing is simpliciter certain ways at moments—and so is constrained by those moments—at which it does not exist, in virtue of existing (i.e., EXISTING) at other moments. This is problematic because a moment, an entity that constrains a thing with the capacity to be incompatible ways, constrains by being the entity in relation to which that mutable thing is, for every contradictory pair of ways it could be, one of those two ways. By being so constrained, a mutable entity can make a determinate contribution to the world. If a thing is determinately certain ways with respect to a moment, m, and, hence, is constrained by m, in that the thing is different

---

[25] See Footnote 19 of Chapter 3.

with respect to *m* from how it is at other moments, standing in the appropriate relation to *m* is necessary. The appropriate relation is that of *existing at*. Merely existing (EXISTING) at some other moment does not suffice for that thing to be related to *m* in the appropriately intimate way needed to be constrained by *m*. Thus, something that does not exist at *m* could not be simpliciter certain ways at *m*.

Even overlooking the inconsistent accounts of things and of change required by moving spotlight views, there is another compelling objection to them. On any view, like these, on which there is mere qualitative heterogeneity in temporal reality, there is now a single moment qualitatively distinguished from all the other equally real eternal moments (standing in permanent temporal relations). In an instant, a distinct moment is qualitatively distinguished from all others. Some account, however, is still needed of this crucial transition, of one equally real moment replacing another as the sole distinguished moment. In other words, some account of temporal differentiation, of the world going from *thus* to *as so*, is still needed. There must be some explanation of why this incontrovertible phenomenon whereby time itself is revealed and one has the singular experience of temporal reality that one does occurs at all. The only appropriate basis of such an explanation—like any apt account of any phenomenon—is the things in the world.

Were there a genuine temporary temporal property of moments, for example, presentness, one might have the means to account for temporal differentiation. The world goes from *thus* to *as so* because of presentness: this property is so natured as to qualify for an instant a unique moment before qualifying an instantaneously later one. But examining the traditional passage view in light of McTaggart's Paradox provides good reason to reject such a property (by which moments would change). On moving spotlight views, then, there is no echt temporal property of presentness, rather 'presentness' is a term that refers to whatever distinguishes all those things at the moment supposed to be unique. On Sullivan's theory, this is the property of having a spatial location. On Cameron's, "there is no fundamental property of presentness," "presentness" is just derivative upon how things are simpliciter.[26]

On neither view are the means available to account for temporal differentiation. Although Sullivan posits a "flow of time" in terms of spatial location,

---

[26] See Cameron 2015: 172.

she provides no account of this flow.[27] I do not see how the property of having a spatial location could itself account for why only certain things (to wit, all those at a given moment) have this property or, more importantly, why in a moment all those things lose it, as certain others (just those at the next moment) gain it. Cameron maintains that there is "genuine passage" on his theory and accounts for this in terms of "the nature of things fix[ing] that they used to, and will be, other than they are."[28] But this provides no insight whatsoever into why a thing goes from how it is simpliciter to how it will be when it in fact does. I do not see how any other property or any other permanent arrangement of things could account for the world going from *thus* to *as so*. Therefore, even if moving spotlight views were not inconsistent, they would be objectionably incomplete.

§8.2. Ontological Transience: Absolute Annihilation, Ceasing to Be Simpliciter

Moving spotlight views, like the traditional passage view, are inconsistent. The allure of such views is that they are supposed to account for both the indisputable constancy and inconstancy in the world by positing temporary—inconstant—qualitative heterogeneity among an array of eternal entities in permanent—constant—relations. But incoherence is an unavoidable consequence of the definitive commitments of any such view. The world in time, therefore, is not merely qualitatively heterogeneous.

If this is so, and the world in time must be heterogeneous (§7.4.), the heterogeneity in temporal reality must be more stark than merely qualitative. It must be, then, with respect to the existence of things, for if this heterogeneity does not arise from *how* a thing is (that is, the ways a thing is), it can only arise from *whether* a thing is. Consequently, there is *ontological transience*: a thing can either come into being or cease to be simpliciter. If a thing can cease to be simpliciter, it can exist at a moment and, at another, fail to be in the world in every way.

---

[27] See Sullivan 2012: 167.
[28] See Cameron 2015: 168.

§8.2.1. An argument that at least some things cease to be simpliciter

In the preceding chapter, I argue that the world in time is not ontologically homogeneous on the grounds that its being so is incompatible with the experience one has of temporal differentiation, that is, of the experience one has of the world going from *thus* to *as so*. Those same grounds are sufficient to undermine an—admittedly odd—account of temporal reality on which it is ontologically heterogeneous, but merely because some one eternal moment (or thing) is *permanently* qualitatively temporally distinguished from all others. Such an account might be one on which some (eternal) moment, say, a hundred years ago is the only moment that bears the peculiarly temporal property of presentness, bearing this property permanently, while all other moments bear the properties of pastness and futurity relative to it. Rather, the heterogeneity of the world in time must involve a *temporary* distinction: anything that is now temporally distinguished from all others must come to fail to have this distinction.

Given that the heterogeneity of temporal reality involves a temporary distinction, if there were no ontological transience—more specifically, if no thing ever ceased to be simpliciter—any account of the world in time would be inconsistent. Say some entity, *e*, a moment or some other kind of thing, is temporally distinguished, but is not permanently so. Eventually, then, *e* is not temporally distinguished. When *e* is *not* so distinguished, that *e is* so distinguished cannot be so. This would be inconsistent. Thus, when *e* is not so distinguished, whatever thing, *e* itself or a mode of *e* or a state of affairs partially constituted by *e* or a fact involving *e*, etc., that accounted for *e* being temporally distinguished cannot still exist. This thing must cease to be simpliciter, and so there is ontological transience.[29]

§8.2.2. Another argument that at least some things cease to be simpliciter

I now present an even more direct argument for ontological transience based on one's awareness of certain things in the world. Most temporal entities

---

[29] Were the traditional passage view and moving spotlight views not to include a commitment to ontological transience, their inconsistencies would emerge more directly. Cameron accepts ontological transience with respect to states of affairs. See Cameron 2015: 170.

change and eventually cease to be, or they certainly seem to. One eats an apple and that apple seems to go out of existence. With something like an apple, though, one is not in a position to know with certainty when it exists. One's relationship to the apple might be as direct as possible—one might be acquainted with it, and so, in that context, not be aware of the apple were it not to exist. Still, this is consistent with the apple being hidden from one, in a different context, and therein one not being in the position to know whether the apple exists. Indeed, the apple is ontologically independent of one, in that given what it is, it can exist in one's absence. That the apple nonetheless exists even when it appears to have ceased to be is, then, not beyond doubt.

Consider, however, one's awareness of being appeared to whitely (because one is facing a white wall) or of a pain in one's finger. In such cases, one's awareness is a mental mode, a particular way that only one's mind could be, and one is related to that mode. Such modes are things. These are things, unlike apples, that are ontologically dependent on one or, more specifically, on one's mind. One need not think that all such modes are *self-intimating*, in the sense that if they exist, one must be aware of them, but if any of these modes are self-intimating—and my chosen examples plausibly are so—one can have direct grounds for accepting ontological transience in the world. If at some moment, m_1, one is aware of a pain in one's finger and the mode that is this awareness is indeed self-intimating and then, at m_2, one is no longer aware of this pain, then one has sufficient grounds for concluding that that mode has ceased entirely to be. Unlike an apple, if such a mode exists, it is accessible to one regardless of where one is or when one is. Were the mode to exist at all, one would have to be aware of it—one is not aware of it, so it does not exist. There is, therefore, ontological transience.

§8.2.3. The scope of ontological transience

There is ontological transience in the world, then, at least insofar as some things cease to be simpliciter. This raises the question of the scope of such transience: what things cease entirely to be and how this contributes to the structure of the world in time.

As has been shown, the world in time is ontologically heterogeneous, and so some moment is distinguished from all others. In light of the arguments against the ontological homogeneity of temporal reality, this distinction is apparent between two moments, m_1 and m_2, when the world is *thus* and then *as so*. Given the arguments of the preceding sections, the distinction is with respect to *whether* something exists, rather than a merely qualitative distinction, one regarding the way(s) a thing is. Say this moment, now, is m_2, when things are *as so*. This indicates that there is some difference between the two moments, m_1 and m_2, regarding whether some thing exists. Obviously, this moment, m_2, exists, as do all the things surrounding one, and they exist at this moment, so the pertinent ontological difference has to be with respect to m_1.

When some thing exists at m_1, that moment when the world was demonstrated by 'thus,' it exists no differently from anything that now exists at m_2, when the world is *as so*. The things at any moment are as real as at any other. Thus, if the difference between m_2 and m_1 were merely pertaining to some thing at m_1 and whether that thing exists, then, since, when the world was demonstrated by 'thus,' that thing existed in the same way that any thing at m_2 now does, the difference would have to be that thing ceasing to be simpliciter at m_1. Such ontological difference, like synchronic change, would require something to be so at a moment and subsequently fail to be so *at that very moment*. This is impossible. However, whatever occurs *subsequent* to a moment occurs at a distinct moment. This sort of ontological difference with respect to merely some thing *at* m_1 is also impossible. The ontological difference between m_2 and m_1 must, therefore, pertain to m_1 per se. Since m_2 exists, it follows that m_1 does not. This is the only non-qualitative, non-relational, ontological difference there could be between the two moments themselves.

The foregoing considerations are totally general, and so apply to any two consecutive moments. Hence, whenever the world goes from being *thus* to *as so*, the moment at which it was demonstrated by 'thus' ceases to be simpliciter. And the moment at which it was demonstrated by 'as so' ceases to be simpliciter when the world becomes *as such* (and so forth). A mutable thing must exist at a moment, since that that thing, which has the capacity to be incompatible ways, is determinately certain ways is in relation to a moment. If moments prior to this one, now, cease to be simpliciter, and some mutable thing that once clearly existed appears not to exist now—despite one being in similar epistemic conditions to those in which one would be aware of such a thing were it to exist uncontroversially—these are strong grounds for accepting that that thing, too, has ceased to be simpliciter. The scope of ontological transience, then, is considerable. Not only do moments cease entirely to be part of reality, but many mundane things (including mental modes) do as well.

§8.2.4. Ontological transience and temporal differentiation

Theories of the structure in temporal reality, like the traditional passage view and moving spotlight views, that posit mere qualitative heterogeneity in a world in which all things exist permanently can provide no insight into why the world goes from being *thus* to *as so* as it incontrovertibly does. Such theories, which are inconsistent, are, then, also objectionably incomplete in that they provide no account of this phenomenon of temporal differentiation. Recognizing ontological transience and its scope—that each moment ceases to be simpliciter and with it many mundane things—provides significant insight into this phenomenon.

When the world is *thus*, this moment has a salience that all others lack; and when this moment, now, is *as so*, *this* moment has a salience that no other has. The experience of temporal differentiation, therefore, involves a crucial transition in salience from one moment to another. The ontological basis of this transition is the most enigmatic aspect of temporal differentiation when one first seriously reflects upon the phenomenon in the effort to explain it. Any adequate explanation of temporal differentiation must account for the transition, yet initially how any thing in the world could do so is not clear. What must be accounted for is how—in concert—each thing in time changes or ceases to be or just remains as it is, so that what is *thus* becomes *as so* and what was salient is no longer, having been supplanted by what now is. Seemingly, no thing could coordinate so flawlessly such a constant and complicated shift in *all this*.

However, once one recognizes that this—and *every*—salient moment ceases to be simpliciter, a satisfying account of the transition of the world from *thus* to *as so* is available. Each thing that now exists is ontologically dependent on this moment. Given that this moment ceases to be simpliciter, each of these mutable things must either cease to be or come to be related to a distinct moment that constrains that thing so as to make a determinate contribution to the world. At this distinct moment, a mutable thing, with its capacities to be incompatible ways, might remain the same or change with respect to some of these ways. There is, therefore, not some thing in the world that coordinates everything now in time to transition simultaneously, so that a distinct moment thereby comes to be salient. But since each thing that now exists, contributing to the world being *thus*, is dependent on this moment, its loss requires each of these things to be otherwise—to itself cease to be or, if it persists, to come to be related to (and so constrained by) a different moment in a distinctive way. This moment then becomes the unique salient moment.

These considerations illuminate temporal differentiation and in particular the crucial transition from one moment to the next that has often been regarded as so mysterious. They do so in a way consistent with radical ontology, for what explanation of temporal differentiation is provided here is simply in terms of certain things and what and how they are. In this case, the relevant things are transient moments and mutable entities. Nevertheless, the foregoing is not a complete account of temporal differentiation. It does not provide insight into the moment that comes to be salient once this one, now, ceases to be simpliciter. In particular, it provides no account of how such a moment is prior to its becoming the unique salient one or whether it is any way at all; more generally, it provides no insight into what, if anything, there is in time subsequent to this moment, now. Once these issues are addressed, one can provide a complete explanation of the phenomenon of temporal differentiation. (I provide this in §9.2.1.)

§8.3. What the Foregoing Reveals About the Structure of the World in Time

If the heterogeneity of temporal reality and the inconstancy in the world are to be accounted for by means of moments—including this one, now—ceasing to be simpliciter, then this has further important consequences regarding the appropriate specific account of the structure in temporal reality. Given that moments (and at least some of the things at them) cease to be, another class of views of the world in time must be rejected.

§8.3.1. Growing block views must be rejected

There are theories of temporal reality, so-called *growing block views*, on which this moment, now, and everything that precedes it, each moment and everything that exists at any of these, is equally real; subsequent to this moment, now, though, there is literally nothing—no moment, no things, nothing whatsoever.[30] However, in an instant, there is a novel moment.

---

[30] See Broad 1923; Adams 1986; Tooley 1997; Forrest 2004.

Such views, then, recognize ontological transience with respect to moments (among other things), but only their coming into being simpliciter. Once they exist, they exist permanently.

On such views, the world in time is clearly ontologically heterogeneous. This moment, now, bears a distinction that no other moment does. It is, momentarily, the boundary of temporal reality. It bears this distinction only temporarily before a wholly novel moment comes to be after it. Although growing block views acknowledge ontological transience, the sort of transience included here is incompatible with anything ever ceasing to be simpliciter. The world just comes to include more and more things; no thing is ever lost. Considering only the world going from *thus* to *as so*, growing block views are structurally similar to the traditional passage view and moving spotlight views: there is a moment at which the world is *thus*, then one at which it is *as so*, and the only difference between these two moments is that when the world is *as so*, this moment has a qualitative distinction that the earlier moment lacks. Growing block views, then, have the same problems that views that posit mere qualitative heterogeneity in temporal reality have. Either this moment, now—the "present" moment—must change per se, when it ceases to be the boundary of temporal reality (but it cannot) or, if "presentness," what makes this moment distinctive, is to be characterized in terms of how all the things that exist at this moment when it is the boundary of reality are, these things must undergo synchronic change when a novel moment becomes the boundary of reality (but such "change" is impossible). Growing block views, despite including ontological transience and, hence, significant inconstancy in temporal reality, are untenable, and for the same reasons that the traditional passage view and moving spotlight views are.

Of course, the problems with growing block views are even more obvious than this. I argue above that the appropriate account of the structure in temporal reality must include the sort of ontological transience whereby things cease to be simpliciter, lest the account be inconsistent. Yet growing block views explicitly exclude such transience. Moreover, I argue that moments themselves must entirely go out of existence. A definitive feature of growing block views, though, is that whereas moments come into existence simpliciter they never cease to be. Therefore, growing block views must be rejected.

The considerations in Chapter 7 show that the general view of the world in time on which it is ontologically heterogeneous is correct. The considerations in this chapter provide constraints on the appropriate specific account of temporal reality. Even if a view recognizes the ontological heterogeneity in temporal reality, if it posits merely qualitative differences among permanently existing things, the view is incorrect. Even if a view recognizes ontological transience in the world, unless this transience admits things ceasing to be simpliciter, the view is incorrect. Hence, the ontological heterogeneity of the world in time is profound, requiring inconstancy that involves things ceasing to be in the world in every way. Part of the allure of the traditional passage view, moving spotlight views, and growing block views, however, is the seeming capacity of such theories to account not only for the inconstancy in the world, but also for the constancy herein. If, as I maintain, many moments and things cease to be simpliciter, seemingly any means to account for this constancy are lost. This is not so (as I show in Chapter 11). Before taking this up, though, there is more to be done to clarify the structure in temporal reality in order to provide the appropriate specific account of it.

9
Absolute Becoming and the Contingency in the World

The arguments of the preceding chapter show that there is nothing prior to this moment, now. However, in experiencing temporal differentiation, not only does one experience the world as *thus* and then *as so*, one also experiences it *as such* and *such* and so forth. There must, then, be more to the basis of the phenomenon than this moment, now, and some moment that has ceased to be simpliciter. There must be some thing(s) else to account for the continuity in temporal differentiation. Reflecting on this continuity indicates that the world as it now is is, although complete, not exhausted: *all this* remains latent. There *could* be more to the world or, perhaps, there *will be*. What more there could be, however, would seemingly be different from what is or has been. Presumably, what is to be includes *contingency*, an openness such that incompatible alternatives are possible. These considerations raise the question of what the structure in temporal reality subsequent to this moment, now, is. They also raise the question of the relation between the world in time and this contingency, in particular, how the contingency is included among the things in temporal reality.

The primary purpose of this chapter is to answer these questions. In doing so, I complete the account of the structure in the world in time presented in the last chapter, providing an account of what is subsequent to this moment, now, to complement that account of what is prior to this moment. Given this structure, and the ontology underlying this inquiry, the only contingency in the world arises from what now is: although nothing could now be otherwise than it actually is—so everything *must be just as it is*—in some cases, a thing could be otherwise (than it now is) at some moment yet to be. Likewise, although all there now could be (in time) is what there is at this moment, there might be more (or less) at some moment yet to be. Contingency arises *through* a moment, *m*, with the actualization, at a distinct moment, of the potential of the things at *m*; contingency and, hence, incompatible alternatives are not present *at* any moment. There is, therefore, a crucial connection between contingency and temporal differentiation.

I begin by considering views of the world in time on which there are moments subsequent to this one, now. New applications of arguments from preceding chapters show that these views are incorrect: there are no later moments. From this conclusion, in combination with previous ones, that this moment, now, is the only moment in temporal reality follows. Of course, as noted above, there is more to the structure in temporal reality than a single moment, for one's experience of the world is not momentary; one persists with a continuous experience of temporal differentiation. An account of what underlies this experience is given in terms of time itself and of *absolute becoming*, whereby moments come into being simpliciter. The discussion of absolute becoming completes my account of the ontologically heterogeneous structure in temporal reality and enables me to explain fully the phenomenon of temporal differentiation. I conclude the chapter, and Part III of this book, by examining the modal status of the temporal entities and their arrangements underlying this account of the metaphysics of time and, relatedly, the relation between contingency and time.

§9.1. The Structure of the World in Time Subsequent to Now

One of the conclusive arguments against the view that temporal reality is ontologically homogeneous turns on recognizing that if there were other moments (at which one existed) as real as this one, now, that did not differ in any peculiarly temporal way from this moment, then one's experience of the world in time would be a farrago and so quite different than it in fact is. In competition with one's experience of this moment, now, with its distinctive salience, would be one's experience of all other moments at which one exists, for these moments and whatever exists at them—including oneself and one's experiences—are supposed to be no less real than this moment. To comprehend what such a farrago of competing experiences of distinct, equally real, and salient moments would be like, is hard, but that such experience would be chaotic in ways that one's actual experience at this moment, now, is not is clear.

Whether equally real moments are prior to or subsequent to this moment, now, makes no difference to this argument. In either case, were there such moments, one's experience of the world would be a farrago, chaotic in ways that it patently is not. Thus, if the world in time does indeed include moments subsequent to this, these moments must be distinguished in some peculiarly temporal way from this moment, now. In other words, the structure of moments beginning with this one must be ontologically heterogeneous. Those moments subsequent to this one, now, must bear some temporal property—call it *futurity*—that this one lacks. This property might be the basis of an explanation for why the moments that have it are not salient in the same way that this moment, now, is although they are no less real.

However, given this sort of qualitative ontological heterogeneity, some of the arguments of the preceding chapter are pressing. Those arguments, which maintain that a moment itself cannot change and that synchronous change is not possible, were used to demonstrate that there are no moments *prior* to this one, now. Essentially the same arguments indicate that there are no moments *subsequent* to it either.

§9.1.1. Arguments from change in a moment and synchronous change applied again

There is certainly this moment, now (when the world is *thus*). That there are moments subsequent to this one, too, is not implausible. Reflecting on the world in time, one might think that either one will wake at six o'clock tomorrow morning or one will not; so there is, i.e., IS (tenselessly), that moment, subsequent to now, at precisely six tomorrow morning at which one is just waking up or is not. That moment might be epistemically inaccessible, it might now be impossible to know exactly what one is doing at it, but, one might think, it is no less part of the world than this moment, now.

Assume, then, that there are moments subsequent to this one. Even if there are, this moment, now, is nonetheless unique. It is, one might also assume, present and so has a salience—presumably in virtue of its presentness—that no other moment has. Moreover, since there are no moments prior to it, it is distinctive in being the one moment not later than another; in other words, it is the first in a temporal ordering of moments. Given temporal differentiation, the presentness of this moment, now, whereby it is distinctive, is only temporary. This moment ceases to be simpliciter, and some other moment comes to be present as its predecessor once was. If the moment that comes to be present exists (i.e., EXISTS) subsequent to this moment, now, it exists (i.e., EXISTS) without being present. If that moment, which is not present, comes to be present, then it itself must undergo change. However, I demonstrate above (§8.1.1.2.) that no moment per se can undergo change.

As I argue above (§8.1.1.2.), one moment cannot exist at another. Change requires the bearing of incompatible properties by one and the same thing. Since bearing incompatible properties requires a thing to exist at distinct moments, if one moment cannot exist at another, a moment cannot bear incompatible properties and, hence, cannot change. Furthermore, I argue above (§8.1.1.2.), there is no thing, such as a hypermoment, that a moment exists at or in relation to in such a way that that moment can bear incompatible properties. In that discussion, I use these arguments to show that a moment that is supposed to exist prior to this one, now—a moment bearing pastness—cannot have changed from being present to being past. Here I use the arguments to show that a moment that is supposed to exist subsequent to this one, now—a moment bearing futurity—cannot change from being future to being present. That essentially the same arguments are applicable in both cases should not be surprising, for in both a moment is supposed to change (and change with respect to its temporary temporal properties). What exactly the putative change is makes no difference, if a moment cannot change at all.

In light of the arguments of the preceding chapter against the traditional passage view and the moving spotlight theory, when the world goes from *thus* to *as so*, the moment at which it was demonstrated by 'thus' ceases to be simpliciter. Its doing so does not require that the moment that comes to be present undergo any change per se. Still, if there are moments subsequent to this one, the things existing at the moment that succeeds this one (if not the moment itself) must undergo some change, lest there be no account of one's experience of temporal differentiation. When the world goes from being *thus* to *as so*, the things that are the basis of the world being *as so* must come to have features that they lacked. They come to be accessible with a vividness that they did not have previously, though they were no less real. So if this moment, now, is present, its presentness is derivative on the features of the things that exist at it. However, if the things at a moment change as that moment comes to be unique among all equally real moments, as the present moment or the first, subsequent to no other, then those things must change synchronically. Thus, a thing that exists, i.e., EXISTS, at a moment lacking certain features—namely, whatever features confer the uniqueness of this moment—must come to have those features *at that very moment*. As I argue above (§8.1.2.3.), such "change," which involves but a single moment and incompatible properties, is incoherent. Consequently, there can be no such change. If this is so, a moment existing subsequent to this one, now, does not come to be temporally unique, i.e., the present moment, by the things existing at that moment undergoing changes.

Temporal reality is ontologically heterogeneous, at least one moment is unique, bearing a temporal property or having some distinction that separates it from any other moment. As temporal differentiation makes indisputable, the distinction of this unique moment is borne only temporarily—momentarily—before a different moment comes to bear it. If there are moments no less real than this one, now, but subsequent to it, each of these moments is, i.e., IS, as it is (IS). Each of these moments, however, is temporally related to this one, now; each is later than it. Eventually, therefore, some one of these moments must come to be unique in the way this moment, now, is. No moment is (IS) unique in the way this moment now is, that is, no other moment is present. Yet I have just argued that no moment subsequent to this one, now, can itself change to become present. Nor can the things that exist at any such moment change in such a way that they are different at that moment. Consequently, no moment can come to be present derivatively upon changes in the things that exist at that moment. There is no other way for a moment, which is supposed to exist (i.e., EXIST) subsequent to this one, to become present. Hence, there is no existing (EXISTING) moment that comes to be as this moment, now, is. Since any moment that exists subsequent to this moment—any future moment—would eventually have to become as this moment, now, is—to wit, present—I conclude that there are no such moments. There are no moments subsequent to this one, now, just as there are none prior to it.

Nevertheless, obviously, this is not the last moment of time. Certainly some moment becomes present. The upshot here is that temporal differentiation does not involve change, from futurity to presentness or any other properties, among equally real moments. This result should not be surprising. It is arrived at by a rehearsal of essentially the same considerations as those employed above to argue against the traditional passage view and the moving spotlight theory, whereby temporal differentiation is supposed to involve change, from presentness to pastness, among equally real moments. Formally, a thing going from present to past is no different from a thing going from future to present. Therefore, an account of temporal differentiation is still needed, one that illuminates how *all this* can go from *thus* to *as so* despite there being no future moments (and no moment later than this one, now).

§9.1.2. Rejection of any structure subsequent to this moment, now

The apt account of temporal differentiation is constrained by the structure in temporal reality, which includes time itself and all temporal entities, those things ontologically dependent on time. A complete view of this structure is now available: there is this moment, now, which comes from time. (Little more can be said about how a moment comes from time, beyond noting that time is just the thing that yields moments. Each thing simply is what it is and does what it does (see §5.4.). There are no moments prior to it; there are no moments subsequent to it. Considerations in the previous chapter exclude a view of the structure in temporal reality on which it comprises a series of equally real moments, some of which are prior to this one. In the preceding section, I apply essentially the same considerations to demonstrate that the structure in the world in time is not a series of moments that begins with this one, now. These considerations, however, rule out many more views of the structure in temporal reality.

There are a variety of views that posit more structure to the world in time subsequent to this moment than merely a series of moments related by the earlier than (or later than) relation. On such views there are a number of, perhaps infinitely many, equally real moments set to succeed this one, now, as the unique present moment. There are, as well, a number (perhaps infinite) of equally real moments set to succeed the successor of this one, and the one after that, and so forth. The notion often employed to illustrate such views is that of a tree with many intricate branches: each moment is related to many moments analogously to the way that the trunk of a tree is related to its many branches and subsidiary stems. Storrs McCall propounds the most developed example of a view of this variety, and it has come to be known as a *shrinking tree view* of the structure in temporal reality. In developing the view, he introduces and objects to others that include a branching structure of moments subsequent to this one.[1]

---

[1] See, in particular, McCall 1994: 4–5. For references to discussions of a branching future, see Footnote 4.

On McCall's account, temporal reality includes moments at which every development of how things now are consistent with the laws of nature is real. If that I wake at six o'clock tomorrow morning is consistent with the laws of nature, given the way the world now is, and that I do not wake then is also consistent, the world includes a moment at which I do wake tomorrow morning at six o'clock and one at which I do not. Both of these moments (and myriad others) are temporally related to this moment, now, by a series of intermediate moments. As this moment, now ceases to be present, some subsequent moment comes to be distinguished as the unique present one. (On McCall's view, although moments cease to be present, no moment at which the world is as it is ceases to be simpliciter. This detail, although problematic for the reasons discussed in the previous chapter, can be overlooked for present purposes.) All other sequences from the moment that ceases to be present that do not include the one that becomes present cease to be simpliciter. As each later moment comes to be distinguished as present, more of the world in time ceases to be (simpliciter). Thus, the structure in temporal reality is that of a continuously shrinking tree: as different moments come to be present, some of the enormous structure of the world in time, "branches" at which alternative goings-on occur, "fall off," ceasing to be simpliciter.

This shrinking tree view, and any relevantly similar to it, is untenable. Regardless of how complicated the posited structure subsequent to this moment is, or how exactly it is supposed to be arranged, a defining feature of this sort of view is that some moment just as real as this one, now, but which lacks its unique temporal status, comes to have this status. This, however, is precisely what is ruled out by the foregoing considerations: neither any moment, nor the things existing at some moment, can change in such a way that that moment can come to be present or to have the unique temporal status of this moment, now. Even if one denied that these subsequent moments were as real as this one, now, suspending for the nonce the principle that there is only one way to exist and, hence, be in the world, this would not make this sort of view of the world in time any less problematic. Whatever ontological status a subsequent moment had, that moment would have to change to become as real as this moment, now. Yet a moment cannot change. Similarly, whatever ontological status the things at such a moment had, those things would have to change synchronically, they would have to change at the very moment at which they exist, so that moment could become as real as this moment, now. Yet things cannot change synchronically.

Therefore, I conclude that no view that posits structure in the world subsequent to this moment, now—be it a mere series or some arrangement of things much more elaborate—is correct.

The motivation for entertaining such views is more than the plausibility, noted above, that either one will wake at six o'clock tomorrow morning or one will not, which many take to suggest that there now is (IS, tenselessly) a subsequent moment at which one is waking or is not. Rather the primary motivation is an appreciation of the current latency in reality: the world is complete yet not exhausted. There *is* no more, yet there *could be*. That there *will be* more is almost universally presumed. What more there could be, however, is not complete, nor even determinate, in that incompatible alternatives are both possible. This openness in the world, this contingency, is widely thought to be aptly captured by a non-linear, branching array of subsequent moments at which different things and, thus, different goings-on exist (EXIST). If all views that posit a structure of moments subsequent to this one, now, are to be rejected, some alternative account of this contingency in temporal reality is needed. Any such account must be consistent with that of temporal differentiation, and the constraints on both are severe. Both must be compatible with a world in time that includes little more than this moment, now, the things that exist at it, and time itself.

§9.1.3. Temporal entities and the extent of the world in time

When the world goes from *thus* to *as so*, there is a difference between the moment at which it was demonstrated by 'thus' and the one at which it is now *as so*. The world in time is, then, ontologically heterogeneous, at least one moment is unique, bearing a temporal property or having some distinction that separates it from any other moment. This moment, now, is the distinctive one. By this point, what distinction exactly this moment has is clear: it is the only moment that exists in any sense. There is no moment prior to it, nor any subsequent to it. The structure in temporal reality is, therefore, quite sparse.

The uniqueness of this moment, now, is ontological, rather than qualitative, in that it is distinctive just in being at all, not in some way that it is. There is no peculiarly temporal property that this moment—or anything existing at it—has that distinguishes it from other things in temporal reality. To call this moment 'present' is not apt, then, for the term is supposed to refer to some thing that bears a special temporary monadic temporal property that only this moment, now (or something existing at it) has. Moreover, there is no relational property of presentness. If there is only a single moment and nothing is present at it, no thing is present relative to that moment or any other thing. If there is no presentness, there is no pastness nor futurity either. These temporal properties are supposed to be had in relation to what is present: pastness is supposed to be a property of a moment (or a thing at such a moment) had after it is present; futurity is supposed to be a property of a moment (or a thing at such a moment) before it is present. If nothing is present, then nothing can have these other properties. The presumption that there are (or must be) such temporal properties is a consequence of accepting an incorrect account of the world in time, one on which temporal reality is thought to contain much more structure (in particular, many more moments) than it in fact does.

Not only are there not the familiar temporary monadic (or relational) temporal properties, there are fewer temporal relations than widely—if not universally—presumed. If there is only this moment, now, there is no moment earlier than it, nor any moment later than it. If there are no such moments for things to exist at, then presumably nothing is derivatively earlier than or later than anything else. This corroborates the conclusion that there is no property of pastness or futurity, for whatever were past would at least have to exist earlier than this moment, and whatever were future would at least have to exist later than it. One upshot of these considerations is that, say, the event of my birth, which occurred at a particular moment many years ago, is not earlier than the event of my now writing, at least not in the sense that the former event and the moment at which it occurs bears the *earlier than* relation to the latter and the moment at which it occurs. If the claim that my birth precedes this moment, now, is to be regarded as literally true, then it cannot be construed as a description of such structure, to wit, moments standing in some temporal relation. The basis of its truth, which is crucial to the indubitable constancy in the world, must be some thing(s) other than those moments and the things existing at them. (I take up such issues in Chapter 11.)

In general, and as odd as it sounds, nothing is earlier than anything else, and nothing is later, for nothing stands in these temporal relations— nor could anything. However, there is the temporal relation of existing at a moment, which each mutable thing bears to any moment at which it exists, and the relation of simultaneity, which all things existing at a moment bear to each other. Therefore, the only temporal entities there are, in addition to time itself, are a single moment, a host of mutable entities (with the particular ways they are), and the temporal relations that these mutable entities bear to this moment and each other. Setting time per se aside, the entire structure of the world in time comprises this one moment and the mutable temporal entities simultaneously existing at it.

§9.2. Ontological Transience: Absolute Becoming, Coming to Be Simpliciter

That the foregoing considerations regarding the world in time—which result in a catalog of exactly what temporal entities there are—are not themselves a complete account of the metaphysics of time or even of temporal reality is obvious. In confronting the world in original inquiry, one experiences it as *thus* and then *as so* and, given this temporal differentiation, one can confront the world again and again in original inquiry. One's experience of the world is, then, not limited to this moment, now. A comprehensive and satisfactory account of the metaphysics of time must explicate this phenomenon of temporal differentiation. The continuity of one's experience of the phenomenon reveals the latency now in the world and its associated contingency. These phenomena, too, must be explicated. Given the connection between them, one might expect a unified account of all three, that is, an account of the contingency in the world in terms of temporal differentiation and the latency of what now exists. Indeed, such an account is forthcoming based upon the things in temporal reality: time itself and what now exists. However, a fully satisfactory account of the metaphysics of time must also explicate the constancy in the world, for this constancy is no less indubitable than the inconstancy one experiences via temporal differentiation. If the extent of temporal reality (beyond time itself) is merely a single, transient moment and what exists thereat, though, there is not the means *in time* from which to develop the needed account of constancy. Thus, more things are required for this account. I resolve these matters concerning the constancy in the world in Chapter 11. But here I am finally in a position to provide a full account of temporal differentiation and to thereby illuminate the indubitable inconstancy in the world.

§9.2.1. What temporal differentiation is

This one moment, the only one that exists, does not exist permanently (or eternally). It has its distinctive status—of being the unique moment—only temporarily. In an instant, it ceases to be simpliciter. Of course, however, the world in time does not end with it: another moment immediately follows. Although this novel moment follows the first, it is not *later* than it. The relata of any relation, temporal or otherwise, must exist if that relation is to hold. Yet each moment exists in the absence of any other, so the relations of earlier than and later than cannot hold (though that one thing follows another can be true without the former standing in any relation to the latter). The preceding arguments demonstrate that this novel moment did not exist (EXIST, tenselessly) priorly. It does not bear any relation to its predecessor, because its predecessor no longer exists; nor did it bear any relation when that other moment existed, for then this moment did not exist. This novel moment comes to be simpliciter. It does not come from nothing, of course, it comes from time itself, the thing that yields moments. Moreover, it comes as it does, uniquely, in no relation to any other moment, because of time itself, which orders moments. Time does so by continuously yielding instantaneous moments (each of which ceases to be simpliciter).

This coming to be simpliciter of a moment is *absolute becoming*.[2] In general, a thing becomes absolutely when it comes to be from in no way being in the world. The becoming of a moment is absolute in another way, to wit, that the coming to be of this temporal entity is not relative to some moment. It is the coming to be *of* a moment and does not occur *at* any moment. Thus, the absolute becoming of a moment does not occur in time. Although any moment stands in a relation to time itself, this is no peculiarly temporal relation: a moment is not earlier than or later than time or even simultaneous with it (time does not exist at a moment and to exist simultaneously is to exist at the same moment). Rather, the relation between a moment and time itself is that in which anything stands to its source, and so need not be peculiarly temporal at all.

---

[2] This term is introduced in Broad 1938, Volume II, Part 1, §1.22. Broad explicitly distinguishes absolute becoming from any sort of qualitative change, so I believe he has in mind the phenomenon I characterize in the text. However, Steven Savitt (2002) interprets Broad quite differently. According to Savitt, Broad takes absolute becoming to be the ontological homogeneity of temporal reality. See §7.3.2. above. I think Savitt's interpretation is mistaken, but exegesis of Broad is not my concern here.

Absolute becoming is of the utmost importance to understanding temporal differentiation and its ontological basis. Essential to temporal differentiation is the continuous and ineluctable coming to be simpliciter—and immediate ceasing to be simpliciter—of the (instantaneous) moments yielded by time. The ceasing to be simpliciter of one moment accounts for the crucial transition of the world to the next moment (§8.2.4.). Hence, no less important to temporal differentiation are all the many mutable things that exist in time, that is, at moments, that make this transition. These things have the capacity to persist, to exist at many moments. They also have the capacities to be incompatible ways: red at one moment, brown at another; sitting, then standing; young and, eventually, old. These mutable things and how they now are account (in part) for *all this* being *thus*. Now *these* mutable things, some of which persisted and changed, some of which persisted as they were, some of which are wholly novel account (in part) for *all this* being *as so*. Thus, the changes in the world that one experiences are accounted for by the persistence of mutable things and the manifestations of their capacities to be incompatible ways realized by the absolute annihilation and becoming of moments. The continuousness of the absolute annihilation and absolute becoming of moments underlies the continuity of one's experience of the world going from *thus* to *as so* to *as such* and so forth.

Here, then, is the full account of temporal differentiation. This account, like any acceptable explanation of any structural phenomenon, is in terms of things and their relations. In this case, temporal differentiation is accounted for in terms of time itself, the distinct transient moments it yields and the mutable things that exist at these moments. The world goes from *thus* to *as so* because of what time is, what moments are, and what mutable things are. Note that temporal differentiation does not involve any temporary temporal properties (nor the temporal relations of earlier than or later than). Furthermore, although temporal differentiation involves change, it involves ontological transience and, hence, more than mere qualitative differences in temporal reality. The inconstancy one experiences via temporal differentiation is, therefore, of two varieties: the ontological transience of moments and other things, coming to be simpliciter, ceasing to be simpliciter—as well as the changes of mutable things, one and the same thing being a certain way at one (transient) moment and an incompatible way at a distinct (transient) moment.

The absolute becoming of moments is necessary for change, yet moments coming to be simpliciter do not involve change in anything. Indeed, this phenomenon does not even occur at a moment and so does not take place in time. The absolute becoming of moments is, therefore, not a *process*, for, presumably, any process must involve changes in some thing(s) over time. The absolute becoming of moments is, rather, an essential concomitant of time, one whereby anything can exist at a moment at all; and so is that by which there can be any process or, more generally, any change whatsoever. Given that the absolute becoming of moments is no process, there is no question about the rate at which it occurs. There is, consequently, no question regarding the rate at which temporal differentiation occurs. This is significant because of the long-standing objection to views that acknowledge significant inconstancy in the world based on the question of the rate at which this inconstancy occurs (§7.1.1.). Customarily, the objection has been directed at views that take temporal reality to be merely qualitatively heterogeneous (e.g., the traditional passage view and moving spotlight views) with the question of how fast time passes, that is, how fast a moment goes from being, say, future to present to past. Recently it has been maintained that the objection applies to any view on which the world in time is inconstant.[3] In light of the foregoing discussion, however, this objection can simply be discarded. It is premised on the assumption that what underlies the inconstancy in the world is merely change or some process involving moments standing in temporal relations. This assumption is incorrect and only seems plausible if one fails to recognize the absolute coming to be—and absolute ceasing to be—of moments and, hence, what temporal differentiation actually is.

Although there is only this moment, now, that there are moments is nonetheless true. There are moments in that there is a kind of thing, *moment*, that is multiply instantiated. Each moment is an instance of this kind. The kind is never instantiated simultaneously, and could not be and, more generally, the world could not include distinct moments. The kind is no less multiply instantiated for this, however. There is this moment, now ... and this one ... and this and so forth. When any moment comes to be, though, its predecessor has ceased to be.

Moments are the only temporal entities that come into being not in relation to a moment. There are other entities that come to be, yet not in (temporal) relation to a moment—not *at* a moment—but these are *atemporal*. Such atemporal entities, some of which are crucial to explicating the constancy in the world, are discussed in detail below (§11.3.). All other temporal

[3] Olson 2009: 3.

entities that come to be, viz., all mutable entities, can only come into being at a moment. (The two temporal relations, the *at* relation and *simultaneity* are, like time itself, eternal, that is, without an origin, and so do not come into being at all.) The relational existence of each mutable thing is overlooked in many contexts and so, say, a tree might be characterized as green (simpliciter) or in bloom (simpliciter), when really it is only green at m_1 or in bloom at m_2. Although the tree is, in itself, a tree and organic and living, it is not, per se, green or in bloom. It has the capacity to be both green and not green and in bloom and not in bloom; in itself it is neither of any contradictory pairs of ways it can be. What is so with respect to a tree is so for mutable things in general. Thus, that a mutable thing is determinately, for each contradictory pair of ways it can be, one of these two ways is only in relation to a moment.

Consequently, and importantly, given this account of the structure in temporal reality—on which there is ever but a single instantaneous moment in the world—to characterize, once and for all, how things are at a given moment is possible. On some accounts of the world in time (e.g., the traditional passage view, moving spotlight views, growing block views), how the world is at a moment, m, is supposed to change constantly; m itself is taken to change or the things at m are taken to change (constantly). Were this so, then there could be no account of how the world is at m simpliciter, and so there could be no constancy in the world—yet there indubitably is. However, since on the account of the world in time propounded here, a moment, m, exists and then entirely ceases to be, m is never otherwise than it is. Therefore, to accept, at any moment that comes to be, that it is true that things were (or ARE, tenselessly) at m just as they are for the instant that m exists is appropriate. This point is key to ensuing discussion of the constancy in the world and its ontological basis in Part IV. Before turning to such issues, though, a different one must be addressed.

§9.3. Necessity, Contingency, and the World in Time

I have propounded an account of the structure in temporal reality on which all there is in time (beyond, of course, time itself, the at relation and simultaneity) is this moment, now, and the mutable things existing thereat. Temporal differentiation reveals the latency at this moment; there could be more than what now is. Reflecting on how things now are, and that there could be more to *all this*, there seems to be nothing precluding a host of incompatible alternative arrangements of things yet to be. When considering oneself as an agent, a thing capable of contributing in accordance to reasons or other norms to what more there could be, to regard the world as open to such incompatible alternatives is important. I might wake at six o'clock tomorrow morning to go to the gym or sleep in; I might help the person in need or selfishly retain my resources. Each mutable thing, as a natured entity, must be certain ways essentially. However, for every other way that mutable thing is, it has the capacity to be the contradictory of this way. Given my capacities and those of other mutable things, there are seemingly the means in the world for contingency, an openness such that incompatible alternatives are possible. Whether in fact there is such contingency, though, and, if there is, what its ontological basis is and how prevalent it is must be determined.

Fatalism is a view of the world on which there is no unactualized possibility and, hence, no contingency.[4] Few philosophers, if any, now accept fatalism. In contemporary discussions of metaphysics, widespread contingency—this possibility of incompatible alternatives—is universally taken for granted. Many accept that things *now* could be otherwise, that given the way the world is at this moment, things *now* could be different. What is accepted is that things could be different, not merely in the *epistemic* sense that for all one knows things are in fact otherwise than how one takes them to be, but in an *ontological* sense: that even though things are at this moment certain ways, these things now could be incompatible ways *at this very moment*. Hence, most philosophers accept that whatever is true now could be false now. Indeed, most even accept not only that incompatible alternatives are now possible, but that they are possible subsequent to this moment, now, and even prior to this moment.

I argue this is mistaken. Each thing must be precisely as it is (now), and every true claim is necessarily true. There is, nevertheless, contingency in the world, it just arises in a way different than most recognize and is less prevalent. The common view of contingency is a consequence of misguided

---

[4] To some, the term 'fatalism' might suggest that what is to be has a preordained outcome, that although there might be many different ways for *all this* to evolve, these differences are irrelevant, for all ways lead to the same ordained outcome. However, understanding fatalism in this way requires someone or something to ordain what is to be. The fatalism I discuss has no such theistic requirement. Note that *necessitarianism* is not an apt name for the fatalism I reject. Although I reject the latter, and so accept there is unactualized possibility, i.e., contingency, in the world, I maintain nonetheless that everything is necessarily just as it is and, thus, that every true claim about the world is necessarily so—and this view might perspicuously be called 'necessitarianism.'

(or unexamined) assumptions regarding the basis of possibility in the world. On this view, alternative possibilities are possible at a moment, this one, now, or any other. I maintain, however, that incompatible alternatives are *never* both possible, that is, at no moment can a thing be different than it is. There is, then, some dispute regarding the modal status of what now is, whether it must be as it is or need not be so. Settling this dispute reveals how the world at this moment is complete, yet not exhausted and how the things in time are latent. These considerations provide an account of contingency, revealing the important relation between the possibility of incompatible alternatives and temporal differentiation, and thereby illuminating the necessity of what now is. Such an account of contingency is needed, therefore, for a complete account of the metaphysics of time—and of *all this*, more generally.

§9.3.1. The basis of possibility and the necessity in this moment, now

Often, the contingency in the world is contrasted with the necessity herein. A state of affairs, that is, an arrangement of things, is necessary if that arrangement *must*—without qualification—be. Thus, a contingent state of affairs is supposed to be an arrangement of things that is and yet need not be. It need not be in that an incompatible state of affairs *could*—without qualification—exist in its stead. Those who accept this account of contingency often characterize it as one on which the things in the world could be otherwise than they in fact are. This characterization is misleading, because although, in a sense, things could be otherwise than they in fact are, that any existent arrangement of things is not necessarily so is incorrect. There are, then, alternative accounts of contingency. Distinguishing them is requisite to understanding the structure in reality and to discerning the relation between contingency and time.

As noted above, many philosophers take it for granted that if the world is now a certain way, it nevertheless—at this very moment—could be otherwise. Hence, many presume that incompatible alternatives are now both possible. This is an account of contingency on which there is *synchronic possibility*. Contingency is supposed to occur *at* a moment, m, and so what actually is need not be, for there are ever so many incompatible arrangements that could (simpliciter) exist at m. Each moment is supposed to be overlain, as it were, with myriad alternatives, i.e., possibilities, just one of which is actual. This familiar account of contingency and when it is located is, I argue, mistaken.

To see what is wrong with synchronic possibility and, hence, any account of contingency that includes it, one must consider what the ontological basis of the possibility in the world is. The basis of such possibility is whatever makes it so that a certain arrangement of things, e.g., two substances standing in some relation to one another or one substance bearing a certain quality, could or might be. Nota bene: what makes it *so* that a certain arrangement of things is possible must be distinguished from what makes a representation of the possibility of that arrangement *true*. The latter crucially involves some (true) representational entity, whereas the former does not. Thus, the ontological bases of possibilities are not necessarily the truthmakers of modal claims (regarding possibility). This distinction between what makes the world so and what makes claims about it true is pivotal to a comprehensive and satisfactory account of the metaphysics of time (§11.1.2.). Here, however, I merely articulate the distinction in order to clarify in what sense exactly there is contingency in the world.

The familiarity and glibness of talk of *possible worlds* might lead one to believe that they have something to do with the basis of possibility. This is misguided. If a possible world is supposed to be a multitude of related things just like this world, then it can provide no insight into how these (actual) things could be. If a possible world is supposed to be a maximal representation depicting an alternate complete arrangement of things, then a possible world is illuminating only if it is consistent with the actual bases of possibility, with what indeed could be so. In either case, a possible world is removed from what makes it so that some arrangements of things (and not others) could be. One might think, then, that the *concepts* one employs or what one is able to *conceive* provides the basis of possibility. But this, too, is misguided. Concepts are the means one has of sorting and then representing the things in the world. How one (accurately) conceptualizes these natured entities is certainly dependent on how they could be, rather than vice versa. Conceiving is some representational act or other, one supposed to present what is possible;[5] as such, successfully conceiving depends on what could be and is not its basis. Thus, concepts and conceiving are representational in a way that precludes them from being what makes it so that certain arrangements of things could be.

---

[5] I am quite dubious of conceiving as a theoretically fruitful activity. See Fiocco 2021.

All there is are things, so the basis of any phenomenon, in this case, the presence of possibility in the world, is some thing(s) or other. So whatever these ontological bases are, they must be things and ones intimately related to what is made to be possible. Suppose, then, that it is possible for a given thing to be a certain way. A red apple, for instance, could be brown. There is some thing that accounts for this possibility. In this case, it is not the apple as a whole, for most of the apple (e.g., its stem, flesh, core) and most of how it is (e.g., tart, firm, fragrant) are irrelevant to its color. So some feature of the apple, pertaining to its color, accounts for its possibly being brown although it is in fact red. The most straightforward suggestion as to what this feature is is also, I maintain, the most insightful. What accounts for the possibility of the apple being red when it is brown is, I submit, the *capacity*—or *power* or *disposition* (I use these terms interchangeably)—of that apple to be different colors. In general, it is the capacities of things that determine how they could be.[6]

A capacity just is a quality, a way a thing is, that makes possible the thing that has this capacity relating to another thing. With respect to qualities, a certain capacity enables a thing that is one determinate way to be an incompatible way from a range of determinates of the same determinable. If a thing does not itself have the capacity to be related to some other, nothing could make it be so-related. Capacities are, then, inherently modal, in that they pertain to what could or must be, and cannot be explicated in terms of things that are not modal. But, then, no thing can be explicated in terms of some other. The view I am proposing is a sort of *modal dispositionalism*, a view on which all possibility arises from the actual capacities of things in the world.[7] Such views are contested,[8] but that some version of modal dispositionalism is the only tenable account of the basis of possibility in the world seems obvious to me. Given what things are, each thing is fundamental. Insofar as some phenomenon that requires explication is modal—and, clearly, the presence of possibility is—its explication can only be via things that are modal.

---

[6] Thus, I accept that among the things there are are irreducibly modal capacities, qualities of things that determine how the things that bear them interact with others and so could be. For an insightful systematic discussion of an ontology that includes such capacities, i.e., powers, see Williams 2019.

[7] For similar views, see Borghini and Williams 2008 and Jacobs 2010. These authors develop their views in terms of the truthmakers of modal claims. For the reasons noted in passing above, and those to be presented in greater detail in subsequent discussion, I believe carefully distinguishing between what makes some phenomenon so and what makes one's claims about that phenomenon true is important.

[8] See, for example, Wang 2015.

Capacities are not just the most apt things to account for possibility, they seem to be the only things.

If the ontological basis of the possibility in the world is the capacities of things, then there is no synchronic possibility. A thing that exists at a moment might have a capacity to be incompatible ways, but nothing has a capacity to be incompatible ways *at one and the same moment*. If something did, that thing could be simultaneously, say, (entirely) red and (entirely) not red or standing and not standing, and this is impossible. Rather, some thing with a capacity to be incompatible ways has a capacity to be one of any number of incompatible determinate ways, of a given determinable, *at some moment or other*. At any moment, though, that thing is constrained to be but one of the incompatible determinate ways it can be, and, at that moment, makes a determinate contribution to the world with respect to that way. Once that thing with this capacity is this way, the capacity is realized and manifested. The capacity makes possible that thing being incompatible ways, but the realization of that capacity at a moment—and, hence, that thing being a certain way it could be—precludes all ways incompatible with how that thing is thereat. If it is to be one of the other ways it is capable of being in virtue of that capacity, it can only be so at a distinct moment. Therefore, incompatible ways are not now both possible, despite the capacity of a thing to be both, because this capacity only enables a thing to be incompatible ways at distinct moments.

A consequence of this is that if a thing is one way at a given moment, m, and has not the capacity to be an incompatible way at m, then, given that the basis of possibility is the capacities of things, that that thing be otherwise than it is at m is impossible. It must be just as it is at m—and at any other moment at which it exists. Thus, for example, an apple that is red at a moment could not be brown at that moment, despite its capacity to be different colors. If it is to be brown, which it very well could be, it can only be so at a different moment. When it is red, it is necessarily red, and when it is brown, it is necessarily brown. The same is so for each thing and every way that thing is.

Although each thing is necessarily as it is when it is that way, it does not follow that each thing is essentially all the ways it in fact (necessarily) is. A thing is essentially some way only if its being that way is attendant upon its very existence, that is, only if it is that way simply given what it is and because it is at all. A thing can be a certain way necessarily at a moment, m, although not essentially that way, precisely because it has the capacity (at m) to be an incompatible way at some moment other than m. So, say, an apple that is red and material at m is necessarily red (at m) and necessarily material (at m).

It is essentially material, for, given what it is—an apple—it must be so; however, it is merely necessarily red (at m) for given its capacity to be different colors, it could be, say, brown at a distinct moment. No apple is essentially the color it is, nor does any apple have the capacity to be other than material.

There is, therefore, no synchronic possibility: every thing must be as it is at any moment it exists.[9] All the capacities of everything that exists at this moment are fully realized, and so every determinate way anything could now be is actually so. The world at this moment, now, is necessarily just as it is and so the world in time is, in this way, *complete*.

§9.3.2. The necessity of the past

One might object to the conclusion that the world is now complete—that each thing is, at this moment, necessarily every way it is and, hence, every way it could be is actually so—holding that incompatible alternative arrangements of things are in fact now possible. One might do so by claiming that had things gone otherwise, things would now be different than they actually are. This might seem consistent with conceding that the ontological basis of possibility is the capacities of things and that nothing has the capacity to be incompatible ways at one and the same moment. Things, one might claim, would now be different, had the capacity of any thing been realized in some way incompatible with the way it actually was, and so how things are at this moment need not be just as they are.

This line of objection might seem compelling, for that what has been so at moments that once were is not necessarily as it was is generally presumed. Indeed, this presumption is de rigueur in contemporary discussions of the modal status of the structure in the world, having been adopted by many of the most eminent metaphysicians of the late 20th century. Consider:

> Surely Socrates could have been born ten years later. Surely he could have lived in Macedonia, say, instead of Athens. And surely he could have stuck to his stonecutting, eschewed philosophy, corrupted no youth, and thus

---

[9] Although synchronic possibility seems to be universally accepted in contemporary discussions of metaphysics, that such acceptance has not always been the case is worth noting. Indeed, Simo Knuuttila maintains that the acceptance of synchronic possibility marks the divide between ancient and modern notions of modality. (See 1981: 236.) Knuuttila argues that John Duns Scotus was the first to defend synchronic possibility (see 1993, 1981); others, such as Stephen Dumont, maintain that the notion was present in a previous generation of theologians (see 1995: 151). For further discussion, see Normore 2003.

escaped the wrath of the Athenians. None of these properties is essential to him.[10]

Certainly Nixon might not have existed if his parents had not gotten married, in the normal course of things.[11]

Most of the things commonly attributed to Aristotle are things that Aristotle might not have done at all. In a situation in which he didn't do them, we would describe that as a situation in which *Aristotle* didn't do them.[12]

But things might have been different, in ever so many ways. This book of mine might have been finished on schedule. Or, had I not been such a commonsensical chap, I might be defending not only a plurality of possible worlds, but also a plurality of impossible worlds, whereof you speak truly by contradicting yourself. Or I might not have existed at all—neither I myself, nor any counterpart of me. Or there might never have been any people. Or the physical constants might have had somewhat different values, incompatible with the emergence of life. Or there might have been altogether different laws of nature; and instead of electrons and quarks, there might have been alien particles, without charge or mass or spin but with alien physical properties that nothing in this world shares.[13]

[There is the] intuition (which many of my opponents share) that a particular material artifact—say, a particular wooden table which we may call 'Woody'—could have originated from matter slightly different from its actual original matter m^* (while retaining its numerical identity, or its *haecceity*) but not from entirely different matter.[14]

This presumption that things could have gone differently remains prevalent in more recent discussions.[15] Despite its prevalence and pedigree, the presumption is misguided. Assume, contrary to what I argue above, that there are (ARE, tenselessly) moments prior to this one, now. Were there such moments, then they, with everything existing at each one, would be *the past*.

---

[10] Plantinga 1974: 61.
[11] Kripke 1980: 48.
[12] Kripke 1980: 61.
[13] Lewis 1986: 1–2.
[14] Salmon 1989: 5.
[15] It is made, for example, in Borghini and Williams 2008 and Jacobs 2010, cited above.

If the past could be otherwise than it in fact is, then some thing existing at one of the moments prior to this one, now, could be different than it actually is. However, a moment that stands in the earlier than relation to this one, now, is no different in kind from this moment for standing in that relation. Nor are the things at that prior moment different in nature from those existing now for standing in a temporal relation (or, for that matter, a relation of any kind). In light of these considerations, that the ontological basis of possibility at any moment is the same as what it now is is plain, namely, the capacities of the things existing at that moment. I argue above, though, that once a thing is a certain way at a given moment, any capacity that thing has to be incompatible ways is realized in such a way that precludes that thing from being any way incompatible with the ways it actually is. So, however a thing is at any moment prior to this one, it must be that way. The past could not have been otherwise, then, and there are no possible prior differences in the arrangement of things to yield differences at this moment, now.

If one is glib about possibility, casually invoking possible worlds without considering whether what is thereby represented is really possible or assuming that whatever is conceptually coherent or "conceivable" is possible, that things could have been otherwise or even that how things now are need not be so might seem correct. But if one takes seriously that every phenomenon has an ontological basis among the things in the world, one can see that there is much less possible than is usually taken for granted. Things as they now are must be so. Moreover, if there were moments prior to this one, now, things thereat would be necessarily just as they are. Of course, though, I argue above that there are no such moments, nothing stands in the earlier than relation to this moment (or anything else).

One upshot of there being literally nothing prior to this moment, the one most relevant to present purposes, is that any attempt to undermine the conclusion that the world is now complete by adverting to differences that could have been is futile. There are, however, other consequences relevant to a comprehensive and satisfactory metaphysics of time. First of all, if how things are at each existent moment are necessarily just as they are, yet each moment ceases to be simpliciter, what must be, need not be permanent. In other words, what is necessarily so need not always exist; what must be as it is in temporal reality need only be as permanent as this instantaneous moment. If a thing must exist, then that thing cannot fail to be (and, hence, is permanent). However, the world is not now complete because the things that now exist must exist; rather, the world is now complete because the arrangement of things that is now so—the structure at this moment—must be as it is. The capacities of each thing that now exists are fully realized and so every determinate way a thing could now be is actually so. This is compatible with many of these things and, thus, this structure ceasing to be simpliciter momentarily. Recognizing this is important to understanding the modal status of the structure in temporal reality.

Yet if this moment, now, ceases to be momentarily, and there is literally nothing prior to it—and, hence, no past, at least not in the natural sense of all those moments (and the things existing at them) preceding this moment, now—then there appears to be no ontological basis for the indubitable constancy in the world. Consequently, there seems to be no basis for the truth of claims about what has ceased to be, and certainly some claims about what has been are true, even necessarily so, whereas others are false. If an account of the metaphysics of time is to be satisfactory, it must include some explication of the constancy among *all this*. What has been argued so far suggests that the ontological basis of this constancy is not in temporal reality, wherein one finds the basis of the indubitable inconstancy in the world. This should be expected though, for what is inconstant, as temporal reality is, cannot also be constant. This problem of finding a suitable basis for the patent constancy in the world is addressed in Chapter 11.

§9.3.3. Contingency and the openness of what is to be

The world at this moment now is complete. There is no past in any familiar sense, yet were there, it too would be complete. I argue that there is nothing subsequent to this moment, now. It might seem, then, that there is no contingency in the world. But this is not so. In general, if there is contingency, things could be otherwise than they in fact are. One way for things to be otherwise requires that at least some arrangement of things need not be, that an incompatible arrangement of things could exist in its stead. Contingency in this sense involves synchronic possibility, incompatible states of affairs both being possible at the same moment. I argue, though, that given the ontological basis of possibility in the capacities of things, there can be no synchronic possibility: whenever things are, they must be just so. Thus, if contingency required synchronic possibility, there would (and could) be none in the world, and fatalism would be correct.

I noted above, however, that there are alternative accounts of contingency. Things could be otherwise in a more mundane sense than one requiring synchronic possibility. Things could be otherwise than how they now are simply in that they could change, and incompatible alternatives regarding how they might do so are both possible. These incompatible alternatives are not possible at this moment or any moment (for there is only this moment, now). Nevertheless, these incompatible alternatives are both possible simpliciter in that either could be at some moment that comes to be. Such contingency occurs only because there is (IS, tenselessly) no moment subsequent to this one. Were there such a moment, it would constrain anything existing at it to be but one of the incompatible ways that thing is capable of being for each determinable way that thing is (and once that thing were those ways, it would be so necessarily). Such contingency occurs, moreover, because a moment distinct from this one, now, could—indeed, must—come to be. Were it not possible that there be a novel moment at which either of the incompatible alternatives might be, neither alternative would be possible after all.

Therefore, there is contingency in the world, despite the completeness of *all this* at this moment. Contingency comes not *at* a moment, but *through* one, via the inevitable coming to be of a novel moment. A moment is not overlain with an infinite array of possibilities; any moment is, in itself, fully realized as is each thing existing thereat. Any moment is, then, complete in that the arrangement of things, which includes how each thing is, is utterly determinate and necessarily just as it is. Nevertheless, things could be otherwise—and incompatible alternatives possible—because a new moment comes to be and things could be different at that moment than they now are. The contingency in the world arises from the capacities of things being realized in different ways from moment to moment, that is, via temporal differentiation. Therefore, the openness that arises from this contingency, and contingency itself, are dependent on the absolute becoming of moments which, of course, depends on time itself.

Given that there is no moment—or anything else—subsequent to this moment, now, there is nothing to what is usually taken to be the future. There literally is no future. Of course, this claim is not as ominous as it sounds, for although there is not anything subsequent to this moment, new moments come to be (and must, given what time is). Given that there is nothing later than now, any claim about how things are subsequent to this moment is without truth-value: there is nothing to account for either the truth or the falsity of such a claim. Despite appearances, any such claim is just not evaluable with respect to truth and, hence, falsity. Claims about what is subsequent to this moment are, then, indeterminate in this radical way.[16] Moreover,

---

[16] Indeterminacy can be explicated in different ways. See, for example, the discussion of the "unsettledness" of the future in Cameron 2015: §§5.3–5.5. Cameron endorses a different view of this unsettledness than the one I accept.

although each thing must be as it is when it is—and so necessarily all things are as they are—that anything *had to be as it is* does not follow. Incompatible alternatives are both possible from this or any other moment. The necessary arrangement of things at each moment, the completeness of the world, does not necessitate that anything is preordained or fated to be as it comes to be necessarily as it is. There is, therefore, a genuine openness in what is to be. What is to be comes to be openly in virtue of a merging of how things are, chance and choices made by agents at a novel moment.

There is no future in that there are no moments (or things existing at them) existing subsequently to this moment, now. Nonetheless, anticipating what is to be is appropriate. To anticipate what is to be, is merely to acknowledge temporal differentiation and that what is to be has an ontological basis in the capacities of things that now exist. To regard what is to be as the future is a mistake, for what is to be is not anything at all, though to speak of what is to be in terms of "the future" is, perhaps, not infelicitous. Although there is nothing prior to this moment and nothing subsequent to it, there is an asymmetry concerning what has ceased to be simpliciter and what is to be. There are correct ways to regard and speak about what is no more, so there must be some basis for this correctness (even if it is not anything that exists in time). In contrast, there are no similarly correct ways to regard or speak about what is to come. Given the openness of what is to come—an openness that what has ceased to be lacks—to care about what is to come in ways that one does not care about what is no more is fitting. Therefore, the past, whatever it is, and the future, i.e., what is to be, should be regarded differently.

What is now is clearly different from both the past and what is to be. This moment now, and everything at it, exists, that is, is so. What was is not so; what is to be is not so. Without time, there would not be moments, transient moments that come to be and cease to be simpliciter, thereby enabling change, but also allowing other temporal entities to come to be and cease to be (simpliciter). The things at this moment and their capacities, all of which must be just as they are, are, with each moment yielded by time, the bases of change—and how things change is yet to be determined. Incompatible alternatives are yet possible. Time is, therefore, essential to any openness in the world. So without time, not only would there be no temporal differentiation and, hence, inconstancy in the world, there would be no contingency either.

PART IV
THE SPECIFIC ACCOUNT OF TEMPORAL REALITY
Transient Presentism and Its Limitations

10
Temporal Reality and Inconstancy

In a moment of inquisitiveness, one might confront the world, the totality encompassing one, and wonder. One might wonder what *all this* is or whether it is anything at all, and this prompts the question of what a thing—any thing whatsoever—is. Such a general question, if it is to be answered in an appropriately critical way, requires a special method of inquiry, one I characterize in Part II as *original inquiry*. In taking up this method, one finds the world one confronts is *thus*, myriad ways, comprising countless distinctions and, as such, clearly differentiated. The world is *thus*, and then is also *as so*, myriad ways, yet now comprising countless novel distinctions. Hence, the world is differentiated in distinct modes. These modes, by this point in the discussion, can be characterized as differentiation now, *at a moment* and *temporal differentiation*, differentiation *through moments*, viz., *all this* going from *thus* (at one moment) to *as so* (at a distinct one).

Time, I argue above, is the thing that accounts ultimately for these two modes of differentiation. Its prominence at the outset of wholly critical inquiry indicates its importance to the *structure in reality*, all the things there are, inclusive of the relations in which things stand. Insofar, then, as one aspires to gain insight into the world and the structure therein, time itself is an all-important focus of inquiry. All those things that depend for their existence on time are the *world in time*, i.e., *temporal reality*. There are two general, mutually exclusive views regarding the world in time. The purpose of Part III is to articulate these views and demonstrate which of the two is correct. There is the general view of temporal reality on which it is *ontologically homogeneous* and the one on which it is *ontologically heterogeneous*. On the former, when the world goes from *thus* to *as so*, the moment at which it is *thus* and the one at which it is *as so* do not differ ontologically nor with respect to any temporal property. Neither of these moments is distinguished in any peculiarly temporal way. On this view, there are (infinitely) many moments, all of which are equally real; each is *earlier than* some moments and *later than* others, with all these temporal relations holding permanently. On the latter general view, on which the world in time is ontologically heterogeneous, when the world goes from *thus* to *as so*, the moment at which it is *thus* and the one at which it is *as so* do differ, either ontologically or in some peculiarly temporal way. There might be (infinitely) many moments; but at least one moment is unique, bearing a distinctive temporal property or having some other distinction that separates it from any other moment.

The view that temporal reality is ontologically homogeneous is incorrect. Not only is it incompatible with one's experience of the world as revealed in original inquiry, it simply does not have the means to account for the indisputable phenomenon—the world going from *thus* to *as so*—underlying this experience. I argue that temporal differentiation, this indisputable phenomenon, can only be accounted for by means of ontological difference. The world in time is, therefore, ontologically heterogeneous. Yet there are many specific accounts that elaborate this general view of temporal reality. Having examined a number of these, I maintain that the only tenable account is one on which there is but a single moment, a moment that bears no peculiarly temporal property (such as *presentness*), nor stands in either familiar temporal relation (viz., *earlier than* or *later than*) to any other moment or anything else. In temporal differentiation, there is an ontological difference between the moment at which the world is *thus* and the one at which it is *as so*: the latter exists, whereas the former does not. Hence, all there is to the world in time, in addition to time itself, is this moment, now, the mutable things that exist thereat, the relation of simultaneity that holds among these things and the existing at relation. This is clearly an account on which the world in time is ontologically heterogeneous, for this moment, now, is distinguished in being the unique moment.

There is nothing that will be, that is, nothing that exists (or EXISTS tenselessly) subsequent to this moment, now; nothing that was, that is, nothing that exists (or EXISTS) prior to this moment. What now is is wholly determinate and complete. It is complete yet not exhausted, for although there *will not be* more in time, there, of course, *could be* more.[1] Not at this moment, nor at a subsequent one (for there are none), but at some novel

---

[1] Note that there *could have been more* is not so. Had there been more than there in fact is, this moment, now (that is, the multiplicity of things existing thereat or one of the things included in this multiplicity) would have had to be different than it actually is. But everything that exists is now necessarily just as it is. This 'could have been' locution is, I think, sometime used as an infelicitous way of expressing the point, which I accept, that what is to be is open, that the goings-on at some moment are not set prior to the coming to be of that moment. However, from this point about the openness of what is to be, this past-directed claim that things could have been different—that what is now might have been otherwise—does not follow.

moment that comes to be. This moment, now, exists but for an instant, and is replaced by another. This account of the world in time, which surely seems meager to some, is suggestive of *presentism*, a somewhat notorious view (or number of views) regarding the metaphysics of time. The purposes of this chapter are to elaborate my account of temporal reality by examining it vis-à-vis presentism, to consider whether it can satisfactorily account for the obvious *inconstancy* in the world—as evidenced by the coming to be of things, the multitudinous changes among them, and their ceasing to be—and to determine whether it and its attendant explication of temporal differentiation suffice as an account of the metaphysics of time.

To these ends, I first discuss what presentism is supposed to be and consider to what extent the account of temporal reality I am propounding is appropriately regarded as presentist. This is worth considering because presentism is open to some obvious and formidable objections. Whether my account is presentist is a surprisingly nuanced issue, for presentism, it turns out, is neither a single view nor even a unified class of them. Although the account I am propounding rejects what is standardly the definitive ontological claim of presentism, that *only present things exist*, I believe it is nonetheless appropriate to regard it as presentist. This account, which avoids all the objections usually directed at presentism, provides the optimum explication of the inconstancy in the world. Nevertheless, it is open to a most pressing objection, one associated with several often leveled at presentism, concerning the constancy in the world. The objection, I acknowledge, is conclusive. This acknowledgment, however, does not present grounds for rejecting my account of the world in time; rather, it reveals that a comprehensive and satisfactory account of the metaphysics of time includes more than merely an account of temporal reality.

§10.1. On Presentism

Presentism is familiar from discussions of the metaphysics of time. It is usually glossed simply as the view that *only present things exist*. This view is sometimes defended as commonsensical or intuitive, but more often it is derided as clearly untenable. According to the account of temporal reality I am propounding, there is but a single, transient moment: this one, now. Some might take my account to be merely an eccentric statement of presentism; if the two are not the same, there certainly seems to be an affinity between them. Thus, examining presentism, and the connections between it and my account of the world in time is worth doing, for many think presentism is easily refuted. If my account were presentism or if the former were relevantly similar to the latter in the ways supposed to be problematic, this would require addressing the objections frequently leveled at presentism.

It turns out an understanding of presentism per se is not possible, for there is not a single view, nor even a unified position captured by the usual gloss. There are many incompatible views that are put forth as presentism or, at least, presentist. The account of temporal reality that I am propounding is so unlike any of these that it raises the question of whether it should be regarded as presentist at all. Although the point is debatable, and merely terminological, I conclude that my account is aptly regarded as presentist, for the view of the world suggested by the usual gloss is quite similar to the account of temporal reality I accept—though I do maintain the former is significantly incomplete.

§10.1.1. The triviality objection

Perhaps surprisingly, some deny that examining presentism is even worthwhile, if presentism is simply the view that only present things exist. For if this is the view, it is thought to be either trivially true or patently false.[2] It is thought to be trivially true if 'exist' in the usual gloss of presentism is construed as *tensed*, because in this case the view would be that only present things exist now, i.e., presently. In other words, presentism would be the view that only present things presently exist, and this is a claim that no one would deny. On the other hand, if 'exist' is construed as *tenseless*, in the sense of pertaining to this moment, now, as well as to any moment before or after it, presentism would then be the view that only present things—those at this moment, now—exist, existed prior to this moment, or will exist subsequent to it. Such a view is thought to be patently false, because that there are things, like Caesar or some dinosaur, that once existed but now do not, and others, like a lunar colony or my first grandchild, that will exist yet now do not is taken for granted.

---

[2] The best discussion of this so-called *triviality objection* is Crisp 2004. The objection is presented in passing (and perhaps introduced) in Lombard 1999.

I do not find this objection incisive. Any presentist rejects that the world in time is ontologically homogeneous, and so many deny that there are other moments and things thereat that are just as real as this moment, now, and the things existing at it (though not all presentists deny this, as seen below). Such presentists may claim that although Caesar, for example, once existed, he has since ceased to be simpliciter. One who objects that presentism is patently false assumes, then, there are (or ARE, tenselessly) things, e.g., Caesar, some dinosaur, a lunar colony, etc., that many presentists deny exist.[3] Whether there are, in any sense, things at moments other than this (or any other moments) is by no means obvious—as the contention in discussions of the correct general view of the world in time indicates—and so to regard either the claim that there are indeed such things, or the claim that there are not, as incontrovertibly true is not correct. Therefore, presentism, with the 'exist' of its usual gloss construed as tenseless, is not patently false, and so is a view worthy of examination.[4]

There is, however, a much more perspicuous way of interpreting the claim that only present things exist. On this interpretation, 'exist' is to be understood without reference to any particular moment or temporally at all, and so is not taken to be either tensed or tenseless. To exist, in the relevant sense, is to exist *simpliciter*. Some philosophers suggest that this notion is unclear.[5] But to exist simpliciter is simply to be among the things there are, that is, to be in the world. It is to enjoy the being requisite for anything to bear any quality or to stand in any relation whatsoever. Indeed, I maintain that there is only one way of being (simpliciter), so any notion of existence relativized to some thing or restricted in some other way marks a merely theoretical—a conceptual or otherwise representational—distinction, rather than an ontological one (§4.3.2.). Given this understanding of existence, presentism might be regarded as the view that the only things in the world are the present ones, to wit, those at this moment, now. Call the crux of this view—everything is at this moment, now—*the standard presentist thesis*. This is the bold thesis that at least some presentists endorse and at which the opponents of presentism balk.

---

[3] Ulrich Meyer is clearly doing this when, in maintaining that presentism is trivial (or untenable), he asserts, "Yet if [Caesar] did exist then he does exist at some past time, and therefore does exist temporally [i.e., within temporal reality]" (2005: 214).

[4] This triviality objection is persistent, despite this rather obvious response to it (a version of which is given in Crisp 2004). For additional discussion of the objection, see Deng 2018; Tallant 2014; Stoneham 2009; and Meyer 2005.

[5] See, for example, Meyer at 2005: 214–215.

§10.1.2. The multiplicity of "presentist" views

Standard presentism is the view that adopts the standard presentist thesis. Several philosophers accept this view.[6] One of my purposes here is to elaborate my account of the world in time by examining it vis-à-vis presentism as the latter has been developed in recent discussions of the metaphysics of time. However, the matter of comparison is more involved than simply comparing my account with standard presentism. There is a bewildering multiplicity of views put forth as "presentism" that are incompatible with the standard presentist thesis (and, hence, standard presentism). If I am to elaborate my view vis-à-vis contemporary presentism, these other views must be considered, too.

Thus, there are presentist views that deny that there is but one moment of the same kind as the present one, i.e., this one, now.[7] Consider the *moderate presentism* of Francesco Orilia, on which only present *events* exist, though there are not only past and future moments, but familiar objects existing at past moments.[8] Or the presentism espoused by Dean Zimmerman, according to which only present *objects* exist, yet there is a space-time manifold, a "four-dimensional, invisible, permeable cosmic jello,"[9] comprising many moments, including this one, now. According to these views, there are many moments. There is another presentist view, though, according to which there is not but one moment, because there are no moments at all. This is so-called *existence presentism*, which Jonathan Tallant attributes to Trenton Merricks and adopts himself[10] and which is supposed to be a view not about what exists or when things exist, but about what it is to exist. To exist is to be present, that is, the property of existence is identical to the property of presentness.[11]

There are also presentist views according to which, although there *exists* nothing that is not present, there nevertheless *are* things, such as moments

---

[6] See, for example, Crisp 2007, 2005, 2003; Bourne 2006a, 2006b; De Clercq 2006; Markosian 2004; Hinchliff 2000, 1996; Bigelow 1996.

[7] There are standard presentist views, such as the ones held by Crisp, Markosian, and Bourne, according to which there are many moments. These views, however, make a distinction between the one *concrete moment*, namely, the present moment, i.e., this one, now; and the many *abstract moments*, which exist presently, that represent what was and what will be.

[8] Orilia 2016: 589–590.

[9] Zimmerman 2011: 200.

[10] See Tallant 2014 and Merricks 2007: 124–125.

[11] This is the most straightforward way to construe the view. At 2014: §3.3, Tallant offers other ways of interpreting the view on which existence, i.e., presence, is not a property at all.

and things thereat, that do not now exist. Such views invoke the Meinongian distinction between *existing*, on the one hand, and *subsisting* or *having being* or *being real*, on the other. Michele Paolini Paoletti proposes such a view,[12] which he dubs *Meinongian presentism*, and a similar view is suggested by André Gallois.[13] Arthur Prior espouses a presentist view on which the present moment is real and what precedes it is unreal, in one way, and what succeeds it is unreal, in another way.[14] What is unreal does not exist, but it is not without ontological standing; it is nonetheless in the world. Quentin Smith proposes a presentist view on which there are not, as Prior suggests, three ways of being in the world (viz., being past, existing now, and being future), but an infinite number of them. According to Smith's *degree presentism*, "[t]he degree to which an item exists is proportional to its temporal distance from the present; the present, which has zero-temporal distance from the present, has the highest (logically) possible degree of existence."[15] So what just occurred or what is just about to occur exist slightly less than what now does, but what occurred a million years ago (or will come to be in a million years) exists much less. There is also a presentist view that whereas it does not make an ontological distinction among ways of being in the world, does make one in terms of fundamentality. This is the *priority presentism* of Sam Baron, according to which "only present entities exist fundamentally ... past and future entities exist, but they are grounded in the present."[16] Hence, past and future moments and the things thereat exist—they are no less real than this moment, now—they are just less fundamental than it.

None of these presentist views is consistent with the standard presentist thesis; most are mutually incompatible. What this shows is that there is no single view of presentism, nor even a presentist position comprising different views unified by a common thesis.[17] The above views share merely a name or the principle that there is something distinctive about this moment, now. (This principle, however, commits one to little more than the general view that temporal reality is ontologically heterogeneous.) Nonetheless, comparing my account of temporal reality to these "presentist" views is worthwhile, for doing so allows me to develop the account by clarifying its

---

[12] Paoletti 2016.
[13] Gallois 2004.
[14] Prior 1970.
[15] Smith 2002: 120.
[16] Baron 2015: 325.
[17] Jonathan Tallant demonstrates this point in his unpublished paper, "There's No Such Thing as Presentism," which has informed the present discussion.

commitments. Moreover, further consideration of these views provides the means of answering the question of why there is such a proliferation of "presentist" views at all. This answer underscores the constraints on any satisfactory account of the metaphysics of time.

In accordance to the principles of radical ontology, in particular, that the world just is all things, each thing existing and fundamental, the account of temporal reality I am propounding precludes any distinction in existence per se and any ontological priority (and, hence, levels of reality). An account of any temporal phenomenon must, therefore, be in terms of (existent) things—none of which is any more or less fundamental than another—standing in some relation(s). One of these things must be a moment, for a moment is needed to constrain mutable things that have inherently capacities to be incompatible ways. Yet there cannot be more than one moment, for two (co-)existent moments is irreconcilable with one's experience of the world. There are, furthermore, no grounds for holding that the one moment there is bears any peculiarly temporal property, such as presentness. Finally, my account of the world in time is compatible with there being things that exist, but not in time (for example, time itself); the standard presentist thesis, though, is the claim that *everything* exists in time, more specifically, at this moment, now. My account of temporal reality is, therefore, inconsistent with all of the varieties of presentism canvassed above.

Nevertheless, I think calling my account 'presentist' is suitable. Any term of art can be used as one sees fit (though clarity does enjoin at least some explication). Whether I call the account of temporal reality that I am propounding 'presentism' or 'presentist' is, then, not a substantive issue. Still, my account, like any of these varieties of presentism, regards this moment, now, as paramount to an account of the metaphysics of time. Moreover, as discussed below, my account is inspired by, to some extent, the same considerations as any of these other views and is susceptible to a pressing objection, one associated with several often leveled at standard presentist views. A thing is *transient* when it both comes to be (simpliciter) and ceases to be (simpliciter). A conspicuous feature of my account of the world in time is the transience of the single existent moment, the one at which all things in temporal reality exist. So call this account *transient presentism*. The suitability of regarding transient presentism as presentist becomes more apparent when one considers why, in the first place, there is such a proliferation of presentist views. (If one disagrees and thinks calling my account of temporal reality 'presentist' is unsuitable, one may call it *momentary transientism*.)

§10.1.3. Presentism and structure

That the standard presentist thesis, viz., everything is at this moment, now, has its adherents is not shocking. What is now so has a vividness and corollary cogency that other moments (and things existing at them), were there such, could not have. Thus, when proposing an account of the metaphysics of time—or a theory of the world—to include the claim that there are only presently existing things is plausible to many philosophers. Notice, however, that this is merely a thesis about what exists.[18] Such a bald ontological thesis provides no insight into how the things claimed to exist relate. Yet any satisfactory account of the metaphysics of time must provide some insight into how things relate, for such an account is supposed to illuminate the ontological basis of one's experiences of a world that includes time, in particular, experiences of the inconstancy and constancy in the world.

When one confronts the world in original inquiry, one is not merely presented with the world as *thus*, a portion of what now exists; one is also presented with the world *as so*, a distinct array of things. To be presented with both is to experience the inconstancy in the world. However, both also prompt an experience of constancy. The ontological basis of these experiences is, of course, things in the world (it could be nothing else). Any presentist view is supposed to be an account of the metaphysics of time; any such account, if it is to be satisfactory, must provide some explication of the relations among these things—mutable things, moments, time itself, etc.—in such a way as to explain the experience of the indubitable inconstancy and the experience of the no-less-indubitable constancy. One can expect the bases of such seemingly incongruous experiences to be quite complex.

The proliferation of presentist views is a result of the different attempts to put forth a position that acknowledges the cogency of what is now so—by maintaining that this moment, now, is in some way unique—while also positing sufficient structure—things and relations—to account for one's experiences of the world. Most "presentist" views are incompatible with the standard presentist thesis because it is assumed that providing such an account requires more in temporal reality than what there now is. Thus, there are the views that admit more moments or non-existent things or less fundamental things.

---

[18] Presentism is introduced and discussed as an ontological thesis in Ingram and Tallant 2018.

Transient presentism (or momentary transientism) has the same inspiration as any of these presentist views. Although I recognize the uniqueness of this moment not because of the vividness of what is now so, but on grounds that demonstrate it can be the only moment in the world, I nonetheless concur with the proponent of any presentist view that this moment, now, is indeed special. Moreover, my stated objective from the outset of this inquiry has been to provide a comprehensive and satisfactory account of the metaphysics of time, one that explains both the inconstancy and constancy in the world. Transient presentism, however, explicitly denies that there is any structure in temporal reality beyond what there is among the things that now exist. Whereas others believe to posit more in temporal reality to provide a satisfactory account of the metaphysics of time is necessary, I explicitly maintain there is and could be no more. This makes urgent the questions of how transient presentism—so ontologically sparing with its single transient moment—accounts for the inconstancy and for the constancy in the world.

§10.2. Dynamism and Inconstancy

Some philosophers object that any standard presentist view, one according to which everything is at this moment, now, is incapable of explaining the inconstancy in the world. Were this so, transient presentism, according to which there is but a single moment, would seem also to be open to similar objection. However, I believe that any objection of this sort is based on a misunderstanding of how *all this* is inconstant and, consequently, of what must be in the world to explain this inconstancy. The inconstancy is a result of temporal differentiation, which involves absolute becoming, absolute annihilation, and change. Although *dynamism* is crucial to temporal differentiation, the phenomena of dynamism and of inconstancy are distinct.

Accounting for these phenomena is necessary for any comprehensive account of the metaphysics of time. Doing so reveals where in the world exactly the bases of inconstancy are to be located. As becomes clear, there is more underlying inconstancy than simply dynamism. Nevertheless, given what these bases are, a single moment is sufficient to accommodate them, and so transient presentism, with its one moment, does have the means to explain the inconstancy in the world. Indeed—and this is not obvious—there can be dynamism without change and, hence, dynamism at no moment at all.

§10.2.1. Change, ontological transience, and dynamism

In modern discussions of time, philosophers have often claimed that dynamism *is*, or involves essentially, temporal passage, the gain and loss by moments (or the things existing at them) of temporal properties, viz., futurity, presentness, and pastness. As I argue above (Chapter 8), this is false. There is and could be no phenomenon of temporal passage; indeed, nothing even instantiates one of the temporal properties. Yet in the world going from *thus* to *as so*, there is certainly some change. There are different diverse arrays at the distinct moments and so at least a change in one's mental states reflecting different experiences of the world. One might think, then, that even if dynamism does not involve temporal passage, that is, change of moments, it nonetheless necessarily involves change in some other thing(s)—or that dynamism *just is* change.

Change, one thing bearing incompatible properties at distinct moments, contributes to the inconstancy in the world, because it requires some difference in what exists or difference in how things are related. If to be dynamic is to be able to bring about such differences, then change indicates dynamism. But dynamism and change are distinct phenomena. Were temporal reality ontologically homogeneous, it could include change, still it could not include the dynamism this world actually does. This world is dynamic in that it includes change, yet it is also dynamic because of the continuous absolute becoming and annihilation of distinct transient moments (and at least some of the things existing at them). Such ontological transience, which obviously requires difference in what exists or difference in how things are related, *involves no change*, yet indicates dynamism no less than change does. There is, then, more to the inconstancy in the world than just change. However, just as change alone is not sufficient for the inconstancy in the world, neither is mere ontological transience. Original inquiry reveals both dynamic phenomena.

Temporal differentiation, the world going from *thus* to *as so*, involves both dynamic phenomena contributing to the inconstancy in the world. The issue at hand is whether the dynamism in temporal differentiation can be accounted for in a world in which there is but this moment, now. Clearly it can be. One of the upshots of Part III is that the distinct moments required by temporal differentiation are transient, each existing for but an instant and not together. They cannot exist together. Consequently, the moments are in no way related (a fortiori, they stand in no temporal relation). One comes into being and the other ceases to be. So the absolute becoming and ceasing to be of moments in temporal differentiation can be accounted for in a world in which there is only a single moment. The basis of this much dynamism, at least, is compatible with transient presentism—indeed, such structure is the crux of the view.

This point, however, can be obscured by the way that some philosophers understand inconstancy, and its underlying dynamism, in a world supposed to contain but a single moment. Thus, Huw Price claims that "One major component of the intuitive idea of the passage of time [i.e., temporal differentiation] is that it involves a distinguished but continually variable 'present moment'—a single 'box' or 'frame', whose contents are continually changing. One version of this idea is at the heart of *presentism*, a view which holds that the present moment is *all there is*—that the past and future simply don't exist."[19] A "single 'box' or 'frame'" that is "continually variable" suggests there is one persisting moment, which provides the forum for all the goings-on of temporal reality—a moment that changes insofar as these goings-on do. Any such view is incoherent; moments cannot persist (§8.1.1.2.). But the inconstancy in the world does not need to be underlain by a unique, persisting platform. An instantaneous moment is enough to sustain temporal reality until that moment ceases to be and is replaced by a distinct one.

Still, some philosophers maintain that this sort of view, with its single moment, is itself incoherent, if the world is inconstant. The problem is supposed to be that given the world in time is not inexorably *thus*, that is, given there is temporal differentiation, then there must be another moment—yet it is definitive of this view that there is but one moment, this one, now.[20] Of course, a view on which the world includes *only* this moment, now *with* some other moment is incoherent. This is not, however, how things are according to transient presentism. On this account, the world only ever includes a single moment. It does not include this moment, now, *and* some other that will be; there is never anything that will be. The world does include time, though, which yields a distinct instantaneous moment as this one ceases to be.[21] Any view of temporal reality that explains the inconstancy in the world by means of distinct moments, must account for the source of these moments and the

---

[19] Price 2011: 277.
[20] See Leininger 2015: 730. Leininger attributes a similar concern to Price, see Footnote 8.
[21] Again, to demand an account of *how* time yields moments is like demanding an account of *how* sets have members or *how* a proposition, i.e., an abstract representational entity, represents. There is no such account. (See §5.4.) Time is simply the thing that yields moments—and orders them (by continuously yielding instantaneous moments that cease to be).

relations among them, if any. Although standard presentist views are objectionable on the grounds that they fail to provide such an account, transient presentism is not.

So there is ever only a single, transient moment. This moment... and this one (with time itself) suffice to account for the basic ontological transience in temporal differentiation. There is more to the inconstancy in the world than the coming to be and ceasing to be simpliciter of things, however; there are also countless changes. Even if one concedes that a single moment is compatible with ontological transience, one might object that but one moment is insufficient to account for change. Lisa Leininger maintains that the changes in this inconstant world require a "direct comparison of existing states of affairs at different moments" and, consequently, that "at least two moments be drawn in the picture of the totality of what exists in the world."[22] Leininger is mistaken. Although change does require distinct moments, it does not require that these moments co-exist. Change merely requires a persisting thing be one way at one moment and an incompatible way at a distinct moment. When that persisting thing is the latter way, it certainly need not *also* be the former way. Indeed, the assumption that it does have to be both ways (or, at least, *is* both ways) leads to a contradiction and the putative problem of temporary intrinsics (§8.1.1.2.). One can avoid this putative problem simply by holding that the only way(s) a thing is is how it is at this moment, now, even if it is true that it were incompatible ways at some other moments. If that this thing was, at some moment that has ceased to be, an incompatible way, is true, then this thing is changed and there is change in the world.

Of course, if to hold that a thing *was* an incompatible way at a moment that has ceased to be is correct—and it must be, if there is a changed thing—there must be some basis in reality for the correctness of this claim. This crucial issue recurs below. For present purposes, I need only point out that an adequate account of this correctness does not (and cannot) require that the moment at which the thing was an incompatible way be just as real as this moment, now. Change, like the ontological transience of moments (and other things), is compatible with an account of the world in time on which there is only a single moment. Both dynamic phenomena underlying the inconstancy in the world require distinct moments, but neither requires that moments ever co-exist. Dynamism is, therefore, compatible with the account of temporal reality provided by transient presentism.

[22] Leininger 2015: 730.

§10.2.2. Dynamism as actualizable potential

The ontological transience of moments (and things existing at them) and change are both dynamic phenomena, together accounting for the inconstancy in the world, that is, the differences in what exists and how things are related. By this point, what ontological transience and change are is clear; the same is not so in regard to dynamism itself. The question of what dynamism is is especially perplexing when one recognizes that the (continuous) coming to be and ceasing to be simpliciter of moments is dynamic, yet does not and cannot involve change. Even if transient presentism is compatible with dynamism, the account is incomplete without some explication of this key phenomenon. As the discussion below illustrates, an insightful explication of dynamism has further value in revealing certain distinctions that are central to a comprehensive and satisfactory account of the metaphysics of time.

In order to explicate dynamism, one must first recognize what in the world is dynamic. The world itself is not dynamic—nor is it static. The world is a multiplicity of things and, as such, is not itself a thing; strictly speaking, then, the world is no way at all. Although the world is not itself dynamic, there is nevertheless dynamism in the world. The basis of this dynamism, like the basis of any phenomenon, either is some thing or is some things standing in some relation(s). Thus, at least some things are dynamic and the inconstancy in the world arises from these things.

Dynamism is indicated via change. Yet it is also indicated via ontological transience, more specifically, through the continuous coming to be and ceasing to be simpliciter of moments, which does not involve change. The common basis for both of these dynamic phenomena is the *actualizable potential* of things. Some things have the potential (or capacity or power) to contribute more to the world than themselves or to contribute otherwise than they actually do. Such contributions add to the world, either in terms of what there is or how those things are, and so are the source of inconstancy. Dynamism is the broad capacity that such things have to make these additions to reality; dynamism is, then, an intrinsic quality of certain things. Mutable things have dynamism and so are dynamic, in that they are capable of being incompatible ways at distinct moments. A mutable thing changes when, from one moment to the next, this capacity to be otherwise is realized. Thus, when an apple changes from red to brown, this, the actualization of the capacity of that apple to bear a different determinate color (from a certain range) than the one it was bearing, is a manifestation of the general actualizable potential of the apple. The continuous coming to be and ceasing to be simpliciter of moments does not involve change. It does, however, involve the actualizable potential of a thing, namely, time, per se. Although time is not a mutable thing and so is not capable of being incompatible ways—it must be just as it is—it is nonetheless dynamic, for it has the potential to contribute more to the world than itself. Time is the thing that yields moments; the actualization of its potential to add to reality results in an instantaneous, transient moment coming to be.

Therefore, dynamism is the general actualizable potential of a thing to add to the world. In many familiar cases, dynamism manifests via change, but it does not have to. In at least one crucial case, that of time itself, it does not. In this case, dynamism manifests via the absolute becoming of a moment. Perhaps time is the only thing that is immutable but nonetheless dynamic (if so, this is merely another distinctive feature of this unique and sui generis thing). Were all mutable things to cease to be—so there was nothing that changed or could—the world would be no less dynamic given the necessary existence of time itself. It follows that not only does a thing not have to change to be dynamic, it need not even exist at a moment. The question, then, of when a thing is dynamic is not incisive. A mutable thing is dynamic at every moment it exists; time is not dynamic at any moment. Being dynamic is not some action performed by a thing at some moment or other; nor is it some process manifested over several moments. Being dynamic is just being a certain way, to wit, having actualizable potential.

§10.2.3. Independent bases of inconstancy (and of constancy)

A mutable thing is essentially mutable. Time, which exists at no moment and cannot change, is essentially each way that it is. If a thing is dynamic, then, it is so essentially and, consequently, is dynamic just in existing. Each thing is fundamental in that what it is and how it is essentially is beyond explanation. Thus, there are things that are fundamentally dynamic. There are, I argue below (§11.3.), also things that fundamentally lack dynamism. These things are static and essentially lack actualizable potential and, hence, cannot contribute any more to the world than what they are (and how they are essentially). Such things are complete and inert. The world includes both dynamic and static things. Just as dynamic things are crucial to the inconstancy in the world, static things are crucial to the constancy. This is important to recognize if one is to understand how reality is both fundamentally dynamic and static.

Although the dynamism and stasis inherent in things are centrally important to the structure in reality, these qualities do not suffice to account for the inconstancy and constancy in the world. Another pair of contradictory qualities is no less important, to wit, *transience* and *permanence*. A thing is transient if it (comes to be and) is susceptible to ceasing to be; a thing is permanent if it is not susceptible to ceasing to be, if it must continue to exist once it exists. Note, for this is important below, having an origin, that is, coming into existence is compatible with being transient and also with being permanent. The relevance of transience to accounting for inconstancy is obvious in light of the importance of the coming to be and ceasing to be simpliciter of moments (and things existing at them) to inconstancy.

This distinction between transience and permanence is independent of the one between dynamism and stasis. As observed above, although time does not (and cannot) change, it is nonetheless dynamic. As a necessarily existing entity, time has no origin and must continue to exist; it is permanent. Time is, therefore, both dynamic and permanent. So a dynamic thing need not be transient, in other words, dynamism is compatible with permanence. Consequently, transience is not a condition of being dynamic. This is interesting, for one might have thought that permanence and dynamism were contradictories, that whatever is permanent is not dynamic and vice versa. Yet this is not so. Dynamism and permanence are actually independent ways for things to be. There is, therefore, nothing paradoxical about the permanent dynamism of time manifested by the continuous yielding of instantaneous moments.

So there is at least one dynamic thing that is permanent. There are, obviously, dynamic things that are transient, as well. Any familiar mutable thing—a person, an apple, a cell phone—is an example of such. Each of these exists at a moment; its dynamism, its general capacity to be otherwise, manifested by the changes through which it persists. There are static transient things. A moment is both static and transient, having no capacity to be otherwise and ceasing to be. (Such absolute annihilation is, of course, not a change.) Finally, there are static permanent things, ones that might or might not have an origin, but must continue to exist and have no capacity to be otherwise than what they are (and how they are essentially) throughout their existence. Such things are discussed in detail in the next chapter, for they are crucial to explicating the constancy in the world and, hence, to a comprehensive and satisfactory account of the metaphysics of time.

What is needed to account for the inconstancy in the world are time itself, the moments it yields, and the host of mutable things that exist at these moments. Some of these things, time and the mutable things, are dynamic, contributing to the world beyond what each is (and how each is essentially). Some of these things, any moment and presumably most familiar mutable things, are also transient, susceptible to ceasing to be. Time itself, being dynamic, yields transient moments. These things, with mutable entities, are the ontological bases of temporal differentiation. The mutable things existing at this moment, now, and persisting from this moment to another, can bear different properties at these different moments and, hence, change. All this is consistent with the account of the world in time provided by transient presentism. Indeed, not only is that account the optimal one, for it is the only one that can explicate the transition of the world from *thus* to *as so*, it is also the only one consistent with the world one confronts in original inquiry.

Therefore, transient presentism is compatible with and has the means to explain the inconstancy in the world. The constancy of the world, one expects, is explicated by means of things that are not merely static—as is this moment, now—and not merely permanent—as is time itself—but are both static and permanent. There is, however, nothing in the world in time, as it is according to transient presentism, that is both ways. Although this account of temporal reality is compatible with such things being among *all this*, any there are are beyond its purview. This provides the grounds for a conclusive objection to transient presentism as a comprehensive and satisfactory account of the metaphysics of time.

§10.3. Objections to Transient Presentism

Transient presentism offers the best—indeed the only—account of inconstancy and yet also acknowledges some permanence and stasis in the world. To this extent, it is promising as an account of the metaphysics of time. However, transient presentism is open to an objection associated with ones often directed at views that maintain there is no more to temporal reality than a single moment. The objection pertains to the indubitable constancy in the world. After considering some other, futile objections, I acknowledge that this one pertaining to constancy is conclusive, showing that transient presentism itself is unacceptable as a comprehensive and satisfactory account of the metaphysics of time.

§10.3.1. The different motivations for holding standard presentism and transient presentism

Views like standard presentism and transient presentism, according to which the world in time includes but a single existent moment, are quite controversial as accounts of the metaphysics of time. Indeed, they all face insuperable objection of one sort or another. In light of this, one might consider why anyone would hold such a position in the first place. Any position that is poorly motivated and faces insuperable objection can hardly be taken seriously. Standard presentist views have often been introduced as the "commonsense" or "intuitive" account of the metaphysics of time and initially justified on these grounds.[23] Thus, proponents maintain such a view is likely true or, at least, should be taken seriously because it seems to be true. Many philosophers regard such motivation for holding a view as flimsy and, consequently, regard such views as dubious, even before careful consideration.

Above (§10.1.3.), I observe that what is now so has a vividness and corollary cogency that other moments (and things existing at them), were there such, could not have. Thus, a view on which there is but this moment, now, is plausible. Plausibility does not confer justification, however. I concur, then, with those who dismiss claims about common sense or intuition as providing any real justification for an account of the metaphysics of time—or an account of anything whatsoever. I do not think there is an insightful, probative faculty of common sense (common sense is, if anything, a merely statistical phenomenon among groups often chosen arbitrarily); nor do I think one's intuitive capacities can arbitrate directly among arcane or controversial views. In the context of discussing the appropriate means of arguing for the correct general view of temporal reality (§7.1.1.), I briefly consider "common sense" and "intuition" but then set them aside. The notions have played no role in the intervening discussion and, hence, are no part of my justification for or defense of transient presentism.

---

[23] See, for example, Bigelow 1996: 36; Sider 2001: 11; Markosian 2004: 48; De Clercq 2006: 386; Tallant 2009.

None of the commitments of transient presentism is taken for granted or adopted merely because it seems right. Rather, the ultimate justification for this account of temporal reality is one's experience of the world in original inquiry, that is, the experience of the world as *thus* and of going from *thus* to *as so*. It is this experience that justifies, in the end, the rejection of the general view that the world in time is ontologically homogeneous. It is this experience that yields the account of a thing as a natured entity that informs the accounts of time itself, of a moment and of change that underlie the rejection of the view that the world in time is merely qualitatively heterogeneous. The grounds for the account of the world in time on which there is but a single transient moment that (absolutely) ceases to be as a distinct transient moment (absolutely) comes to be could not be deeper or more direct. The motivation for accepting transient presentism, therefore, could not be more compelling, coming as it does from an origin as purely critical as possible, one that makes no presuppositions about *all this*—or *all this* going from *thus* to *as so*.[24] Given these considerations, if there are objections to the account, these (and their presuppositions) must be scrutinized, for discarding the objections is much more feasible than is rejecting transient presentism.

§10.3.2. The Special Theory of Relativity

The foregoing considerations are relevant to assessing one of the most familiar objections to any account of temporal reality that includes just a single moment, to wit, this one, now. Any such account is supposed to be incompatible with Einstein's Special Theory of Relativity (STR), a theory central to modern physics. The incompatibility is supposed to be straightforward and decisive.

On the standard interpretation of Einstein's theory, simultaneity is relative to inertial frames of reference. Thus, what is happening at the same moment as some event depends on a feature of that event, to wit, its velocity. Since different events at any given moment can have any number of velocities, this standard interpretation requires a Minkowskian space-time,

---

[24] Of course *inquiry*—and a fortiori *original inquiry*—cannot be entirely presuppositionless, given that it has norms and involves reflection and reasoning, that is, the making of inferences and the drawing of conclusions. But the principles I adopt to conduct original inquiry are compelling given the world, which is not distorted by these principles; their adoption is posterior to one's unadulterated confrontation with *all this*. See §3.5.

a four-dimensional manifold, in which there are infinitely many moments, no one of which is privileged. In other words, the standard interpretation of STR commits one to the view that temporal reality is ontologically homogeneous.[25] Consequently, there is not one moment—this one, now—at which everything happening in time occurs and at which everything in time exists. If this is a consequence of STR, the theory is clearly incompatible with transient presentism (and any standard presentist view).

STR is well-confirmed and universally accepted among mainstream physical scientists. It is known to be well-confirmed and universally accepted by those who are not scientists, but regard empirical inquiry as the primary, if not the only, way of acquiring knowledge of the world. Hence, in light of the apparent incompatibility between STR and any account of the world in time on which there is only this moment, now, many dismiss the latter out of hand. The (supposedly) clear incompatibility of a metaphysical theory with an established, authoritative empirical one is supposed to be irrefutable grounds for rejecting the former. This conclusion is, however, too quick and simplistic.

This dismissive conclusion simply ignores that physical theories are underdetermined by evidence. Like any physical theory, STR has background assumptions—about what is in the world, how these things are, how they interact, etc.—that ought to be evaluated. Like any other physical theory, there are interpretations of STR that make different background assumptions that nonetheless account equally well for the empirical data relevant to evaluating the theory. According to transient presentism, the world in time includes but a single moment, this one, now. This account requires, then, *absolute simultaneity*, that anything happening in time occurs at this moment, and so what is simultaneous with any event is simultaneous with all events (regardless of the features, including the velocities, of those events). The standard interpretation of STR requires one to reject absolute simultaneity in favor of a relativized notion that commits one to the background assumption that the world in time is ontologically homogeneous. So, with respect to the tenability of transient presentism, the crucial question is whether there is an interpretation of STR on which simultaneity is absolute and, hence, compatible with the background assumption that there is but a single moment.

---

[25] Rietdijk 1966 and Putnam 1967 are the *loci classici* of the arguments that the Special Theory of Relativity requires a view of temporal reality on which it is ontologically homogeneous.

Indeed there is, the so-called Lorentzian interpretation.[26] The details of this interpretation are not relevant, other than that it is consistent with absolute simultaneity and with a Newtonian space-time. A Newtonian space-time, in contrast to the Minkoswkian one required by the standard interpretation, is compatible with the background assumption that there is but a single moment. The two interpretations, despite the different background assumptions, account for the empirical data equally well. There are no empirical—no physical—grounds, then, for preferring one interpretation of STR over the other. Still, the two interpretations are not simply equivalent and their differences have led some to maintain that the standard interpretation is preferable. Were this so, there would remain a significant problem for transient presentism (and any other account of the world in time that requires absolute simultaneity).

The issue, then, is what exactly these differences are between the two interpretations. The differences are in terms of posited structure or, relatedly, what must be regarded as brute or inexplicable in regard to how matter behaves as it moves through space and time (or space-time).[27] But these differences are subtle and their upshots inconclusive. So much so that Craig Callender concludes weakly:

> [A]ll else being equal, one ought to prefer the Einstein-Minkowski interpretation to the Lorentzian interpretation. Positing otherwise unnecessary unobservable structure—absolute simultaneity—does violence to Occam's razor. But is all else equal? If the case for tenses [i.e., heterogeneity in temporal reality] is elsewhere strong, that may tip the balance over to the Lorentzian interpretation. The Lorentzian picture is logically consistent and empirically adequate, after all. What are a few lost explanatory virtues in contrast to _____ (fill in the blank with whatever [heterogeneity in temporal reality] explain[s])?[28]

Of course, the case for the general view of temporal reality on which it is ontologically heterogeneous is strong, as is the case for the particular account of the world in time offered by transient presentism. As discussed above, the

---

[26] William Lane Craig (in his 2001) appears to be the first to urge a Lorentzian interpretation of STR in order to defend a particular metaphysical account of the world in time.
[27] For illuminating discussion, see Callender 2008; Balashov and Janssen 2003; and Janssen 2002.
[28] Callender 2008: 53.

grounds for adopting the latter are not slight, based on mere "intuition" or some parochial considerations. Rather, the account is justified on the basis of a critical confrontation with the world in original inquiry. If one insists on the traditional interpretation of STR and, consequently, on the view that temporal reality is ontologically homogeneous, one is in an untenable position. One is insisting on a view that is incompatible with one's indubitable experiences in a world that goes from *thus* to *as so*. There can be no theoretical consideration that offsets such a flaw in one's account of the world, regardless of whether one's theory is physical or metaphysical. Science and metaphysics are compatible, and there is no need to deny STR. Overall considerations, though, indicate that one must reject the standard interpretation of the theory in favor of one, like the Lorentizan (or some other), that is consistent with absolute simultaneity. Transient presentism, with its particularly secure position with respect to the world, requires this.

§10.3.3. The insurmountable problem(s) of constancy

None of the preceding objections undermines transient presentism. This account of the world in time is clearly not trivial. It is compatible with dynamism and transience and has the means to explain the indubitable inconstancy in the world in terms of the persisting mutable objects at this transient moment, now (and at this one and at this, and so forth). Although the account recognizes but a single moment in the world, and so requires the absolute simultaneity of all goings-on in time, transient presentism is nevertheless compatible with the Special Theory of Relativity. Still, since transient presentism does, like any standard presentist view, maintain that there is little more to the world in time than this moment, now, and what exists at it, the account is open to an objection associated with one that has been raised many times in different ways against any such view of temporal reality. The objection, once clarified, is straightforward and compelling and, I believe, does show conclusively that transient presentism is unacceptable as a comprehensive and satisfactory account of the metaphysics of time.

The objection to any view of the world that includes but one moment, as just noted, has been raised in different ways. Yet none of these applies directly to transient presentism. Thus, some would object to transient presentism, as they do to standard presentism, on the grounds that the account does not have the means to accommodate *cross-temporal relations*, that is, relations holding between things existing at different times, i.e., moments.[29] A relation relates things; thus, if a relation holds, both relata existing must be so. If, however, all there is to the world in time—besides time itself, the at relation and simultaneity—is this moment, now, and the things thereat, then there are no familiar relations among temporal entities other than those that hold at this moment. Yet many take that there are such relations among things one or both of which do not now exist to be obvious, to say the least. For example, if Napoleon was 5'7" tall and one is 6', that one bears the *taller than* relation to Napoleon is presumed. If one will have a grandchild someday, that one stands in the *forebear* relation to that child is presumed. Likewise, if Aristotle was more wise than Kant, the former is presumed to stand in the *wiser than* relation to the latter. There are widely supposed to be ever so many such relations. If transient presentism is correct, though, there cannot be any. This upshot is supposed to be exceedingly implausible and an indication of the incorrectness of any view from which it follows.

This general problem of cross-temporal relations is often developed in particular ways and these more specific considerations presumably would also be presented as objections to transient presentism (as they are to standard presentism). For instance, some maintain that one's talk about things that once existed but no longer do (or will exist, but do not yet) requires *reference*. Reference is a semantic relation holding between a linguistic expression and a thing in the world. If this relation holds, both relata must exist. According to transient presentism, however, there are no things that once existed but no longer do (or will exist). Since that one can and does refer to such things is taken for granted, this line of reasoning is thought to reveal a significant problem for views like transient presentism. Similarly, some maintain that obviously one has a host of propositional attitudes (e.g., belief, knowledge, hope, fear, desire, etc.) about unique things that once existed but no longer do (or will exist, though do not yet). Such attitudes are supposed to involve *singular propositions*, that is, propositions that (on some views) have as constituents the very things they are about. Such attitudes would, therefore, require the existence of the unique things they are about. Since, again, according to transient presentism, the only mundane things in time are the ones that exist at this moment, now, these considerations are supposed to reveal a significant problem for such an account of temporal reality. Finally,

---

[29] For discussion of this objection, see, for example, Adams 1986: 321–328; Quine 1987: 197–198; Bigelow 1996; Davidson 2003; Markosian 2004; Crisp 2005; De Clercq 2006.

and relatedly, there are, certainly, true claims about what once was but is no longer. Many also take to be obvious that there are true claims about what will be but is not yet. These claims are supposed to be *made true* by things that exist at moments other than this one, now; in other words, there is supposed to be a relation of *truthmaking* that clearly holds and entails that there are things existing at moments prior to or subsequent to this one. Insofar as transient presentism precludes any such thing, these considerations are supposed to reveal a problem for this account of the world in time.[30]

Although there is indeed an insurmountable problem for transient presentism, it is not the general one of cross-temporal relations or any of the specific variants of this putative problem. The justification for transient presentism ultimately comes from original inquiry and principles informed by such basic confrontation with the world. The grounds for this account of the world in time are, therefore, particularly strong (as noted in the preceding section). On this account of temporal reality, the only moment is this one, now, and the only mundane things are the ones thereat. Consequently, there simply are no familiar or temporal relations between things that do not both exist at this moment. Claims to the contrary do not and cannot have epistemic grounds as strong as does this consequence of transient presentism. Claims that there are cross-temporal relations (between things that do not now both exist) are often just taken to be obviously true or "commonsensical" or "intuitive," but I do not regard such claims as having any epistemic force. Or these claims are the consequence of a theory of reference or of singular propositions or of truthmaking that does not have its basis in original inquiry—and no such theory can undermine transient presentism. This account of the world in time is a constraint on any theory, for what is revealed via original inquiry constrains (any) inquiry. As discussed above with respect to STR, any theory that contradicts transient presentism must be revised to accord with this account of temporal reality. Thus, for example, perhaps speaking about things that once existed but no longer do does not require reference, perhaps one's attitudes and representation of the world involves far fewer singular propositions than many presume (or a different understanding of such propositions). (In Chapter 11, I give an account of

---

[30] For discussion of these specific variants of the problem of cross-temporal relations, see, for example, Adams 1986: 315–322; Fitch 1994; Keller 2004; Markosian 2004; Merricks 2007, 2012: 64–67; Crisp 2007; Kierland and Monton 2007; Sanson and Caplan 2010; Cameron 2011; Mozersky 2011; Tallant 2013; Ingram 2016; Ingram and Tallant 2018.

truthmaking that does not require the existence of things at moments other than this one, now.)

Nevertheless, to maintain that one is taller than Napoleon, if one's height exceeds the one that Napoleon had is by no means implausible; nor is to hold that many comparisons between things that no longer exist are apt the least bit implausible. Moreover, to maintain that any claim about what was once so is as apt as any other or that there is nothing beyond a claim itself to distinguish those that are apt from those that are not is exceedingly far-fetched (I have argued elsewhere that it is incoherent[31]). What makes all of these claims so plausible is one's most basic engagement with the world. When the world goes from *thus* to *as so*, any claim that the world was not as demonstrated by 'thus' is simply unacceptable—so implausible as to be incomprehensible. If, in the transition of temporal differentiation, the world going from *thus* to *as so*, a thing ceases to be, to maintain that that thing never was or that it was not as it was when it did exist is no less unacceptable. The indubitable constancy in the world, as revealed in original inquiry, is, then, what makes these claims that posit cross-temporal relations compelling. The critical confrontation with the world in original inquiry indicates that there are constraints on any account of how the world *was*, on *how things were*. These constraints pertain to the moment that has just ceased to be and, hence, to any moment that has ceased to be. These constraints, applying to what is no more, can neither change nor cease to be. If there are such constraints and so there is some account of what was so, then this account, like any explicable phenomenon, must be in terms of things. This indicates the insuperable problem with transient presentism itself being a comprehensive and satisfactory account of the metaphysics of time.

There are constraints on what was. To think that these constraints require cross-temporal relations or things at moments other than this one, now is mistaken. But what is not a mistake is that *there are such constraints in the world*—denying this would be inconsistent with what is revealed via original inquiry. If there are these constraints on what was and these are or are based upon things that neither change nor cease to be, then such constraints are incompatible with the world in time as characterized by transient presentism. Each moment is transient, so each moment ceases to be. Each temporal substance (other than a moment) is dynamic; all of these, except time itself, are mutable and so can change, even if some of them do not. The inconstancy

---

[31] See Fiocco 2013.

of the world in time makes it inimical to the constancy revealed by original inquiry and required by the constraints on what was. So the crucial problem for transient presentism is that this account of the world in time does not have enough structure to account for the indubitable constancy in the world. Every substance in time (excluding, of course, time itself) ceases to be or can change and, hence, temporal reality does not include the permanent and static things required for constancy. There is just no accommodating such things *in time*, there is no basis for constancy herein, so this problem for transient presentism is insuperable. Transient presentism is not a comprehensive and satisfactory account of the metaphysics of time.

Rather than abandon this view of the world in time, however, what this crucial objection shows is that there is more to an account of the metaphysics of time than an account of the structure in temporal reality. The indubitable constancy in the world cannot be based on what is temporal, in time. It must be based on other things: ones that are *atemporal*, without time. Therefore, in order to provide the sought-after account of the metaphysics of time, one must complement an account of temporal reality with an account of atemporal reality.

11
Atemporal Reality and Constancy

Transient presentism accounts for the inconstancy in the world in terms of the continuous absolute becoming and annihilation of an instantaneous moment and the mutable things that exist thereat. This is the only account of one's engagement with the world in time consistent with the principles of radical ontology. There is, however, a conclusive objection to taking transient presentism to be a comprehensive and satisfactory account of the metaphysics of time. The objection is directed at the inability of this account of temporal reality to provide an ontological basis for the constancy in the world. What makes the account apt as an account of the inconstancy in the world—there being nothing more in time than time itself, the at relation, simultaneity, and mutable entities constrained by a transient moment—is precisely what makes it incapable of providing any basis for the constancy. There is, according to transient presentism, simply no thing in temporal reality and, a fortiori, no structure in temporal reality that is stable in the way that constancy demands.

Yet an account of this constancy is needed, for it, no less than inconstancy, is incontrovertibly in the world. This is apparent from the outset of inquiry. Moreover, the satisfactoriness of the sought-after account of the metaphysics of time depends on this account being able to explain both the inconstancy and constancy in the world. Since the constancy in the world cannot be explicated in terms of transient or dynamic temporal entities, to regard constancy as temporal at all is misguided. Nevertheless, this phenomenon, like any other, must be accounted for in terms of some thing(s) or other in the world. What constancy reveals, then, is that there is more to *all this* than the world in time. Although there is no more to what exists in temporal reality than those few things enumerated above, there is more to *all this* than what exists in time. The ontological basis of inconstancy is among such things. Therefore, what is needed to provide a comprehensive and satisfactory account of the metaphysics of time is a theory of the *world without time*, that is, an account of *atemporal reality*, one that comports with and complements transient presentism, the apt theory of temporal reality.

Given the importance of constancy, to examine the phenomenon anew in order to ascertain what exactly is to be explained by an account of this constancy and, hence, what an appropriate ontological basis of it is is worthwhile. So I begin by considering the constancy in the world from the perspective of original inquiry. I then examine *timelessness*, existence outside of—without—time. Some philosophers maintain that there is no feasible account of existing outside of time, others that nothing does so or could. The account I give in Chapter 5 of time per se, however, enables me to provide a straightforward and non-metaphorical account of timelessness. I maintain that there are indeed things that exist without time. Although some of these atemporal entities have no origin and, as such, did not come into existence, not all lack an origin. Thus, some things *come into existence*, but *without time*. This phenomenon of *atemporal becoming* might initially seem incoherent, yet it is not, and is of the utmost importance to this inquiry. Lest one worry that to rely on things outside of time when theorizing is frivolous because such things would be unknowable, I present some epistemological considerations to the contrary. In conclusion, I propound an account of the constancy in the world. The ontological basis of this constancy is *simple facts*, static entities that come into existence outside of time and exist permanently atemporally. Since a comprehensive and satisfactory account of the metaphysics of time turns on these unfamiliar entities, I consider them in some detail.

§11.1. Constancy in Original Inquiry

In the preceding chapters, my focus is on the inconstancy in *all this*, made striking by the world going from *thus* to *as so*. The conspicuousness of the phenomenon and its putative mysteriousness have made it the source of the contention in discussions of the metaphysics of time. By focusing on it, I am able to demonstrate the appropriate general account of the world in time—temporal reality is ontologically heterogeneous, rather than homogeneous—and the apt specific account, to wit, transient presentism. But this specific account of the world in time is not, in itself, a comprehensive and satisfactory account of the metaphysics of time: it simply does not have the means to explain the constancy in the world. This constancy cannot just be dismissed. Both it and inconstancy are equally plain, equally indisputable, from the point of original inquiry. Nevertheless, one's experiences of the two are rather different.

To experience constancy in original inquiry, once again confront the world as merely the impetus to inquiry. From this singular perspective, this all-encompassing totality is just a diverse array, one that is *thus*. It is *thus* ... then *as so*. This irrefragable transition indicates the inconstancy in the world—as does the transition from this moment to this one and this and so forth. If one passively engages *all this*, to be struck by this inconstancy is easy. To be gripped by the constancy in the world, however, one need only reflect, once the world goes from *thus* to *as so*, on whether to accept that things were as they were when demonstrated by 'thus' is appropriate; or, to put the point differently, on whether to accept that things ARE (tenselessly) as they ARE when demonstrated by 'thus' is appropriate. (I discuss the tenseless formulation of this point below.) Just as that things are now *as so* is manifest—so manifest as to be indubitable—that things were as they were when demonstrated by 'thus' is manifest (and indubitable). Although accepting that things were as they just were involves active reflection, the appropriateness of accepting this is obvious, even compelling, simply in confronting the world—in the same way that that one is presented with a diverse array is obvious and compelling when initially confronting the world in original inquiry. In neither case is what is so apparent assumed rather than *given*. Therefore, what makes the constancy in the world, like the inconstancy, indisputable is one's engagement with things in the world.

To consider things going from *thus* to *as so* is to consider in a general way the inconstancy and constancy in the world. The foregoing points about constancy can be corroborated by considering this phenomenon in specific detail. So consider the world now as it is *thus*. Included in what is *thus* is a cardinal sitting, singing, on an evergreen branch outside my window. At this moment, m_1, the bird must be just as it is, it could not (now) be otherwise. Still, it has the capacities, among innumerable others, to stop singing, take flight, shift on the branch, turn its head. As the world goes from *thus* to *as so*, going from m_1 to the moment m_2, the bird stops singing. At m_2, to hold that this silent bird has never sung is flatly incorrect; on the contrary, to accept that the bird has sung is appropriate. More particularly, to hold that the bird was not—or IS (tenselessly) not—singing at m_1 is flatly incorrect and to accept that the bird was singing at m_1 is appropriate. In other words, at m_2, that the bird was singing at m_1 is true. The appropriateness of accepting the bird was singing at m_1 is the appropriateness of recognizing that the bird was singing at m_1 is true. The truth of this claim is patent, so patent as to be undeniable. In engaging with (at least) this cardinal singing (at m_1) then stopping (at m_2), the truth (at m_2) that the bird was singing at m_1 is obvious and cogent and no mere assumption. What makes it so cogent, then, must be one's engagement with some thing(s) or other in the world.

There is nothing special about the moments or things considered in this specific case. Thus, these considerations generalize to everything that is so at any moment. For whatever is so at some moment, m, at any moment that comes to be, that that thing was so at m is true. How things are at any moment produces everlasting constraints on what is appropriate to accept about the world with respect to that moment, that is, what is true at that moment. These constraints, the ontological basis of abiding truth, must be something or other in the world. Whatever they are, they are accessible in original inquiry and engagement with them is what provides one with the indubitable experience of constancy in the world.

§11.1.1. The bases of constancy are not among the sparse structure in temporal reality

The question crucial to understanding constancy is what these everlasting constraints on what it is appropriate to accept about the world—the ontological bases of abiding truth—are. If one takes this constancy seriously, as one must, and so feels the force of this question, one can readily acquire a sense of the urge to regard the world in time as ontologically homogeneous and the initial plausibility of this view. If each moment were as real as every other, with nothing at any moment ever changing or any moment itself ceasing to be, then the constraints on what is appropriate to accept about how the world is at any given moment are those very moments and the things existing at them. Thus, if that that cardinal was singing outside my window at m_1 is now true, the basis of this truth would be that bird and its song as they are (i.e., ARE) at m_1, a moment earlier, though no less real, than this moment, now. But, of course, the world in time is not ontologically homogeneous (§7.4.). Temporal reality is heterogeneous and in a particularly sparse way.

At this moment, m_2, that that cardinal was just singing outside my window at m_1 is undeniably true. Yet that transient moment, m_1, has entirely ceased to be. So that moment and any feature of it cannot now underlie the truth that the cardinal was singing outside my window at m_1. Moreover, at m_2, the cardinal is not singing, it now is (and must be) silent. Hence, no obvious way the bird is is the basis of the truth that it was singing outside my window (at m_1). No moment other than m_1 is relevant to this truth, nor is any mutable thing other than the cardinal. All there is to temporal reality, though, beyond time itself (and the two momentary temporal relations), is this moment, now, the mutable things existing at it and the particular ways these things are. If none of these is suitably stable, then seemingly there are no bases of abiding truth in time.

Still, some who accept that the structure in temporal reality is as sparse as this maintain that the bases of abiding truth are to be found therein.[1] Consider again the bird outside my window: now, at m_2, when this bird is silent, to accept that the bird was singing at m_1, a moment that no longer exists, is certainly appropriate. Some maintain that accepting the bird was singing (at m_1) is appropriate because the world itself now bears the property *having been such that this bird was singing at* m_1, so the world with this property is the basis of the truth of the relevant claim.[2] But the world itself is not a thing and so bears no properties. Others might maintain that the basis of the truth that the bird was singing at m_1 is the bird and its properties, for one might suppose the bird to bear, at m_2, the property *having been singing at* m_1. However, this property, which characterizes how a thing *is* in terms of how it *is no more*, that is, in terms of how it was at a moment that has ceased to be, is rather dubious. Moreover, and more importantly, sooner or later the bird ceases to be and, once it does, this basis of the truth of the relevant claim, according to this proposal, is no more—and yet that the bird was singing at m_1 is nonetheless true.[3] Yet others maintain that everything in time, including this bird, is made from eternal atoms and so the stable basis for the truth of the claim that the bird was singing at m_1—now, at m_2, and at every moment to be—are these everlasting atoms, wherever they might go, and their property *having made this bird as it sang at* m_1. This proposal, too, though, relies on a dubious property (and questionable substances!) and so is unsatisfactory.[4]

---

[1] Such philosophers, then, accept that there is, for standard presentist views, a concern about grounding that must be addressed. They should not take this to be a version of the problem of cross-temporal relations, however, for they should acknowledge there are no such relations. See §10.3.3.

[2] See Bigelow 1996.

[3] Sanson and Caplan, in their 2010 paper, consider and reject such a proposal, for reasons different than the one I give above. Sider (2001: 41) considers and rejects properties, like *having been singing at* m_1, that "'point beyond' their instances."

[4] For this *atomic presentism*, see Keller 2004: 99–101. Keller also proposes an account of stable truthmakers in terms of *uninstantiated thisnesses*, i.e., *haecceities*, that presently exist instantiating dubious properties. See Keller 2004: 96–99.

Indeed, any account according to which the ontological bases of abiding truth are among the sparse structure of the world in time must be unsatisfactory.[5] This is simply because every temporal entity—excluding the at relation and simultaneity, which are clearly of no use here—is mutable, dynamic, or transient. No thing in temporal reality, therefore, is stable in the way that would make it suitable to be the basis of abiding truth and, hence, to account for the constancy in the world. If one is unwilling to accept dubious properties of mutable things (or questionable substances), one must look elsewhere for these bases. If they are not things among the world in time, they must be things *without time*. There is, then, more to *all this* than what exists in time.

§11.1.2. Being so versus being true

What is undeniable in one's experience of the constancy amid *all this* is not that things remain as they were—this bird that was singing is now silent—but that to accept that things once were a certain way, one incompatible with how they now are, is appropriate. What makes accepting this, that things were otherwise is true, appropriate does not need to be those things themselves, indeed, as shown above, it cannot be.

This last point reveals a key distinction. There is a difference between what *is* or, perhaps more illuminatingly, what *is so* in the world and what *is true* about the world. More exactly, there is a difference between what is so with respect to a thing (or things) and what is true about that thing. What is so with respect to a thing requires that thing to exist; what is true about a thing does not. This is because truth is a representational phenomenon, that is, a phenomenon involving a presentation of a thing as being a certain way. What is represented as being so-and-so, not only does not need to be so-and-so, it need not exist at all. Being, i.e., being so, in contrast, is in no way representational. As a representational phenomenon, then, truth might involve some thing other than what is presented as being a certain way, and

---

[5] Another strategy some presentists employ turns on an untenable account of a moment as a maximally consistent set of propositions whose truth-values change. All such "moments" are supposed to exist now—however this is to be understood—and nevertheless stand in the temporal relations of being earlier than and later than. See Crisp 2007, 2003; Bourne 2006a, 2006b; Markosian 2004; Davidson 2003.

what else it involves might be of principal importance to the phenomenon. So a representation that a thing is (or was) a certain way might be appropriate to accept, that is, be true, if there is something other than the thing so represented that makes that representation appropriate to accept. What this *truthmaker* is might not, initially, be clear, but what it does is: it accounts for why accepting a given representation as apt is appropriate.

In light of this distinction, if (at m_1) that cardinal is singing is so, then (at m_1) the cardinal existing (and singing) must be so. If (at m_2) the cardinal being silent is so, then (at m_2) the cardinal existing (and being silent) must be so. If now, at m_2, that the cardinal was singing at m_1 were so, then, at m_2, the cardinal existing, singing, at m_1 must be so. If now, at m_2, that the cardinal was singing at m_1 were so, then not only must m_2 exist, m_1 (with that singing cardinal) must exist, as well. The latter moment, of course, would not exist *at m_2*, but it would exist (that is, EXIST, tenselessly), nonetheless; m_1, and the singing cardinal that exists at it, would stand in the *earlier than* relation to m_2 (at which the cardinal is silent). However, now, at this moment, m_2, no other moment exists and the cardinal is (and must be) silent. That the cardinal was singing at m_1 is, therefore, *not* so. Nevertheless, that the bird was singing at m_1 is now *true* with respect to this silent bird (and about m_1, which no longer exists). So there must be some truthmaker involving neither m_1, which does not exist, nor the bird, which is silent and itself transient, for this claim. Whatever makes a claim true exists, the basis of any phenomenon must be in the world, and so what is true is true in virtue of what is so. Still, what exactly is so to make this claim about the cardinal true—and any other claim about moments distinct from this one, now—is, to say the least, not obvious.

If one does not recognize the distinction between what is so and what is true, then, given one's awareness of the constancy in the world, to reject that there are other moments and things existing at them that exist in the same way as these things, now, seems impossible. But with the distinction, one can see that this constancy can be consistent with transient presentism. To be consistent with this account of the world in time, the basis of abiding truths about the inconstant world, about transient moments and mutable things, must not be temporal entities. Therefore, in order to have a complete and satisfactory account of the metaphysics of time, some account of the world without time is needed to discern what exactly therein is the ontological basis of the constancy amid *all this*.

§11.2. Timelessness and the World Without Time

If there is nothing in temporal reality that could account for the indubitable constancy in the world, this constancy is not a temporal phenomenon; it is, rather, *atemporal*. The basis of constancy must be among those things that are not significantly related to time, that is, on what exists *without* or *outside time* and so is timeless. Although some notion of timelessness is employed in certain (metaphysical or theological) contexts, and so is not wholly unfamiliar, the notion is rarely, if ever, explicitly and literally characterized. Consequently, it and the corresponding notion of *atemporal reality* might seem inscrutable. In this section, I consider some animadversions concerning timelessness and reject them.

§11.2.1. Attempts to reject timelessness altogether

Some philosophers object that nothing could exist without time, because the very notion of timelessness is incoherent. The basis of this objection is the presumption that the English verb 'to exist' is inherently temporal. Thus, there are those who maintain that 'exists' admits only of a "tensed" use, one that refers to the moment of utterance, or a "tenseless" one, which refers to the moment of utterance or some moment prior or subsequent to it. In either case, to assert that something exists is thereby to relate it to some moment or other and, hence, place it in time. Those who find trivial the claim that only present things exist construe 'exist' in this disjunctive way (§10.1.1.). To say, then, that something is timeless is to say both that it is significantly related to time—because that thing must be related to some moment and, hence, be in time—and is not significantly related to time—because that thing is, in some sense, outside time. This is a contradiction.[6]

When considering the so-called triviality objection to "presentism" (§10.1.1.), I maintain there is no reason to think that 'exists' must be construed as temporal. I argue above (§4.3.2.) that there is only one way of being (*simpliciter*): to exist *simpliciter* is to be among the things there are, that is, to be in the world. It is the being requisite for anything to bear any quality or to stand in any relation whatsoever and so to make any contribution to *all this*. To contribute in this way need not require, in general, a

---

[6] Jonathan Tallant rejects timelessness on these grounds, see 2014: 498–499.

particular and significant relation to any one thing, including time. So to maintain that a thing exists, though does not stand in any such relation to time is not incoherent. In fact, if a thing is to relate to a moment—or anything whatsoever—that thing must first be relatable at all and so exist *simpliciter*. Therefore, 'exists' may be understood as being in no sense temporal, without having reference to any particular moment, and so is not necessarily tensed or tenseless. The notion of timelessness is, therefore, not incoherent.

Even if one concedes that this notion is coherent, one might still hold that there are no timeless things. Existing without time is certainly incompatible with change. Against the existence of timeless things, then, one might object that everything changes (or could) and, thus, there is nothing without time. I argue above that time itself is a thing that does not and cannot change. I argue as well that there are moments and that moments, which enable change, do not and cannot themselves change (I also consider below, other things that cannot change.) So I believe that all things do or could change is demonstrably false.[7]

§11.2.2. Two incorrect views of timelessness

The notion of timelessness is coherent and it appears to be false that all things could change and, hence, must exist in time. Indeed, I maintain there are timeless things. So what is needed now is an account of what to be timeless is, what it is to exist without time. As noted above, considerations of timelessness arise in certain metaphysical contexts, usually in connection to theological issues. As a result, there are a couple traditional views of what to be timeless is. I think these views are incorrect and can obscure the apt one needed for a complete and satisfactory account of the metaphysics of time. Examining these incorrect views in order to discard them is, then, worthwhile.

The impetus for examining the world without time is to discern therein the ontological bases of the constancy in the world. These bases, underlying abiding truth, must at least be immutable. However, on one traditional view, timelessness as *eternality*, being timeless is compatible with changing.

---

[7] Quentin Smith argues that all things, including "abstract" ones such as propositions, exist in time. See Smith 1998: 157–161. His argument for this, however, relies on dubious claims. Thus, for example, he maintains that when I cease to believe a certain proposition, p, this is a change in p.

A thing is eternal if it exists and has no origin. To characterize an eternal thing as one that *always* exists, that is, exists at every moment is natural, but a thing that has no origin might exist at every moment or none at all. If an eternal thing exists at any moment, this is because that thing has the capacity to be both of contradictory ways and, hence, must be constrained so as to make a determinate contribution to the world. If it has this capacity, the eternal thing can change (even if it does not). An eternal thing, then, could be constantly changing, different at every moment. Being eternal—merely lacking an origin—does not guarantee the immutability required by the timeless bases of the constancy in the world. Therefore, eternality must be rejected as the apt account of timelessness.

There is another traditional view, timelessness as *sempiternality*, on which timeless things are taken to be immutable. A thing is sempiternal if it exists unchanging at each moment. So on this view, a timeless thing exists at a moment—and, hence, in time—it just cannot change. This view, however, is worse than paradoxical; given what a moment is, it is incoherent. A moment is an entity that constrains a thing that has the capacity to be both of contradictory ways, making that thing be one of those two ways and thereby enabling it to make a determinate contribution to *all this*. For a thing to exist *at* a moment is for that thing to be so constrained. Anything that exists at a moment, then, can change (even if it does not). Immutable things can stand in many relations to a moment, but they cannot stand in the relation *existing at*. Thus, if timeless things are immutable, as they must be if the bases of the constancy in the world are to be without time, sempiternality must also be rejected as the apt account of timelessness.

§11.2.3. The world without time

Considering sempiternality indicates that what is timeless and, hence, immutable cannot exist at a moment. In considering eternality above, I noted that a thing that is eternal, that is, lacks an origin might exist at no moment at all. This might suggest that what to be timeless is, is to be eternal and yet exist at no moment. This suggestion is doubly incorrect. The discussion above demonstrates that being eternal is not sufficient for being timeless; subsequent discussion demonstrates that it is not necessary either (perhaps surprisingly, I maintain there are timeless things that have origins). Moreover, just as the ontological bases of the constancy in the world must be immutable, they must be permanent, as well; the bases of abiding truth cannot cease to be. There are, however, things that exist at no moment and yet are transient, that is, cease to be. The most obvious example of such a thing is a moment itself. No moment exists *at* a moment and each exists only instantaneously before entirely ceasing to be. So not existing at a moment is not sufficient for timelessness. This conclusion is worth elaborating.

A less obvious example of a thing that exists at no moment and yet is transient is any mode, i.e., particular quality, of a mutable thing. Consider some such mode, say, the whiteness of this shirt. This mode cannot, given what it is, exist in the absence of the mutable thing it modifies (to wit, my shirt). This mutable thing, like any other, is ontologically dependent on time (because the shirt must exist at a moment, which is itself ontologically dependent on time). If the mode is ontologically dependent on the mutable thing and the latter is ontologically dependent on time, the mode is as well. This point is confirmed by considering what such a mode is: in this case, a mode is the particular way, of two contradictory ways a mutable thing is capable of being, that that mutable thing is in virtue of being constrained by a moment; it is the thing whereby that mutable thing makes the determinate contribution it does (with respect to that particular way) at a moment. So at least some modes are temporal entities. Yet no mode has the capacity to be contradictory ways—a particular quality that were other than it is would be a distinct particular quality—and so no mode could be constrained by a moment. Thus, no mode could exist at a moment. Nevertheless, once this mutable entity changes with respect to the relevant quality (say the shirt fades), that mode ceases entirely to be and, hence, is transient.

If what is timeless is to be appropriately stable as to provide the bases of the constancy in the world, what is timeless must not only be immutable, it must also be permanent (and not merely not exist at a moment). But even being immutable and permanent does not suffice for the stability requisite to underlie the constancy in the world and, hence, to be timeless. There is at least one thing that is immutable and permanent and yet dynamic. This is time itself. Time does not change, it does not have the capacity to be contradictory ways, yet it ceaselessly contributes to the world more than itself—namely, this moment and this one and this one, and so forth—and so is dynamic. Any dynamism is incompatible with the bases of the constancy in the world; what is timeless must not merely be immutable, seemingly it must be static. Therefore, what is timeless must be both static and permanent. This stands to reason for a thing that is both static, that is, can contribute no more to the world than what and how it is, and permanent, that is, cannot cease to be and so must exist, is an apt basis for constancy, for abiding truth.

So timeless things are static and permanent. This provides some insight into how these things are (and must be) but provides no account of what things in the world are like this. When one considers all the things that are dynamic or transient or both, one recognizes that despite great differences among such entities, among mundane mutable things, modes, moments, and time itself, they nevertheless share a common feature: they are all ontologically dependent on time. This suggests that what is neither dynamic nor transient—what is static and permanent—is what does not ontologically depend on time. (The only exceptions to this appear to be the at relation and simultaneity, which are themselves static and permanent yet depend for their existence on time.) This is fitting. What is timeless, what exists without time, is what is ontologically independent of time. What such an *atemporal entity* is does not require that it exist with time. Of course, such a thing does not and could not exist in the absence of time, for time must exist. This co-existence with time, however, is coincidental rather than guaranteed by what that atemporal entity is and a significant relation of dependence.

§11.3. Atemporal Reality: The Things Independent of Time

Atemporal reality is all those things—atemporal entities—that are ontologically independent of time. This is a literal account of atemporal reality, one that does not rely on a mere spatial metaphor to distinguish those things "without" (in one sense) or "outside of" time, from those things "within" it. To appreciate the account requires one have informative accounts of what time itself is and of what ontological dependence is. These are provided in prior discussion.

These things ontologically independent of time, atemporal entities, are static and permanent. A thing that is static, one that cannot contribute more to the world than what and how it is, would be a different thing were it dynamic, one that can contribute more to the world than what (or how) it is. So any thing that is static is so essentially. Likewise, any thing that is permanent, and so could not cease to be, is essentially permanent. Atemporal entities, then, are not static and permanent because of their independence from time;

there can be no explanation for why any thing is as it is essentially. Rather, these things can exist without standing in a significant relation to time because they are what they are and, hence, as they are essentially, including being static and permanent. Such entities are merely more things amid *all this*. They just do not stand in certain relations to some things (e.g., time or this moment, now) that others, such as temporal entities, do. So the world without time need not be regarded as inscrutable; the things therein are not different in any alien way. One might worry, however, that despite merely being more things, atemporal entities are less accessible than other more familiar, temporal ones. I address such epistemic concerns below.

§11.3.1. Some examples of atemporal entities

I now introduce some of the things in atemporal reality. An atemporal entity, being static, is essentially each way it is and so must be these ways. If indeed a thing must be as it is with respect to every way it is, an argument that it is some way, for example, atemporal, really can do no more than direct one's attention to that thing in order to appreciate it as what and how it is—and so must be. (Any assumption that such a thing is not as it is, given that it must be each of those ways, is just an assumption that a thing is not itself. One cannot expect to get far by such means.) Hence my ambition, with respect to these exemplars, is merely to direct one's attention toward them, rather than to *argue* that they are atemporal.

As static and permanent, an atemporal entity cannot contribute more to the world than what and how it is and it cannot cease to be. There is a variety of things that are plausibly atemporal. Assume there are numbers. Any given number, say, 2, like any natured entity, has a range of properties. Some of these, such as being even or being prime, are distinctively numerical, being borne only or ultimately by numbers; others, like being abstract (i.e., non-spatial) are borne by other kinds. Any number also stands in countless distinctively numerical relations, such as being greater than or being evenly divisible by. Were a number to bear any different property or stand in any different relation, it would either not be the number it is or be no number at all (thus, no number could be concrete). A number, then, does not have the capacity to contribute anything to the world other than what and how it is. Insofar as one understands what a number is, that no number could cease to be is apparent. So numbers are atemporal entities.

There are different views of what propositions are, but at least on some accounts of such things, they are plausibly atemporal. Assume that a proposition is a non-linguistic, abstract representational entity. Any given proposition, say, that Aristotle is a philosopher (at moment, m), has a range of properties. Some of these, like being about Aristotle or being truth-apt, are had only by representational entities; others, like being abstract, are borne by a wider variety of things. Any proposition also stands in a number of relations, notably ones involving entailment, to wit, necessarily, if one proposition is true, so is another. Were a proposition to bear any different property or stand in any different relation, it would either not be the proposition it is or be no proposition at all (thus, no proposition could fail to be truth-apt). A proposition, then, does not have the capacity to contribute anything to the world other than what and how it is.

On some views, propositions are *unstructured* non-linguistic, abstract representational entities and, hence, lack constituents.[8] Insofar as one understands what such a proposition is, that it could not cease to be is apparent. On other views, propositions are *structured*, having as constituents different things. Hence, there are singular or Russellian propositions that include as constituents the things they are most straightforwardly about.[9] Given the example above, on this view, Aristotle himself would be part of the relevant proposition. On other views of structured propositions, their constituents are properties or Fregean senses or other such abstract entities. Since, as I just maintained, a proposition is static, any constituent it has it has essentially. If the constituent of a proposition ceases to be, then, so too does that (structured) proposition. Consequently, on not all accounts are all propositions atemporal, but on some accounts, to wit, ones according to which propositions are unstructured or do not have as constituents any transient things, they are.

The numbers 2, 42, and 51 and the propositions that Aristotle is a philosopher (at m), that Napoleon is 5'7" (at m), that Eleanor Roosevelt is a humanitarian (at m) are all examples of atemporal substances. A mode, a way for a thing to be, clearly does not have the capacity to be contradictory ways, so no mode could change (a mode that were in any way different would not be the mode it is). Nor could a mode, a way for a thing to be, contribute more to the world than it does and be a mode. Modes are, then, static. Whether a mode

---

[8] I am considering a view of unstructured propositions along the lines of Bealer 2006, rather than the one found in Stalnaker 1987 and Lewis 1986.
[9] See, for such a view, Salmon 1986.

is atemporal turns on whether what that mode qualifies is. The modes of the atemporal substances just considered, for instance, the particular primeness of 2, the particular truth-aptness of that Eleanor Roosevelt is a humanitarian (at m), are examples of atemporal modes. There are, of course, also temporal substances, such as this photograph of me and my family and the tree outside my window, and temporal modes—ones that cease to be—such as the particular glossiness of this photograph and the particular verdancy of that tree. This shows that the distinction between temporal and atemporal does not align with certain categories, but that the distinction can pertain to things of the same category. Moreover, the distinction pertains both to things that are qualitative, ones that qualify (i.e., characterize) others, and things that do not.

Still, a (non-qualitative) substance and a (qualitative) mode are both particular, in the sense that both are instances of a thing—viz., a kind and a property, respectively—rather than instantiable things themselves. When one considers such universal things, all of them appear to be atemporal. Consider some property, perseverance or blueness, for instance. Such a thing accounts for how distinct, but exactly similarly natured modes go together with respect to how they are. Each property, as a natured entity, is itself certain ways: abstract, instantiable, and, perhaps, distinctive ways associated with the unique role that that property has in accounting for how certain modes go together. No property, however, has the capacity to contribute anything to the world other than what and how it is. Were a property to contribute to the world other than what or how it is—were it, say, to be ways incompatible with any associated with its unique role or to be not instantiable, it would not be the property it is or would not be a property at all. Each property might also, perhaps, stand in certain relations to other properties. But were any one of these to be otherwise, that property seemingly would not be the property it is (for example, if blueness were to be more similar to perseverance than to greenness). So each property is static. Some might believe, along traditional Aristotelian lines, that a property exists *in rebus* and, hence, could not exist in the absence of any thing that has that property. On this account, some properties, at least, are transient, ceasing to be when all the things that bear that property cease to be. I reject this sort of Aristotelian account, however. Given the existence of modes and the epistemic views I discuss below (§11.3.3.), I see no grounds for holding it. Therefore, insofar as one understands what a property is, that no property could cease to be is apparent. Properties, then, are evidently static and permanent and so atemporal. The same seems to be so for all (universal) relations, with the exceptions of the at relation and simultaneity, which depend for their existence on time and so are temporal entities.

That each kind is also atemporal is maybe less clear. Consider some kind, *human being* or *television*, for instance. Such a thing accounts for how distinct, but exactly similarly natured substances go together with respect to what they are. The considerations I present in support of the claim that properties are static can be offered, mutatis mutandis, in support of the claim that kinds are. One might object, though, that some kinds evolve or, at least, change. For instance, certain characteristics are now more common among human beings than they were three hundred years ago and televisions today are different in many respects from those produced four decades ago. These observations are obviously correct. However, they do not indicate change, either in kinds, or their instances. What these observations show is that many kinds have the capacity to have instances that differ significantly with respect to the ways they are. Indeed, what a kind is is the basis of an account of how things that are ever so different are nevertheless the same. Consider a television manufactured in 1973 and another in 2018. The designs of, the materials used to make, even the functionality of the two televisions are different and yet they are similarly natured and so both are of the same kind, viz., *television*.

§11.3.2. Atemporal becoming

Seemingly, kinds and properties are all atemporal. That they are all eternal, though, does not follow. That the property of perseverance, say, or the kind *television* has no origin, that each has co-existed with every moment (though, of course, not *at* any moment), is quite far-fetched. Coming to be—having an origin—is compatible with being ontologically independent of time and, hence, with being static and permanent. This phenomenon of atemporal becoming is of the utmost importance to a complete and satisfactory account of the metaphysics of time, for it provides the means of reconciling continuous inconstancy with the constancy that is no less in the world.

Coming into existence, yet outside of time, might seem incoherent. If so, this is presumably because one has incorrect presumptions regarding what to come to be is. Thus, one might be presuming that coming to be involves change and so is dynamic in a way that makes it incompatible with atemporal reality. Becoming, however, does not involve change in what comes to be. An entity that comes into being is not first one way—non-existent—and then a different way—existent—having persisted through some change. Rather, without coming to be, a thing is nothing at all; it comes to be without having been in any way. It is only once it exists that it is (or can be) any way at all.

Any moment, though dependent on time, comes to be absolutely; it comes to be without having been in any way. The continuous absolute becoming and absolute annihilation of instantaneous moments is, in part, the ontological basis of temporal differentiation. Other things come to be, but given what they are can only come to be in relation to a moment—*at* a moment—and so in this way are also dependent on time. Such things, mutable entities, have in themselves the capacity to be contradictory ways and so must be constrained in order to make a determinate contribution to *all this*. However, there are yet other things that are essentially every way they are and so lack the capacity to be contradictory ways. They are, moreover, ontologically independent of time. Such static and permanent things cannot be significantly related to a moment and, consequently, do not come into existence at a moment. They, nevertheless, come to be among the things in the world. Therefore, a thing can be static, and so immutable, and even permanent and yet still come to be. Such a timeless, i.e., atemporal, thing has an origin, but not *at any moment*; it comes to be, but *outside of time*.

Atemporal becoming yields some thing, but this is a difference without change. This novel thing, though not in temporal reality is nonetheless among *all this*; more specifically, it is among the things in atemporal reality. Some atemporal entities are plausibly eternal: 2, the proposition that time exists, the property of being abstract, the kind *moment*. These things have no origin. Yet there are other atemporal entities that surely do. Consider the proposition that I [MOF] am sitting here at the University of California, Irvine at 11:33 in the morning on February 10, 2020, or the property of perseverance or of blueness or of solubility or of being left-handed or of softness or of being nutritious or of being a fan of the New York Yankees or the kind *human being* or *television* or *water*. None of these things were among those in the world at the formation of the physical universe. Each came to be without having been in any way.

That a thing that comes into the world but at no moment comes into the world from *nothing* does not follow—no more than this would follow for a thing that comes into the world at a moment. Each thing has its source among the things in the world. Note that even if a thing could not come to be in the absence of some other thing(s), that the former is ontologically dependent on the latter in the sense that it could not be what it is in the absence of the former does not follow. I could not have come into existence without (among other things), my mother and yet I am not ontologically dependent on her. So even if the property of being left-handed could not come to be in the absence of some relatively sophisticated embodied agent, a mutable and, hence, temporal entity, that this property is ontologically dependent on that temporal entity, and so is temporal itself, does not follow.

In this connection, to try to time, as it were, the coming into existence of an atemporal entity is a mistake. To think that the existence of some new property or kind comes into being simultaneously with the coming to be of its first instance, that original mode or substance, might be tempting. Temptation here should be resisted, for this way of regarding the phenomenon is misleading. The coming to be of the two entities, the new kind and its first instance, say, is not simultaneous, because to be simultaneous is to occur at the same moment. In this case, however, one entity—that individual substance—comes to be at a moment, the other—its universal kind—comes to be, but at no moment at all. Both come into existence, but that the two origins are simultaneous is literally false, even if the two come into the world together. As atemporal, the kind bears no significant relation to time.

Nevertheless, since each moment comes to be simpliciter, exists but for an instant, then ceases to be, the world that includes a particular moment is unique. There is, then, a way of characterizing the unique world that first includes a thing that comes to be outside of time by making reference to the distinctive moment that that world also includes. Of course, that world, that singular collection of things, no longer exists, so the question of why one representation of that world rather than another is apt must be settled. This is, though, just another manifestation of the key problem, regarding constancy, of taking transient presentism to provide a complete and satisfactory account of the metaphysics of time. If this problem can be solved, then there are correct ways of characterizing the world that first includes an atemporal entity.

§11.3.3. Epistemic access to the world without time

Before examining the constancy in the world in light of the foregoing discussion of atemporal entities and atemporal becoming, to consider first an epistemic objection that one might have is important. Assume there are things that exist without time. All the examples I give of such things are abstract, in the sense that they do not exist in space. Presumably, all atemporal entities are abstract (in fact, I do think this is the case). Atemporal entities, then, exist outside of space and time. If this is correct, then one might object that such things are unknowable; consequently, an account of some phenomenon in terms of such things is, at best, dubious, if not sheer fantasy. Hence, if one's account of *all this* or, more particularly, of the metaphysics of time relies on atemporal entities, then—if that account is to be at all credible—one must address how such things can be known.

The objection arises from a widespread and familiar strict empiricism. On such a position what is not knowable via the senses is not knowable at all. One's sense faculties operate only on things with locations, ones that exist in space or space-time. Thus, what has no location is not sensible and, according to the empiricist, unknowable. I acknowledge that no atemporal entity is sensible. Nevertheless, I do not think that such things are unknowable. I am no empiricist. I reject empiricism on ontological grounds. Given that the world comprises innumerable fundamental natured entities related in myriad more and less significant ways, certain accounts of the relations between minds—and, consequently, inquirers—and other things that are incompatible with empiricism are available, if not enjoined. Radical ontology has, then, epistemological consequences. I have illuminated and discussed some of these consequences in other work.[10] Here I merely present, in brief, pertinent upshots of those discussions in order to show why this objection regarding the unknowability of atemporal entities is unfounded.

Certainly among the things there are in the world are minds, where a mind is simply a fundamental natured entity with the capacity of *intentionality*, that is, the capacity to present some thing so as to be considered. Intentionality enables the engagement between a conscious being—a thing with a mind—and the world, and so this capacity is crucial to epistemology, an account of the appropriate (with respect to some norm, for example, truth or revelation) engagement between a conscious being and the world. Elsewhere, I demonstrate that each thing, in principle, can be thought of or referred to and, consequently, that for a mind to passively engage a thing must be possible.[11] Intentionality, then, like other capacities, can be realized both actively and passively. A conscious being can actively direct its mind

---

[10] See Fiocco 2019b, 2017, 2015.
[11] See Fiocco 2015.

toward something, thereby engaging that thing (in thought)—or a conscious being can passively receive something as that thing impresses itself upon the mind of the conscious being.

Acquaintance is the immediate relation that holds between a mind and a thing as the result of the passive realization of the capacity of intentionality.[12] I maintain there are varieties of acquaintance. There is *perception* and, hence, I am a proponent of a *direct realist* account of this phenomenon. (Indeed, I think the correct account of epistemology requires a *naive realist* account of perception, one on which one's engagement with things via perception is not merely direct, but non-representational, i.e., simply relational.)[13] There is also, for lack of a better term, *intuition*. The distinction between these species of acquaintance turns on whether what the mind engages has a location—is in space—or does not. Making this distinction is de rigueur given the hegemony of empiricism in contemporary discussions of epistemology and, because of the place of this position, seemingly has an outsized importance. The distinction is, however, of no epistemic importance.

The reason the distinction between perception and intuition has no epistemic importance is that a mind is capable of engaging with things, *all* things. A thing in space—or time—is no different qua thing from something outside of space (or time). Both are natured entities and so both make some contribution to *all this*. Of course, things in space (or time) bear certain properties and stand in certain relations that things without it do not. But how one thing is related to some particular other thing—space, time, my house, the State of California, etc.—has no bearing on the ontological standing of either thing and, hence, no bearing on the ability of a mind to engage it intentionally. A thing outside of time is no more epistemically inaccessible than a thing outside my house. A mind can, in principle, be acquainted with either, even if the former is imperceptible and can only be intuited; in both cases, a mind just needs to be appropriately situated to encounter that thing. A thing intuited can be confronted and examined and appreciated for what and how it is just as a thing perceived can.[14] Intentionally and so epistemically both phenomena are equivalent (even if the two have distinct

---

[12] See Fiocco 2017.
[13] See Fiocco 2019b.
[14] Note that the account of intuition characterized here is relational or objectual, rather than representational: a mind relates directly to the thing it intuits in such a way that that direct engagement is constitutive of the intuition. This account differs, then, from one on which an intuition is a sui generis propositional attitude, one whereby a proposition is presented as seeming true. For the latter sort of account, see Bealer 2002, 1998; Bengson 2015; Chudnoff 2011; Huemer 2005.

conscious feels or are accompanied by different physiological processes). Therefore, atemporal entities, as things, are knowable and, hence, acceptably included in one's theories.

§11.4. The Constancy in the World

In original inquiry, one experiences the world transitioning from *thus* to *as so*. The ontological basis of this transition is temporal differentiation, one instantaneous moment absolutely ceasing to be and another absolutely coming to be, with other temporal entities changing, coming to be, or ceasing to be. According to transient presentism, all there is to the world in time is time itself; the two momentary temporal relations, viz., the at relation and simultaneity; this moment, now; and all the mutable entities (and their modes) existing thereat. The transition from one transient moment to the next, with all the dynamic or transient things that persist through it or cease to be from one moment to the other or come to be at the latter, are the bases of the indubitable inconstancy one experiences in the world.

Yet, in this same transition, from the world being *thus* to *as so*, one can also experience an unshakable stability. Once the world goes from *thus* to *as so*, to maintain that the world was never as it was when demonstrated by 'thus' would be flatly incorrect. Likewise, if something is in the world and then, now, has ceased to be, to maintain that that thing never existed would be flatly incorrect. Considering either case indicates the indubitable constancy in the world. What makes accepting that that thing existed or that *all this* was as it was when demonstrated by 'thus' appropriate underlies one's experience of this constancy. The basis of this experience, as discussed above, is not a permanent moment (there is none), nor familiar things remaining the same (most do not), nor immutable things in time (any [non-relational] thing in time is either mutable or transient)—indeed, there is nothing in time that is suitably stable to be the basis of one's experience of constancy. These bases are, then, among the static and permanent things that exist without time.

Above, I present some examples of atemporal entities. None of these things, nor any combination of them, however, is plausibly what makes appropriate accepting that something was a certain way when it is no longer that way (or has ceased to exist). What makes appropriate accepting that something was a certain way is the basis of the abiding truth that that thing was that way. No (universal) property, for example, makes true that this silent cardinal was singing a moment ago. Therefore, the bases of abiding truth—those things that underlie one's experience of constancy—must be atemporal entities other than the ones already considered.

§11.4.1. Simple facts

So consider again the cardinal outside my window. At this moment, now, m_2, it is silent, yet a moment ago, at m_1, it was singing. To accept that this bird was singing at m_1 is appropriate, for to maintain that the bird was not singing at m_1 is flatly incorrect. There is, therefore, clearly a constraint on how one ought to take the world to be. Such a constraint indicates—indeed *is*—a thing. Call the thing that constrains how one ought to take the world with respect to this bird and its song at m_1 the *simple fact that this bird was singing at* m_1.[15] This simple fact is what makes true that the bird was singing at m_1. Since this is an abiding truth—at every moment henceforth that this bird was singing at m_1 is (and must be) true—the thing that makes it true is the basis of one's experience of constancy in regard to this bird and its song at that moment. Given that this simple fact does not exist in time, and so is static—it has no capacity to be otherwise than it is—and permanent—it does not cease to be—it is indeed a suitable basis of this constancy. Of course at, say, the moment of my birth, to accept that this bird was singing at m_1 was not appropriate. This only shows, however, that the simple fact has an origin; it comes into being. Thus, simple facts, like other examples of atemporal entities discussed above, come into being outside of time.

Obviously, there is nothing special about this cardinal, its song or the moment, m_1. One can generalize, then, from the foregoing considerations: what makes appropriate accepting certain claims about how some thing is at a given moment is that these claims are made true by simple facts, whereas those claims inappropriate to accept are not made true in this way. So other examples of simple facts are *the simple fact that there is no anteater in my office (at* m*), the simple fact that I am not eight feet tall (at* m*), the simple fact that the branches on the tree outside my window are moving in the breeze (at* m*)*, and *the simple fact that Eleanor Roosevelt is a humanitarian (at* m*)*, where *m* is a moment, this one, now, or some other.

---

[15] I discuss simple facts at length in Fiocco 2014.

A simple fact is *simple* in that it has no constituents. It certainly has no temporal constituents and seems to have no atemporal ones either. Thus, there is no transient thing (such as a bird) whose annihilation would make a simple fact cease to be. Although a simple fact is ontologically independent of the things represented by a claim it makes true and, hence, can exist in the absence of those things—just as many representational entities are ontologically independent of the things they ostensibly represent—a simple fact is in no way representational. A simple fact is a (non-representational) *fact* in that it is an entity made by some thing(s) in the world. A simple fact is not made to be in the sense that its very existence derives from or is supported by another thing; given that each thing is fundamental, no thing is made to be in this sense. Nevertheless, a simple fact is made to be in the same way as is any thing with an origin: it is the product of some thing(s) or other. So when, at some moment, m_1, some thing or other has a particular mode or when some things stand in a certain relation, the simple fact that that thing has that mode at m_1 (or that those things stand in that relation at m_1) comes into being. It does not come into being *at* m_1, but it comes to be part of the world that includes m_1. Unlike m_1, though, which is a part of only that world—that very multiplicity of things—the simple fact is a part of distinct multiplicities of things, such as the world that includes m_2. The simple fact is the permanent (and static) trace of things being as they are at a given moment.

Because the world is in part inconstant, what is so, what exists, is continuously different. Since what is appropriate to accept with respect to the things in the world, that is, what is true with respect to these things depends on what is so, what is true is continuously different. It is continuously different in that there are novel truths—and new truthmakers—in each world that includes a new moment. The truths, i.e., truth-bearers, and truthmakers come into being outside of time. Still, there is nothing happening in the world outside of time; nothing is changing. A thing coming to be is no change and atemporal reality is a multiplicity of things and, hence, nothing itself, so it cannot change. Once some truth exists, though, it and the simple fact that makes it true are part of each world that includes a new moment. So those simple facts are part of the world that includes this moment ... and this ... and this; though, of course, these simple facts do not persist, for they do not exist in time, *at* these moments. In this way, these truths and truthmakers are part of the world evermore and why simple facts are the apt basis of one's experience of constancy.

A simple fact, like that this bird was singing at m_1, makes true evermore that this bird was singing at m_1. In each new world that contains a novel transient moment, this claim about this bird is true. Only in this sense is saying that this claim *will be* true or will *always* be true apt. The future tense here should not be taken to indicate that at each future, i.e., subsequent moment, this claim is true, for there are no future or subsequent moments. A future moment is one that bears the property of being future; a subsequent moment would be one that is later than this moment, now, and so stands in a temporal relation to this moment, now. But there are no such moments; there is only this one moment, now. This is why there are no true claims about what will be other than those that are about what is or has been. Nor should the future tense be taken to suggest that what is so at each new moment is what makes the relevant claim true—its truthmaker is not at any moment at all.

Likewise, to say at this moment, now, that the bird *was* singing (at m_1) is apt. But the past tense here should not be taken to indicate that at some past or prior moment this claim is true, for there are no past or prior moments. Nor should the past tense be taken to suggest that what is so at some past moment—or at any moment whatsoever—is what makes this claim true. The simple fact that this bird was singing at m_1 does not make *so* this bird was singing at m_1. That would require this bird, its song, and the moment, m_1 (two of these things do not exist). Nonetheless, this simple fact does make *true* that the bird was singing at m_1. To accept that these things *were so* because of this simple fact, which is itself so, a unique thing that exists without time as a consequence of those things having been so (in time) is appropriate. Note, and these comments hold for any simple fact, that one may call this the simple fact this bird was singing at m_1 or the simple fact that this bird is singing at m_1 or the simple fact that this bird SINGS at m_1. How one names the simple fact is not relevant to what it is; its name is purely heuristic. Hence, the simple fact, this atemporal entity, is not tensed or tenseless any more than other simple facts are negative or conjunctive or what have you.

The ontological basis of constancy is the simple facts that exist and come into being. Constancy is, then, not a temporal phenomenon at all. (Nonetheless one can experience it and thereby recognize it at a moment.) These simple facts provide sufficient structure for all true claims about what is and has ceased to be. Thus, there are simple facts about things that now exist yet have changed from how they were and there are simple facts about things that are no longer. Simple facts, moreover, underlie the truth of descriptions regarding what are mistakenly taken to be "cross-temporal" relations, that is, seeming relations between things that now exist and ones that do not or seeming relations between things that never existed with one another. There are, then, the simple facts underlying the truths that Aristotle was a philosopher (at m), that I am now taller than Napoleon was (at m) and that World War I preceded World War II. The simple fact that Aristotle was a philosopher (at m) underlies the first truth. What underlies the second are the simple fact that I am 6' tall at this moment, now; the simple fact that Napoleon was 5'7" (at m); and the simple fact that 6' is a larger height than 5'7". The third truth is made true by the simple facts that World War I existed at moment, m, and that there are no simple facts in the world that included that very moment that underlie true claims about World War II. Simple facts underlie all claims about the temporal world in similar ways.

There are compelling reasons for accepting simple facts. Elsewhere,[16] I argue that—on pain of contradiction or incoherence—there must be something or other in the world that makes each true claim true. Setting aside any consideration of constancy or inconstancy, there are many patent truths for which there are no patent truthmakers among familiar entities. Thus, consider the truth that at this moment there are only three pens on my desktop or that there is now no anteater in my office. In regard to the former, there is nothing about these pens or my desk and its top that excludes there being something else upon it; these things are compatible with there being, say, a book also on the desk, in the sense that all the former could exist just as they are and yet that there are only three pens on my desktop be false. Hence, there must be some other thing that accounts for why accepting that at this moment there are upon my desk only three pens is appropriate, that is, why that at this moment there are upon my desk only three pens is true. I maintain that this thing is the simple fact that there are only three pens on the desktop (at this moment).

Once one considers again the inconstancy in the world, there is even more reason for recognizing simple facts. For these pens and this desk at some moment cease to be and things here in my office come to be arranged differently, yet evermore that there are only three pens on my desktop at m is true. In addition, though, to these considerations are those grounds provided directly by one's experience of the world. When one hears this bird singing at m_1 and finds it silent at m_2, one is aware with certainty that to accept that this bird was singing at m_1 is appropriate. This awareness is not without a basis; there

---

[16] See Fiocco 2013.

is some thing that accounts for it. This is the simple fact that the bird was singing at m_1. So as one engages perceptually this silent bird now at m_2, one is, at this moment, acquainted—intuitively—with the simple fact that it was singing at m_1, a simple fact that is real and in the world though not at this moment. One is literally confronting this simple fact, one is acquainted with this thing and just as there can be no better grounds for the claim that there is a bird before one is so than seeing (or hearing or touching) the bird, there can be no better grounds for the claim that this bird was singing a moment ago than immediately engaging what is in the world that makes this true, namely, the simple fact that the bird was singing at m_1.

A simple fact is a thing, a natured entity. It is, therefore, a constraint in (or on) the world. So the claim now, at m_2, that this bird was singing at m_1 is true and to accept that things were such that this silent bird was singing at that moment is appropriate is no mere assertion—not mere insistence—that things were that way. There is an ontological commitment here: to something so, in the world, that makes this claim true. One's awareness of this thing, the simple fact that this bird was singing at m_1, and other such simple facts, is what underlies one's experience of the constancy in this world. Even as one now, at m_2, confronts this silent bird, one can confront the simple fact that it was otherwise and that there are grounds evermore for the truth that it was singing at m_1.

Simple facts are not familiar entities (although one engages them quite often!). However, they should not be resisted on this ground alone. One should not take oneself to be familiar with every sort of thing in the world prior to inquiry, and so unfamiliarity should not in itself be suspicious or odious. There are compelling grounds for recognizing simple facts—I maintain there must be something that makes any truth true and, furthermore, one can be directly aware of the constraints in the world regarding what was so—and no real grounds for rejecting them. Qua things, simple facts are no different than others; most features a simple fact has, coming into the world, existing atemporally, being abstract, being permanent, etc., are shared by many others.

Still, one might demand an account of why the simple fact that this bird was singing at m_1 is the simple fact it is. But each thing, being fundamental, just is the very thing it is; so there is no informative answer to why a simple fact is the simple fact it is. Likewise, one might demand an account of how this simple fact makes true a representation. But each thing, being fundamental, just is the constraint it is and just does what it does. A tree does what trees do because it is a tree and the maroon mode of my pants appears as it does and qualifies my pants as it does simply because of what it is. There is nothing odd or different about simple facts on these scores. A simple fact makes true the representation(s) it does because it is a simple fact and the very simple fact it is. If one thinks there is some thing better suited to be the truthmaker for a claim or, in particular, something better suited to be the truthmaker for the claim that this bird was singing at m_1, one has to recognize that all seemingly plausible alternatives—this bird, its song, the moment, m_1—are transient or dynamic or both in ways that render them incompatible with the abidingness of truth. Simple facts are perfectly suited as truthmakers. Of course, this alone might make some suspicious of them. If this is so, however, one needs to recognize that this is nothing distinctive about simple facts: each thing is perfectly suited to constrain the world as it does, for each thing is perfectly suited to be itself.

Things, the temporal ones, come and go, but some things, the atemporal ones, go on and on. Both sorts of things are included in *all this*. Among the atemporal entities is a structure of simple facts that accounts for the constancy in the world of which one can be aware. Simple facts, like any other things, are suitable for a mind to be acquainted with, and one merely needs to engage, amid the indisputable inconstancy in the world, these permanent and static traces of what is so to experience the indisputable constancy also in the world. Atemporal entities, including simple facts, complement the temporal entities recognized by transient presentism, the apt account of the world in time. With this account of temporal reality and the foregoing account of atemporal reality, one finally has the things for a complete and satisfactory account of the metaphysics of time.

PART V
CONCLUSION
The World in Its Entirety

12
All This and Why It Matters

One is amid *all this*, and curiosity might lead one to wonder what any—or all—of it is. If one does ask what all of it is, that is, asks what *the world* is, and insists on an answer that comes directly from *all this*, rather than from presumption about what it is or ought to be, then, with some effort, one can attain an answer: *all this* is a multiplicity of things, every thing there is. Nothing more, no thing less.

Such an answer might sound vacuous. Of course that is what the world is, one might demur, it could not be anything else. Clearly, the world, this all-encompassing totality, could be nothing less. The account of it as all things, however, is hardly trivial—if one appreciates what a thing is. A thing, as revealed via *original inquiry*, is a natured entity, an inherent constraint that just is, and just is what it is and how it is essentially. No thing is made to be by some other thing or made to be what it is or how it is (essentially), and so each thing is, in this sense, fundamental. There is no accounting for its existence or its existing, as it exists (although there might be some explanatory account of how it came to be), and no explanation of that thing per se. The best account one can have of some thing is an illuminating description of it and how it relates to other things. Any thing necessarily exists with others and interacts necessarily as it does with yet others. That there are such things is, prior to a critical investigation, not obvious. Each thing accounts, in part, for how the world is *thus*; all things together are the basis of a complete explanation for how the world is as it is: *thus*.

There is *all this*, which is *thus* . . . and *all this*, which is *as so*. It is then *as such* . . . and *as such* and so forth. This transition is irrefragable, given in confronting *all this* in original inquiry. An account of all things that does not acknowledge and explain it is no real account at all. Such an account, therefore, must explain not only how *all this* is *thus*, but also how there could be more than *all this*: it must be an account of every thing and then some. Since the world is merely a multiplicity of things, it is not itself a thing. Hence, in this transition, there is no change in the world per se. *All this*, this multiplicity of things, which is *thus*, is simply a distinct multiplicity than this, which is

Time and the World. M. Oreste Fiocco, Oxford University Press. © Oxford University Press 2024.
DOI: 10.1093/oso/9780197777107.003.0012

as so. This world is literally a different world than what was demonstrated by 'thus.' Differences between the two must be accounted for in terms of the things each comprises.

Central to such an account is time itself. Time yields the moments needed for *all this* to go from *thus* to *as so*. This phenomenon, temporal differentiation, reveals the indubitable inconstancy and constancy in the world. These phenomena, like all others, must be accounted for in terms of the things in the world. The ontological bases of the inconstancy are dynamic things, which can contribute more to the world than just as they are—all except time do so by changing—and transient things that cease to be. The bases of the constancy in the world are the static, permanent things that can contribute nothing more to what is than they themselves, just as they are, and cannot cease to be. Time is crucial for understanding these phenomena, too. The novel moments that time provides are what enable dynamic things to change, realizing their capacities to be incompatible ways, and that enable transient things to cease utterly to be. The timelessness of static, permanent things, their independence from time, is what helps illuminate what these (atemporal) things are. There is some continuity between the multiplicity that is *thus* and this distinct multiplicity, which is *as so*, because of the dynamism or permanence of some things. However, the worlds cannot be identical because of the necessary permanent dynamism of time itself; time continuously yields a novel moment, which immediately ceases to be.

Therefore, confronting the world in original inquiry allows one to discern the contour of *all this* in significant detail, to recognize the boundaries of reality. Reality—the world—is these things: some that have origins (and, hence, came to be) or do not; that are dynamic or are static; that have the capacity to change and become otherways or do not; that are transient and might cease to be or are permanent and cannot. Pivotal to it all is time itself, for some things depend on time, via the unique moment there is, and some do not. This is the structure in reality, things standing in relations (which are themselves things) to other things; this is the extent of the world. One can, in principle, be acquainted with any of these things and every phenomenon must be accounted for by them.

So here, among these innumerable things, is the basis of all inquiry. The importance of this result turns on the account of what a thing, any thing whatsoever, is. This account is attainable only by taking up a wholly critical discipline, one that provides an evaluable account of a thing while taking nothing for granted about *all this*. I call this discipline *metaphysics*. Resolving the distinctive problem of metaphysics—attaining, without presuming anything about the world, the correct account of a thing—requires a novel methodology, to wit, original inquiry. In original inquiry, one simply confronts the world, this encompassing totality, recognizing that it is diverse and so constrained. That *all this* is constrained in a unique way, *thusly*, is given, not assumed. Considering what could constrain it so, one is able to apprehend what a thing is, a fundamental natured entity. The ineluctable transition in *all this* reveals a singular constraint herein, time itself. By scrutinizing the world, going as it does from *thus* to *as so*, one is able to discern the structure in reality and its extent, all these things within and without time.

This is what metaphysics via original inquiry delivers, to wit, the framework of *radical ontology*. One might be moved by these results or be totally unimpressed. If one is curious about nothing, then, of course, this wholly critical metaphysics is worthless. If one is curious about *all this*, then the importance of this metaphysics is plain: it provides one with an insightful, albeit general, account of what the world is and what it comprises. But even if one has no interest in reality in this way, metaphysics has significant value. This is because such wholly critical metaphysics is inquiry that demonstrates there could be successful inquiry at all and divulges the framework in which it must be conducted. It does so by showing that there are (fundamental) things in, constraints on, *all this*. Since a thing just is essentially certain ways and relates as it does necessarily to some other things, there are ways that thing is, including relations in which it stands, that are independent of any consideration of it. Insofar as the goal of inquiry is a view of the object of that inquiry *in itself*, that is, unadulterated by one's prejudices or by one's very act of inquiry, such metaphysics shows that the sine qua non of this goal—a thing that just is and is what it is and as it is essentially—is there. One needs the accounts of a mind and of epistemology that complement radical ontology (§11.3.3.) to see how successful inquiry can, in fact, be realized, but without things, natured entities, such inquiry would be impossible. Without things, inquiry would be mere sport.

Wholly critical metaphysics is worthwhile, therefore, because it shows that inquiry is worthwhile in that it has ends that are not arbitrary. Such metaphysics is, in this respect, a scientific, rather than performative or creative, enterprise. It is directed at discovery, at an object independent of the activity itself—the structure in reality—and has a particular methodology (namely, original inquiry) adopted precisely because it conduces to revealing this object. The success of metaphysics is determined, then, not merely by standards intrinsic to the activity itself, but by an object there regardless of the activity. What it reveals, a world of things, natured entities standing in relations, is what would be revealed, via original inquiry, in any context, from any perspective. Metaphysics pertains to anything, anywhere, anywhen, including those things independent of space or time, and so, pursued correctly, is an activity that can be completed definitively, once and for all, for a thing qua thing does not change. Even when one and the same thing comes to have qualities incompatible with ones it had, it does not change as a thing. Moreover, *all this* is distinct from ... *all this*, but every multiplicity of things is a multiplicity of things: things standing in relations (which are themselves things) to things. This world, or any, is just so many natured entities, joints to carve, the bases of any knowledge or understanding. Some individual things change and some come and go, but things in general as the objects of inquiry and the bases of its success do neither. Consequently, theorizing about the structure in reality need not be, through and through, mere discourse and ideology arising from some arbitrary process or other.

Generality is essential to the success and significance of a wholly critical metaphysics and so it would be ruined by the limitations demanded by any ordinary theory. A theory is a representational account of some thing or some phenomenon. As such, it requires discrimination (of its object) and, hence, certain concepts, means of classifying and organizing what is in the world. To avoid stultifying discrimination, this metaphysics begins with what is so, rather than with what is true (or taken to be). In other words, it does not begin with some representation, neither a theory nor even a single claim, to be confirmed or rejected, but with what is there to be represented, to wit, the world. One confronts *all this*, which is *thus*, and scrutinizes, via acquaintance, the things that make the world *thus* (and then *as so*). Key here is recognizing the diversity in the world (this requires no specific discrimination) and recognizing that this has a basis in what is. The upshot is insight into what such a basis must be, a natured entity, an inherent constraint, and what the world is, a multiplicity of these things. There is, therefore, a universality at the outset of wholly critical metaphysics, a lack of discrimination and concomitant conceptualization, which is all-important to the enterprise. This (initial) eschewal of concepts is indicated by the reliance on ostension by means of demonstratives at the beginning of such metaphysics, at the point of original inquiry, and throughout when unconditioned, unqualified engagement with the world is needed. Such language—*all this* which is *thus*...

then *as so*—is employed to direct one, without the conditions required by concepts, to attend just to what is there to be represented, conceptualized, and theorized. Hence, wholly critical metaphysics is pre-conceptual and pre-theoretical and so can transcend and underlie theory.

This conditionlessness of metaphysics via original inquiry is likely obscured by any presentation of the discipline, including the one in the present context. Here, I am describing some things, the world, that need not be described and expressing the means, wholly critical metaphysics, whereby *all this* can be understood. Doing so, of course, requires language and, hence, conceptualization. But presenting a subject matter by linguistic, conceptual means does not make what is so presented itself conceptual, and the structure in reality is not. So simply confronting *all this*, without taking anything for granted, does not have to be conceptual (or conceptualized) either. Furthermore, this metaphysics, despite not being conditioned by concepts at its origin, the point of original inquiry, can nonetheless produce a theory and theoretical framework. This discipline alone can yield the only universal theory, a collection of principles consistency with which constrains all inquiry with respect to any subject matter. Thus, this metaphysics, when complete, does involve certain concepts, e.g., *all, diversity, thing, natured, distinct, multiplicity, world, mode of differentiation*, etc. Note, however, that all these concepts are introduced in light of what is not exogenously conditioned or qualified, viz., what is given—*all this*—and defined in terms of it. The resulting theory, radical ontology, is significant because it bears on every thing, providing guidance and restrictions on any attempt to account for any thing (or phenomenon).

Principal to radical ontology is the concept of a thing. Every thing falls under this concept and so any thing whatsoever is a fundamental natured entity. Hence, in inquiring about some thing in the effort to understand it, one need not look for what makes that thing be or be what it is (or how it is essentially). This is important because many modern investigations are directed at what some thing "really" or "ultimately" is, that is, at what makes that thing exist or do what is distinctive of it. This is misguided. A thing just is and just does what it does. Each thing must co-exist with others, but the latter do not—indeed, cannot—make the former exist. One might be led, when investigating some thing, to other things. These others, however, are just more things. They might illuminate one's initial object of inquiry by being essentially or necessarily related to it, or by showing how that thing interacts with others in more or less attenuated ways, but what they cannot do is *explain the existence* of that initial thing (even if they do clarify *what* that thing is).

Merely appreciating what a thing is, then, constrains inquiry, as do the principles that follow from recognizing that *all this* is nothing more than a multiplicity of things. Some of these principles, regarding the uniformity, compulsoriness, determinacy, and non-fragmentariness of being a thing, are introduced above (§4.3.). If, when piqued by some phenomenon, one purports to account for it in terms involving things that do not exist or exist yet are not determinate in every way, one should reconsider, for one's account is incompatible with the world and, consequently, cannot be right. Or if one presents some theory on which it is inscrutable exactly what thing(s) the theory is a theory of, that theory should be rejected, for every (apt) account must have a basis among the things in the world. Thus, the concept of a thing and its associated principles are the ground rules of inquiry in that they provide the conditions on making sense of any thing, where doing so requires some understanding of what a thing is (or how it is essentially) or how certain things relate. Violating these rules might not produce obvious gibberish, but one's claims are nonetheless nonsensical, for in the end they do not reach *all this* and, hence, are unconstrained by it. In this case, one's claims are mere noise.

The purview of wholly critical metaphysics is total and this generality is the grounds of the definitiveness (i.e., what allows it to be done once and for all) and the significance of the discipline. Yet this scope is also the grounds of its limitations. Such metaphysics reveals what a thing, any thing, is, it does not reveal, for the most part, what things exist. Nor does it reveal, in great detail, how particular things relate to or interact with one another. This metaphysics, then, leaves unanswered nearly all of the most-meaningful or interesting questions one might have upon finding oneself amid *all this*. This discipline itself cannot disclose whether God exists, whether one has free will, what a good life is, or whether there are values or numbers or even ghosts, trees, or tables. What it does demonstrate is what such things would be were they to exist: each would be a (fundamental) natured entity, an inherent constraint, one that makes a unique contribution to the world being *thus*. It also shows that things can co-exist and interact only in ways consistent with their being things. Thus, this metaphysics reveals the extent of the structure in reality, not by showing what things exist, but by making clear what a putative thing would have to be in order genuinely to be. Other inquiries in others disciplines are needed to discern what exactly there is in the world. These disciplines are *metaphysical*—though not *metaphysics* per se—in that they are directed at illuminating what some thing (or kind) is consistent with radical ontology, the all-inclusive framework of wholly critical metaphysics.

Radical ontology provides a definitive account, in significant detail, of the world in general, but this account is not remotely complete in particulars. Metaphysics via original inquiry shows that *all this* is innumerable things, but not which ones. For the most part, then, it is not about producing specific accounts or making sense of individual things. As a consequence, this metaphysics can provide little insight into how individual things or kinds interact and so must be silent on (most) such interactions. Relatedly, given persons' interests and needs, they can respond to *all this* in ever so many ways, combining certain things, ignoring others, and, in some cases, creating new things, including such artifacts as genders, races, classes, and institutions. Metaphysics itself provides no guidance on how these activities, and the conceptualizations requisite for them, ought to proceed, even as it lays bare the ontological bases that make such activity possible. One can connect the dots, so to speak, in whatever ways one sees fit; wholly critical metaphysics merely demonstrates there are set dots (of various categories) to be connected. Presumably, the questions that are most pressing to inquirers in their daily lives turn on these activities, undertaken by oneself and others—but such metaphysics itself is of little use in answering them. Although the discipline has profound implications, the understanding it provides of specific meaningful issues is quite limited. This metaphysics, therefore, is probably not going to change one's life.

Wholly critical metaphysics is primarily general; it is, however, not devoid of particular conclusions (hence, the subtle qualifications throughout the preceding discussion). The method of this metaphysics is original inquiry. Such inquiry begins by confronting *all this*. In addition to the world, this inquiry requires an inquirer (*this* inquirer) and the means of inquiring, of presenting something, to wit, a mind (*this* mind). Since inquiry is a process, involving the phenomenon of *all this* going from *thus* to *as so*, it also requires distinct moments (*this* one . . . and *this*) and, thus, time, the unique thing that yields them. This much of the world is given via original inquiry and so metaphysics, founded on such inquiry, does reveal the existence of certain things. In taking up original inquiry, one, with a particular mind, is placed in the world at a particular moment and these things, while not wholly irrelevant to an effort to understand the structure in reality, are far less important than time itself. Despite their individuality, there is nothing special about this inquirer or this mind or this moment; any other instances of these kinds would do to undertake original inquiry. There is, though, something especially revelatory about time. It, that very thing, is crucial to any and every inquiry—and, more generally, to any happening *whatsoever*—and plays a distinct and central role in structuring *all this*.

The salience of time is apparent through the indubitable inconstancy and constancy in original inquiry, but its importance might be less obvious. Metaphysical inquiry reveals that there is no single thing that better illuminates the structure in reality than time itself. If one could know and understand each thing this structure comprises, one would have a thorough understanding of the world. Even so, such understanding would immediately become obsolete, for although *all this* is determinately complete, there could—and must—be more. Despite its completeness, the world is not exhausted, indeed it is inexhaustible. And when the more comes, there is literally a new world. Grasping the ephemeralness and inexhaustibility of *all this* is necessary for understanding the world, and the basis of both is time. Time is not a container, nor inert structure, a passive forum in which things evolve or phenomena occur. It is, rather, an immutable, yet dynamic, necessarily existing thing, the thing that essentially and, hence, inextinguishably yields novel (instantaneous, transient) moments. In doing so, it enables change, allowing the realization of dynamic capacities inherent to the things constrained by a moment to contribute more to *all this*. Yet it also enables the annihilation of these things. The stasis and permanence of certain things in the world is, moreover, best understood in terms of their independence from time. Time is the unique thing relation to which provides insight into not only every thing and every happening, but also the structure in reality, inconstant and constant.

Therefore, the metaphysics of time, the discipline that critically examines time itself and all temporal phenomena (that is, things in relation to time) reveals the extent of the world in important ways that go beyond metaphysics per se. The impetus for the former discipline is temporal differentiation—*all this* going from *thus* to *as so*—and, with it, the inconstancy and constancy in the world given in original inquiry. Examining the inconstancy provides an account of temporal reality, all those things that cannot, given what they are, exist in the absence of time. On this account, *transient presentism* (or *momentary transientism*), there is ever but a single moment. There is no moment in relation to this one, now, and so no past moments and no subsequent ones. Consequently, there is no thing, either moment or otherwise, earlier than this moment or later than it. Every mutable thing in time exists now. This is the breadth of temporal reality and so *all this* is not spread out in time (though, of course, some things can persist, exist at distinct moments). Since the world is complete and this moment constrains every thing that has the capacity to change and so be otherwise, each thing must be just as it is. This is the height of the structure in reality, there are herein no incompatible possibilities, so the world is not spread out in any modal sense. What is possible is latent in what exists and can only come to be through the dynamism of time. But there is more than the structure in time, examining the undeniable constancy in the world leads to an account of atemporal reality, those things independent of time. These things, some of which have origins, that is, come to be, exist permanently and without the capacity to contribute more to the world than they themselves, just as they are. *All this* is, then, both temporal and atemporal. A complete and satisfactory account of the metaphysics of time must include both an account of temporal reality and an account of atemporal reality. The failure to recognize this has been the dominant problem in modern discussions of time and its associated phenomena.

Metaphysics via original inquiry reveals the ontological extent of the structure in reality; the metaphysics of time reveals its temporal and even modal extent. In addition, then, to the wholly general constraints on inquiry that the former discipline provides, the latter provides more specific constraints that acknowledge the existence of the unique thing time. Just as part of the value of wholly critical metaphysics comes from revealing what the structure in reality is, and part from providing ground rules for all inquiry, part of the value of the metaphysics of time comes from revealing the structure in temporal and atemporal realities and part from providing further, more specific ground rules of inquiry. These more specific principles follow from the principles of radical ontology given the particular things and kinds revealed by the metaphysics of time. Among them is the principle that no thing is (ever) constrained by what exists at some other moment (for there are no other moments). The consequences of this principle alone are enormous: they include that determinism, on any traditional construal of the doctrine, is false; that one can have no moral obligations to future generations; that there can be no time travel, on any familiar depiction. Another significant principle is that every thing must be just as it is—until it is not, and so every truth is necessary. Some things can change or cease to be, some can do neither, but every true claim about this world, whether it pertains to some thing(s) within time or without, is necessary. Any theory of any phenomenon that turns on synchronous possibility, i.e., possibility at this moment (rather than through it) is, then, mistaken. There are certainly other principles of radical ontology that follow from metaphysics and the metaphysics of time together, I make note of these two because they are, perhaps, the most heterodox.

All this, the structure in reality, is a multiplicity of things. However, *all this* is ephemeral—yet lasting—and so one cannot understand what this structure is without recognizing time, and the crucial role it plays with respect to all these things and the indubitable inconstancy and constancy among them. An account of the world, then, would be neither comprehensive, nor insightful, without an account of time itself. The two accounts are even more intimately related than these observations show. Since temporal differentiation and time are apparent in the world from original inquiry, the origin of wholly critical metaphysics and the metaphysics of time is the same. Indeed, an examination of time, the sole indispensable substance revealed in original inquiry, is continuous with metaphysics. Thus, an inquiry into the world must include an inquiry into time and, given that time is a thing, a critical inquiry into time cannot be completed without the critical inquiry into the world that provides an account of what any thing is. Metaphysics displays, through demonstrating what a thing is, the primary (general) ground rules of inquiry, but insofar as inquiry is a certain sort of phenomenon, namely, a process, these primary rules need to be supplemented. As just indicated, the metaphysics of time is arguably the most important means of supplementing them. This more focused discipline displays constraints on inquiry by demonstrating the temporal and atemporal structure in reality, the bases of dynamism and transience, stasis and permanence. Once one has satisfactory accounts of both time and the world and so understands what *all this* is, what things are, what time in particular is and how time relates to all the things herein, one has a clear view of the means and limits of inquiry. Metaphysics-cum-metaphysics of time provides a full account of the ontological, temporal, and modal extent of reality, making clear how any process can occur and, specifically, how inquiry goes and how it may go—but where it must end.

In general, metaphysical inquiry, inquiry conducted in accordance to these limits, reveals what some thing or phenomenon is, how it relates to certain other things and, hence, what could be with respect to it. Such inquiry is necessary for understanding that object of inquiry and to propounding a theory of it. But that is all such inquiry can do or provide. Since no thing itself is *ameliorative*—it just *is*—no account of what a thing is (or even an account of *all this*) can itself be progressive or liberating or, for that matter, regressive or repressive. Thus, metaphysical inquiry, which is merely directed at revealing what is so, cannot itself make things better (or worse). Truth alone will not set one free. What is progressive or regressive, beneficial or harmful are the ways one responds to the things there are—what one makes of and from these. Metaphysics provides no guidance on how to respond to things, beyond the need to appreciate, insofar as one wants to get things right, what is there. Surely some ways of responding to these things are better than others, in a practical, rather than theoretical, sense. So, after satisfying oneself that one has the correct answer to the question of what *all this* is, or what *this* thing is, one might now wonder what to do with it.

If one is curious about such practical matters, and considers what is to be done given this structure in reality, one might be perplexed anew, if not dismayed or, worse, horrified. Things are not good, and not going well, for too many people. Although metaphysical inquiry per se, even when it make more perspicuous what is so with respect to some thing or phenomenon, cannot be ameliorative, it does not have to be idle. Where original inquiry begins is with *all this* and where it ends is with *all this*—but with a clearer view of what is here to deal with, with an understanding of things and the constraints they are and the constraints they impose; and more focused metaphysical inquiry can provide insight into what *this* fundamental thing here is, what its source is, what it does and can do. How one proceeds depends on one's interests and needs and one's vision, yet what one can do is constrained by what is herein. Now one can look to see what exactly is here, which individual things, what kinds, what phenomena, for one needs to know the essential features and capacities of what is in order to know what can be improved and what cannot, and so to acquire an inkling of how to affect change. Although some of this structure is wondrous, some is inappropriate, some abhorrent. If one finds this, and is dissatisfied with how things are, one can try to change things so another world is less reprehensible. If making a better world is the goal, what the present inquiry shows is that realizing it must start now, with these things.

References

Adams, R. 1986. Time and Thisness, *Midwest Studies in Philosophy*, 11: 315–329.
Aristotle. 2000. *Metaphysics, Books* B *and* K *1–2*, translated and with commentary by A. Madigan (Oxford: Oxford University Press).
Aristotle. 2018. *Physics*, translated and with introduction and notes by C.D.C. Reeve (Indianapolis, IN: Hackett Publishing).
Armstrong, D. 1997. *A World of States of Affairs* (Cambridge: Cambridge University Press).
Armstrong, D. 1989. *Universals: An Opinionated Introduction* (Boulder, CO: Westview Press).
Balashov, Y., and M. Janssen. 2003. Presentism and Relativity, *British Journal for the Philosophy of Science*, 54: 327–346.
Barnes, E. 2010. Ontic Vagueness: A Guide for the Perplexed, *Noûs*, 44: 601–627.
Barnes, E., and R. Cameron. 2009. The Open Future: Bivalence, Determinism and Ontology, *Philosophical Studies*, 146: 291–309.
Baron, S. 2015. The Priority of Now, *Pacific Philosophical Quarterly*, 96: 325–348.
Bealer, G. 2006. Universals and the Defense of *Ante Rem* Realism, in P.F. Strawson and A. Chakrabarti (eds.) *Universals, Concepts and Qualities: New Essays on the Meaning of Predicates* (Aldershot and Burlington, VT: Ashgate), pp. 225–238.
Bealer, G. 2002. Modal Epistemology and the Rationalist Renaissance, in Gendler and Hawthorne 2002, pp. 71–125.
Bealer, G. 1998. Intuition and the Autonomy of Philosophy, in DePaul and Ramsey 1998, pp. 201–239.
Bealer, G. 1996. *A Priori* Knowledge and the Scope of Philosophy, *Philosophical Studies*, 81: 121–142.
Beer, M. 2010. Tense and Truth Conditions, *Philosophia*, 38: 265–269.
Bengson, J. 2015. The Intellectual Given, *Mind*, 124: 707–760.
Bennett, K. 2016. There Is No Special Problem with Metaphysics, *Philosophical Studies*, 173: 21–37.
Bennett, K. 2011a. By Our Bootstraps, *Philosophical Perspectives*, 25: 27–41.
Bennett, K. 2011b. Construction Area (No Hard Hat Required), *Philosophical Studies*, 154: 79–104.
Bigelow, J. 1996. Presentism and Properties, *Philosophical Perspectives*, 10: 35–52.
Booth, A., and D. Rowbottom (eds.). 2014. *Intuitions* (Oxford: Oxford University Press).
Borghini, A., and N. Williams. 2008. A Dispositional Theory of Possibility, *Dialectica*, 62: 21–41.
Bourne, C. 2006a. A Theory of Presentism, *Canadian Journal of Philosophy*, 36: 1–24.
Bourne, C. 2006b. *A Future for Presentism* (Oxford: Oxford University Press).
Broad, C.D. 1938. *An Examination of McTaggart's Philosophy*, Volume II, Part I (Cambridge: Cambridge University Press).
Broad, C.D. 1923. *Scientific Thought* (London: Routledge and Kegan Paul).
Callender, C. 2008. Finding "Real" Time in Quantum Mechanics, in William Lane Craig and Quentin Smith (eds.) *Einstein, Relativity and Absolute Simultaneity* (London: Routledge), pp. 50–72.
Cameron, R. 2015. *The Moving Spotlight: An Essay on Time and Ontology* (Oxford: Oxford University Press).

Cameron, R. 2011. Truthmaking for Presentists, in K. Bennett and D. Zimmerman (eds.) *Oxford Studies in Metaphysics*, Volume 6 (Oxford: Oxford University Press), pp. 55–100.

Chalmers, D. 2012. *Constructing the World* (Oxford: Oxford University Press).

Chalmers, D. 2009. Ontological Anti-Realism, in Chalmers, Wasserman, and Manley 2009, pp. 77–129.

Chalmers, D., R. Wasserman, and D. Manley (eds.). 2009. *Metametaphysics* (Oxford: Oxford University Press).

Chisholm, R. 1973. The Problem of the Criterion, in *The Foundations of Knowing* (Minneapolis: University of Minnesota Press, 1982), pp. 61–75.

Chudnoff, E. 2011. What Intuitions Are Like, *Philosophy and Phenomenological Research*, 82: 625–654.

Coope, U. 2001. Why Does Aristotle Say That There Is No Time Without Change?, *Proceedings of the Aristotelian Society*, 101: 359–367.

Correia, F., and B. Schnieder (eds.). 2012. *Metaphysical Grounding: Understanding the Structure of Reality* (Cambridge: Cambridge University Press).

Craig, W.L. 2001. *The Metaphysics of Relativity* (Dordrecht: Kluwer).

Craig, W.L. 1998. McTaggart's Paradox and the Problem of Temporary Intrinsics, *Analysis*, 58: 122–127.

Crisp, T. 2007. Presentism and the Grounding Objection, *Noûs*, 41: 90–109.

Crisp, T. 2005. Presentism and "Cross-Time" Relations, *American Philosophical Quarterly*, 42: 5–17.

Crisp, T. 2004. On Presentism and Triviality, in D. Zimmerman (ed.) *Oxford Studies in Metaphysics*, Volume 1 (Oxford: Oxford University Press), pp. 15–20.

Crisp, T. 2003. Presentism, in M. Loux and D. Zimmerman (eds.) *The Oxford Handbook of Metaphysics* (Oxford: Oxford University Press), pp. 211–245.

Dasgupta, S. 2016. Metaphysical Rationalism, *Noûs*, 50: 379–418.

Davidson, M. 2003. Presentism and the Non-Present, *Philosophical Studies*, 113: 77–92.

Deasy, D. 2018. Philosophical Arguments Against the A-Theory, *Pacific Philosophical Quarterly*, 99: 270–292.

Deasy, D. 2015. The Moving Spotlight Theory, *Philosophical Studies*, 172: 2073–2089.

De Clercq, R. 2006. Presentism and the Problem of Cross-Time Relations, *Philosophy and Phenomenological Research*, 72: 386–402.

DePaul, M., and W. Ramsey (eds.). 1998. *Rethinking Intuition: The Psychology of Intuition and Its Role in Philosophical Inquiry* (Lanham, MD: Rowman and Littlefield).

Deng, N. 2018. What Is Temporal Ontology?, *Philosophical Studies*, 175: 793–807.

Deng, N. 2013a. On Explaining Why Time Seems to Pass, *Southern Journal of Philosophy*, 51: 367–382.

Deng, N. 2013b. Fine's McTaggart, Temporal Passage, and the A versus B Debate, *Ratio*, 26: 19–34.

Dummett, M. 1975. Wang's Paradox, *Synthese*, 30: 201–232.

Dummett, M. 1960. A Defense of McTaggart's Proof of the Unreality of Time, *Philosophical Review*, 69: 497–504.

Dumont, S. 1995. The Origin of Scotus's Theory of Synchronic Contingency, *Modern Schoolman*, 72: 149–167.

Dyke, H. 2003. Temporal Language and Temporal Reality, *Philosophical Quarterly*, 53: 380–391.

Dyke, H., and J. Maclaurin. 2002. "Thank Goodness That's Over": The Evolutionary Story, *Ratio*, 15: 276–292.

Evans, G. 1978. Can There Be Vague Objects?, *Analysis*, 38: 278.

Feser, E. (ed.). 2013. *Aristotle on Method and Metaphysics* (New York: Palgrave).

Fine, K. 2012a. What is Metaphysics?, in Tahko 2012a, pp. 8–25.

Fine, K. 2012b. Guide to Ground, in F. Correia and B. Schnieder (eds.) *Metaphysical Grounding: Understanding the Structure of Reality* (Oxford: Oxford University Press), pp. 37–80.

Fine, K. 2005. Tense and Reality, in Kit Fine *Modality and Tense: Philosophical Papers* (Oxford: Oxford University Press, 2005), pp. 261–320.

Fine, K. 2001. The Question of Realism, *Philosophers' Imprint*, 1: 1–30.

Fiocco, M. Oreste. 2021. The Epistemic Idleness of Conceivability, in O. Bueno and S. Shalkowski (eds.) *The Routledge Handbook of Modality* (New York: Routledge), pp. 167–179.

Fiocco, M. Oreste. 2019a. Each Thing Is Fundamental: Against Hylomorphism and Hierarchical Structure, *American Philosophical Quarterly*, 56: 289–301.

Fiocco, M. Oreste. 2019b. Structure, Intentionality and the Given, in Christoph Limbeck-Lilienau and Friedrich Stadler (eds.) *The Philosophy of Perception and Observation: Proceedings of the 40th International Wittgenstein Symposium* (Berlin: De Gruyter), pp. 95–118.

Fiocco, M. Oreste. 2017. Knowing Things in Themselves: Mind, Brentano and Acquaintance, *Grazer Philosophische Studien* 94: 332–358.

Fiocco, M. Oreste. 2015. Intentionality and Realism, *Acta Analytica*, 30: 219–237.

Fiocco, M. Oreste. 2014. On Simple Facts, *Res Philosophica*, 91: 287–313.

Fiocco, M. Oreste. 2013. An Absolute Principle of Truthmaking, *Grazer Philosophische Studien*, 88: 1–31.

Fiocco, M. Oreste. 2009. Temporary Intrinsics and Relativization, *Pacific Philosophical Quarterly*, 91: 64–77.

Fitch, G. 1994. Singular Propositions in Time, *Philosophical Studies*, 73: 181–187.

Forrest, P. 2004. The Real but Dead Past: A Reply to Braddon-Mitchell, *Analysis*, 64: 358–362.

Frischhut, A. 2015. What Experience Cannot Teach Us About Time, *Topoi*, 34: 143–155.

Gale, R. 1968. *The Language of Time* (London: Routledge and Kegan Paul).

Gale, R. (ed.). 1967. *The Philosophy of Time: A Collection of Essays* (New York: Anchor Books).

Gallois, A. 2004. Comments on Ted Sider: *Four-Dimensionalism*, *Philosophy and Phenomenological Research*, 68: 648–657.

Gendler, T., and J. Hawthorne (eds.). 2002. *Conceivability and Possibility* (Oxford: Oxford University Press).

Gödel, K. 1944. Russell's Mathematical Logic, reprinted in his *Collected Works: Volume II: Publications 1938–1974* (New York: Oxford University Press, 1990), pp. 119–141.

Hawley, K. 2002. Vagueness and Existence, *Proceedings of the Aristotelian Society*, 102: 125–140.

Heller, M. 1990. *The Ontology of Physical Objects: Four-Dimensional Hunks of Matter* (Cambridge: Cambridge University Press).

Hinchliff, M. 2000. A Defense of Presentism in a Relativistic Setting, *Philosophy of Science*, 67: S563–S574.

Hinchliff, M. 1996. The Puzzle of Change, *Philosophical Perspectives*, 10: 199–136.

Hirsch, E. 1986. Metaphysical Necessity and Conceptual Truth, *Midwest Studies in Philosophy*, 11: 243–256.

Hoffman, J., and G. Rosenkranz. 1997. *Substance: Its Nature and Existence* (London: Routledge).

Hoffman, J., and G. Rosenkranz. 1994. *Substance Among Other Categories* (Cambridge: Cambridge University Press).

Hofweber, T. 2009. Ambitious, Yet Modest, Metaphysics, in D. Chalmers, R. Wasserman, and D. Manley (eds.) *Metametaphysics* (Oxford: Oxford University Press), pp. 260–289.

Huemer, M. 2005. *Moral Intuitionism* (New York: Palgrave Macmillan).

Hume, D. 1739. *A Treatise of Human Nature*, edited by L.S. Selby-Bigge (Oxford: Oxford University Press).

Ingram, D. 2016. The Virtues of Thisness Presentism, *Philosophical Studies*, 173: 2867–2888.

Ingram, D., and J. Tallant. 2018. Presentism, in Edward N. Zalta (ed.) *The Stanford Encyclopedia of Philosophy* (Spring 2018 Edition). https://plato.stanford.edu/archives/spr2018/entries/presentism/.

Jackson, F. 1998. *From Metaphysics to Ethics: A Defence of Conceptual Analysis* (Oxford: Oxford University Press).

Jacobs, J. 2010. A Powers Theory of Modality: Or, How I Learned to Stop Worrying and Reject Possible Worlds, *Philosophical Studies*, 151: 227–248.

Janssen, M. 2002. Reconsidering a Scientific Revolution: The Case of Einstein *versus* Lorentz, *Physics in Perspective*, 4: 421–446.

Johnson, D. 2013. B-Theory Old and New: On Ontological Commitment, *Synthese*, 190: 3953–3970.

Keller, S. 2004. Presentism and Truthmaking, in D. Zimmerman (ed.) *Oxford Studies in Metaphysics*, Volume 1 (Oxford: Oxford University Press), pp. 83–104.

Kierland, B., and B. Monton. 2007. Presentism and the Objection from Being-Supervenience, *Australasian Journal of Philosophy*, 85: 485–497.

Kim, Jaegwon. 1994. Explanatory Knowledge and Metaphysical Dependence, *Philosophical Issues*, 5: 51–69.

Kim, J., and E. Sosa (eds.). 1999. *Metaphysics: An Anthology* (Oxford: Blackwell).

Knuuttila, S. 1993. *Modalities in Medieval Philosophy* (London and New York: Routledge).

Knuuttila, S. 1981. Time and Modality in Scholasticism, in Simo Knuuttila (ed.) *Reforging the Great Chain of Being: Studies in the History of Modal Theories* (Dordrecht: D. Reidel), pp. 163–257.

Koslicki, K. 2018. *Form, Matter, Substance* (Oxford: Oxford University Press).

Koslicki, K. 2012. Varieties of Ontological Dependence, in Correia and Schnieder 2012, pp. 186–213.

Koslicki, K. 2008. *The Structure of Objects* (Oxford: Oxford University Press).

Kripke, S. 1980. *Naming and Necessity* (Cambridge, MA: Harvard University Press).

Ladyman, J., and D. Ross. 2007. *Every Thing Must Go: Metaphysics Naturalized* (Oxford: Oxford University Press).

La Vine, M. 2016. Prior's Thank-Goodness Argument Reconsidered, *Synthese*, 193: 3591–3606.

Leininger, L. 2015. Presentism and the Myth of Passage, *Australasian Journal of Philosophy*, 93: 724–739.

Le Poidevin, R. 2007. *The Images of Time: An Essay on Temporal Representation* (Oxford: Oxford University Press).

Le Poidevin, R. 2003. *Travels in Four Dimensions: The Enigmas of Space and Time* (Oxford: Oxford University Press).

Le Poidevin, R. (ed.). 1998. *Questions of Time and Tense* (Oxford: Clarendon Press).

Le Poidevin, R., and M. MacBeath (eds.). 1993. *The Philosophy of Time* (Oxford: Oxford University Press).

Lewis, D. 1993. Many, but Almost One. In John Bacon, Keith Campbell, and Lloyd Reinhardt (eds.) *Ontology, Causality and Mind: Essays on the Philosophy of D.M. Armstrong* (Cambridge: Cambridge University Press), pp. 23–38.

Lewis, D. 1992. Critical Notice of Armstrong, *A Combinatorial Theory of Possibility*, *Australasian Journal of Philosophy*, 70: 211–224.

Lewis, D. 1986a. *On the Plurality of Worlds* (Oxford: Blackwell).

Lewis, D. 1986b. *Philosophical Papers*, Volume II (Oxford: Oxford University Press).

Lewis, D. 1983. New Work for a Theory of Universals, *Australasian Journal of Philosophy*, 61: 343–377.

Lombard, L. 1999. On the Alleged Incompatibility of Presentism and Temporal Parts, *Philosophia*, 27: 253–260.

Lowe, E.J. 2014. Grasp of Essences Versus Intuitions: An Unequal Contest, in Booth and Rowbottom 2014, pp. 256–268.

Lowe, E.J. 2013a. Essence and Ontology, in Novák, Novotný, Sousedík, and Svoboda 2013, pp. 93–111.
Lowe, E.J. 2013b. Neo-Aristotelian Metaphysics: A Brief Exposition and Defense, in Feser 2013, pp. 196–205.
Lowe, E.J. 2009. *More Kinds of Being* (Oxford: Wiley-Blackwell).
Lowe, E.J. 2008. Two Notions of Being: Entity and Essence, *Royal Institute of Philosophy Supplement*, 83: 23–48.
Lowe, E.J. 2006. *The Four-Category Ontology* (Oxford: Oxford University Press).
Lowe, E.J. 2002. *A Survey of Metaphysics* (Oxford: Oxford University Press).
Lowe, E.J. 1998. *The Possibility of Metaphysics* (Oxford: Oxford University Press).
Lowe, E.J. 1989. Impredicative Identity Criteria and Davidson's Criterion of Event Identity, *Analysis*, 49: 178–181.
Ludlow, P. 1999. *Semantics, Tense, and Time: An Essay in the Metaphysics of Natural Language* (Cambridge, MA: MIT Press).
Maddy, P. 2007. *Second Philosophy: A Naturalistic Method* (Oxford: Oxford University Press).
Maddy, P. 2001. Naturalism: Friends and Foes, *Philosophical Perspectives*, 15: 37–67.
Markosian, N. 2004. A Defence of Presentism, in D. Zimmerman (ed.) *Oxford Studies in Metaphysics*, Volume 1 (Oxford: Oxford University Press), pp. 47–82.
Markosian, N. 1993. How Fast Does Time Pass?, *Philosophy and Phenomenological Research*, 53: 829–844.
McCall, S. 1994. *A Model of the Universe: Space-Time, Probability, and Decision* (Oxford: Oxford University Press).
McCall, S. 1976. Objective Time Flow, *Philosophy of Science*, 43: 337–362.
McDaniel, K. 2009. Ways of Being, in D. Chalmers, R. Wasserman, and D. Manley (eds.) *Metametaphysics* (Oxford: Oxford University Press), pp. 290–319.
McTaggart, J.M.E. 1927. *The Nature of Existence*, Volume II (Cambridge: Cambridge University Press).
McTaggart, J.M.E. 1908. The Unreality of Time, *Mind*, 17: 457–74.
Mellor, D.H. 1998. *Real Time II* (London and New York: Routledge).
Mellor, D.H. 1981. *Real Time* (Cambridge: Cambridge University Press).
Meinong, A. 1904/1960. On the Theory of Objects (Über Gegenstandstheorie), in Roderick Chisholm (ed.) *Realism and the Background of Phenomenology* (New York: Free Press) pp. 76–117.
Merricks, T. 2013. Three Comments on *Writing the Book of the World*, *Analysis*, 73: 722–736.
Merricks, T. 2012. Singular Propositions, in Kelly James Clark and Michael Rea (eds.) *Reason, Metaphysics, and Mind: New Essays on the Philosophy of Alvin Plantinga* (Oxford: Oxford University Press), pp. 61–81.
Merricks, T. 2007. *Truth and Ontology* (Oxford: Oxford University Press).
Meyer, U. 2005. The Presentist's Dilemma, Philosophical Studies, 122: 213–225.
Mozersky, J. 2014. Temporal Predicates and the Passage of Time, in N. Oaklander (ed.) *Debates in the Metaphysics of Time* (London and New York: Bloomsbury), pp. 109–127.
Mozersky, J. 2011. Presentism, in C. Callender (ed.) *The Oxford Handbook of Philosophy of Time* (Oxford: Oxford University Press), pp. 122–144.
Normore, C. 2003. Duns Scotus's Modal Theory, in Thomas Williams (ed.) *The Cambridge Companion to Duns Scotus* (Cambridge: Cambridge University Press), pp. 129–160.
Novák, L., and D. Novotný (eds.). 2014. *Neo-Aristotelian Perspectives in Metaphysics* (New York and London: Routledge).
Novák, L., D. Novotný, P. Sousedík, and D. Svoboda (eds.). 2013. *Metaphysics: Aristotelian, Scholastic, Analytic* (Frankfurt: Ontos Verlag).
Oaklander, N. 2012. A-, B-, and R-Theories of Time: A Debate, in A. Bardon (ed.) *The Future of the Philosophy of Time* (London: Routledge), pp. 1–24.
Oaklander, N. 2002. Presentism: A Critique, in H. Lillehammer and G. Rodriguez Pereyra (eds.) *Real Metaphysics: Essays in Honour of D.H. Mellor* (London: Routledge), pp. 196–211.

Oaklander, N. 1993. On the Experience of Tenseless Time, *Journal of Philosophical Research*, 18: 159–166.
Oaklander, N., and Smith, Q. 1994. *The New Theory of Time* (New Haven, CT: Yale University Press).
Oderberg, D. 2007. *Real Essentialism* (New York and London: Routledge).
Olson, E. 2009. The Rate of Time's Passage, *Analysis*, 69: 3–9.
Orilia, F. 2016. Moderate Presentism, *Philosophical Studies*, 173: 589–607.
Paoletti, M. 2016. A Sketch of (an Actually Serious) Meinongian Presentism, *Metaphysica*, 17: 1–18.
Paul, L. 2010. Temporal Experience, *Journal of Philosophy*, 107: 333–359.
Phillips, I. 2009. Rate Abuse: A Reply to Olson, *Analysis*, 69: 503–505.
Plantinga, A. 1974. *The Nature of Necessity* (Oxford: Oxford University Press).
Price, H. 2011. The Flow of Time, in C. Callender (ed.) *The Oxford Handbook of Philosophy of Time* (Oxford: Oxford University Press), pp. 276–311.
Prior, A.N. 1970. The Notion of the Present, *Studium Generale*, 23: 245–248.
Prior, A.N.1968/2003. *Papers on Time and Tense*, in Per Hasle, Peter Øhrstrøm, Torben Braüner, and Jack Copeland (eds.) (Oxford: Oxford University Press), 2nd edition.
Prior, A.N. 1968. Changes in Events and Changes in Things, in Prior 1968/2003, pp. 7–20.
Prior, A.N. 1967. *Past, Present and Future* (Oxford: Oxford University Press).
Prior, A.N. 1959. Thank Goodness That's Over, *Philosophy*, 34: 12–17.
Prior, A.N. 1958. Time After Time, *Mind*, 67: 244–246.
Prosser, S. 2007. Could We Experience the Passage of Time?, *Ratio*, 21: 75–90.
Putnam, H. 1967. Time and Physical Geometry, *Journal of Philosophy*, 64: 240–247.
Quine, W.V. 1987. *Quiddities: An Intermittently Philosophical Dictionary* (Cambridge, MA: Harvard University Press).
Quine, W.V. 1985. Events and Reification, in E. LePore and B. McLaughlin (eds.) *Actions and Events: Perspectives on the Philosophy of Donald Davidson* (Oxford: Basil Blackwell), pp. 162–171.
Quine, W.V. 1953a. Reference and Modality, in W.V.O. Quine, *From a Logical Point of View* (Cambridge, MA: Harvard University Press), 3rd edition, pp. 139–159.
Quine, W.V. 1953b. Three Grades of Modal Involvement, in W.V.O. Quine, *The Ways of Paradox and Other Essays* (Cambridge, MA: Harvard University Press), Revised and enlarged edition, pp. 158–176.
Ramsey, F. 2006. Ramsey's "Note on Time", in M. Galavotti (ed.) *Cambridge and Vienna: Frank P. Ramsey and the Vienna Circle* (Dordrecht, the Netherlands: Springer), pp. 155–165.
Raven, M. 2011. Can Time Pass at the Rate of 1 Second Per Second?, *Australasian Journal of Philosophy*, 89: 459–465.
Rea, M. 2003. Four-Dimensionalism, in M. Loux and D. Zimmerman (eds.) *The Oxford Handbook of Metaphysics* (Oxford: Oxford University Press), pp. 246–280.
Rietdijk, C.W. 1966. A Rigorous Proof of Determinism Derived from the Special Theory of Relativity, *Philosophy of Science*, 33: 341–344.
Ritchie, K. 2020. Social Structures and the Ontology of Social Groups, *Philosophy and Phenomenological Research*, 100: 402–424.
Rorty, R. 1979. *Philosophy and the Mirror of Nature* (Princeton, NJ: Princeton University Press).
Rosen, G. 2010. Metaphysical Dependence: Grounding and Reduction, in B. Hale and A. Hoffmann (eds.) *Modality: Metaphysics, Logic, and Epistemology* (Oxford: Oxford University Press), pp. 109–135.
Rovane, C. 2013. *The Metaphysics and Ethics of Relativism* (Cambridge, MA: Harvard University Press).
Rovane, C. 2012. How to Formulate Relativism, in C. Wright and A. Coliva (eds.) *Mind, Meaning, and Knowledge: Themes from the Philosophy of Crispin Wright* (Oxford: Oxford University Press), pp. 238–266.

REFERENCES

Ruben, D. 1990. *Explaining Explanation* (New York and London: Routledge).
Russell, B. 1908. Mathematical Logic as Based on the Theory of Types, reprinted in his *Logic and Knowledge: Essays 1901–1950*, edited by Robert C. Marsh (London: George Allen & Unwin, 1956), pp. 59–102.
Sainsbury, M. 1994. Why the World Cannot Be Vague, *Southern Journal of Philosophy*, 33: 63–82.
Salmon, N. 1989. The Logic of What Might Have Been, *Philosophical Review*, 98: 3–34.
Salmon, N. 1986. *Frege's Puzzle* (Cambridge, MA: MIT Press).
Sanson, D., and B. Caplan. 2010. The Way Things Were, *Philosophy and Phenomenological Research*, 81: 24–39.
Savitt, S. 2002. On Absolute Becoming and the Myth of Passage, in C. Callender (ed.) *Time, Reality, and Experience*, The Royal Institute of Philosophy Supplement 50 (Cambridge: Cambridge University Press), pp. 153–167.
Schaffer, J. 2010. Monism: The Priority of the Whole, *Philosophical Review*, 119: 31–76.
Schaffer, J. 2009. On What Grounds What, in D. Chalmers, R. Wasserman, and D. Manley (eds.) *Metametaphysics* (Oxford: Oxford University Press), pp. 347–383.
Schlesinger, G. 1982. How Time Flies, *Mind*, 91: 501–523.
Shoemaker, S. 1969. Time Without Change, *Journal of Philosophy*, 66: 363–381.
Sider, T. 2011. *Writing the Book of the World* (Oxford: Oxford University Press).
Sider, T. 2001. *Four-Dimensionalism: An Ontology of Persistence and Time* (Oxford: Oxford University Press).
Skow, B. 2012a. Why Does Time Pass?, *Noûs*, 46: 223–242.
Skow, B. 2012b. "One Second Per Second", *Philosophy and Phenomenological Research*, 85: 377–389.
Skow, B. 2009. Relativity and the Moving Spotlight, *Journal of Philosophy*, 106: 666–678.
Smart, J.J.C. 1980. Time and Becoming, in P. van Inwagen (ed.) *Time and Cause: Essays Presented to Richard Taylor* (Dordrecht: Reidel), pp. 3–15.
Smart, J.J.C. 1967. Time, in P. Edward (ed.) *The Encyclopedia of Philosophy* (New York: Macmillan), pp. 126–134.
Smart, J.J.C. 1949. The River of Time, *Mind*, 58: 483–494.
Smith, Q. 2002. Time and Degrees of Existence: A Theory of "Degree Presentism", *Royal Institute of Philosophy Supplement*, 50: 119–136.
Smith, Q. 1998. Absolute Simultaneity and the Infinity of Time, in R. Le Poidevin (ed.) *Questions of Time and Tense* (Oxford: Clarendon Press), pp. 135–183.
Smith, Q. 1993. *Language and Time* (Oxford: Oxford University Press).
Stalnaker, R. 1987. *Inquiry* (Cambridge, MA: MIT Press).
Stalnaker, R. 1976. Possible Worlds, *Noûs*, 10: 65–75.
Stoneham, T. 2009. Time and Truth: The Presentism-Eternalism Debate, *Philosophy*, 84: 201–218.
Sullivan, M. 2012. The Minimal A-Theory, *Philosophical Studies*, 158: 149–174.
Tahko, T. 2013. Metaphysics as the First Philosophy, in Feser 2013, pp. 49–67.
Tahko, T. (ed.). 2012a. *Contemporary Aristotelian Metaphysics* (Cambridge: Cambridge University Press).
Tahko, T. 2012b. In Defence of Aristotelian Metaphysics, in Tahko 2012a, pp. 26–43.
Tahko, T., and E.J. Lowe. 2015. Ontological Dependence, in Edward N. Zalta (ed.) *The Stanford Encyclopedia of Philosophy* (Spring 2015 Edition). http://plato.stanford.edu/archives/spr2015/entries/dependence-ontological/.
Tallant, J. 2015. The New A-Theory of Time, *Inquiry*, 58: 535–560.
Tallant, J. 2014. Defining Existence Presentism, *Erkenntnis*, 79: 479–501.
Tallant, J. 2013. Time, *Analysis Reviews*, 73: 369–379.
Tallant, J. 2009. Presentism and Truth-Making, *Erkenntnis*, 71: 407–416.
Tallant, J. Unpublished. There's No Such Thing as Presentism.

Thomasson, A. 2009. Answerable and Unanswerable Questions, in Chalmers, Wasserman, and Manley 2009, pp. 444–471.
Thomasson, A. 2007. *Ordinary Objects* (New York: Oxford University Press).
Tooley, M. 1997. *Time, Tense, and Causation* (Oxford: Oxford University Press).
Torre, S. 2009. Truth-Conditions, Truth-Bearers and the New B-Theory, *Philosophical Studies*, 142: 325–344.
Twardowski, K. 1894/1977. *On the Content and Object of Presentations* (Dordrecht: Springer).
van Inwagen, P. 2013. What Is an Ontological Category?, in Novák, Novotný, Sousedík, and Svoboda 2013, pp. 11–24.
van Inwagen, P. 1990. *Material Beings* (Ithaca, NY: Cornell University Press).
Wang, J. 2015. The Modal Limits of Dispositionalism, *Noûs*, 49: 454–469.
Wiggins, D. 2001. *Sameness and Substance Renewed* (Cambridge: Cambridge University Press).
Wiggins, D. 1968. On Being in the Same Place at the Same Time, *Philosophical Review*, 77: 90–95.
Williams, C. 1996. The Metaphysics of A- and B-Time, *Philosophical Quarterly*, 46: 371–381.
Williams, D.C. 1951. The Myth of Passage, *Journal of Philosophy*, 48: 457–472.
Williams, N. 2019. *The Powers Metaphysics* (Oxford: Oxford University Press).
Williamson, T. 2007. *The Philosophy of Philosophy* (Oxford: Blackwell).
Williamson, T. 2002. Necessary Existents, in A. O'Hear (ed.) *Logic, Thought and Language*, The Royal Institute of Philosophy Supplement 51 (Cambridge: Cambridge University Press), pp. 233–251.
Wilson, J. 2010. What is Hume's Dictum, and Why Believe It?, *Philosophy and Phenomenological Research*, 80: 595–637
Yablo, S. 2009. Must Existence-Questions Have Answers?, in Chalmers, Wasserman, and Manley 2009, pp. 507–525.
Zimmerman, D. 2011. Presentism and the Space-Time Manifold, in C. Callender (ed.) *The Oxford Handbook of Philosophy of Time* (Oxford: Oxford University Press), pp. 163–244.
Zimmerman, D. 2008. The Privileged Present: Defending an "A-Theory" of Time, in T. Sider, J. Hawthorne, and D. Zimmerman (eds.) *Contemporary Debates in Metaphysics* (Oxford: Blackwell), pp. 211–225.
Zimmerman, D. 2005. The A-theory of Time, the B-theory of Time, and "Taking Tense Seriously," *Dialectica*, 59: 401–457.

Index

For the benefit of digital users, indexed terms that span two pages (e.g., 52–53) may, on occasion, appear on only one of those pages.

absolute annihilation, 211–16, 230, 289
absolute becoming, 220, 273, 289
   coming to be simpliciter and, 228–32
   of moments, 229–31, 257–58
absolute simultaneity, 266–68
acute perplexity, 3–4, 5–6, 8, 10, 13–14, 20, 39–40
all this, 3–20. *See also* world; world, going from *thus* to *as so*
   Cartesian method and, 14–15
   change and, 107–8
   constancy and, 273
   engagement with, 181–82
   as impetus to inquiry, 5–6, 7, 16–17, 71–75, 120–21
   Kant and, 15–16
   metaphysics and, 33–38, 39–40, 42–43, 44, 50, 52–53, 57–59, 95, 304–7, 308–10, 312–13
   moments in, 128–29, 131–32, 181–82
   in original inquiry, 5–12, 33, 72, 73–74, 76, 110, 118–19, 136, 156, 167–68, 304, 309–10, 313
   presuppositionless inquiry into, 7–8, 16
   as structure in world, 92–100, 111, 312
   as *thus*, 9, 74–76, 87, 303–4
   time and, 12, 121, 122–23, 132, 133, 146, 304, 310, 312
   See also world; world, going from *thus* to *as so*
all this, thing and, 10, 60–61, 76–77, 102–3, 128–29, 303, 308
   being a thing as uniform, 110–11
   categories of, 107–10
   constancy and inconstancy and, 11–12, 16–17
   explicative account of thing, 69–70
   impetus to inquiry and, 71–74
   moment and, 128–29
   original inquiry on, 10–12, 71–74, 76, 82, 86–87, 106, 207–8

   properties of world and, 104–6
   relatedness of things, 62, 143
   thing as natured entity, 79–80, 83–84, 93–94, 207–8
   world as plurality of all things, 102–6
Aristotle, 53, 55–58, 64–65, 66–67, 98–99, 108–9, 134–35, 286
Armstrong, David, 95–96
atemporal becoming, 288–90
atemporal entities, 284–94, 299
atemporal reality
   metaphysics of time and, 272, 310–11
   temporal reality and, 272, 273, 310–11
   things independent of time, 284–93
   timelessness and, 280–84

Baron, Sam, 252–53
Bealer, George, 51, 52–53, 54
being, 65–66
   Aristotle on, 66–67
   thing and, 65–67
   of thing as compulsory, 111–12
   of thing as determinate, 112–15
   of thing as not fragmentary, 115–16
   of thing as uniform, 110–11
Being, 18
being so *versus* being true, 278–79
Bennett, Karen, 41–43, 43n.10, 64n.2, 96n.11
Broad, C.D., 199

Callender, Craig, 267
Cameron, Ross, 199–200, 202–4, 205–7, 208–11
Carnap, Rudolf, 44–45, 49–50
change
   all this and, 107–8
   constancy and, 158
   differentiation and, 124–27
   dynamism, ontological transience and, 257–59, 260–61
   metaphysics of time on, 126

change (*cont.*)
  moments and, 121–22, 127, 128–29, 134, 191–211, 221–24, 230–31, 232, 259–60, 263, 265
  ontological homogeneity and, 159–60
  Parmenides on, 125–26
  synchronic, 205–7, 217
  synchronous, 221–24
  temporal differentiation and, 128–30, 147, 174–75, 177–78
  thing and, 126–27, 130, 133, 134, 259
  time and, 132–35, 145, 176
common sense, 9–11, 13, 164–65, 264
constancy, in world, 156–57, 231–32, 293–99
  being so *versus* being true, 278–79
  change and, 158
  insurmountable problems of, 268–72
  in original inquiry, 274–79, 293
  simple facts and, 294–99
  structure in temporal reality and, 276–78
  transient presentism and, 268–72
  world going from *thus* to *as so* and, 293
constancy and inconstancy, in world, 8–9
  all this, things and, 11–12, 16–17
  experience of, 156–57
  independent bases of, 261–63
  metaphysics of time on, 142–43, 153–54, 155, 157–58, 168–69, 241, 255
  original inquiry on, 9–10, 142, 228, 255, 271–72
  temporal differentiation and, 228, 304, 310–11, 312
  transient presentism on, 256, 273, 274–75
  world going from *thus* to *as so,* 156–57, 310–11
contingency, 219–20, 226, 228
  necessity, world in time and, 232–43
  openness of what is to be and, 241–43
Craig, William Lane, 198
critical inquiry, 35–36, 37–39
cross-temporal relations, 268–71

Dasein, 18
Dasgupta, Shamik, 80–82
Deasy, Daniel, 199–200
Descartes and Cartesian method, 14–15
differentiation, 124–27. *See also* temporal differentiation
dynamism, 149, 154–55, 158
  as actualizable potential, 260–61
  change, ontological transience and, 257–59, 260–61
  inconstancy and, 256–63
  of thing, 260–63
  transience, permanence and, 262–63

Einstein, Albert, 265–66, 267
empiricism, 63, 98–99, 291, 292
essentialism, 79nn.19–20, 80–81, 94, 99–100, 208–9
Evans, Gareth, 113n.32

fatalism, 233, 233n.4
Fichte, Johann Gottlieb, 16
Fine, Kit, 53–54

Gallois, André, 252–53
growing block views, of temporal reality, 190–91, 216–18

Hegel, G. W. F., 16
Heidegger, Martin, 18
Hume, David, 15, 45, 94
Husserl, Edmund, 17
hypermoments, 197–98, 222

impetus to inquiry
  all this as, 5–6, 7, 16–17, 71–75, 120–21
  the world as, 4–5, 70–76
inconstancy, in world, 153, 156, 174–75
  constancy and, 8–10, 11–12, 16–17, 142–43, 153–54, 155, 156–58, 228, 241, 255, 256, 261–63, 271–72, 273, 274–75, 304, 310–11, 312
  dynamism and, 256–63
  moments and, 149–50, 263
  ontological basis of, 173–75
  presentism and, 248–49, 256–63
  simple facts and, 295, 297–98
  temporal differentiation and, 173–75, 176–77, 248–49, 257–58
  transient presentism on, 273, 274–75
  world going from *thus* to *as so,* 274–76
  See also constancy and inconstancy, in world
intentionality, 98–99, 136–37, 291–92

James, William, 70

Kant, Immanuel, 15–16, 45, 49–50, 53, 63

Ladyman, James, 46–48, 49, 50
Leininger, Lisa, 259
LePoidevin, Robin, 177
Lewis, David, 94
Lorentzian interpretation, of STR, 267–68
Lowe, E.J., 56–57, 69, 79n.20, 108–9
Ludlow, Peter, 165

Maddy, Penelope, 49–50
making so, 296
making true/truthmaking, 269–71, 278–79, 295–96, 297, 298–99
Maudlin, Tim, 156
McCall, Storrs, 224–25
McTaggart, J.M.E., 148, 151, 190–91, 201, 204–5
McTaggart's Paradox, 166, 193–94, 195–99, 202–3, 204, 210
Mellor, D.H., 150, 151–52, 176–77
Merricks, Trenton, 41–44, 252
metaphysics
  all this and, 33–38, 39–40, 42–43, 44, 50, 52–53, 57–59, 95, 304–7, 308–10, 312–13
  as autonomous, 51–58
  contemporary, critique of, 40–58
  deflationary views of, 41–50
  distinctive problem of, 37–40
  as first philosophy, 55–58
  as hodgepodge, 41–43
  naturalized, 45–50
  need for novel method and, 58–59
  on thing, 34–37, 75, 255, 308–9
  traditional, 40–41, 42–44, 46–47, 51, 56, 58, 65–66
  wholly critical, 36, 37, 39–40, 42, 44, 50, 51, 58–59, 84, 104, 137, 305–6, 308–10
metaphysics of time, 191
  atemporal reality and, 272, 310–11
  on change, 126
  on constancy and inconstancy, 142–43, 153–54, 155, 157–58, 168–69, 241, 255, 273, 310–11
  controversy regarding, 147–61
  original inquiry and, 121–22, 135, 141
  on phenomena attendant upon time, 122–23
  presentism and, 248–50, 255, 264
  primary issue regarding, 161–62
  radical ontology and, 311–12
  temporal differentiation and, 121, 123–24, 135, 147, 156, 228, 310–11, 312
  on temporal reality, 141–42, 165, 187–88
  transient presentism and, 271–72, 273
  wholly critical, 121–22, 123, 135, 137, 165
  on world going from *thus* to *as so*, 122–23
minimal A-theory, of temporal reality, 199–201, 208
Minkowskian space-time, 265–66, 267
mode of differentiation, 23–24, 120–21, 126, 127–28, 135, 141
momentary transientism. *See* transient presentism

moment/moments
  absolute becoming of, 229–31, 257–58
  in *all this*, 131–32, 181–82
  change and, 121–22, 127, 128–29, 134, 191–211, 221–24, 230–31, 232, 259–60, 263, 265
  contingency and, 241–43
  hypermoments, 197–98, 222
  inconstancy and, 149–50, 263
  now, 220–21, 223, 224–27, 231, 232–33, 234–38, 239–43, 248–49, 255, 258–59, 265
  ontological transience of, 259–60
  possibility and necessity in this moment, now, 234–38
  presentism and, 258–59
  properties of, 144–45
  temporal differentiation and, 128–32, 178–80, 185–87, 223–24, 229, 230–31, 248, 257–58, 259
  in temporal passage view, 195–98
  temporal relations between, 184–87, 227–28, 229, 231–32, 293
  time and, 121–22, 127–32, 134, 135–36, 144–46, 229
  transient presentism on, 256, 293, 310–11
  world going from *thus* to *as so* and, 158, 159–60, 161, 176, 178–80, 184–88, 215–16
moving spotlight views, of temporal reality, 190–91, 198–211, 222–23
Mozersky, Joshua, 174
myth of passage, 170–73

naturalism, 45–50
necessity
  contingency and, 232–43
  of the past, 238–41
  possibility and, 234–38
Newtonian space-time, 267

Oaklander, Nathan, 174, 176–77
ontic vagueness, 112–14
ontological dependence, 42–43, 64–65, 96–98, 143–44, 284
ontological transience
  absolute annihilation, ceasing to be simpliciter and, 211–16
  absolute becoming, coming to be simpliciter, 228–32
  change, dynamism and, 257–59
  temporal differentiation and, 215–16, 228, 229–32
openness of the future, 241–43

original inquiry, 14
  on *all this*, thing and, 10–12, 71–74, 76, 82, 86–87, 106, 207–8
  all this in, 5–12, 33, 72, 73–74, 76, 110, 118–19, 136, 156, 167–68, 304, 309–10, 313
  on constancy and inconstancy, 9–10, 142, 228, 255, 271–72
  constancy in, 274–79, 293
  metaphysics of time and, 121–22, 135, 141
  radical ontology and, 106–7, 110, 121–22, 136, 305
  on thing, 110, 111–12, 255, 303
  as wholly critical, 11–12, 84–91
  world going from *thus* to *as so* in, 120, 124–25, 128, 136, 141, 293
Orilia, Francesco, 252

Paoletti, Michele Paolini, 252–53
Parmenides, 125–26
Paul, Laurie, 156, 177
perception, intuition and, 292–93
perplexity, 3–4, 5–6
possible worlds, 105, 106, 235, 240
presentism, 12, 152, 249–56
  dynamism, inconstancy and, 256–63
  in metaphysics of time, 248–50, 255, 264
  multiplicity of views, 252–54
  standard, 252, 253–55, 256, 258–59, 264–66, 268–70
  structure and, 255–56
  triviality objection to, 250–51, 280–81
  See also transient presentism
presuppositionless inquiry, 7–8, 16, 76, 90–91, 265n.24
Price, Huw, 257–58
Principle of Sufficient Reason, 11–12, 80–82
Prior, A.N., 165, 252–53

Quine, W.V.O., 44–45, 94

radical ontology, 92–93, 104, 106–16, 254, 273
  means and limits of inquiry and, 116–19
  metaphysics of time and, 311–12
  original inquiry and, 106–7, 110, 121–22, 136, 305
  thing and, 106–16, 146, 307–8
Ramsey, Frank, 174
reality
  metaphysics on, 33–34
  structure in, 63–65, 92, 95–96, 312, 313
  See also all this; atemporal reality; temporal reality; world
Reichenbach, Hans, 49–50

Reinhold, Karl Leonhard, 16
relativism, 115–16
Ross, Don, 46–48, 49, 50

Savitt, Steven, 174
Scholasticism, 63, 98–99
Shoemaker, Sidney, 134
shrinking tree view, of temporal reality, 224–26
simple facts, constancy and, 294–99
Skow, Bradford, 156, 199–200
Smart, J.J.C., 156, 171–72, 176–77
Smith, Quentin, 252–53
Special Theory of Relativity (STR), 265–68, 270–71
Spurrett, David, 46–48, 49, 50
standard presentism, 252, 253–55, 256, 258–59, 264–66, 268–70
STR. *See* Special Theory of Relativity
structure
  presentism and, 255–56
  in reality, 63–65, 92, 95–96, 312, 313
  subsequent to this moment, now, 224–26
  in temporal reality, 141–42, 163, 164, 170, 173–74, 179, 182, 192, 193, 215, 220–28, 232–33, 272, 276–78
  in the world, 62, 92–102, 103, 111, 312
Sullivan, Meghan, 199–201, 206–7, 208–9, 210–11
synchronic change, 205–7, 217
synchronic possibility, 27–28, 234–35, 237, 238, 238n.9, 241–42
synchronous change, 221–24

Tahko, Tuomas, 57
Tallant, Jonathan, 252
temporal differentiation, 121, 127
  absolute becoming and, 230–31
  change and, 128–30, 147, 174–75, 177–78
  constancy, inconstancy and, 228, 304, 310–11, 312
  experience of, 167–69, 175–78, 182, 192
  inconstancy and, 173–75, 176–77, 248–49, 257–58
  metaphysics of time and, 121, 123–24, 135, 147, 156, 228, 310–11, 312
  moments and, 128–32, 178–80, 185–87, 223–24, 229, 230–31, 248, 257–58, 259
  mutable things and, 263
  ontological basis of inconstancy and, 173–75
  ontological homogeneity and, 170–78, 188–89
  ontological transience and, 215–16, 228, 229–32

passage of time and, 163–64, 168, 170–73
time and, 136–37, 141
as world going from *thus* to *as so,* 124–25, 128, 135, 138, 147, 156, 163, 167–69, 173–75, 178–80, 185–87, 210, 212, 219, 223–24, 248, 257–58, 271, 293, 310–11
temporal entities, extent of world in time and, 226–28
temporal reality, 121–22, 137–38, 143–46
atemporal reality and, 272, 273, 310–11
constancy and, 276–78
growing block views of, 190–91, 216–18
McTaggart's Paradox and, 193–94, 195–98
metaphysics of time on, 141–42, 165, 187–88
minimal A-theory of, 199–201, 208
moving spotlight views of, 190–91, 198–211, 222–23
necessity, contingency and, 232–43
ontological heterogeneity of, 160–61, 163, 166, 169, 183, 190, 212, 213–14, 223, 226, 248, 267–68, 276
ontological homogeneity and, 158–60, 163–65, 166, 170–89, 202, 265–66, 274–75
ontological transience and, 211–16, 228
presentism and, 248–49, 250, 253–54, 255
qualitative heterogeneity in, 191–211, 221
shrinking tree view of, 224–26
STR and, 265–66
structure in, 141–42, 163, 164, 170, 173–74, 179, 182, 192, 193, 215, 220, 232–33, 272, 276–78
structure of, subsequent to now, 220–28
temporal entities and extent of, 226–28
time and, 138, 141–42, 146–47
traditional passage view of, 190–98, 199–200, 222–23, 257
transient presentism on, 264–65, 269–72, 273
temporal relations, 123, 144–45, 146–47, 148–50, 163
cross-temporal relations, 268–71
between moments, 184–87, 227–28, 229, 231–32, 293
thing/things, 4–5, 10–11
actualizable potential of, 260–62
atemporal entities, 284–94, 299
being and, 65–67
being a thing as compulsory, 111–12
being a thing as determinate, 112–15
being a thing as uniform, 110–11
being of thing as not fragmentary, 115–16
categories of, 107–10, 132
change and, 126–27, 130, 133, 134, 259

defining, 60
dynamism of, 260–63
essentialism on, 208–9
existence of, 130
explicative account of, 68–70, 71, 72, 73–74, 76, 79–80, 101–2, 108, 117
Heidegger on, 18
metaphysics on, 34–37, 75, 255, 308–9
mutable, 145–47, 214, 215–16, 230, 231–33, 260–63, 273
as natured entity, 76–84, 93–94, 104, 107, 109–10, 111–12, 207–8, 209
ontological transience and, 211
original inquiry on, 110, 111–12, 255, 303
question of what a thing is, 61–69
radical ontology and, 106–16, 146, 307–8
structure in the world and, 95–96, 111
time and, 128, 132–35, 137, 141, 143–44, 145–46, 261–62
transience and permanence of, 262–63
world and, 36, 60, 70–77, 78–80, 102–3, 104–6, 303
world as plurality of all, 102–6
See also all this, thing and
Thomasson, Amie, 67–68n.9
time
all this and, 12, 121, 122–23, 132, 133, 146, 304, 310, 312
change and, 132–35, 145, 176
confronting, 122–27
as key to a second mode of differentiation, 121
moments and, 121–22, 127–32, 134, 135–36, 144–46, 229
mutable things and, 263
passage of, 163–64, 168, 170–73, 190–91
temporal differentiation and, 136–37, 141
temporal reality and, 138, 141–42, 146–47
thing and, 128, 132–35, 137, 141, 143–44, 145–46, 261–62
world and, 105–6, 135–38, 143–47, 157–61, 178–89, 216–18
world without, 280–84
See also metaphysics of time
timelessness
atemporal reality and, 280–84
attempts to reject, 280–81
incorrect views of, 281–82
traditional passage view, of temporal reality, 190–98, 199–200, 222–23, 257
transcendental argument, 15
transience, permanence and, 262–63

transient presentism, 257–60, 263, 293
  constancy and, 268–72
  on constancy and inconstancy, 256, 273, 274–75
  metaphysics of time and, 271–72, 273
  moment in, 256, 293, 310–11
  objections to, 263–72
  standard presentism and, 254, 256, 258–59, 264–66, 268–70
  STR and, 265–68, 270–71
  on temporal reality, 264–65, 269–72, 273

wholly critical inquiry, 5–8, 9, 14, 20
  metaphysics as, 36, 37, 39–40, 42, 44, 50, 51, 58–59, 84, 104, 137, 305–6, 308–10
  metaphysics of time as, 121–22, 123, 135, 137, 165
  original inquiry as, 11–12, 84–91
Williams, D.C., 156, 170–71, 173–74
Williamson, Timothy, 54–55, 200
world, 33–35, 36
  becoming, 88
  as impetus to inquiry, 4–5, 70–76
  language and, 165
  as plurality of all things, 102–6
  structure in, 62, 92–102, 103, 111, 312
  thing and, 36, 60, 70–77, 78–80, 102–3, 104–6, 303
  as *thus,* 10, 74–76, 78–79, 83–84, 88, 93–94, 103, 107, 110, 115, 179–80, 303
  time and, 105–6, 135–38, 143–47, 157–61, 178–89, 216–18
  See also constancy, in world; inconstancy, in world
world, going from *thus* to *as so,* 9, 135–36, 267–68
  constancy, inconstancy and, 156–57, 310–11
  constancy and, 293
  inconstancy and, 274–76
  metaphysics of time on, 122–23
  moments and, 158, 159–60, 161, 176, 178–80, 184–88, 215–16
  ontological heterogeneity of temporal reality and, 160–61
  in original inquiry, 120, 124–25, 128, 136, 141, 293
  temporal differentiation as, 124–25, 128, 135, 138, 147, 156, 163, 167–69, 173–75, 178–80, 185–87, 210, 212, 219, 223–24, 248, 257–58, 271, 293, 310–11
  time in the world and, 143, 146
  traditional passage view on, 192
world in time. *See* temporal reality

Zimmerman, Dean, 252